To Adam Enjoy the book — come for a visit.

The Brass

It's a bit of England where good companionship is the order of the day

by

Robert Wright

Robert Wright

WRIGHT STUFF PRESS, LLC

Cover photograph
    by Mary Izett
Cover photographs: Wood Panel and Horse Brass
    by Dick Kaiser
Rear cover photograph
    by Michael Flynn, CAMRA SW London
Cover Design
    by Matthew Barron

ISBN-10: 0-578-13141-2
ISBN-13: 978-0-578-13141-2

Library of Congress Control Number: 2013917853

Printed in the United States of America
by
Wright Stuff Press, LLC
1221 SW 10th Avenue, #505
Portland, Oregon 97205

Dedication

The Brass is dedicated to the memory of Donald Allen Younger, publican for over 34 years of the Horse Brass Pub in Portland, Oregon, until his death in 2011. He was brilliant, eccentric, gruff and giving, and loved his pub and his regulars. His iconic British pub is considered the cathedral of Oregon's craft beer revolution, Don its archbishop. He promoted charitable events born at the Horse Brass Pub that continue to this day. In his memory, all royalties from the sale of *The Brass* will be donated to Sisters of the Road in Portland, Oregon. This charity, which helps the homeless, was close to Don's heart.

Contents

Preface

It was by chance I discovered the Horse Brass Pub. It was the most English of pubs that I had seen in the United States. After returning from an Air Force assignment in England in the early '80s, I had sought and sampled many establishments that chose to call themselves pubs. Entering *this* pub, I was stopped dead in my tracks as I gazed across a warm, inviting, familiar scene: soft lighting, cluttered British décor, conversations at wooden tables over pints of beer, dark wooden bar with beer engine levers, seated patrons speaking easily with the barman, and dartboards with people engaged in friendly games. All that was missing was a coal fireplace with a pub dog sleeping nearby. The feeling was one that I had experienced many times before in cozy English village pubs; I knew it well. It swept over me as I stood in the doorway. I was home.

A real pub is not created easily or quickly, nor should it be. Just including "pub" in a name, or adding some English-looking decorations, does not make a public establishment a public house. It would be a start, but much more is required—a concerted, honest, well-meaning effort on the part of many people over time to ensure comforting surroundings: publican, workers, patrons, regulars, good beer, a little serendipity, some synergy, and maybe a dose of something beyond our understanding. This was a real pub. I knew it without asking.

I was very fortunate to have lived in England for three years, right next to Royal Air Force (RAF) Mildenhall, the base where the United States Air Force had assigned me. I fell in love with the public house, known as a pub to villagers who considered it their living room, their lounge, their social center. Pubs were quiet, warm, inviting places to meet with friends and neighbors over a pint of good English beer and maybe a game of darts. While stationed there, I inadvertently crossed a line one Saturday afternoon. This brought into focus for me what it meant to be a regular.

The pub I enjoyed very often was the White Hart. It was in the center of the village of Mildenhall, very close to the medieval shopping square that dated back to the 1400s. Without realizing it, I had become a regular, not only by frequency of visits, but by feeling quite at home there, conversing with villagers, throwing darts on the pub team, having a few pints. I had gotten to know quite well some of the villagers, and the publican and his wife who lived above the pub. He had served in the Royal Navy.

On a road into the village was a quaint-looking pub, the Volunteer Arms. I drove on that road often en route to the White Hart. Through the small-paned windows, the interior of the Volunteer Arms looked warm and inviting. One day I just had to stop in for a look and a pint. It was indeed a pub. The publican cheerily poured me the pint of Guinness I had ordered. Pint in hand, I went to a dart board to practice; I needed it. While at the board, the publican of the White Hart came in. Both publicans worked on the upcoming schedule for the dart league. Then *my* publican turned and saw me. With as serious a voice as he could muster, he said, "Bob! What the bloody hell are you doing here? The White Hart is your local. It's a sad day when I have to go out and fetch my regulars."

Both publicans let out hearty laughs as my face turned red. Patrons joined in the laughter as they watched this embarrassed Yank twist in the wind. It was all good fun, but I felt like someone who had been caught cheating on his wife. The terms "regular" and "local" took on new meanings for me.

My wife and I visited Portland often, the city of our births with many family members there. On the first visit after returning from the United Kingdom, I found an English-styled pub down by the Willamette River, the Elephant and Castle. One night, a Portland dart player and I were engaged in a game at this pub, over a pint of good beer, of course. I cheerily described my time in England. He politely listened to my enthusiastic, lengthy descriptions of England and her pubs and suggested, "Oh, you need to see The Brass."

Unsure if I had heard him correctly, I asked, "The what?"

"The Horse Brass Pub. It's across the river, near Mount Tabor on Southeast Belmont Street."

I called a cab. I knew about Mount Tabor as my wife had grown up near there. But I did not have the address of the pub, so I simply requested, "Please take me to the Horse Brass Pub."

The driver looked back, smiled and said, "Sure. It's a great place."

He drove me there, and the embrace of the Horse Brass Pub has endured.

The following trips home always included visits to the Horse Brass. I became acquainted with its publican, his friendly staff and the regulars, some over games of darts with pints of good brews, just like I'd had back in England. When final retirement arrived from a post-Air Force job, my wife and I returned to Portland for good, to be near family—daughters, sons-in-law, and grandchildren. My wife was unaware that family now included those at the Horse Brass. Not surprisingly, the frequency of my visits to this pub increased—a lot. I joined one of their sponsored dart teams and played in a Portland league. I was on my way to becoming a regular. Just like a new business that eventually becomes a true pub, this patron status is not achieved just by saying it or by spending a lot of time there. It has to become your third place, your home away from home.

To keep the creative juices flowing in retirement when not at the Horse Brass, I wrote and published a book of hopefully interesting and humorous memoirs. This was a different tangent for me, having been a nerdy scientist most of my life. I celebrated the publication of my first book by signing copies and giving them to fellow dart players, employees and regulars at the pub. One evening, while sitting at the regulars' table, with a pint or two under my belt, someone suggested that somebody should write the story of the Horse Brass Pub. Eyes glanced at me, being the closest thing to an author at the table at that moment.

I hesitated. But on impulse, I agreed to give it a go. By this time I realized that The Brass was not only the most English of pubs that I had visited in this country, but that it had something very special, even beyond that of an old English pub. The story of this pub not only deserved to be told, it needed to be told. This would take a bit of focused work of a type that I had not done before. A few days later, I sat down, blank notebook in hand, and asked some regulars about the early days of the pub. Facts and tales crossed over the table in considerable amount as I scribbled furiously, trying to keep up. There was more here than I had imagined, much more. In the following months and years, I interviewed many people and spent time in archives to unearth the stories of people and events centered upon this Southeast Portland neighborhood over the course of nearly 40 years, stories that extended to very English roots.

Before starting in organized earnest, I thought it prudent and appropriate to speak to the owner, Don Younger, the publican of the Horse Brass Pub, to ask his approval for the intended book and to do my first real and most important interview. I knew he loved his pub and its people, and they loved him. He was very intelligent, considerably eccentric and an iconic figure in Oregon's craft beer industry. I did not know him well. But I knew him well enough to know not to interrupt his conversations with patrons at the bar. I was advised that the best time to meet with Don was on a Saturday morning when he came in to look over the books and tend to the business end of the establishment.

The very next Saturday, my wife and I went to watch our grandson's basketball game on a rainy Portland January morning. We treated him and our son-in-law to an early lunch at the Horse Brass Pub. We sat in the approved area for young people. The waitress came over, welcomed me by name and took our order. I asked if the publican was in. She said that I had just missed him by a few minutes; he had left early for some reason. I just made a mental note to come out on some other Saturday morning, with no particular urgency in mind.

During the following two weeks, the publican very unfortunately found himself in and out of a local hospital because of an accidental fall. He'd had to return there because of complications. All of this was unknown to me. I came to the Horse Brass on a Sunday evening to play darts, have a pint and just enjoy the company of my friends. What I found instead were patrons in a very somber mood with sober news, standing vigil. Early in the morning of the following day, the deeply respected and dearly loved publican died.

Acknowledgements

My gratitude is sincerely extended to the following people, without whom the story of the Horse Brass Pub absolutely would not have been possible. Their time and patience are greatly appreciated. Special thanks are extended to Fred Eckhardt for finding and allowing the use of his documented personal interviews of Don Younger, the interviews I never had. Lastly, I owe special thanks to my wife of 49 years, Janice, for her patient review and editing of the manuscript.

Victor Atiyeh
Aaron Barnard
Diana Barnard
George Bieber
Leslie Bourbeau
Philip Bourbeau
Jay Brandon
Greg Bundy
Martin Butler
Joy Campbell
Bud Clark
Clay Connolly
Brian Dutch
Fred Eckhardt
Jillian Flynn
John Foyston
Bob Garnes
Ian Griffiths
Arthur Hague
Richard Housman
Rosa Housman
Jack Joyce
Robert Luster
James Macko

John Maier
Rick Maine
Tom May
Theresa McAreavy
Michael McCormick
Brian McMenamin
Michael McMenamin
Edward Meyo
Richard Ponzi
Jon Reid
Katina Reynolds-Reid
Ronald Roberts
Robert Royster
Paula Snoddy
Burton Tinsley
Jeffrey Tooze
Ruth Tooze
Debbie Urwin
Terry Urwin
Dennis Vigna
Martin Weller
Kurt Widmer
Robert Widmer
Susan Winterlich

Introduction

Don Younger was sitting at his usual spot at the bar in his public house, cigarette in hand, reading about a beer-centered event taking place in Portland, Oregon, that week. He had been the publican of the Horse Brass Pub for over two decades. He was also part of the Oregon craft beer revolution then in full swing. Since the revolution's very beginning, he had been an incessant promoter of craft beer, microbreweries and brewpubs, while being a good steward and maintaining the British soul of his pub.

There was a beer festival that week, one of many such annual events in Portland, now called Beervana. Home brewers, owners of craft beer microbreweries, brewpub owners and those that just enjoyed really good beer swirled around Portland and the pub. Don was proud to see that his Horse Brass was featured in the event's literature.

Don took a sip of award-winning Younger's Special Bitter, the beer of his pub named in honor of his departed brother, and took a long drag on a strong cigarette as he spoke to a close friend. A young, eager fellow walked in and easily spotted Don with his distinctive, shoulder-length hair, beard and mustache. He boldly walked right up to Don, rudely interrupted and introduced himself. He was a reporter. Certainly, getting an interview with Don Younger at the Horse Brass Pub would net a sure-fire publishable story about beer. He had many questions carefully outlined in the little notebook he held. Without being asked, he initiated the conversation, "Mister Younger, I want to compliment you on how extraordinarily well you've done selling beer."

Don flinched. Annoyed, he set down his cigarette and pint and did an incredulous double take at this fresh face. What the young man heard was Don's gravelly voice, "Do you think all I do is sell beer?!"

The young man's eyes widened. Don's fairly loud reply got the attention of some regulars and other patrons nearby. Don continued with a very short, blunt, oblique lecture about beer, his pub and his role in Oregon's craft beer revolution, "You can buy beer at the fucking grocery store! This place isn't about selling beer! Young man, this is the Horse Brass Pub!!"

That brought the interview to an abrupt end. They stared at each other for what seemed like an eternity to the reporter. His face reddened a bit as he tried to think of what to ask next, considering the context within which Don had placed him. He looked down at his list of questions. None fit that wrapping. He took a deep breath, sighed and turned away. Rejected in public, he headed towards the door. He had heard a few things about the renowned Don Younger and his pub. Apparently he had not heard enough. From that brief exchange he learned a lot more.

Before leaving, he stopped at the front door, turned back and looked around at the warm, authentic English interior of the pub. People were drinking beer alright, but there was something else going on which he did not quite understand. He made a mental note that selling beer was not the sole objective at the Horse Brass. Back at his desk in the publication's office, he did some research that should have preceded his visit to the pub. He uncovered its basic dogma: "It's a bit of England where good companionship is the order of the day."

The Brass is the story of a real and rare world-famous jewel, cut and polished by time and people, lodged in the midst of the Northern Willamette Valley. Its story is a journey through time with people from two countries. It is primarily a summary of the individual oral histories of the principals, supplemented by research. The story allows for a bit of the mystical, so as not to dismiss this aspect as possibly having had an influence on the Horse Brass Pub.

In the main, the story is about the pub's events and people, their history, their character and their motivations, which are the *soul* of this pub. Many people have touched the pub in one way or another, from simply stopping in for a good beer and conversation to those whose life stories centered around The Brass. How the pub became the Horse Brass Pub of today is left for the reader to conclude, based on the facts and stories presented herein.

Hopefully, *The Brass* will inspire and motivate the passing of the baton to future generations of publicans, managers, regulars, patrons, bartenders, wait staff, cooks and brewers. Younger patrons, who become well-grounded in the history and spirit of The Brass and have the proper attitudes and intentions, may find themselves seated at the regulars' table, warmly welcomed into the family of this pub.

Author's Notes:

Representative dialogue, otherwise known as literary journalism or creative nonfiction, is used occasionally in this narrative to help frame some historical settings and give readers further insight into the personalities of those involved. As paraphrased, they are based on interviews with others; such dialogues may not be verbatim accounts.

The recollections and facts uncovered doing research for this book dealt with far more than just the business aspects of running a successful pub. Rent, labor, food, beer and bookkeeping are all very important components of any pub, tavern or bar. However, these topics are better suited for bottom-line, business-minded people. Intentionally, this story of the Horse Brass Pub does not include the details of the financial stresses and successes of the pub. That story is left for others to tell. Due attention has been paid to obstacles and circumstances that could have sidetracked and prevented the evolution of the pub.

Some readers may find expletives that could offend. They are not included gratuitously nor to sensationalize the narrative but rather to help convey the personalities, emotions and passions of some of the people involved in the story. To have removed them would have denied the reader full understanding and appreciation of the characters.

The Brass is an independent work. The current owners of the Horse Brass Pub were neither involved in its preparation nor have they promoted it. There is no affiliation with them or endorsement by them of this book. *The Brass* is a story inspired by and based on the interviews of others who were involved in and had touched the life of the pub, to the best that their memories recalled. (Accuracy in the reporting of historical information by a bunch of drinkers after 20+ years cannot and should not be expected—comment from an interviewed, longtime regular.)

The basic story of the Horse Brass Pub is covered in Parts I, II and III. The underpinnings of the story are expanded upon in Parts IV and V. Part VI points to the future.

To those who love the Horse Brass whom I have not located in the press of time, my apologies. Please know that you were part of its story. Whatever your touch, your hand was also on the tiller of the ship.

PART I

Farewell

THE WAKE

It was a Sunday afternoon at the pub. Casual patrons, regulars and others who found a home and family there came in as sunset turned to evening. Some came to find a game of darts, others to have a good beer and converse with friends. Soft light, golden walls, dark wood, horse brasses and the soul of England again wrapped around them, as they had done for many people for the past 34 years.

But that evening was much different. News and rumors from friends and family at the hospital had spread. People spoke in low, unbelieving tones, slowly shaking their heads, hoping it was not true. Stories were being told over pints of beer and shots of whiskey. Others arrived after hearing the news. They came to the only appropriate place to stand vigil, in the publican's home, their home. Well past midnight, as the family of the pub finally left, a short, stout English gentleman with a heavy accent pointed back to the pub and declared, "It's more English than anything we've got back home."

One of the pub's barmen stepped out into the rear parking lot. Overcome with grief, he shook his fist towards the sky and angrily shouted, "Why? Why?! *Why*?!!"

Sadly, the inevitable arrived. Early in the morning of January 31, 2011, the beloved publican died.

The following week, editorials, letters to the editor, and tributes appeared in the city's newspapers. They spoke of his leadership and contributions to Oregon's and the Pacific Northwest's craft beer industry and of his Horse Brass Pub, now known worldwide. Through this publican's love of people, place and beer, this softly worn, welcoming space had become an icon in the city of Portland. In deference to the modern age, e-mails of condolence and remembrance preceded the regular mail. All were printed, posted, and otherwise shared. A member of the family of the pub created a large collection of memorable photographs of people and places, mostly of the publican, his pub, and its twinned pub in London. The collage was hung by the dart board that's next to the wall with old barrelheads from across the Atlantic Ocean, one of which shared the publican's family name—Younger.

In the following days, people sat around the regulars' table and reality set in. In memory, some ordered pints of Younger's Special Bitter, cask-conditioned.

3

Others added a shot of Macallan 12 Scotch whiskey. One question hung in the air. When?

Where was known absolutely, without question; the Horse Brass Pub would have another wake. The date was finally set. They were told by one of the longtime regulars. He had known Don Younger and his pub for many years, decades. Again, it would be on a Sunday.

Portland provided the people, special people, as it always had from the very beginning. It now provided weather for the mood. Very cool, damp air drifted in from the Pacific Ocean, with overcast grey clouds that bestowed light rain on this February gathering. Family and close friends arrived early that morning for the wake, collecting inside, making ready. Relatives, regular patrons, and the larger extended family of the pub arrived later to grieve, console and celebrate with pints in hand, as Don would no doubt have wanted and expected from his patrons, his staff and, most certainly, his regulars.

Everyone soon held a pint of the special bitter. Some preferred it cask-conditioned. This bitter had been designed specifically for this pub, as requested by Don, by the brewmaster of the famed Northwest brewery, Rogue Ales. This special, award-winning beer had been given the family name in remembrance of Don's younger brother, who had passed on tragically and unexpectedly in his prime. The pub enfolded all of them now, as it always had, but this time with a special embrace that provided comfort as well as the familiar, somewhat spiritual force that encouraged one of the most revered and basic of human needs — companionship.

The original white-plastered walls and ceiling were now golden brown, like a well-used Meerschaum pipe, from years of smoke from pipes, cigars and cigarettes used by the patrons, the regulars, and certainly by Don; cigarettes were a favorite pastime of his. Tobacco smoke was now banned in such public places by government decree. But the residue of curling, drifting smoke and, more importantly, the feelings and character of the people who had created this smoke, still permeated the place.

The walls and ceiling also carried history: World War II photographs of Winston Churchill and RAF Spitfires used in the Battle of Britain; British and RAF Flags; a photograph of the now-deceased Queen Mum "pulling a pint" in an English pub; and a splendid painting of the late Princess Diana, painted by an artist that had been both a longtime regular and a waiter at the pub. Artifacts on the walls traced the love of its regulars and those seasoned into the family of the pub. Some were photographs, drawings or engraved plaques of those now deceased, on the East Wall reserved for them.

The dark-stained wood floors supported and rough-hewn wood beams and posts surrounded tables, chairs, stools and benches. Some of these had been purchased from English pubs; some had held parishioners on Sunday mornings in an English church. The historical artifacts, photographs, old tables and benches had been acquired in England by a Portland native, an Anglophile who, some 20 years earlier, had returned from an Air Force assignment there with an English wife and young son. With a true love and understanding of English pubs, he had designed and remodeled this space, decorated it, and named it before Don purchased the business in 1976.

The worn wooden tables had held many pints and bottles. They also secretly overheard many conversations and the tales told over them, here and back in England. Positioned high in one corner, a bust of William Shakespeare watched over all of this, approvingly. Shiny brass amulets of much greater meaning, gathered in England, were affixed to posts or hung on leather straps—the horse brasses. From Celtic times, such things protected a horse and its rider from evil forces. Later, they adorned the harnesses of horses pulling wagons, some loaded with British beer. They now provided, or hinted at, protection and good luck. All these adorned the centerpiece of a neighborhood family, a family that now extended well beyond Portland, to people and places with British roots and the love of Britain.

Even though he had departed from his family, the spirit of Don Younger remained, infused in everything. Over the years, the publican and his pub had merged into one thing. It had become absolutely impossible to speak about one without thinking or speaking about the other. The people that came this day could feel his presence as they spoke of him and his pub. Known only to a very few, the box with his ashes had been placed out of sight before people arrived, under his favorite spot at the bar where he usually sat and held sway. At this place, he had provided memorable and often blunt advice, mostly given privately and directly, in his very distinct voice, with cigarette in one hand, pint of bitter in the other, and a shot of Scotch whiskey on the bar to punctuate his discourse.

Don's beliefs—the faith and canons of the pub—remained and could be felt:

- It's a bit of England where good companionship is the order of the day.
- It's not about the beer. It's about the *beer*.
- If it was any more authentic, you'd need a passport.
- When you walk through that door, you're a stranger no more

—at the ol' Horse Brass!

Somberness mixed with laughter, as stories of the pub and its owner were told and retold. Some took to the open microphone. Their eulogies were laced with tales, both humorous and profound. The history of pub and publican were full, rich and deep, and had touched all in the room in one way or another. Many of those present were the pioneers of Oregon's craft beer industry. They spoke of what Don Younger and his Horse Brass Pub had meant to them and the craft beer revolution.

A longtime regular and gifted artist, James Macko, stepped to the microphone. Some of his art now hung on the walls of the pub. He condensed the relationship between Don Younger and beer with a raised pint and a simple declaration, "Don took us from Bud to wiser."

A British pop-rock bandleader of some renown stepped forward and spoke of the meaning that the Horse Brass and its publican held for him. Martin Weller had cancelled scheduled public performances in England and had flown thousands of miles to be a part of Don's final sendoff. Drawing from a time not too long ago, when Britannia ruled the waves, Martin raised a pint in a farewell toast: "To Don and the Horse Brass, and all who sailed in her."

Testimonies and stories had been received from across North America, and from England to New Zealand. These were printed and displayed for all to read. A number of them had come from an English pub in a southwest borough of London, a historic pub strongly twinned with The Brass for over 25 years. It was well known there that Don was a heavy smoker, who enjoyed a good cigarette with good conversation. An English pub regular over there put forth his view of Don's death, saying that Don probably had to breathe pure oxygen in the hospital, with no cigarette smoke in it, and that, in disgust, Don left his body and headed out to a bar for a drink and was having such a good time that he just forgot to come back.

Some members of the family of the pub brought in a unique touch of their own, with the approval of the immediate family. A few wondered if this was appropriate, but certainly the publican would have approved of, and even encouraged, this gesture. Two life-size photographic cutouts of him had been made, affixed to firm backings so they could be stood upright. A full-height one was placed in the corner by a pair of well-used dart boards; the other one, his upper half, was placed on his barstool. This upper-body image of his smiling and bearded face, framed by his signature long, white hair, showed him holding a pint of his favorite bitter, as was often his wont. People posed next to these likenesses and had their photographs taken. Others, as have been done in wakes of legend and tradition, stepped up close with a final, personal toast, nodding the glass in the direction of his image, as if he were still sitting or standing there. For some, he *was* still very much there.

At traditional wakes, the body of the deceased was normally laid out in the parlor of the house where the person had lived, or sometimes placed in his or her favorite chair, or stood in the corner of the deceased's lounge, the living room. Neighbors and friends would gather in the house and there would be plenty of food and drink, as the deceased host would have wanted. People came to socialize and remember; a traditional way to celebrate a person's life, ensuring a good and proper sendoff. This often meant a final farewell toast by the body.

This publican was given a special sendoff this day, good and proper. But unlike the living room in a private home, this pub would be visited often for a long time afterwards. For those attending, it was their living room too, maybe even more so. They surely felt his presence, soaked into every fiber of the place, and knew that he and his spirit would live on when they stopped by for a pint, or the companionship he had fostered. The publican would be remembered, his pub now his shrine.

Musicians came that had known Don and had performed there, friends with banjos, guitars, flutes, and song—standing next to the piano that had accompanied cheerful songs and laughter of gatherings in days past. Yes, those were the days, now remembered and talked about with a happy reverence. A prominent balladeer, Tom May, with guitar and flute, sang the songs that had filled the pub time and again. With special tribute, the words of the "Ballad of the Horse Brass Pub" flowed out over the crowd, a ballad Tom had written especially for this pub years earlier.

After that a bagpiper appeared, a lone piper in a plaid kilt, which was expected and appropriate. Bagpipe music had filled the pub for weddings and wakes. People quieted as a haunting refrain from Scotland filled the room. Tears filled eyes. It was a poignant reminder of Don's love of Britain that spread from Land's End to John O'Groats. The publican, an American with distant roots to that land, had become an absolute Anglophile. He had adopted the British Isles, and they him.

Over the years, the publican had acquired a taste for a special liquid from Scotland—Macallan 12-year-old single malt Scotch whiskey, carefully distilled and aged north of Edinburgh. But this drink, like the patrons of the pub, also required companionship; its companion was found by the publican in a special bitter, Younger's Special Bitter. Many there that day knew of Don's later fondness for a small glass of Macallan 12, chased along by a pint of this special amber drink, all to warm his heart, foster companionship, and liberate good conversation. So deep were the roots of this tradition that the wake required special planning. The exact count was lost, but over one hundred bottles of Macallan 12 were purchased, and nearly all were consumed. This purchase was felt across the city as well; the State of Oregon's liquor stores in the area ran out of this aged, Scotch whiskey because of the wake's demand.

It would take some time before the liquor stores, and the mourners that day, would recover.

Two of Don's close friends arranged for a large marquee that covered almost all of the parking lot out back and accommodated many. The beer there was provided by Don's fellow publicans. Food was provided, inside and out. This was a wake to be remembered. Ales and bitters were drunk, with occasional stronger spirits to emphasize what the publican had meant to them. A toast was prepared inside the pub. Small glasses were filled with Macallan 12. The clear golden liquid was distributed. Under the tent, glasses were filled with Pacific Northwest brews as other bagpipes signaled the well-planned toast.

At precisely 3 pm, music, song and talk ceased as all were alerted. Pints of bitter or shots of Macallan 12 were held high as a single toast was proposed, outside and in: "To the caveman!" This toast had been made many times before in this pub, a tribute to Don's deceased brother who had created it. With one voice, the response swelled in crescendo from the congregation; honor and sorrow spilled out with, "To the caveman!"

This same toast had started in New Zealand that day, given at the same local hour, as carefully planned. As the Earth slowly turned and time marched east to west, the toast was repeated, again and again, binding distant corners of the world to this public house. Then it was given at the Horse Brass Pub.

More toasts were made around the pub, some in more private gatherings of people that knew Don in their special way. The family of the pub gathered around their usual table. Their toasts gave the publican a heartfelt send-off.

Late in the evening, people hugged and slowly drifted away with misty eyes. When day was done, it was estimated that more than fifteen hundred people had come to bid Don Younger farewell. As they departed, some hesitated and glanced back at the sturdy, red-brick building that encased and protected their public house. Others wondered briefly just what miracle had happened in their midst over the years to transform this area into a living place that beckoned good-hearted people into its warm interior. They looked up at the sign, a larger wooden version of a horse brass found inside. It hung over the entry door; the pub's name, on the horseshoe over the horse's head, announced to all with understated elegance: HORSE BRASS.

Friends of the Horse Brass Pub and friends of Don Younger were not done, having set other wheels in motion. Two months later, copies of the April/May 2011 Anniversary Issue of the *Celebrator Beer News* arrived. It contained special tributes to Don Younger and his legendary pub. The *Celebrator* is for people who really know and love their beer—those that make it, those that drink it. Don Younger was certainly one of them, but he was also a key, energetic, persistent man who promoted good beer and helped the craft beer industry in the Pacific Northwest. The *Celebrator*, widely distributed throughout the United States and Canada to thousands of readers, had a full-page collage of photographs taken at the wake, around a memorial article about Don Younger. On the facing page, there was a full-page photograph of Don from an issue four years earlier, which had honored his 30 years at the helm of the Horse Brass Pub.

The April/May 2011 issue of *London Drinker* also carried a long obituary and tribute to Don. It spoke about his strong connections with London through the Prince of Wales pub in Merton, near Wimbledon. *London Drinker* is published on behalf of the London Branches of the Campaign for Real Ale, Ltd.

Like the enduring twinning of the Horse Brass Pub and the Prince of Wales, some 25 years earlier, the *Celebrator Beer News* and the *London Drinker* were now twinned in soul and purpose—in tribute to Donald Younger.

Don accomplished much in his life, whether reasoned, eccentric, planned or just touched by the hand of fate and good people. His mark is deeply etched on the history of Portland. He reached out and moved the hearts of his staff, his friends, his regulars—the whole family of the pub. The pub has done so much for so many, and it has the infused capability to continue doing so. Donald Allen Younger, the publican, has physically died, but his spirit lives on in his pub—the Horse Brass Pub.

PART II

In the Beginning

OLD BELMONT SQUARE

Before written or oral histories, what is now known as the Northern Willamette Valley of the State of Oregon was a caldron. Volcanic eruptions, steaming cinder cones and fuming vents all gave birth to buttes, mounts and incredible natural beauty. The area cooled.

A massive ice age flood cut a gorge through the volcanic mountain range to the east. Rains swept in from the enormous stretch of water to the west. A verdant cover grew.

The first people came, likely descendants of those that crossed an ancient ice bridge far to the northwest. They gathered, hunted and settled. Some clustered in a clearing, a communal area on the banks of a river that flowed north through a broad valley to join a great river from the east that flowed through the abraded cut in the mountains. On a crest of the western hills, their leaders met in council. They wondered with awe at the majestic, snow-covered volcanic peak far to the east. The Multnomah tribe called it Wy'east. Later, a nautical British explorer named the beautiful peak after a British Royal Navy admiral of the day, Samuel Hood.

Between Mount Hood and Council Crest in the West Hills, there lay smaller hills, dormant volcanic cinder cones. Tribal elders wondered about their spiritual origins as well. One dome-shaped hill was thought to have been named Mount Tabor by a later settler, the son of an Episcopal Methodist pastor, an Oregon City pioneer that arrived in 1848. His spiritual texts and sermons described the dome of Mount Tabor, or Har Tavor in Hebrew. Events of enormous

Mount Tabor, 2011, east of Downtown Portland from West Hills, Mount Hood above the clouds
Courtesy of Library of Congress
Highsmith archive, LC-DIG-highsm-12108

spiritual meaning were believed to have occurred on Har Tavor near the Sea of Galilee, half a world and centuries away.

While similar in shape, the Mount Tabor of Oregon had more trees than its namesake in the Holy Land due to the wetter climate of the Willamette Valley. Like Har Tavor, Oregon's mount was gently rounded. It had had no hard edges and was further softened by its nap of tall evergreen trees.

Native inhabitants and the early pioneers both sensed that the wooded Mount Tabor and its surrounding gently-sloping apron meant something special.

Inexorably, more people arrived from the east. Encampments grew into a city that spread from the river towards Mount Tabor. Properties were measured, staked and recorded. Streets were planned, named and paved, connecting workers and families that chose to live near the ancient volcanic cone. Modest wood-framed houses were built on the grid of streets for people that labored for their livelihood, built on rich sediment that lay over ancient compacted cinders from the depths.

Rains filtered down through the ancient silt, sand and volcanic ash to subterranean levels. The water formed an underground aquifer, spreading out and seeking the surface, the surface of land in the morning shadow of Mount Tabor. Springs dotted the land, feeding small streams and rivulets sloping towards the river, drainage left untouched until settlers left their mark.

The veil of Portland's unique character—grey, wet days from fall to spring—lay over the area. Following beautiful summer weather, this annual re-nourishment bestowed a gentle character to the neighborhood. All grew in the cool, damp weather and mild social climate. People and families of varying disposition and intent were drawn to Portland, but its persistent veil was there to filter them out; some remained, some moved on. The people of this neighborhood were accepting as they welcomed newcomers without judgment. Working people filled the neighborhood next to the main thoroughfare. Over time, there would be a gestation that gave birth to a special place, and with this birth there would be pains.

A small section of land lay relatively untouched until the early part of the twentieth century. Soon, there were owners of small lots, according to property ownership laws patterned after those in England. Those settlers built structures, houses and small business buildings. Houses were built on the south side of an east-west thoroughfare named Southeast Belmont Street and to the east of Southeast 45th Avenue. With due regard for Mount Tabor, the street name was appropriate, "beautiful mountain" in French.

Years later, some buildings lay nestled amongst deteriorating older houses. One building had an atrium garden in its center. It caught the eye of Walter Lincoln Tooze IV, then president of Seaport Shipping in Portland. Walter had attended Mount Angel Seminary, north of Silverton, Oregon, and well south of Portland. But Walter decided the priesthood was not for him. Yet, he had absorbed the basic philosophy of their teaching. After that, Walter worked as a messenger boy at Seaport Industries while working his way through Portland State University to a degree in Child Psychology. But the import-export business had more allure for Walter, so he formed his own company of Tooze and Associates. He became so successful in that venture that Seaport Industries merged with his growing company, and he became president of Seaport Shipping, an international freight forwarding business.

Walter had a keen eye and a good ear for business and, more importantly, honest people. Up to this time, Walter had dreamed of owning commercial buildings with spaces for lease and having his office in one of them.

Like many Americans, Walter's lineage traced back to England. For him, it was to Clayhanger in Devonshire. In the early 1800s, two brothers named William and James Tooze left their small village and their local public house and emigrated to the young, fresh United States of America with its Constitution inspired by England's Magna Carta. The Tooze family descendants spread in number and location. Some headed west to Oregon. Walter Lincoln Tooze I was born in the Willamette Valley, attended Mount Angel Seminary, served in World War I and was a candidate for the United States Congress. He became the 66th Associate Justice of the Oregon Supreme Court. All Tooze family members in America descended from William or James from Clayhanger, including Walter Lincoln Tooze IV.

Walter had his Seaport Shipping office in the Pacific Building in downtown Portland. When the building was sold, the office lease offered by the new owner was not to Walter's liking. There was a vacant plot of land near Mount Tabor, to the south and east of the intersection of Southeast Belmont Street and Southeast 45th Avenue. Next to that land were two one-story, '50s-styled buildings connected together that were for sale for a good price. Walter purchased and renovated them and leased them out as offices. With future expansion in mind, he called them Building One and Building Two; he dreamed of buying the corner vacant lot. It, too, came up for sale. He was determined to buy it and construct a building there, and he did.

The corner lot was covered with scruffy grass, weeds, scrub bushes and a few small trees. Neighborhood children played there. In a corner of the lot was a small wooden shed used for dropping off bundles of newspapers for young boys who delivered *The Oregonian*, one of the main daily newspapers of the growing city. The vacant lot was the center for distributing printed news to the surrounding residents.

Walter wanted to erect Building Three on the lot. He started the process for a building loan at a local bank. Quite sure of himself, he started excavating the lot for a building with a basement *before* the loan had been approved. The loan officer was a bit surprised when he came out to check out the site and found a newly dug hole in the ground. He called Walter and asked, "What are you doing?! You don't have the money yet."

Walter confidently replied, "I'm building a building. I know you'll approve the loan." As predicted, he got the financing and Building Three was completed. A bank was the first tenant.

Up the street, towards Mount Tabor, there were a couple of old commercial buildings and old vacant houses. Walter continued buying property in that direction. Existing structures were torn down and Building Four was built, but without a basement. City engineers advised of the risks as there were a spring and a small creek that flowed right through the property. To accommodate the natural spring water, drainage tiles were laid and covered with a concrete slab, the base for the floor above. Water from the spring merged with rainwater from the paved surface of the rear parking lot and flowed through a drainpipe into the city drainage system. Unfortunately, the drain piping under the parking lot was installed with a flaw that restricted flow. When Portland's rain was heavy and persistent, the shallow area around the drain grate just outside Building Four's back door would fill with water to within a fraction of an inch of coming into the building. Four decades would elapse before the drainpipe would be repaired. Until then, people coming and going through this rear exit had to pay special attention, taking a small leap over this pedestrian water hazard. It would take on a special meaning to some.

Buildings Three and Four were separated by a pedestrian plaza from the street to the parking lot constructed out back. He covered the plaza by a second floor that connected the office spaces of the two buildings, making it a tunneled pedestrian passageway.

Expansion according to Walter's dream continued eastward towards Mount Tabor. He purchased an existing building, his Building Five. It had a special feature that really appealed to Walter. "What sold me was an atrium garden in the middle of the building. I had it completely gutted and went to colonial and old traditional." [1]

Between Building Four and Building Five, Walter had a driveway built from the street to the rear parking lot. As before, he added a second floor that connected Building Five to the second floor of Building Four. That covered the driveway, making it a car tunnel.

Walter built his dream office in the basement of Building Five, next to the atrium. His Seaport Shipping office had a nautical motif: old oak wood finishes, fireplaces, a sauna, wet bar, tall leather wing back chairs, built-in TV, and antiques. Around the basement level of the atrium, Walter built out and leased the remaining spaces. They became Old Belmont Country Store, a contract post office and Old Belmont Kitchen with an old-fashioned ice cream parlor.

Walter had never been to Colonial Williamsburg, but photographs of its buildings had made an impression on him. The fronts of taverns, homes and public buildings in Colonial Williamsburg were right next to the sidewalk, with small-paned windows.

Walter named the connected collection of buildings Old Belmont Square. He applied the Colonial Williamsburg architecture to Buildings Three and Four, which also meant that the necessary parking lot would be in the back and not visible to passing motorists or pedestrians. With a bank on the corner, and either a restaurant or tavern in Building Four, Old Belmont Square became the center of a village.

Building Six followed across Belmont Street, a beautiful three-story brick structure with the same external architecture. Walter's dream was complete.

Building Four was a stout-looking, two-story structure with a red brick exterior, black wrought iron gate at the entrance, framed by a dark-painted wood mantel with paned windows on either side. This building fit the Colonial Williamsburg character of Old Belmont Square. The tunnels were there more for function than form. Walter wanted to use as much of the land area as possible, with office spaces over the tunnels. The driveway and passageway tunnels were needed for access to the rear parking area to support tenants and businesses that leased the buildings' spaces, for their employees and patrons. They reminded some of the architecture found in the French Quarter of New Orleans with its tunnels leading to interior gardens, shops and cafés hidden from the street. Walter knew that it was better to make the parking lot a little less convenient in order to not clutter the architecture as seen from the street and sidewalk, a basic design consideration quite different than that found in the strip mall of the day.

The architecture of the collection of buildings added to the character of the surrounding blue-collar neighborhood. Like spaces in the other buildings, Building Four was easily leased by referral during its construction. For available space in Old Belmont Square, advertising was not necessary. One look at the architecture, the neighborhood and the out-of-sight parking lot made the business potential obvious.

Building Four was completed in 1973. It was destined for much greater significance than the sterile reference to the number of a building built in sequence as part of a larger plan for Old Belmont Square. Walter knew that the ground floor unit, with its Colonial Williamsburg face, with a hint of the New Orleans French Quarter, would make a very nice home for a tavern, bar or themed restaurant. As a keen businessman, he always kept his eye on what was happening in the city. The old Hoyt Hotel in Downtown Portland had been closed in 1972 and was destined for destruction. Walter knew well the atmosphere in the hotel's Barbary Coast Lounge, bathed in the light of gas lamps, anchored by a beautiful wooden bar, all reviving the heart and feel of the Gay Nineties. That bar had seen a lot in the lounge, a home away from home for some of Portland's more interesting citizens. A bit of negotiation—Walter was good at that—and the old, wooden back bar was his. It found its way onto the ground floor of Building Four, bringing with it a fair bit of Portland's history. Old Belmont Square and Building Four would become the social center of the neighborhood, in both soul and character. But there were some bumps in the road leading there. The first business in Building Four's ground floor was a pizza tavern, the Gaslight Tavern of Belmont. It also offered live music to stimulate its customers. Gaslight-looking lamps were installed outside, adding the ambience of an earlier time, which was very fitting since the old bar inside had been surrounded by gas lamps at its previous home in the old Hoyt Hotel.

Opening night was exciting. A virtual riot of people packed the place. People from the neighborhood came in with their children. Walter and his wife, Ruth, helped out their new tenants that night, pouring beer and taking orders. While the pizza and beer were good and the business owner eager to succeed, the Gaslight Tavern was slow to catch on. It met the fate of many start-up restaurants and taverns, burdened with the complex vagaries that make or break such a business. Soon, it became more lucrative to sell it.

The Gaslight Tavern of Belmont was soon purchased by the owner of the Hook and Ladder Tavern. He was previously a representative in the State of Oregon Legislature and a fireman before that.[2] Not surprisingly, the Gaslight Tavern was renamed the Firehouse Tavern and transformed into a cabaret and advertised as such with more live music, dancing, and wine. This was trending towards a different ambience, one with unintended consequences. It turned into something quite different and eventually strained the relationship with the neighborhood, to say the very least.

Some months later, the owners brought in new management and the tavern was remodeled. A large dance floor replaced the game area. Music from local rock bands now catered to a younger, hirsute crowd with much hustling of drinks and dance partners.[3]

It became a rock and roll tavern that sold beer and just happened to sell pizza, rather than a tavern that sold pizza and just happened to have beer. That distinction was important. This new type of business was not designed with the neighbors or neighborhood in mind, except solely as a source of customers and profit. It was another gathering place, but mostly for young people from different parts of the city, guided more by moments of opportunity and unthinking hormones than fraternity. The food, drink and stimulating music were mere preludes for more private meetings away from the establishment.

The business owner and his friends happened to like motorcycles, powerful two-wheeled vehicles, some made by the venerable Harley-Davidson company. They also liked the life-style that sometimes came with powerful motorcycles, close-knit groups that rode together celebrating life in unique and colorful ways on the road and at their favorite watering holes. The Firehouse Tavern attracted customers of this ilk. They were usually not content to just quietly discuss matters of life, love and manhood while sipping good ale.

The Firehouse Tavern evolved unintentionally into a biker bar, a tough biker bar right in the middle of a quiet village. This added a unique character to the area and a certain zest for life. But the things that spilled out into the street from this new establishment did not square with its surrounding neighborhood in the morning shadow of Mount Tabor. Often, too often, the early morning calm was interrupted by the sound of revved-up Harley Hogs demonstrating their owners' testosterone levels. Muscle cars with powerful engines, and little in the way of mufflers, also shattered the night's calm from the parking lot and from side streets, and denied sleep to neighbors. Loud motorcycles and hot rods were sometimes accompanied by loud, colorful shouting and physical exchanges when there were disagreements over petty issues. Some neighbors thought they remembered hearing the sharp crack of gunshots. Sirens and flashing lights accompanied the results of a knife fight right outside the front door and a shooting nearby that involved customers of the tavern, adding to the nighttime festivities. Neighbors were more than a tad unhappy.

Walter worked with the tenants of Building Four while trying hard to calm the valid concerns of the neighbors. A tough biker bar could find a place in a free society, but certainly not in this neighborhood. He heard complaints of horrific noise, no doubt from the big Harleys and their vocal riders. Some neighbors did not relish that their fences and shrubbery were torn up by frisky patrons of the Firehouse, stumbling back to their vehicles parked in front of neighborhood homes, sometimes blocking their driveways. Often, with just a bit too much to drink, some tired, bleary patrons used the neighbors' streets, sidewalks and lawns for bedrooms and bathrooms before leaving. One woman angrily reported being nearly run over in front of her home on two occasions by drivers drunk from drinking at the Firehouse.

Another neighbor resorted to picketing the Firehouse Tavern in her bathrobe. She was also the catalyst for petitions and letters for over two years, starting with the Gaslight Tavern. Such was the level of her anger, and that of her neighbors, that a local TV station aired a feature story of her in her bathrobe, and the strongly-worded sign she carried, striding defiantly in front of the Firehouse Tavern. Normally, free publicity for a tavern would be a good thing, but definitely not in this case.

Things clearly had gotten way out of hand. The Oregon Liquor Control Commission (OLCC) and the Mayor of Portland received the full force of the neighborhood's written wrath. They very strongly suggested or, more accurately, demanded that alcoholic beverages not be allowed in that retail space—ever! With the onslaught of petitions and letters, and confirmation of alleged activities that violated OLCC rules, action was needed. It was difficult to know which came first, the OLCC's cancellation of the Firehouse Tavern's beer and wine license, or Walter's eviction notice. The band of irate neighbors signed a strongly-worded petition to then-Mayor Neil Goldschmidt and the Portland City Council.

Now the cavernous ground floor space of Building Four lay vacant except for a newly constructed bar, the beautiful historic back bar and a few wooden tables and low padded stools. The petition to the mayor and the city council, and the OLCC's heightened awareness of what had gone wrong at this place, could have put a damper on a potential suitor's desire for running a similar business in this space. Could they get an OLCC license with the neighbors closely watching?

Even so, there were a number of eager business people that wanted to purchase the Firehouse Tavern business, name and all, intent on changing it to a more reputable establishment. However, Walter knew that would never fly with the neighbors, and probably not with the city council and the OLCC. A tavern with the same name at the same location, but under different ownership, would likely still draw the same type of patrons, like flies thinking the same old honeypot was still there. Bikers now knew the neighborhood, and they would still need a place to park their Harleys so they could stride inside to quench their thirst after a long day on the road.

A paying tenant with a very different vision for his building was needed. Walter found one, or rather, one found Walter. He was a man who grew up in Portland and had lived in England some 20 years earlier. This potential businessman knew with conviction that a friendly, quiet establishment that served good beer in a family atmosphere for young and old alike would enhance the character of the neighborhood as its social gathering place, a place where people could find companionship. It would be the social opposite of the Firehouse Tavern. An English pub would fill the void.

Jay Brandon

Where does a dream start? For most, a dream is the result of the sum total of life experience and the hope and expectations for the future. A key ingredient in the early fermentation of the Horse Brass Pub, like barley is to beer, was the dream nurtured in a young, transplanted boy of Scottish heritage.

Jay Brandon's mother and stepfather moved from Indiana to Portland in early 1941. Jay was eight years old at the time and turned nine in September of that year. Within three months, Jay's connection to England, and the formation of his dream, began with a violent start half an ocean away.

Despite being a chilly December day, a quiet Sunday, he was out riding his bike around his neighborhood near Southeast Hawthorne Street. The quiet noontime atmosphere was broken by startled, angry neighbors, pouring out into the street, hollering and yelling something about an attack on the United States Navy base in Hawaii—Pearl Harbor. Jay did not understand, but he sensed it must be something very important. He rode his bike back home as fast as he could and asked his stepfather what this was all about. Having lived for 13 years in the Far East, his stepfather tried to explain to Jay what it meant at the moment, and what it meant for the immediate future.

The effects of World War II swirled around Jay's young life, as it did around all Americans: people volunteering or drafted and marching off to war, rationing, paper and metal drives, buying stamps for war bonds, stretching scarce butter by mixing it with oleo, and the hand delivery of terrible telegrams. For Jay and his childhood friends, there were "the bundles." Young boys found themselves knitting small squares from yarn. Mothers in the neighborhood stitched these squares together into blankets to keep warm the war-weary people who had been bombed from their homes in England, on the other side of the Atlantic Ocean. These were wrapped up as Bundles for Britain and shipped east, hopefully to make their way across the dangerous Atlantic.

All of Jay's uncles served in the war, so Jay felt connected to this indelible epic event. He became very interested in the war, reading much in the papers and watching many newsreels about England and the war in Europe.

The war ended when Jay was in high school in Gresham, Oregon, even though his family had recently moved back into Portland. He was brash and impetuous. Jay insisted on commuting to his Gresham high school where he was part of the "in crowd." He had been the sophomore class president and now had his eye on being student body president. Jay's stepfather put his foot down and directed that Jay transfer to Grant High School. Jay, with all the wisdom of youth, boldly said, "I'll go in the military before I do that!"

His stepfather jokingly replied, "OK, soldier."

Jay took this seriously and made the rounds of all the recruiters during the summer. He was 17 years old at the time and tried to enlist in the United States Marine Corps. An uncle, a Marine who had served in the South Pacific, had been killed in action. But the new United States Air Force nabbed Jay. All that was needed was for his parents to sign off so that he could enlist in the service of his country before his 18th birthday.

Jay was a very bright young man and his capabilities were soon recognized. After basic training and a few short assignments stateside, he was sent to an Air Force school in Omaha, Nebraska, to become a cryptographer, a very difficult specialty. Two three-month temporary duty cryptographer assignments took him to England. Messages during the early days of the Cold War needed encrypting and decrypting, especially when they involved the movement of nuclear weapons.

His first assignment was to RAF Sculthorpe. Having read so much about the war in Europe, he was absolutely thrilled to be in England at the tender age of 19. Jay also felt a strong kinship to this country, as his Scottish ancestors had been a sept of Clan Gordon, a large, powerful family within that clan.

The nearest town of any size near Sculthorpe was Norwich, near the North Sea. That was also where the girls were. He and his buddies soon fell into a weekend ritual. Historic English castles, buildings or manor houses were not on their agenda. Their place of choice was the Samson and Delilah, an English dance hall. Not only would English girls be found there, small bars were at the corners of the large dance floor with seating along the walls. That is where young American airmen met young ladies, as they had done during WWII just a few years earlier. Showing up in uniform also helped break the ice. Jay got to know a group of close friends at the dance hall—Rita, Yvonne and Melba. And they danced. It was all good fun. But Jay had to rotate back to the United States when his 90-day temporary duty assignment was over.

After a short time stateside, Jay was next assigned to RAF Burtonwood between Liverpool and Manchester. Certainly, there were young women in those fair cities. Yet there was something about Norwich and the Samson and Delilah dance hall that drew him back there—Rita, Yvonne and Melba. Norwich was a considerable distance from RAF Burtonwood, but trains remedied that. Another weekend ritual was started. With weekend passes in hand, he and his uniformed fellows made their way to the train station, boarded and headed to Norwich to dance.

Squeezing every hour out of the weekend, they boarded a return train just before midnight on Sunday. With just a bit of beer under their belts, they would sleep on the way back and hopefully be fit for duty in the morning. Trains in those days were not particularly posh affairs, at least not this late-night train. There was no heat in any of the cars except those designated First Class. They did not have First Class tickets, but they went in those warm cars anyway. Jay and his buddies would curl up on the seats, stick their tickets in their Air Force flight caps for the conductor to see, and doze off to the rocking clickety-clack of wheels on rails. Conductors had been through the war and were appreciative of what the Yanks had done. They just stopped, looked at the inebriated airmen with their wrong tickets showing, smiled, and moved on.

Tickets, train trips and dances — Jay rekindled his friendships with those girls from Norwich. As before, time ran out before things got too serious. It was back to the United States again to await orders.

The Korean War broke out, and Jay soon had orders to that conflict. Jay requested, or more accurately begged, to go back to England. Because of his unique military skill and the guiding hand of fate, his orders were cancelled. He wound up with a permanent assignment to England, to RAF Mildenhall on the flat fens of East Anglia, not far from Cambridge — and Norwich, as luck would have it. Soon after his arrival, he made a phone call and boarded a train. Yvonne and Melba met him at the station and informed Jay that Rita was engaged to be married. One thing led to another, and Jay started dating in earnest Yvonne Adams of the original threesome.

They got along famously. She had a great family of mother, father and two brothers. He admired them, and they became quite fond of him. Her father had been away during the war, fighting with the Allies in North Africa. Yvonne and her family had weathered bombing raids on Norwich. They all knew what war was about, and they had not forgotten the sacrifices made by the Yanks to bring the war to a close. Soon, Jay was invited to stay with them on his weekend visits. While he had visited English public houses on earlier assignments, Norwich is where his love affair with pubs began. Like virtually every corner of the British Isles, Norwich had pubs. Jay fell in love twice, first with Yvonne, who would become his wife, and second with pubs.

Sunday was a traditional pub day in Norwich for Yvonne's family. The men would go to their local right across the street, the Artichoke pub. There they would converse and drink from late morning until early afternoon, put on a beer-induced glow, and come back to a warm home where the women of the house had fixed a nice, big Sunday dinner. This was followed by sitting around the coal fireplace in their cozy lounge, occasionally dozing off. They were sure to awaken in time to hit the pub in the evening, usually with Yvonne and her mother. This was also in keeping with tradition and mores, wherein a proper English chap drank in the pub, not in his home. Jay realized that English pubs were not at all like taverns and bars back in the United States. After more pub Sundays and more dates with this wonderful English girl, Jay was hooked. He loved them both.

English pubs were now in his blood. From some pub regulars he learned that a pub was sometimes called "the church with levers." This referred to the long, decorated wooden handles used to pump beer by hand from the cool pub cellar. If a chap visited his local pub in lieu of Sunday church services, a guilty conscience could be soothed a bit if asked of his whereabouts that day. A wink accompanied the answer that he had been to church alright, the church with levers. There was a different religion in those pubs, a warm embracing religion, and Jay felt it. Considering the real value of God-given human companionship found in the social center of the village, a pub could be more of an accepting community than that found in a church that dictated beliefs and behavior.

As his love of English pubs blossomed, so did his love of this lady from Norwich and hers for him. They married in 1951 and moved into a little home, a quaint English cottage in his mind, in the small, old village of Lidgate. Of course, compared to America, all English villages, towns and cities were old. Their first child, a boy, was born there. Jay used his free time to complete some courses at the University of Cambridge, a mere 20 miles away.

Lidgate, being a proper village, had pubs. Jay soon had his own local, and his local had a regular from America. The Star pub was steeped in history, its dwelling having been built in the 1500s. Carved oak beams on the ceiling, stout bressummer beams, supported the upper floor with quarters for the publican and his wife. Its old English style was adorned and protected by horse brasses.

During those magnificent years, Jay thought he was in Heaven without having to get there the hard way. Of course, with visits to his friendly in-laws in Norwich, the Artichoke pub on Sundays, and his local pub in Lidgate without waiting for Sundays, his love affair with pubs grew and grew. On occasional trips throughout the countryside, Jay just had to visit pubs of opportunity—to sample their beer and the all-important companionship found there with the people of the village. He soon realized that pubs were not only the lounge and social center of the village; they were indicative of the very heart of Britain.

Jay could not help but notice that almost all pubs had small, brass decorative items, round or crescent-shaped, about the size of the palm of his hand, hung from plastered walls and roughhewn timbers; some were attached to leather straps. These shiny brass amulets were called horse brasses. There were many different molded designs: horses and other animals, castles, churches, beer kegs, sun, moon, stars, and more. The variety was large indeed. Over a pint, Jay asked about their origin. He studied up on these ubiquitous things scattered throughout the British Isles. Much had been written about the origins of horse brasses and their meanings, some of it superstitious. This was fascinating stuff to Jay. It just might help explain the magic of warm companionship found in a church with levers. Never doing things half-heartedly, he started his own collection of horse brasses and accumulated hundreds of them. Jay purchased them in antique and curiosity shops, at fairs and markets in village squares. These were part of the history of Britain, and part of her pubs.

Jay learned that horse brasses, or at least their meaning, were very ancient things, likely brought to England by European gypsies, or possibly by the Romans as adornments on their horses, attached to the leather harnesses. People in ancient times held superstitious beliefs in the power of the "evil eye," possibly promoted by roaming gypsies who just happened to have antidotes and protective services to sell. Evil and darkness were one in the minds of medieval people, so an amulet with designs related to the worship of the Sun could push away the darkness and protect its owner. Early amulets were hand hewn from workable metals: copper, tin, zinc, and lead. The dawn of the Industrial Age brought foundries and amulets cast from the molten alloy of copper and zinc—brass. In addition to the leather straps of horse harnesses, the amulets were also hung on cottage walls, in manor houses, in pubs. It became common to decorate the leather straps of big draught horses with amulets, sometimes containing the name or logo of the hauling company or brewery that owned them. Some of these big steeds pulled heavy wagons to public houses, delivering wooden barrels of beer. The amulets became commonly known as horse brasses. In the minds of many over the years, horse brasses would provide protection from evil and promote good luck.

Jay's five-year Air Force enlistment ended after nearly three years in England. He moved back to Portland with his family. His military commitment was over. But due to his specialty and his rare security clearance, a three-letter agency of the Federal Government lobbied him hard, trying to convince him to move to Washington, DC. He thought for a moment, realized he was back in God's country, and politely declined to work in the most secretive corners of his nation's capital.

His first job with Pacific Northwest Bell was in 1958, collecting coins from pay phones. Jay wanted something more but did not know exactly what. He left the telephone company. The deep love of pubs and the excitement of England were still very much there, and Jay was restless. But he had to support himself and his family, which by now included four children.

Jay signed on with a wholesale record company. While there, he became good friends with a kind, elderly couple that worked in the shipping department. He was quite interested when they told him about their son, who was building the first real English pub in Portland in an historic building on Portland's near west side, at the corner of Southwest 2nd and Washington. The ground floor of the three-story Waldo Building, built in 1886, was transformed into a pub. The name given the pub spoke to a major road intersection in the London Borough of Southwark, on the south side of the Thames, called the Elephant and Castle. This stemmed from a coaching inn of the same name at that location dating back hundreds of years. The inn was well known, so much so that Shakespeare referred to it in *Twelfth Night*. In latter days, a stop on the London Underground, the Tube, took on the name. For a pub in the center of Portland, what name could be more British?

The couple left the record company to help their son run the Elephant and Castle. They knew of Jay's deep love of England and her pubs, that he had an English wife, and that he knew the local English community. Before it opened, they asked Jay to tend bar at the pub. He became the first bartender there. He relished serving patrons and promoting the companionship and comfortable ambience found in an English pub. He was home.

Early customers thought Jay was the owner. The real owners were content to manage quietly in the background. Jay worked hard to make the Elephant and Castle as authentic as possible, to become the first true English-styled pub in Portland. The owner had done a very good job decorating the place. It included a huge crystal chandelier brought back from Europe after the war. It hung from the high ceiling in the middle of the pub and filled it with unique character, as did the beautiful dark wooden, mirrored bar. Jay knew that furnishings and fittings were important in helping frame the character of a pub. He also knew that the spirit of a pub ultimately came from the people that frequented and worked there.

But money was money, and bills were bills. So, with a wife and four children, Jay returned four years later to a management job at the telephone company and started his steady climb up the company's career ladder, being named the company's public relations representative in 1968. As it turned out, his office was only three blocks from the Elephant and Castle. Like clockwork, he would get off work at the telephone company at 5 pm, walk to the Elephant and Castle, take off his suit coat, put on a colorful vest, tend bar, welcome patrons by name and entertain them until closing time. Jay would get up and go back to work at the telephone company the following morning and repeat the cycle. He liked his job at the telephone company, but he was content and satisfied with his work at the Elephant and Castle. That was an important difference.

A very active sort, unless Jay had many irons in the fire, he became bored. After his return to Portland, he had helped his stepfather start a travel agency, Brandon Travel. Jay was helping run the agency in his spare time. As if Jay did not have enough to do, he had become involved in local English and Scottish societies; he was the business manager of the Portland Scottish Pipe Band, he became Vice President of the local Saint Andrews Society, and served as field steward at local Highland Games. Following in his stepfather's footsteps, Jay also became heavily involved in the Portland Chamber of Commerce. He proved to be an exceptionally hard worker in fund-raising activities for the Rose Festival Association, the Pacific International Livestock Exposition, and the Columbia Pacific Boy Scouts Council. As chairman of the Commerce club, Jay spear-headed membership drives. For his dedication and hard work, Jay was the youngest person ever to be awarded the Chamber's Life Membership Gold Card. In addition, Jay also attended Portland State College.

Twenty years earlier while living in England, he had begun creating a pub in the back of his mind, with the dream of building and running an authentic English pub in Portland. While working at the Elephant and Castle, the pub in his head started to swirl around and around, gaining steam. Jay now had a goal, a dream that the people of Portland would realize and appreciate just how a real pub is different from a tavern or bar, a place where old people can sit alongside young people and both feel at home. Yes, home, a home open to all, a warm and welcoming public place with a family atmosphere. The pub in Jay's mind took shape: design, decorations, colors, lights, bar, beer, levers for his "church" and, of course, horse brasses. He had boxes of them that he had collected while living in England. He had carefully and reverently brought them back, stored them securely, waiting to be hung to work their magic in the pub of his dreams.

Fate conspired to thwart Jay's dream for a while. It was during the early 1970s when he had his first opportunity to fulfill it. There was a little two-story building in Downtown Portland that became available, across the street from the old Multnomah Hotel. Money and partnership were needed. The deal, financially, was almost put together, with a star hockey player from the Portland Buckaroos and a friendly English chap, a printer by trade, to be Jay's business partners. But it did not work out. Or maybe it was not meant to be.

An entrepreneur at heart, Jay found himself involved in all manner of things interesting, and profitable. A man he knew at the telephone company had started a small side business manufacturing and selling Murphy's Magic Wet Weather Windshield Sponges. Basically, these were normal kitchen sponges soaked with a special chemical that when wetted and rubbed on a wet car windshield did a bit of magic. This application supposedly eliminated smearing from windshield wipers and was touted to cause rainwater to sheet in a thin film making it almost possible to drive with inoperative windshield wipers. This man did not have Jay's sales and business management skills, so he sold the small business to Jay. The manufacturing end of the business was transferred to Jay's garage with the use of three old wringer-type washing machines that he purchased. He hired local neighborhood kids to make and package the sponges. Sponges were "washed" in the oscillating tubs, run through the wringer and let dry before packaging. This little side venture put spending money in the pockets of some neighborhood teenagers and netted Jay some extra cash that was put to good use to help finance a more important venture on the east side of town.

Jay did try his hand at the tavern business, to gain some business experience and credibility in the eyes of future creditors or partners when it came time to create the pub of his dreams. It was a typical Portland neighborhood tavern on Sandy Boulevard in Portland's near-east side — the Coach Light. Jay was part of a four-way partnership. Eventually, he bought out the other three and ran the place for nearly two years. Even though the Coach Light was not an English-styled pub, people in the local English and Scottish communities frequented the tavern because of Jay. This further cemented his relationship with these expats who knew what an English pub was all about. Jay eventually sold this tavern. With the profit, he impulsively took his entire family back to England and Norwich for the summer, and he spent a month there with them. To Jay, it was money very well spent. It recharged his batteries, as if that were necessary.

After his return, a better opportunity presented itself, but not to Jay. Because of his work at Brandon Travel and the telephone company, Jay had to reassess his priorities. By now he was the Marketing Manager for Pacific Northwest Bell. His time had to be spread between his job at the telephone company, helping out at Brandon Travel and tending bar at the Elephant and Castle. So he left tending bar there for a time. Unfortunately for Jay, the pub was sold while he was not working there. Jay did not know the owner was considering selling it because it was not widely advertised. Otherwise, Jay would have done everything possible to take over the place, making some modifications, fulfilling his dream of running a pub in Portland. In any event, the Elephant and Castle slipped through Jay's hands.

A while later Jay learned of another opportunity. It was on the east side of Portland, across the Willamette River towards a low hill called Mount Tabor. Jay and his wife made a quick drive to Old Belmont Square and met Walter Tooze. Walt unlocked the door to the unoccupied ground floor and they went in. The interior was kind of blah, just a pizza tavern without any real character to it. To Jay, the space was not perfect, but close. Actually, his original dream was for more than an English pub. It was for a miniature village with little walk-through shops, cheap and cheerful, with the pub at its center. But thanks to Walter Tooze, those aspects of Jay's dream already existed to some degree in Old Belmont Square. Jay would provide the central pub.

Despite the place being dull and cavernous, it did have that nice wooden back bar from Portland's old Hoyt Hotel. Some of the tables and low stools could be used in Jay's pub, but little else was worth keeping. The space was much larger than that found in English pubs. Without modification, it would be decidedly less cozy. He and his wife felt something, though, and thought maybe this could be the blank canvas for the pub in Jay's mind, his dream pub.

Parts of that canvas were the tunnels from the street to the parking lot in back, one for pedestrians and one for cars. Jay had taken many pictures of pubs when he had lived in England to help define the pub in his head. He particularly liked those tunnels, walkways to a rear entry courtyard behind or to the side of the pub. The tunnels of Old Belmont Square helped Jay make his decision.

In the days that followed, there was discussion about the lease cost with Walter Tooze before Jay talked things over with his English wife in earnest. She saw the excitement in Jay's eyes as he outlined how he could convert and decorate this available space. But that would take money, in addition to the monthly lease cost. Unless he found a business partner, his dream pub would not get off the ground.

There was another Jay in Portland, Jay Kileen. He was working in the position that Jay Brandon's stepfather once held at the local Chamber of Commerce. The Two Jays, as they would be known, met to discuss this business opportunity. They visited the empty place on Southeast Belmont and noticed the tunnels. Inside, with Walter Tooze and Jay Kileen, Jay Brandon walked around and described with animated waving hands how he would build out the space, elevate part of the floor, divide the room into smaller areas with low wooden railings, all easily viewed by the bartender. Dark, rough-hewn beams and posts would frame a freshly plastered white ceiling and walls that would hold authentic English artifacts and decorations. And, of course, horse brasses would be hung from the posts and walls.

Jay Kileen thought this over for a while. Jay Brandon convinced him that this establishment would be unique, in the tradition of English pubs, with just a bit of the spirit of the Elephant and Castle, the Artichoke pub, and The Star pub thrown in for good measure. Jay Kileen wanted to oversee the business part of the partnership. He contacted Walter Tooze, despite having learned of the problems caused by the previous, now-evicted tenants, the Firehouse Tavern. He told Walter that he and Jay Brandon wanted to lease the space and convert it into an English pub according to the plans described during earlier visits.

The Two Jays were not the only people interested in leasing the space and running a tavern or bar there. Some other business people wanted to buy that business, lease the space and reopen the tavern. For very good reasons, this would be a hard sell to the justifiably irate neighbors. But the neighbors might just soften to the idea of an English pub in their midst, like the one described by Jay Brandon. After all, a true English pub is the social center and lounge of a village.

In response to problems caused by Firehouse Tavern patrons, wanting to be a good neighbor in general, and as the owner of commercial buildings in their neighborhood, Walter Tooze began hosting coffee-and-donuts neighborhood gatherings in his office. At the initial gatherings, Walter received broadsides from his neighbors, aimed at him and the Firehouse. He definitely knew where they sat on the type of business desired in the now-vacant space. In a nutshell, it was one that did not sell alcohol. He had a solution, a paying tenant and a business that would be welcomed by the neighbors, or at least not initially opposed. Walter contacted Jay Brandon and asked that he open his English pub in the vacant building. But there were hurdles to be cleared. He invited Jay to a February, 1975 coffee-and-donuts meeting with the neighbors. Jay readily accepted, but also discovered that he *had* to attend as Walter's condition for signing a business lease. The irate neighbors, led by neighborhood activists, were there to be convinced. Jay brought some of his horse brasses to show, for luck and for the needed protection. Jay softly gave a brief history of English pubs and the role they play in the life of English villages. He described the pub in his mind, one to appeal to members of the British Commonwealth Society (formed by British expats living in Portland) and the many ex-service men and women that had spent some years in England. The atmosphere would be that of an old English pub, as if you had walked into it during the Second World War or just after the war, as Jay had done. Jay's vision had this pub being the only place in Portland serving authentic English food. The neighbors were surprised to hear that Jay had already contacted Colonel Whitbread, of Whitbread Brewery in London, and was arranging a trip there to purchase old tables, chairs and other things found in old English pubs. Of course, he held up some horse brasses that would adorn the pub and passed them around to be examined by suspicious neighbors. Those brasses worked a little magic.

After another cup of coffee, a few more donuts and considerable discussion, some of the neighbors were convinced, but not all. The signed petition that had been sent to the Mayor of Portland and Portland City Council was thrust into Jay's hands. There would certainly be hurdles.

After the coffee-and-donuts meeting, the woman who had coordinated the original petition went back around the neighborhood and petitioned in *favor* of the English pub. Jay's presentation had resonated with what she thought would be welcomed, or at least tolerated, in their fair neighborhood. She initiated another petition, this one far more favorable to the opening of an English pub in Old Belmont Square.

Jay was not one to waste time and let another opportunity slip though his fingers. He quickly applied for an OLCC Retail Malt Beverage License. The wind to fill the sails of his dream pub was good beer. Even though not the primary reason for visiting a pub, without the ability to sell malt beverages, the number of patrons would be thin.

The administrative wheels were set in motion. But it was noted that the Portland City Council would have more than a passing say on this application, with a neighborhood signed petition against an establishment that served alcoholic beverages sitting on the mayor's desk. A report on Jay's application for a Retail Malt Beverage License, prepared by the Portland Department of Finance and Administration, was scheduled for review on March 13, 1975, by the Portland City Council with public testimony permitted. The department's report had a favorable recommendation, but this was certainly no guarantee of how the council would vote.

Reviews and recommendations by the city council on liquor license applications were routine, often handling the reports on many applications in one session. But the original neighborhood petition sat on this one like a lead weight. And there was an additional complexity, with uncertain consequences, thanks to Jay's earlier eager involvement in city affairs.

Jay knew Mayor Neil Goldschmidt like many people did. However, Mayor Goldschmidt also knew Jay very well, in a way that could prove somewhat awkward. When Neil Goldschmidt was running for mayor in 1972, his main opponent in the primary balloting, R. W. "Bill" DeWeese, needed a little campaign management help. By this time, Jay Brandon's energy and enthusiasm for any task he tackled were well known to those on the Chamber of Commerce and in Portland business circles. Business people and political operatives approached Jay and asked that he take a leave of absence from the telephone company and run DeWeese's campaign. Jay was agreeable, if the telephone company was. They were, and Jay immersed himself in city politics at the mayoral level for the next two months.

The hours were very long. Jay was only getting three or four hours of sleep a night. He worked every day until the polls closed. The voters of Portland spoke; DeWeese's vote tally came up too short. Jay returned to his job at the telephone company. Now he and his OLCC application would be before Mayor Goldschmidt.

Jay strode into City Hall and into the Council Chamber, with some of his horse brasses in a box under his arm. His task was to convince the City Council and Mayor Goldschmidt that he was going to open an establishment not at all like the Firehouse Tavern. This was going to be a true English-style pub, a place that would be a welcome addition to the neighborhood, not a dangerous detriment.

The mayor and council members came into the Council Chamber from their offices in City Hall and took their seats on the dais. Jay sat in the public section with others also waiting to publically voice their opinions to their elected leaders. The chamber was filled with Belmont neighbors. They came with strong feelings about allowing another alcohol-serving business in their neighborhood. The later, more favorable petition resulting from the coffee-and-donuts meeting had been submitted in time. It accompanied the department's report on the application of J C B, Inc. for a Retail Malt Beverage License at "Horse Brass, 4534 S. E. Belmont Street" with the department's favorable recommendation.

When the session started at 2 pm, the first thing on the council's agenda was a report on five liquor license applications. Jay's application could easily have been included in that batch, but it had a much larger case file, including the neighborhood petitions. It deserved separate review and testimony. Despite the positive later petition from some neighbors, four especially vocal women took to the microphone and let fly with public testimony that could frost a pumpkin on a warm fall day:

> "The noise was terrific and they tore up the fences, they tore out shrubbery, they used our streets for bedrooms and they used it for bathrooms and I'm telling you the things that went on there were just out of this world."
>
> "Instead of getting in their cars they would *rrrrr-rrrr*, just roar them out. You couldn't get a night's rest they would make so much noise."
>
> "I have come home occasionally at 1:30 am when the tavern was there and have just barely escaped being killed by the drunk drivers coming out of there."
>
> "If you people issue them a license to have another tavern, we'll have the same things over again and that is something we do not want." [4]

When they had finished, Jay thought citizens' civic pitchforks and torches had been exchanged for the tambourines and axes of a neighborhood temperance movement. The coffee-and-donuts meeting had not been as successful as hoped for in changing everyone's mind towards an establishment in their neighborhood that sold alcoholic beverages. Some had not attended the meeting when Jay had spoken. They focused on the problems caused by the Firehouse Tavern, and the pub of Jay's dreams was being tarred with the same brush. To these women, another alcoholic beverage-selling establishment would result in the same horrific behavior by its patrons. The neighbor who led the charge for the new, favorable petition was unfortunately not able to attend.

At last, it was Jay's turn. As he had done at the coffee-and-donuts meeting, Jay described the pub he planned and how it would benefit the neighborhood. He gave a brief description of the horse brasses and handed around to the council members some of the ones he had collected in England. Surely, he thought, these objects of historical significance, intended to adorn his pub, would put a more positive sheen on his application.

Jay objected to how the OLCC had handled his application thus far. In response to it and letters received from neighbors, they had surveyed around 55 people in the neighborhood, asking if they would mind a tavern opening up at the proposed location — a tavern, not an English pub as described by Jay. Even so, just over 50 percent, 29 of those surveyed said they did not object. This was likely the result of the second, more favorable petitioning of the neighbors after Jay's presentation at the February coffee-and-donuts gathering.

Walter Tooze also testified in favor of the proposed pub. An empty space was not a very good return on his building investment. Walter needed a stable tenant. He and Jay fielded questions, mostly from one council member. There was some legitimate concern about spillover parking in the neighborhood, regardless of whether from a bar, tavern or pub. Walter addressed that and described just-finished additional parking and planned parking on the nearby property he owned. The fate of the pub was at a turning point. The odds were uncertain.

Mayor Goldschmidt spoke, "Unless there is objection from the Council . . . first of all I like the idea. I think it's a super idea and the only issue obviously is whether this place can accommodate it . . ." [4]

He said he would like to drive around the neighborhood to see the parking situation for himself. After more discussion, by unanimous vote the issue was continued until the following week.

In the following days, the mayor and some of the council members went to look over the property and its environs for themselves, always a good thing when making land use decisions. They strolled about and spoke to some neighbors in the process.

The March 20, 1975, city council session on the license application was very short. The roll was called on the issue, resulting in 5 Yeas and 0 Nays for transmittal of Jay's Retail Malt Beverage License application to the OLCC — with a favorable recommendation.[5]

A major hurdle had been cleared, but another lay ahead — the OLCC. Jay now had to appear before the OLCC's Board of Commissioners, a signed application in his hands and now in theirs. The name for Jay's establishment on Department of Finance and Administration's Report to the city council was Horse Brass. Jay, being a resourceful and clever fellow, requested a different name for his pub on the OLCC application form — The Horse's Brass.

The OLCC commissioners were a staid lot. They did not take kindly to Jay's requested name for his pub. It sounding disturbingly close to that part of a horse's anatomy usually attributed to people with limited honesty and poor social skills. The commissioners bluntly made their objections known to Jay. So out came the same stash of horse brasses he just happened to have handy. He passed them around to the commissioners. As they examined them he explained their history, their role in English pubs and as the basis for the requested name for his pub. He made his case with all the outward innocence he could muster, while knowing, with an inner wink, that this pub name would catch on very quickly, especially in Portland.

The OLCC was very well aware of the neighbors' raw feelings and felt that a suggestive name on a public sign in their neighborhood would not be a step in the right direction. After brief deliberation, Jay received a very frank, "With all that's happened to the neighbors around the Firehouse Tavern, how do you think they will take to a Horse's Brass sign hanging outside?! Nice try, but we're not going to approve your application for a place with *that* name."

A number of names were kicked around and negotiated on the fly. One satisfied Jay and the commissioners — they changed a possessive noun to an adjective and added a word of English origin — the proposed name for the place became "Horse Brass Pub." After all, that's what anybody would call one of those historic brass amulets, and a pub named after them would be in keeping with English tradition.

Now the Two Jays, Brandon and Kileen, had the necessary green light to open the Horse Brass Pub. They were motivated to do this quickly, not only for Jay's dream of becoming a publican of an English pub in Portland, but also because now a signed lease and monthly payments were breathing down their necks.

The interior space would have to be remodeled according to the pub in Jay's mind. Equally important, or more so, would be the furnishings and decorations, authentic artifacts to complement the bar, floor, plastered ceilings and walls, timbers and beams. Jay strongly prohibited kitsch. He would not have it. The décor, like his horse brasses, had to come from the origins of the public house—Britain.

BUILDING THE DREAM

In the spring of 1975, Jay Brandon finally had the underpinnings of his dream: a business financial partnership loosely referred to as the "Two Jays," a license to sell wine and beer, and a lease on a ground floor commercial space of a building in the center of a quiet neighborhood in Old Belmont Square. The fulfillment of one dream would enable the fulfillment of another. Walter Tooze now had his own office in his own set of buildings of Colonial Williamsburg design on Southeast Belmont; Jay Brandon would have his English pub. It had been over two decades since he had first tipped a pint in the Artichoke on Sunday pub day in Norwich. Now his pent up enthusiasm was unleashed.

Jay did not have to start from scratch. Ever the energetic optimist, he had been collecting things found here and there around Portland, some bric-a-brac for his dream pub. These had been added to his collection of horse brasses and tucked away for the day he had hoped would come.

One day he was browsing around in the 1874 House Antiques in the Sellwood neighborhood in Southeast Portland. It was one of those love-at-first-sight things. In a corner of the old shop was a curved, leaded-glass affair, a doorway cover. The glass sections were tinted a warm brownish-yellow. He bought it without hesitation knowing it would fit above the back bar in his dream pub. It would also go well with the backlit leaded glass sign he envisioned above the front bar. It would be simply worded, "Public Bar."

Jay had his eye on an artist's depiction of the *Charge of the Light Brigade*, an infamous, disastrous battle fought by ill-led British soldiers during the Crimean War, immortalized by a Lord Tennyson poem by that name. It hung in the barbershop he frequented. The barber, Ian Milligan, played side drum in the Portland Scottish Pipe Band that Jay managed. Plead as he might, Ian was stubborn and would not give it up. Later, with a real pub in Jay's sights, pleading turned to abject begging, and the picture was his to be hung in the Horse Brass Pub.

Not long after receiving the beer and wine license, the Two Jays set to remodeling and building the interior. The large expanse of the previous Firehouse Tavern was certainly at odds with the warm coziness that fostered companionship found in an English pub. There was definitely no need to hire an interior designer; Jay sketched out the floor plan. All those rainy, foggy nights spent in warm pubs throughout England, especially in Norwich, were now in plans on paper. Walter Tooze looked them over and approved this needed modification to his building.

The design sectioned the floor space into smaller areas, each to give patrons the feeling that they were in a small enclave. But there would be no areas hidden from the watchful eye of the barman, to ensure that patrons were served and welcomed. The main entry and the areas on either side would have a raised floor with low steps down to the main floor around the bar.

Wood was ordered and craftsmen retained; some were close friends with an interest in Jay's plans. One weekday, while he was in a telephone company meeting, he received a phone call from Walter Tooze. "What the hell do you want done with all this wood?"

The load of wood had arrived days earlier than expected. Jay's onsite direction was needed. Being a crafty sort, Jay concocted an excuse and left the meeting to take care of an undisclosed emergency. Just like he had done when starting a barman's shift at the Elephant and Castle, he removed his suit jacket and pitched in and helped unload and stack the wood. The wide, thick wood planks were to be the flooring in the raised section of the pub. Stout wood beams would arrive later.

Days passed. Jay was excited. He and his woodcraft volunteers gathered on a weekend when there was no rain forecast. The regular cut wood beams were hefted onto saw horses in the parking lot work area. They were "aged" using an electric wood chisel to give their exteriors a rough, hand-hewn finish, as if an old English adze had been used to shape them. Neighbors certainly noted all this activity, especially those still opposed. But most were cautiously optimistic and looked on with interest. They were witnessing the birth of their neighborhood pub.

The interior walls and ceilings were covered with snow-white plaster that was roughly troweled to give them the look of an old English inn. The raised floor and rough-hewn beams and posts were installed. Low railings were built, set in place over wood slats with a saw cut design. The interior low fencing sectioned off the barn-like interior. Posts and beams were added above the front bar.

Jay and his helpers mixed a concoction of black and brown stain. They mixed and tested until it was just right, just like Jay remembered the dark woodwork in pubs back in England. Some thought it looked close to the color of Guinness beer. It was applied to the wood beams and posts, railings, section fencing and the floors, giving all a dark, warm sheen.

The background on the canvas had been prepared and was now ready for Jay's touch. Tables, chairs, benches and more bric-a-brac were needed. There were some tables and stools left over from the Gaslight Tavern of Belmont and the Firehouse Tavern. But the soul of the pub absolutely had to come from Britain. Jay Brandon would not budge on this.

It had been some time since Jay had been back in England. Jay Kileen's contacts extended well beyond the Portland Chamber of Commerce, all the way to an English brother-in-law who owned pubs and some small hotels in London. This contact was a successful businessman who had connections and was prepared to assist and advise Jay. In late August 1975, Jay was again winging his way back to the country he loved, but not directly. There was a fellow in Switzerland that owed Jay a significant sum of money from one of Jay's other business dealings. He had been slow-rolling the payment behind the buffer of distance. A face-to-face meeting in the Swiss Alps netted Jay the cash he needed for his buying spree in England. Jay could be very persuasive and blunt when necessary.

Jay landed in England and got settled in an old hotel in London. He had a few pints with Jay Kileen's relative at a local pub. Jay carefully noted suggested suppliers and possible sources for the items he sought. Jay Kileen's brother-in-law was definitely a connected chap. On a later day, Jay found himself in the backseat of a convertible Bentley with a driver, along with its owner and his 12-year old son. This luxury automobile was owned by the largest supplier of hotel and restaurant equipment in London. The three of them were being driven through the heart of this great city on a fine day. The top on the Bentley was down. They and the driver discussed possible lunch locations and the merits of having a McDonald's hamburger. A McDonald's fast food restaurant had recently opened in London. Jay's business sense automatically kicked in. He suggested, "You want to get every one of those restaurants you can get your hands on."

Then fate nearly stopped Jay Brandon and the Horse Brass Pub. Jay's search for pub furniture, artifacts and accoutrements, and Jay himself, were almost brought to an abrupt end at the very beginning of his visit. It was about 18 minutes past noon. They had just passed the Hilton Hotel on Park Lane across from Hyde Park in Central London. A few hundred feet later, they were rocked by the shock wave from a large bomb that exploded in the lobby of the hotel, apparently set by the Provisional Irish Republican Army. They, in fact, later claimed responsibility. Two people were killed and 63 were injured. Jay could easily have been one of them, either killed or maimed. What forces were at work that day, moving the hand on the clock of fate just a few seconds, enabling Jay to barely miss the explosion and to continue his quest for a real English pub in Portland?

This terrible event did change the immediate future for Jay. Following that tragedy, security was intense, causing Jay to open his briefcase for inspection everywhere he went. Jay had planned to go to Northern Ireland for possibly less-expensive furniture and artifacts. He prudently changed his mind. Following this near-death experience in London, he bought a British Rail pass and spent three hectic weeks searching and buying.

Most pubs in England at the time were not free houses, that is, those owned totally by the publican, free to serve what the publican thought best for his patrons. Most were owned by large breweries, rather like a franchise operation, because of the prohibitive cost to own a pub outright on one's own. However, this also brought the proviso that only the breweries' brews, or ones they approved, could be sold there.

Without thinking things through very carefully, some bright young lads thought that beautiful old English pubs should be modernized. To speak modernize and pubs in the same breath was oxymoronic, to be sure. In England, modern and pub are at opposite poles. The very soul and essence of an English pub is soaked into its tables and walls from warm conversation with a good pint over many generations, hundreds of years for some. The birthright of some pubs went all the way back to when they had been carriage houses and inns for weary travelers. But all of that was not apparent to some young chaps with fresh degrees in modern business administration. They convinced some beer company executives, but not all, to modernize their pubs to keep up with the times. This required fresh coats of paint, some over old stained beams. Directions came from on high to purchase new furniture and decorations. Pool tables and electronic game machines would intrude on the lanes where darts had been played and intrude on the sensibilities of pub regulars. Fortunately, this modernization trend was reversed some years later. But at the time, this worked to Jay's advantage and to the advantage of the Horse Brass Pub.

Jay discovered that some pubs were going to get new tables and chairs and be rid of those clunky old round wood tables with cast iron bases that dated back to who-knows-when. Never mind that many generations from the village had sat at those same tables and on those same chairs, finding companionship over a good pint of real ale pulled with pump handle by the publican from the cellar. Jay saw the opportunity. In a flash, out came a roll of money to purchase, followed by an agreement to hold the furniture until a *lorry* could be hired to pick it up; £50 to £75 cash on the bar, and a table and chairs were his. Jay also found old wooden barrelheads mounted on pub walls. Some had been painted with the names and logos of the bitter or ale they had once topped. A few had already been removed and were stacked on the floor in a back room. One in particular caught his eye. It showed a top-hatted gentleman with a long white beard and cane, holding a glass mug with an amber bitter with the name of that bitter painted beneath. He recognized the name of that bitter, having drunk it when living in England nearly 20 years earlier. More cash and the barrelheads became part of his stash.

Some pubs had well-used wooden pews that came from Anglican churches, real churches without levers. Other pub artifacts, some fairly old, also found their way into a shipping container on a London dock, to eventually make its way to a Portland dock and into the Horse Brass Pub, a sort of Bundles for Britain in reverse.

Starting December 7, 1941, as a youngster in Portland, Jay had become quite interested in World War II, reading much about the war in the Pacific, in Europe and over England. That, and keeping with his promise to his pub's neighbors, the pub of his dreams would have to have photographs of that period of world history when England's back was against the wall during the Blitz, when the few of the Royal Air Force did so much for so many.

Jay went to the main offices of *The Times* of London and convinced them to let him review their enormous files of black and white photographs of people and events during the war. Of course, photographs of Prime Minister Winston Churchill and Field Marshall Bernard Law Montgomery were among them, as well as photographs of venerable Spitfires and young children boarded on trains leaving for countryside homes to escape the bombs of the Blitz. With permission from *The Times*, he was allowed to make high-quality photographic copies of the ones he selected. These were to be framed to hang on the walls of the Horse Brass Pub back home in Old Belmont Square. Jay's absolute favorite was a photograph of Field Marshall Montgomery standing alongside a life-size oil portrait of himself, confirmation of Monte's famed ego.

What's a pub without authentic levers, wooden handles to drive beer engines to draw real ale from the cool cellar depths? He went to Birmingham and Manchester since that was where most of the pull arms were made. These wooden levers, made by caring English craftsmen, would perform their magic in Portland.

Jay roamed all about England buying lots of authentic artifacts, not just any old bric-a-brac. His keen eye and knowledge of English pubs ensured that the furniture, handles and odd bits would be more than just decoration or functional items. They would bring a real part of England to Portland.

His travels brought him to Liverpool. There he came upon a shop that had four authentic antique gas lamps that had once graced the streets of that fair city. These, too, found their way to that shipping container waiting on a London dock.

Jay then focused on the Royal National Lifeboat Institution (RNLI), a notable charity that saves lives at sea. He was well aware of their service and prestige when he had lived in England. Founded in 1824, it performed lifeguard and life-saving operations over the extensive coastline of the United Kingdom. To help raise funds, many pubs had a small model of their lifeboats on the bar where donations could be deposited. Pub owners would not part with one. Jay even went to an RNLI lifeboat station to beg for one of their model lifeboats to put on the bar at the Horse Brass Pub. But even Jay's silver tongue couldn't convince them at the time, even with the promise to send them the money that people in Portland would put in the little boat. Later, back in Portland, Jay was persistent from a distance and was finally successful. An RNLI donation boat was sent his way and put in a place of honor at the bar. That little boat was not a trivial part of Britain.

Back in Portland, the shipping container was opened and its contents trucked towards Mount Tabor. The old church pews went inside against the walls and railings. Barrelheads and framed World War II photographs were hung. Other bits were installed: sepia-toned photographs of famous universities and rugby teams, posters of distinguished writers and poets, beer and ale advertising signs, and four dart boards. But no pool tables or television sets for sports fans. All this conformed to the cluttered yet clean look he knew so well from English pubs.

The gas lamps from Liverpool were to go outside, now converted to electric bulbs. He had planned to fuel them with natural gas. These lamps would have added authentic exterior charm as had been envisioned for the earlier Gaslight Tavern of Belmont. But city inspectors and the fire chief would not hear of it, public safety being what it was. So they were modified, wired with electric bulbs of color and shape to appear to be soft yellow gas flames. Two were mounted inside to adorn either end of the bar, two outside.

Then, the all-important horse brasses were put up. Some were fastened directly to posts. They stood out against the dark stained wood as intended. Others were on leather straps that were hung on walls. To onlookers and helpers, it was just more English decoration. But to Jay, the spirit that had been forged into those brasses back in England was now in his pub, blessing the floors, beams, posts, everything. The horse brasses that had protected people from the "evil eye" and mischievous forces — travelers, knights, drivers of beer delivery wagons and their horses — would now protect his Horse Brass Pub and maybe add a bit of good fortune.

The World War II English theme that he wanted so very much was now in place, the pub that he had promised the worried neighbors. It had been imbued in him since the time he first set foot on British soil. Now it was in his actual Portland pub, no longer just the pub in his head.

The pump handles from Manchester needed modification. The beer from the kegs in the cooler room would be delivered by pressurized gas through valves at the bar, the taps. As fate would have it, there were two young lads, Rick and Todd, across the street from the pub that took more than a passing interest in the place. They worked in a machine shop and were keen to help Jay adapt the pump handles. They did this using skill and heart. The character of the neighborhood was starting to seep in. The pump handles clicked and worked as needed, appearing to customers that their beer was being pumped by hand from the cool, hidden reaches of the pub.

Jay commissioned a local artisan, a talented man from a nearby small town to make the pub sign to hang outside above the entrance. Like pubs in latter day England, the sign was lit by electric spotlights shining upon it. A garish plastic sign, lit from within, certainly would not do. The sculpted wooden sign was of the head of a horse framed by a horseshoe, all looking very much like a small horse brass of the same design that was mounted on a wooden pillar inside. The sign was painted black with the name HORSE BRASS in raised white letters on the horseshoe. It spoke to people of the pub within. A very key aspect of Jay's design was that the outward look of the pub be subtle. The sign did not shout; rather, it beckoned softly to passersby to come in, that there was a warm home inside.

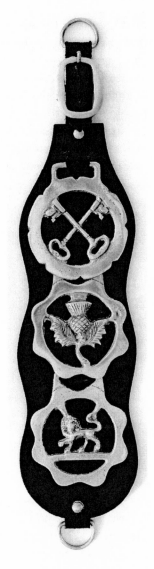

Horse brasses on leather strap
Courtesy of Dick Kaiser

A man that worked for Jay at the telephone company had a father that was quite skilled in the leaded glass craft. At the time, this artisan had done the leaded glass work for a chain of ice cream parlors in Portland that had a Gay Nineties atmosphere. The designs looked like Tiffany glass. This man's handicraft produced the backlit leaded glass sign above the front bar that announced service to all who entered — "Public Bar."

43

One day as Jay was driving up Belmont en route to the Horse Brass, about three blocks before the pub he saw a sign announcing an estate auction that was going on inside an old neighborhood house. Jay stopped, went in, and immediately noticed a set of Tiffany-style leaded glass lampshades that asked to be hung from the ceiling of his pub. The first one came up for auction and Jay bid enough to buy it: $200. The auctioneer said Jay could have the rest for the same unit price if he wanted them. Jay did. The lampshades were soon hung in the Horse Brass Pub. Jay needed a few more hanging lamps of similar character. He managed to find them later, but they were not quite the same nor as expensive.

A horse brass
Courtesy of Dick Kaiser

Finally, he added a heavy solid wood sign on the side of the entry; it was stained dark brown. On it was engraved another business in which he was involved, Brandon Travel. Its phone number was engraved on it as well. It sort of fit the décor and might just help his other business with his stepfather.

Jay worked very hard to ensure the pub in his head was becoming a reality. His high standard was that if Robert Burns himself were alive and stepped into the pub, he would look about and nod his head in approval. Many first-time visitors would do so.

Then there was the beer. Jay stocked every single brand of bottled beer that was available. These included beer from all over the world. The variety of beer at the Horse Brass was impressive, literally from A to Z. Jay boasted that the Horse Brass Pub was the first place in the Pacific Northwest to have Guinness and Whitbread on tap. He also offered a beer certificate to his customers. When each brand of beer had been purchased, the corresponding letter on the patron's beer card was punched. When the card was complete, they would receive a certificate and some beer of their choice, on the house.

More than décor, bottled beer, beer kegs and pump handles were needed before opening day. People were needed, the right people. He had not yet advertised when the pub would open. Jay just put a hire ad in the paper and began interviewing. The ad was straight to the point, "If you still have your British accent, call this number . . ."

At first, he didn't hire anyone with an American accent. The first employees were of English, Irish or Scottish descent. He wanted not only their speaking accents, but much more importantly, he wanted their intimate, direct knowledge of pubs. This would appeal to Portlanders in general, and to the significant expatriate population in and around the city from those same countries. Training bartenders and wait staff in the proper ways of a pub was quite important to Jay. People with heritage of countries with pubs would have a better understanding of what pubs were all about. What better way to further infuse the soul of the British public house into the Horse Brass Pub?

One of the first was Mike Howden. He was born in Britain and was living in Portland. He had done bit parts in movies in the past and was on his way to seek employment in California. He had scheduled a flight to Los Angeles. Three hours before his flight, he saw Jay's hire ad and

Horse Brass Pub entrance
March, 1976
Courtesy of Portland Business Alliance

cancelled his flight without knowing what lay ahead. He certainly had a British accent. Jay ended up hiring him as the night manager of the pub.

Then there was the cricket player from England, Brian Dutch. He and his wife, Betty, and their daughter had recently arrived in Portland. They had been to America twice before and knew some British expatriates in the city, known as expats to Portlanders. That was enough for them. Like others from England, centuries before, with the encouragement of friends they decided to leave their Hemel Hempstead home in 1976 for a life in the United States. Brian originally hailed from the North Kensington area of London, near the royal residence of Kensington Palace. He had played sports as a young lad and had worked as a cellar man in a pub, moving kegs and bottles about. He also had served in the RAF. Brian was quite strong and athletic. He had been pounding the pavement of Portland looking for work, which was scarce at the time. He was feeling pretty low. His English sister-in-law knew about Jay Brandon and his new Horse Brass Pub. The next thing Brian knew, he was sitting across from Jay Brandon and Jay Kileen at a long table at the pub. He had not planned on interviewing for a job in an English pub, especially an English pub in America. In addition to himself, and his accent, he had his treasured newspaper clippings from England. They were of an Englishman quite good at a distinctly English sport, one with rules very puzzling to Americans with its rather flat bat, bales, wickets, stumps, overs and bowlers—cricket.

Brian explained what he was about and what he could do for the pub. He slid his newspaper clippings across the table. With his English accent he said, "Ya' might find these interesting."

Jay Brandon read them with considerable interest. They brought back memories of his time in England. The clippings cited Brian's considerable cricket prowess playing for the South Strathmore Cricket Club. They summarized his impressive record as an all-rounder who had made something like 15,000 runs, had taken some 1,500 wickets and had held about 350 slip catches in his 21-year cricket career. Local British newspapers reported that Brian was quitting cricket and that he, his wife, Betty, and daughter, Susan, were emigrating to America. For his farewell, the South Strathmore Cricket Club presented Brian with a silver cruet set, and Brian, in return, gave the club a silver cup to be presented to the best young player each year. Brian had been a mainstay of the club since he was 15 years old.

English cricket's loss was Jay's gain, the Horse Brass Pub's gain, the neighborhood's gain. Besides being a very honest, intelligent, hard-working and handsome chap, he also brought some experience with meats and a recipe for bangers, a uniquely British sausage that found its way onto the pub's menu. Brian's dad and the local butcher had played together on the village cricket team. Brian learned the butcher's recipe for bangers, a very good recipe, and also learned how to play cricket.

Jay opened the Horse Brass Pub in February, 1976 without any fanfare or advertisements in newspapers. It was a "soft opening." He wanted very much to get things up and running smoothly before advertising. Brian started as the day manager, ordering stock and all the beers and tending the bar. A handsome man, Portland lasses and wives were entranced, some enamored, when he spun around at the bar with, "Wot'll it be for ya, darlin'?" straight from the heart of England.

Within a few weeks, everything was in place and up and running with Brian Dutch tending bar, Betty helping in the kitchen, and trained employees, so Jay placed an ad in the *Sunday Oregonian*, "England on $10⁰⁰ A Day." This ad stated: "If you can't afford England this year . . . there's a bit in your own home town." It further promised "four dart boards and a full line of pub foods (Bangers, Pork Pies, Steak and Onion Pies, Steak and Mushroom Pies, Scotch Eggs and Ploughman's Lunches) and England's Finest Beers: Whitbread's On

Tap, Mackenson & Guinness Stouts, Bass and Whitbread's Ale, Plus Every Foreign Beer Available and Bulmer's Woodpecker Cider." Finally, it offered "An Open Mike for traditional entertainers" and a "Pub Sing-A-Long." [6]

Jay also wanted to take advantage of the popular and traditional annual event that just about everybody everywhere celebrated—Saint Patrick's Day. That year, March 17th fell on a Wednesday. He thought that one day was insufficient for a grand opening; a weekend grand opening would be better. So Jay extended the celebration at the Horse Brass Pub by four days and placed another ad in *The Oregonian*. Guinness was offered at 60 cents for a 12-ounce bottle. That got people's attention. Since Guinness was unavailable on tap in time for the grand opening, the distributor offered to sell a lot of Guinness to Jay in bottles. Jay stocked the cooler with many

Celebrate . . .
St. Patrick's
Day
as only the
IRISH do . . .
GUINNESS
Stout'
Wed. Mar. 17 (St. Patty's) thru Sun. Mar. 21 60¢ 12 oz. Bottle
open "MIKE" for IRISH and traditional entertainers
"OREGON'S ONLY AUTHENTIC PUB"
THE HORSE BRASS
4534 S.E. Belmont Phone: 232-2202

Saint Patrick's Day ad
Courtesy of Jay Brandon

cases of bottled Guinness in anticipation of the big day. To round out the festivities, he also arranged to have Irish pipers on hand.

Jay's Saint Patrick's Day celebration was successful beyond his expectations. The place filled up to the point where he had to call the police to keep people from coming in the door and exceeding the safety limit imposed by fire code regulations. Many of the patrons were from the surrounding neighborhood. The Horse Brass Pub was now on the map and in the welcoming minds of the people of the neighborhood as well as the rest of the city.

Not only did Jay's first employees have British accents, one had 27 years of English culinary experience under his belt. That would round out the Horse Brass Pub as being properly English, one that served "proper" English food. That humble menu grew under Jay's and Brian's guidance.

Jay ordered almost all the food served at the pub from a California-based company. He rented a freezer down by the railroad tracks in Portland's near east side in an area called Produce Row. The prepared, refrigerated food was stored there until portions were brought over and kept in the pub, prepared and warmed to order as needed. His sausage rolls were made by the Tulip Bakery in the Saint Johns neighborhood in Northeast Portland.

Soon a Horse Brass patron could find an array of soups: Oxtail, Scotch broth, French onion, Cock-a-Leekie, and Mulligatawny (a curried dish that spoke to the Jewel in the Crown of England, a continent far away and the reason for the creation of India Pale Ale). A Ploughman's Lunch could sate patrons in the middle of the day. Other items on the menu could satisfy a hearty appetite in the evening. Scones, Scottish shortbreads and tea could be purchased, and if late enough in the afternoon, a sophisticated customer could have a right proper high tea.

Important with any business that relies on the public, Jay needed to maintain and accelerate this initial momentum by getting the word out. He ordered and distributed small, two-sided, 3-inch by 4-inch folded business cards with the British Union Jack in red, white and blue. Since customers would be coming on foot, bus or car, and not by ship, the incorrect direction of true north as shown on the card was inconsequential. The card told the pub's story much better than the Saint Patrick's Day ad. A single sentence spoke to the heart of the Horse Brass Pub: "It's a bit of England where good companionship is the order of the day." For good measure, a quote from Winston Churchill was included, "I leave when the pub closes." The unique tunnel to the rear parking area was shown and labeled on a small street map, the result of Walter Tooze's architecture for Old Belmont Square.

A variant of Jay's business card was a matchbook with an advertisement for the pub on its cover. Matchbook advertising was appropriate for The Brass; like pubs in England when Jay had lived there, smoking was allowed in the Horse Brass, even encouraged.

A young woman was shopping at the Portland Saturday Market on a warm summer day in Old Town, not far from the Elephant and Castle. While at the market, someone handed her one of Jay's Horse Brass matchbooks. Later, she handed it to her boyfriend, soon to be her husband. He escorted her to Old Belmont Square where they found the charm of an English pub and came face-to-face with the Ploughman's Lunch. He was a hearty sort, enjoyed a good meal and figured a big, strong English ploughman would eat a hearty lunch, so he ordered one. He was disappointed when the colorful plate was set before him: sliced bread, pickles, cheese, celery, carrots, sliced apple, a small bowl of chutney, but no meat. By the time he finished it off, he was as well satisfied as any English ploughman out in the fields. This was the first of many Ploughman's Lunches to sate him at the Horse Brass for over 30 years, all washed down with a pint of good beer.

About a year earlier the North American Soccer League had awarded an expansion franchise to Portland. Over 3,000 latent soccer fans in the city suggested names for the new team. Latent arborists and those tied to the forest products industry won out. The Portland Timbers soccer team was born. Many of the players hailed from where soccer was much more popular, England. Jay thought about how to tap into this concentration of British culture and sport. The well-known Naito brothers of Portland owned a red double-decker English bus that was used to promote some of their business ventures. They agreed to rent the bus to Jay. With it, Jay sold packages to the Timbers games. This included meeting at the Horse Brass, warming up for the game with a few pints, boarding the double-decker with its designated driver, and celebrating the ride to the game. Sometimes, a bagpiper would pipe them onto and off of the bus. Part of the package was a free pitcher of beer after the return trip to the pub.

Some of the English expatriate Portland Timbers soccer players started hanging out at the Horse Brass, often joining Jay's revelers after the game. It made them feel like they were home, not only in Britain, but at home in their local, their pub. They were. This added to the pub's authentic ambience, bringing something that could not be purchased.

Jay continued to promote a pub culture along the lines he remembered in England. After all, it was the people that really made a pub a pub. On weekends, Jay would hold sing-alongs, complete with an open microphone. A short Scotsman started showing up at these song fests, joining in with gusto and just the hint of a tear. Before long, songs like "Knees Up Mother Brown" and "A Gordon for Me" rolled through the pub. Mid-week and sometimes on Sunday afternoons, Jay would bring in folk music, jug bands and the like, and of course,

Jay Brandon pulling a pitcher
Courtesy of Jay Brandon and
Portland Business Alliance

the occasional bagpiper. For some time, a man played a musical saw at the Horse Brass. Before long, many from the large British expatriate population in Portland would spend enjoyable hours at the pub. Their culture and spirit were seeping into the pub, just like their cigarette smoke was seeping into the dark wood and fresh white plaster.

Not all the entertainment came from singers and musicians. Some of it came from behind the bar. Jay worked at knowing every patron by name and what they liked to drink. For publicans back in England, this was a common if not necessary trait. But Jay was also an entertainer behind the bar, something he experienced in England and polished at the Elephant and Castle. He joked. He kidded. It was like show time when he was behind the bar. Within the limits of individual personalities, Jay tried to transfer these traits to other barmen that worked at his pub.

To Jay's immense pleasure, he observed that when people came in they loved the place. Some wanted to be more involved and offered an array of services or suitable artifacts to further decorate the pub. One new patron was a hobbyist and model airplane builder. He said that if Jay would buy the model kits, he would build them to be hung from the ceiling. In keeping with the theme of World War II in England, Jay took the man up on his offer. Soon beautiful models of a Spitfire fighter, a Lancaster bomber and other wartime aircraft were hanging from the ceiling.

There was another thing that Jay admired when he lived in England. If not love, it was infatuation from afar when a Morgan sports car went by on the left-hand side of the road, its driver in the right seat. Morgans were made by an old English company founded in 1910 by one Harry Morgan. They were hand built near Birmingham. Certainly, there was no room for a Morgan in the pub. But a number of them parked around the place, with their owners meeting inside, would be a good thing. Jay put an ad in *The Oregonian* asking anybody that had a Morgan, or would like to have one, or was just interested in a Morgan, to call him. Before he started the pub, Jay had owned one. A man that just happened to have a Morgan, a bright yellow one, had been visiting the pub. He saw the ad and stopped by. He and Jay discussed forming a Morgan club. With many feathers in the wind, Jay did not have time, so this fellow became the founding president of the Northwest Morgan Club. In a short time after the pub opened, the club grew to over 15 members, some from as far away as Seattle. What better place for the drivers of a British sports car club to meet than at a British-style pub?

The popularity of the Horse Brass Pub grew over the coming months. It became the daytime gathering place for the tenants and those that worked in Old Belmont Square. They came to the pub for lunch, during breaks and after work. Jay also had satisfied customers from the neighborhood and well beyond. The notoriety of a real English pub in Portland was spreading in the best way possible, from personal recommendations. Patrons realized that this place was like home, a comfortable place to quietly socialize. Importantly, the Belmont neighbors were happy. This was indeed a different place than what had been there before. However, some of the earlier patrons of the Firehouse Tavern thought that this was still the rough and tumble biker bar they had come to love.

Police officers, out of uniform, would often relax after work at the Horse Brass Pub. Some of them were the first to earn the A-to-Z certificate for going around the world in beer. This friendly police presence helped filter and form the early patronage of the pub. One afternoon, the quiet of the pub was interrupted by the deep-throated rumble of powerful motorcycles outside being parked in the curb area and on the sidewalk itself. In strode a group of bikers, replete with black leathers, heavy zippers and the belts and buckles of riding gear. With typical, tough biker bravado, they sat down roughly on Jay's barstools. The metal parts of their riding gear nicked things up a bit. Their "don't mess with me" demeanor and verbal abuse of Jay did not help their situation. Off-duty police were sitting at their favorite spot at the west end of the bar. One of them quietly said, "Jay, hand me the phone." Within a few minutes a couple of Portland police cars were parked out front. On-duty police officers from the East Precinct, in uniform and armed, walked in. They explained to the bikers that this was now a police hangout, and that they just might want to find another place to drink. To emphasize their suggestion, they mentioned that if their motorcycles were not soon moved off the sidewalk, they could bail them out later from the police impound lot. The bikers looked around, realized the stark difference between their lifestyle and the character of an English pub, got up and left, roaring off down the street with a few raised hand gestures. The word must have gotten out. Jay was never bothered by this sort of thing again. Other motorcycle riders continued coming to the pub, but they respected the place. It was a home for them, too.

Eventually, the stress of the new business partnership was starting to take a serious toll on Jay: differing opinions about expenditures and investments, managing employees, and working behind the bar to fill in unexpected gaps. Such things were to be expected with any start-up business. Jay was not surprised at this, and he certainly had the talents to handle any problems. However, he was faced with increasing management responsibilities at the telephone company and was getting a lot of pressure from those above him about his career plans. Jay also had responsibilities at Brandon Travel and was still very active in the local English and Scottish communities. Jay finally realized that he could not do it all; there were only so many hours in the day. Jay had to decide whether to go up the corporate ladder at the telephone company or be a publican.

After talking it over with Jay Kileen, Jay discussed with his wife the selling of his dream, his beloved pub, or maybe finding a seasoned tavern owner to manage the place. She advised him that with four children, he had to set priorities. Jay had had the fun and exhilaration of building the pub in his head, his dream pub, and making that concept a reality in Portland.

He had not yet put an ad in the paper, nor had he any dealings with commercial real estate people; he had not yet even discussed this with Walter Tooze. But the word got out through the local Daughters of the British Empire, of which Jay's wife was a member. A good friend of Jay's wife, also an Englishwoman, was also a member, and Jay's wife brought her into the confidence of Jay's decision. This English friend just happened to have a husband that frequented taverns and who knew the owners of one of his favorite watering holes. It was called Strawberry Fields. The owners were Don and Bill Younger.

Oregon's Only Authentic British Pub

𝔥𝔬𝔯𝔰𝔢 𝔅𝔯𝔞𝔰𝔰 𝔓𝔲𝔟

4534 S.E. Belmont Street
Portland, Oregon

Front of folded business card
Courtesy of Jay Brandon

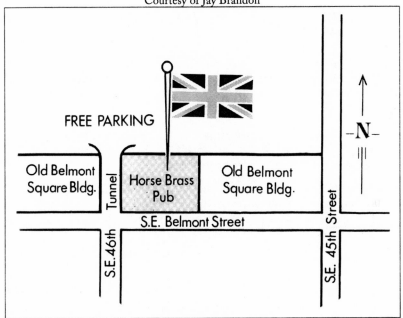

Back of folded business card
Courtesy of Jay Brandon

Horse Brass Pub

Bill of fare

Bangers & Mash	Scotch Eggs	Steak Pies
Sausage Rolls	Pickled Onions	Curries
Pork Pies	Cornish Pasties	Isle Soups
Onion Pies	Stew in a Loaf	Scones

Plus daily specials including sandwiches

Spirits

Beers & Stouts From:

Australia	England
Germany	Holland
Ireland	Japan
Mexico	Philippine Is.
America	Switzerland

Wines & Ciders

Devonshire	Bulmers
Green Hungarian	Rose
Lambrusco	Liebfraumilch
Petit Chablis	Burgundy
Berry Wines	

On Tap

Guinness   Whitbred   Budweiser

Welcome to Our World

We believe you'll enjoy our English beverages and fare, an occasional piano solo . . . a game of darts . . . sing-a-longs . . . and an open mike for those of you with a bit of the entertainer in your blood.

On behalf of Manager Brian Dutch, may I cordially say "welcome to our world." It's a bit of England where good companionship is the order of the day.

For further information, you may ring us at 232-2202. But do come. One visit to the Horse Brass and you will understand what Winston Churchill meant when he said, "I leave when the Pub closes."

Jay C. Brandon, Publican

Inside of folded business card
Courtesy of Jay Brandon

THE YOUNGERS

September 7, 1876, early afternoon; men rode on horseback into the small Minnesota town with business on their minds. That business was to withdraw money from the First National Bank of Northfield, at gunpoint. The James-Younger gang had had well-publicized practice in these types of endeavors. Unfortunately for them, and the bank teller, gunshots rang out inside the bank. The townsfolk quickly realized what was happening. They took to their guns and responded with a hail of bullets. As bank depositors, they did not take kindly to this infamous roving band robbing their bank. Some gang members soon lay dead in the street while the rest fled for their lives. Some were later killed. Some were captured.

Among the latter was Cole Younger, who was supposed to spend the rest of his life in the prison at Stillwater, Minnesota, having pled guilty to avoid the hangman's noose. Apparently, as a model repentant prisoner, Cole was pardoned by the Governor of Minnesota in 1901. Before his death in 1913, Cole Younger openly declared that he had become a Christian, a Christian that was truly sorry for his earlier life of crime.

Years later and miles away on July 11, 1941, in San Francisco, Donald and Virginia Younger had their first child, a great-great nephew of Cole Younger, one Donald Allen Younger. The great aunt of the young Don Younger actually knew Cole Younger and his brothers personally, but she could not easily talk about them for obvious reasons. But the family knew.

About two years later Don's brother, William, was born. Not long after that, the family moved north to Oregon, to live in Gresham, just east of Portland. Seven years later Sue Younger was born, followed by Gail Younger.

The timbre and character of the Younger children were not determined by chance. These apples did not fall far from the family tree. Like everyone else, the two boys and the two girls were the product of their neighborhood, their friends, their schools and, most importantly, their parents. Caring for others was more than just an abstract idea in the Younger home. Virginia made sure that an extra chair was always at the family dinner table. An empty place at the table had varied meanings around the world depending on cultures and traditions. For the Younger family, the chair was there just in case a member of the family had a friend, or had met someone that did not have anywhere to go, or would be by themselves that evening — they could come and have dinner with the Younger family, something that very much made their house a home. Virginia and Donald instilled in their children a sense of obligation to people who were less fortunate than they. That chair and the Youngers had comforted many over the years as the children grew up. When someone was brought there, Virginia would stretch the meal to welcome and accommodate a lonely soul. Her children would all help out and saw their parent's charity.

Virginia was a very good cook and a tolerant teacher in the kitchen, letting her children prepare just about anything they wanted. Her kids loved to cook and eat, and that certainly included Don and Bill.

Very much in keeping with her charitable outlook on life, years later Virginia helped organize and become one of the founding members of the Suburban Neighborhoods Operation Witness Community Action Program — SnowCap. The strong values of the Younger family became infused into this charitable organization. That vibrant and caring organization was, and still is, very active in fulfilling its mission of helping people in need. When in her mid-90s, Virginia died on March 17, 2010 — Saint Patrick's Day. Her wake was attended by well over 200 people. But it was held in a different home, an English pub in Southeast Portland, a pub in the morning shadow of Mount Tabor.

The Younger boys were very close as they grew up in Gresham. During his high school years, like many teenagers, Don knew hard work by doing various jobs from picking strawberries in the summer to bagging groceries at a local Albertsons grocery store.

Don graduated from high school and was a college student for a short time where he excelled at bridge and pinochle as well as his studies. Don also had a mischievous glint in his eye during those formative years, maybe inherited from an older Minnesota branch of the family tree. Despite being underage, he and his friends would somehow find six-packs of locally brewed Blitz-Weinhard beer. They would lug them and a radio to the top of an extinct volcano with an elevation above sea level of 840 feet, Gresham Butte, also known as Walter's Hill. Packs of cigarettes rounded out these excursions on the wooded hilltop. It was out of sight of nosy adults in uniform. But more importantly, they needed the height to receive the signal from a radio transmitter far away. Those transmissions contained the words and recorded rock and roll music offered by a new disc jockey with a raspy voice, Wolfman Jack. Don's distinctive voice was similar, and Don joked about this while trying to imitate the Wolfman. Don also laughed about their being atop a volcano and what would happen to them if it came to life. That would not be the last time Don's life revolved around an extinct volcano in the Northern Willamette Valley.

An inherited physique and a doctor's physical prevented him from volunteering for military service as he had intended, or from being drafted. With that opportunity and possibility put aside, Don applied for a job opening at Lever Brothers, a large company with offices in Portland. They recognized his very quick mind and his keen ability to work with numbers. Don scored so high on their employment exam that their human resources folks wanted to know just who in Lever Brothers had given him a copy. His innate high IQ was revealed. They hired him as an office manager and he started a career climb in the company owing to his honest, hard and accurate work.

When Bill graduated from high school a few years later, he passed his physical and was one of a very few of his friends drafted into the United States Marine Corps. After the intense basic training at Marine boot camp, not surprisingly, Bill found himself in Vietnam. There he completed his one year tour and returned unscathed. He realized that the Marine Corps was a great branch of the Service, but also that it was not for him. While in the service of his country, Bill sent money back for Don to hold for him. He had thoughts of getting a bar or tavern when he got out. He separated and returned to Portland in 1967 to seek his fortune and build his future. He asked Don if he wanted to team up and buy a neighborhood tavern. But Don had a job with Lever Brothers, and at the time, he was more interested in drinking in a tavern than owning one.

Don was doing so well at Lever Brothers they decided to move him to their offices in Los Angeles, California. This was a chance for Don to show his stuff to upper management and see some of the world outside of Oregon. That he did, but he was also introduced to the confines of nine-to-five life in a large corporate building and the courteous Los Angeles drivers during his daily commute. Finally enough was enough, and Bill's offer started looking better and better. So, *adios* California freeways, office cubicles and morning gossip around the coffee pot. Trying to make peoples' lives happier through the production, distribution and sale of soap, toothpaste and syrup, while worthy work for good products, did not quite fit his idea of what he wanted to do with his life.

Don returned to Portland. He and Bill pooled their resources and opened the Mad Hatter in Southeast Portland near the Aladdin Theater, to serve people in a different way. There they provided friendly, honest service, bar food and beer to the neighborhood community and gained experience in running that type of business.

From the look of some of the patrons, some considered it to be a "hippie" bar. It was near a working-class neighborhood, rail yards and warehouses, but also close to a major boulevard. It also attracted people who rode motorcycles. It was also a real rock and roll biker bar, frequented by close-knit groups, such as the Gypsy Jokers. Bill and Don found that they were good guys. But Don advised his customers, "They're the real McCoy. Just don't cross 'em." When that happened, the Mad Hatter or the sidewalks and streets outside could tend to be on the rough side.

The brothers certainly had fertile, quick, energetic minds. Family and friends thought that they both bordered on genius. It would be hard to keep such a partnered pair in check for long. They spread out and made their mark in a variety of business ventures.

They formed the 101st Light Brigade. It was a small shop that carried novelty items, records and interesting smoking paraphernalia. It was known as a head shop in those turbulent, protest days of the late '60s and early '70s. They expanded this business into the Willamette Trading Company and caught the poster and tie-dyed t-shirt craze. They started by publishing a poster called The End of Today. The 101st Light Brigade became one of the company's outlets.

Business was good and expanding. They sought help and brought a young woman onboard to manage the office and monitor the financial and administrative end of things. She was born and raised in Portland. She knew what Portland was all about. Joellen Piluso was a fortuitous hire. Hardworking, honest and loyal, she worked for Don and Bill helping them keep their books, order products, and help them run their other business ventures, which would become more than a few.

Don was a voracious reader with a steel-trap mind. This had been demonstrated when he tested for the job at Lever Brothers. A local community radio station was running a call-in trivia program with teams winning points and prizes. Don joined a trivia team, mostly people from the Willamette Trading Company, a team formed by Joellen. Huddled in an office after work, they dialed furiously to wedge in and answer obscure questions, many about Portland and its history. Clad in team jerseys, they were a motivated, fearsome force in competitive trivia. All of this spawned trivia scavenger hunts. Teams were led around the city by trivia clues found at each location, finally winding up at a picnic for all with six-packs of beer on the tables.

Such quiz programs were becoming quite popular across the country. A local TV station, KGW-TV, started a quiz program; five-student teams from area high schools competed with each other. Owing to the displayed intellect of the chosen students, the program was called High Q. Difficult questions had to be either borrowed from national network programs or created locally.

A friend of Don's at KGW was involved with that show. Somewhere, over a beer or two, they met and Don's quick mind was tapped. Many of the questions used on-air came from Don. He had written and submitted thousands of questions and was very proud of that. Sometime later, Don readily admitted that one of the highlights of his life was when he got to personally meet Alec Trebeck, host of the popular TV show, *Jeopardy*. Don speculated that he would have done well on that program. The managers at Lever Brothers would surely have shared that opinion.

Bill had connections with a friend who owned a record shop. He quickly picked up on the fundamentals of that business. This was quite different than a tavern or the trading company business. What to do? Open Mother Hubbard's music store in Gresham, of course.

Don had a knack for food preparation. He and Bill had learned well in their mother's kitchen. The list of businesses started by these enterprising brothers soon included the Upper Crust, a sandwich shop and deli near the public library in downtown Portland.

Unfortunately, these side ventures did not pan out and they eventually closed down or were sold. But, ever the entrepreneurial optimists, they also sold the Mad Hatter, and with the proceeds and another business partner, became the owners of Strawberry Fields by 1976. It was a larger tavern operation with an expansive food menu. Strawberry Fields was also considered to be a biker bar, but one a little more genteel than the likes of the Firehouse Tavern on Belmont. It was out in the farming country east of Portland, surrounded by fields of strawberries in the summer, a crop grown extensively in that area. The name of their new business fit well. Don and Bill could have picked strawberries around there as young boys during summer vacations.

One of Don's friends from his high school days hung out at Strawberry fields. He and Don had listened to Wolfman Jack at the wooded Gresham hilltop and knew each other quite well. Don's friend had been married to an English woman and was working on his second marriage, also to a woman from England. Another friend also had an English wife. These women were also members of the local Daughters of the British Empire. Connections to England were coincidental and just of casual interest to Don. These buddies were also in the bar business and told Don that they had opened a vibrant, rock and roll kind of place near Mount Tabor called the Firehouse Tavern.

From the English wives, Don later learned that there had been some trouble along the way and that the tavern was now an English pub. They excitedly told him of riding a red English double-decker bus from the pub to the Portland Timbers' soccer games downtown.

"What's the name of this new place?" asked Don.

"The Horse Brass."

"The what?" asked Don.

"The Horse Brass Pub," she said.

Don pulled the cigarette from his mouth and asked, "What the hell is a horse brass? Why would anyone call a bar that?"

Always keeping his hand on the pulse of the tavern and bar business, he just had to check this out. One quiet afternoon, Brian Dutch was tending bar at the Horse Brass. A very interesting looking man—tall, thin, with shoulder length brown hair—walked in. He sat at the bar and Brian asked, "Wot'll be yer' pleasure?"

The customer responded with a hoarse, "Blitz, please."

Brian said, "Sir, we have some fine imported beers. Would you like to try a Bass Ale?"

Don replied with a drawn-out, "Nah. Just gimme a Blitz. I don't want any of that imported crap."

So Brian served up a nice cold Blitz, held out his hand and said, "I'm Brian Dutch. Welcome to the Horse Brass. What's your name?"

"Don, Don Younger. I'm having my car repaired across the street. I thought I'd just drop in for a beer while I waited."

Don had also been to the Elephant and Castle a few times, near the river in downtown Portland. He noticed its distinctive décor and feel, different than a regular bar or tavern. But he and Bill had their hands full at the moment, and they did not fully understand what a pub really was. They understood the Mad Hatter and Strawberry Fields, but an English pub? Not so much.

Don was working at Strawberry Fields one evening. Over a beer with his old high school chum, the English wife mentioned that she had heard the owners of the Horse Brass may be considering selling the place. Don said, "Thanks to you, I know the place. It's across the street from a repair shop I use. I've had a couple of beers there while waiting for my car to get fixed. I've met the English bartender, and I like how they've decorated the place. Do you know the owner?"

"Yes, there are two owners. I can introduce you," answered her husband.

Don inquired, "Can I meet you down there the day after tomorrow? I need some work done on my car again." What better way to wait for repairs to be completed than having a beer at the Horse Brass? Don thought that he would just drop in, get introduced to the owners and discuss business opportunities over a few beers. He would talk to Bill later. What could happen?

The mutual friend told Jay Brandon that a tavern owner named Don Younger would be stopping by the Horse Brass, and he would introduce him.

After dropping off his car, Don walked across the street, stopped under the unique hanging sign he had barely noticed before, gave it a studied look, and walked into the Horse Brass Pub. This time he walked into history. Don spotted his buddy from Strawberry Fields sitting with Jay Brandon and his wife and his partner, Jay Kileen. He walked over to the long table by the bar and introductions were made. There were some pleasantries over beers brought over by Brian, who recognized Don and welcomed him by name like a good pub barman should. After finishing his beer, Don's old friend politely excused himself but left some legal-looking forms behind. Better that business matters be discussed in private, he had thought, and be prepared for any eventuality.

It became quite evident that Don knew much about running a tavern and how to prepare food for customers. Jay Brandon talked about the public houses of England and how his experiences there strongly influenced the interior design and decoration of the Horse Brass. He went on to explain that owning and managing the pub, in addition to his other career and social activities, was getting too difficult. Don quickly pointed out that he was not interested in managing the place or working for others, but that he could possibly be interested in its purchase. That called for more beer.

With pints in hand, a detailed tour of the Horse Brass Pub was proudly given to Don: the walk-in cooler, the beer taps arrangement, the kitchen, the bathrooms, the tunnels to the parking lot out back, and the other buildings of Old Belmont Square. Jay described and pointed out those things that had come from England, especially his horse brasses. Back at the table, there was more beer and discussion that became more detailed and as focused as the pints of beer would allow: cost, financing, timing, employees, and the other underpinnings of a business transfer. The day wore on into evening. Don became increasingly interested, helped along by much beer. That led to a sales contract, of sorts. Figures were scribbled on a napkin. The evolving deal was also sketched out on the forms left behind by his friend and signed at an old round wooden table with cast iron legs that had been in a pub in England. Don, a bit groggy, stuffed some of the papers in his pocket, and with handshakes, bade them a fond farewell.

Don awoke the next morning with the aftereffects of the previous day's social business meeting and a fuzzy recollection of committing to the purchase of a British pub. He rolled over, rubbed his eyes, looked up and saw a beer-stained napkin wrapped in a crumpled piece of paper on his dresser. He groggily stood up, reached over and grabbed the wad of papers, smoothed them out and squinted at them in the morning light. On them were scrawled financial figures, dates and signatures—including his. A cup of coffee and a morning cigarette brought things into better focus. Now it was coming back. He looked again at the apparently agreed-to price. With a more sober mind, he raised his eyebrows and exclaimed, "My God, that's too high! What was I thinking?!"

But Don held to the unwritten honor code of the drinker, "If you can't back up what you did the night before . . . that's when you give up drinking." He was not inclined to do the latter, and he had the integrity learned at the family dinner table. Don thought it best to tell his business partner, his younger brother Bill, that they now had an agreement to buy another business in Portland. Don called him and asked to meet at the Piccadilly Tavern, without explanation. The Horse Brass Pub would not open until later.

At the Piccadilly, Bill asked, "OK, Don, what's this all about?"

"I can't really tell you, but I bought you a present."

"What is it?"

"Well, I'm going to have to show you."

Don looked at his watch, and off they went to the Horse Brass Pub. This was Bill's first visit there. As they approached on foot, Bill noticed the black wooden figure of a horse's head over the front entrance with HORSE BRASS painted in white on a black wooden horseshoe that framed it. As they walked under it and into the pub, Bill hesitated like others had before him when the warm scene of an English pub greeted him.

William Younger's barrelhead
Courtesy of Charles Wells Ltd, UK

Don showed him around, explaining this and that, pointing here and there and at the horse brasses. Bill was suspicious, wondering how Don knew so much about this place. They wound up by a dart board and a number of old wooden barrelheads that were fastened to the wall. On them were painted the names of the beers once held under these barrelheads—old-fashioned forms of advertising back in Britain. Don pointed to a particular one. On it was painted the image of an elderly gentleman with a red vest holding a pint. The painted words spoke of the original contents of the barrel—William Younger's Tartan Bitter. The brewer's name matched his brother's name. Don knocked on the barrelhead and asked, "What do you think of that?"

Bill looked at it and exclaimed, "Wow, that's something. It says William Younger, *my* name. Is that my present?"

Don replied with a straight face, "Yep. I bought it for you, but I didn't know how to wrap it, and since it doesn't come off the wall we got the whole kit and caboodle." Don paused, and with a sweep of his hand across the pub, he added, "This is the wrapping. We just bought a pub." [7]

That barrelhead, discovered by Jay Brandon, had come off the wall of an old pub somewhere in England. It had overlooked and overheard many conversations and had no doubt capped the end of a barrel of very fine bitter. Don's knock on that barrelhead became a knock on a door—a round, wooden portal leading over and back in distance and time to England, its pubs, and great beer. An unseen door had opened for Don and Bill and the neighborhood village around Old Belmont Square. One could almost hear, "Come on in, gents. Wot'll be yer' pleasure?"

Bill did not appear happy, especially when Don unfolded the crumpled papers in his hand revealing the sales price. With all their other business ventures creatively financed one way or another, Bill did not think they should be taking on another business, especially not at that cost. He let Don know, bluntly. A brief silence followed. Remembering their family tree, Don may have considered a sarcastic reply—Hell, why don't we just go and get a quick, no-interest loan from a bank in Northfield, Minnesota?

Don and Bill's conversation was overheard by Jay Brandon and Jay Kileen, who just happened to be in the pub at the time. They came over and all of them sat down at the long table near the barrelhead. Bill was introduced. He immediately set to the awkward task of renegotiating the beer-induced selling price.

Don pleaded a bit, "Hey guys, come on."

Jay Brandon summarized, "If you take over immediately as manager, we'll lower the price. But you're still buying the place." The Younger brothers and the two Jays settled on a lower price, other transfer conditions, and finally agreed, "Deal!" [8, 9]

With considerable afterthought and ingenuity, Don and Bill found the needed money, leaving markers in their financial wake. The Horse Brass Pub would be defined as a holding of the Willamette Trading Company, financially monitored by Joellen on her ledger sheets.

The information on the crumpled paper and napkin was transferred to a more proper sales contract which was signed by all parties. The Younger brothers would become the owners of the Horse Brass Pub business on November 1, 1976. They had never set foot in England nor directly experienced an English public house. They realized that they did not have a clue about running an

English pub, or about those imported beers sold in the Horse Brass. Don did not even like the name of the pub, asking, "Now, tell me again, what is a horse brass?" The only things he knew about England were from what he had read and what he had heard from his friends' English wives.

The deal was closed. Now Don and Bill had an English pub, or at least a very English-looking pub on American soil. By agreement, they had to run and manage the place as an English pub and not make any changes until the OLCC's beer license and the city's business license were approved in their names. That would take about four months.

A few months into this new venture, a bright young fellow came into the Horse Brass, introduced himself and struck up a conversation with Don. Mike McMenamin went on excitedly for a while about his bar near the river, which also served a variety of imported beer. He explained his vision to Don of how good beer served in good, respectable places would transform the tavern business in Portland. He invited Don to come down and see his tavern. Don asked, "What's the name of the place?"

"Produce Row," Mike answered proudly.

A few days later, Don visited Mike at his Produce Row tavern. It was right in the middle of Portland's wholesale fruit and vegetable market near the Willamette River, also not too far from Don's Willamette Trading Company. The coolers, storehouses and truck-loading docks formed this historic area known as Produce Row.

Don walked in and was introduced to Mike's brother, Brian. Don saw that this was not a typical Portland neighborhood tavern. It was different than the Mad Hatter or Strawberry Fields, different well beyond its unique location. It offered a wide variety of foreign beers, draught beers on tap and just about every bottled brand available. This was fueled, in part, by the McMenamin brothers' experiences when they had traveled throughout Europe. Produce Row was quite apart from the typical tavern or bar that had just a couple of taps and a limited number of beers distributed from the big breweries. It felt more like his just-acquired Horse Brass Pub. Regardless, out of habit, he ordered a Blitz.

They all sat at the bar and discussed the future of bars and beer in Portland. It was all very stimulating. This appealed to Don. Like his brother Bill and himself, here were forward-thinking brothers in the same people-serving profession, honestly helping to make life enjoyable. This place was the first of many for the visionary McMenamin brothers. The visits between the McMenamin brothers' establishments and the Horse Brass Pub would be frequent over the coming years. Don had many to choose from as the number of McMenamins' pubs grew. Each of their pubs was unique, yet all of them were bound in common by service to the neighborhood. Eventually, they would be bound by something that would change everything—the craft beer they brewed themselves.

Initially, Don had little intention of keeping the pub. But he kept true to his word and commitment. This was an important aspect of human character to Don. Of great help were Brian and his wife, Betty, who worked in the Horse Brass kitchen. Don had fortunately inherited them as part of the business transfer. Don applied his considerable experience preparing food at his taverns, and he helped rearrange the kitchen a bit while he also learned a thing or two about British food. He was not happy with the English-style sausages they served, something Betty called bangers. They were purchased from a local meat distributor. Brian had a recipe learned back in England, and Don worked with him to put Brian's version of bangers on the menu. They were much better.

During this break-in period, Brian kept trying to get Don to try the foreign beers sold there and to put Blitz aside for a while. Every night after work, Brian would urge Don, "Give Bass a try."

Don replied, "I'll have my Blitz, thank you very much. As soon as I get my license, this place is going back to rock and roll."

Brian would just walk away, slowly shaking his head.

Finally, one evening Don reluctantly acquiesced and had his first pint of Bass Ale. In the late evening embrace of the pub, he took a sip while standing near the sink behind the bar, thinking he would just spit it out. But he rolled it around, carefully savored it, swallowed, looked at Brian and said, "This *is* different."

Maybe there is hope, Brian thought.

Don had considerable experience with the Mad Hatter and Strawberry Fields and was very familiar with Portland's neighborhood taverns. He mused aloud one night where he might put pool tables, the shuffleboard and the pinball machines. There certainly was plenty of room in this pub for such things.

Brian just walked away and again slowly shook his head. The Bass Ale had not yet kicked in.

At Jay's insistence, Don could not change the pub until the licenses came through. Somewhere in the bureaucracy of license approvals, in the stacks of papers on administrators' desks, an unseen hand delayed the process and helped save the spirit of the pub. Don's experience with the Elephant and Castle, McMenamins' Produce Row, and Bass Ale helped as well.

The Portland City Council approved the license application for the Horse Brass Pub by the Willamette Trading Company on March 9, 1977. The vote was unanimous. Mayor Neil Goldschmidt nodded and flashed a brief smile.

Don held the approved business documents as he walked around the empty pub alone very early one morning, taking it all in again. He stopped to look at some of the horse brasses. Alone with his thoughts, he was at a branch point of history. Later that day, Don told Bill, "I feel that something is happening here. I'm not going to change anything. It doesn't make sense, but there's something about this." [8, 9]

Don returned to Produce Row. The bartender asked what Don would like. He almost made his automatic order for a Blitz. But after his first taste at the Horse Brass at Brian's insistence, he proudly announced, "I'll have a Bass Ale, if you please." It tasted even better to Don this time, and he visited Produce Row again and again. The McMenamins' Bass Ale stocks there were noticeably less after Don's visits. Don began to exhibit a trait that would stay with him for the rest of his life, visiting and drinking at other people's bars, taverns and pubs. Was it for the beer? Was it for the look and feel of these places? No, it was because of the people.

Don finally realized that he and Bill were more than just owners of an English-looking place that sold imported beer. Don knew that they were now stewards of something very special in Portland. They also felt that there was something special in the mix—themselves. Don thought that he and Bill should see England and learn about her pubs and beer. Jay Brandon offered to show them around over there and to help make brewery and pub contacts in England that could be helpful; his offer was readily accepted. Leaving Brian in charge, Don, Bill, another close friend, and 17-year old Lisa, one of Jay's children, went to England with Jay cheerfully leading the way.

Of course, Norwich was their destination, where Don was introduced to Jay's English in-laws. Don's contingent was put up in a nearby bed and breakfast; Norwich became home base for Don's first tour of England, pubs and British beer. Don was introduced in proper fashion to Sunday pub day in Norwich with a visit to the family's local, the Artichoke, complete with an afternoon dinner back home, then finishing off the day with everyone—wives, neighbors and friends—back at the pub. That experience was certainly different than any back in Portland.

Jay eagerly escorted the Yank threesome to pub after pub, sampling atmospheres, patrons and, importantly, beer—British style. Don had his first taste of real ale and fell in love with it. He noticed that the barman had used a brass pump at the bar with a long wooden lever, pulling it slowly back and forth a few times to fill his pint. Don took a sip and asked, "What's this?"

The publican proudly replied, "Mate, this is real ale. We've been making and serving it this way for a long time. Some beer-making chaps call it cask-conditioned."

"Cask-conditioned?"

"Yes, Sir. This beer is allowed to mature naturally. It is not pasteurized or filtered, and the cask in my basement for this beer is not pressurized, except for a wee bit of gas from its final fermentation. We don't rush things along; we allow the malt and hop flavors to develop naturally. It's a richer-tasting beer, with more character."

Don slowly finished his pint, thinking—real ale, cask-conditioned.

They travelled throughout the surrounding area known as the Norfolk Broads. This flat, marshy low-lying area was laced with canals and locks that had served as transportation links. Many of the pubs they visited were very old ones, some right by the canals.

The beer found in those pubs was very different than most beers available in America, beers that Don and his friends were accustomed to, taken from a six-pack, ordered at a neighborhood tavern, or served at the Mad Hatter and Strawberry Fields. The sight and taste of a pint drawn slowly from the cool depths of the cellar impressed them. At one dockside pub with a long, narrow canal boat moored outside, an elderly English gentleman sitting next to Don at the bar held up his freshly drawn bitter, admired it against the light, and expressed with admiration, "Now, gentlemen, *that* is a fine pint." The tone and sincerity of this simple statement by that pub regular made an impression on Don. He held his pint up to the light, revealing amber-brown clear liquid, topped by a crown of white foam. It *was* a fine pint. Its soft smell, rich taste and the pub itself, with its own horse brasses, worked their collective magic. This was *real* beer! Beer as it was meant to be, as served in public houses over the ages. There were many varieties, with a full range of flavors and hues, some dark as road tar, others very light, pale yellow or golden brown. Don sampled many.

The beer was captivating to Don, but the social ambience he found in a village pub was compelling. He loved the open warm companionship found in that soft atmosphere, which was sometimes accented with antiques and the musty scent of a well-aged structure. Certainly, there were bars and neighborhood taverns back in Portland where people knew each other, where the bartender and neighbors were friendly. Don and Bill owned a couple. But these pubs were different; not better necessarily, but much different.

In pub after pub, Jay pointed out the horse brasses on the walls, beams and posts. Don realized that every pub he visited had these brass amulets. They were everywhere. Jay, publicans and regulars were more than happy to explain them in depth. Some said that not having horse brasses in a pub was considered as fostering bad luck; more positively, they said that horse brasses brought good luck.

Don took many mental notes, discussed these with Bill; they wanted to learn more. Jay and the publicans they met on the tour were more than happy to oblige. Don and Bill wanted to make sure the employees at the Horse Brass Pub also knew what an English pub was, so that they could continuously work to that end. Of course, they had Brian to smooth over any gaps of personal experience.

While there, Don heard about an interesting organization that had been formed in Britain in 1971 to make sure that real ale and pubs would not wither and be forgotten. It was known as the Campaign for Real Ale, CAMRA for short. Their focus got his attention and caught Don's imagination. CAMRA campaigned for real ale, and in the process campaigned for pubs and drinkers' rights. He made note that he would have to follow up with CAMRA when he returned to Portland.

Along the way, Don carefully observed the attributes of a pub, listened as Jay Brandon, his Norwich family, and those along the way explained their views of the British public house. He took more mental notes and later summarized their meaning in his steel-trap mind.

Jay had advised that to earn God's good grace, always bid a cheerful farewell to employees and fellow patrons when leaving a pub. Don easily got the hang of that simple gesture, having done so many times when leaving Portland establishments.

Don, Bill and Jay also discussed how an English pub and a coffee shop shared some of the same traits as social centers of the neighborhood. However, the gathering times and brews were different. People came to grips with the awakening world each morning with their friends over a cup of hot coffee. While coffee had been around for some time, its influence on companionship was different from a good pint of ale. Like Jay had already known, Don and Bill now realized that the public house was even more than the social center of a village - it contained the very heart of the British people.

On the flight back to America, Don thought about what he had seen and experienced. Foremost, a pub is the landlord's *home*. This was worth repeating to himself, for emphasis; a pub is the landlord's home. The landlord of a pub was also known as its publican, sometimes as its governor or innkeeper; but Don liked the word "publican," the natural extension of "public house." With maybe a little concern, Don also realized that an English pub had elusive qualities. There was not a simple formula for making a real pub. He had learned that a pub was the sum of its staff, its regulars, the village, good conversation, good traditional food, games, songs, a relaxed social environment and, certainly, good beer.

It had taken hundreds of years of tradition to brew and age all these ingredients in England. Some pubs traced their origins all the way back to inns and alehouses along the sides of Roman and Norman roads. Roman engineers had established a good road network in the British Isles which resulted in increased travel. This fostered the demand for roadside alehouses and inns where weary travelers could find shelter and quench their thirst. The Romans finally left the British Isles, suffering from withered support from a crumbling empire. But some of the roadside establishments previously frequented by Roman soldiers persisted. Centuries after their departure, shortly after their conquest of Britain in 1066, the Normans began building a huge network of places of worship throughout the conquered land. Monasteries and abbeys soon began brewing their own beer for sale to pilgrims. Close to the religious buildings, alehouses offered a place where travelers could find lodging and sit with local villagers for a drink and conversation. These evolved into simple drinking establishments called public houses, or pubs, and became central to community life and entertainment.[10]

Don wondered how he could achieve a similar aging for his pub. Portland was a very young city compared to the scale of English history. But the Horse Brass did contain English artifacts that had been in well-aged pubs. Maybe, just maybe, that aging had been transferred and infused somehow into The Brass. Don mentally recounted that a pub is first a home, *then* a place of business, and that a good publican will work hard so that patrons are made to feel very welcome, to feel that they are at home. He was advised that if a publican got the proverbial cart before the horse by reversing these priorities, the elusive, sought-after qualities would unknowingly slip through the owner's fingers and evaporate like yesterday's spilled ale. Contrary to conventional wisdom and business-model thinking, especially in America, a good publican was more interested in running a good pub, for the sake of the village and its people, than for profits. Don thought about that philosophy for a good long while and summarized it—*pub before profit*.

Don thought that his views of the neighborhood tavern might need a little adjustment. He had been told that while good bitter added warmth to pub conversation, a pub was more of a community than a drinking establishment. In a pub, drinking tended to be more incidental and strongly related to companionship, rather than the main reason for coming into a pub. Basically, patrons were advised to drink in polite moderation. One publican had suggested to Don that if an unfortunate person with bad luck felt the need to just drown his or her sorrows, a pub was not the place. But Don thought that maybe it was; companionship with the pub family could help lessen the pain or sorrow of the moment, in a quiet corner with an arm over a weary shoulder. He knew that a good bartender could listen, console and advise when tales of life's woes flowed across the bar. He had done so himself at the Mad Hatter and Strawberry Fields.

Don was also told that since a real pub was the "living room" of the village, its "lounge" in English parlance, manners and protocols for patrons were called for. After all, they were in a home, the publican's home. The expected behavior was obvious and well known to those born and raised in Britain. Foreign visitors, especially brash Yanks, might require some reminders: talk quietly, don't be rude, order in polite and low tones, don't order the barman or wait staff about and, most certainly, don't bully or pick a fight. The rule, when it came to behavior in a pub, was: Don't abuse your publican's hospitality, don't disrespect his place. With his experience at the Mad Hatter and Strawberry fields and at other taverns and bars, Don now thought that some filtering of patrons could become necessary at the Horse Brass Pub.

Hidden in the rich explosion of flavor, with Don's first tasting of real beer in a real public house, was the start of a strong, subliminal link to old England. He carried this back to Portland, never to be forgotten and certainly to be applied at the Horse Brass. When Don and Bill returned to the pub, they sat down with Brian and their few employees and recounted their trip. Don summarized the essence of the English public house and the beer served there. Bill agreed, and Brian affirmed what Don was telling them. Brian did not have to slowly shake his head this time. The pub had been saved.

With his gravelly voice, Don firmly directed: "Make that work here." They did, as did he.

Part III

Sailing
the
Brass Horse

SETTING SAIL AND COURSE
(1977 – 1982)

A ship, its captain, crew, passengers and provisions, and the sea upon which they sail are never constant. As the ship ages and wears, sails and sheets must be replaced, decks and hull caulked, barnacles removed. Yet the fundamental lure of the sea remains. Those aboard for passage change from one sailing to the next, enjoying each other's company, sometimes pitching in and helping the crew when fierce winds blow on stormy seas. After casting off from the dock, sails must be set to power the ship, the course set and standing orders given the crew. The good ship must be manned by able seamen, guided by a seasoned first mate, and captained with a steady view of the horizon and a guiding star. All must be done whether becalmed on a flat ocean, sailing along in fair winds with following seas, or heeled over at exhilarating speed in a gale with decks awash.

The Horse Brass Pub was a stout ship with a keel well laid. Now, a new publican was the captain, and the crew awaited sailing orders. Don Younger would provide them. He had returned from his first-ever trip to England. He and Bill now owned the Horse Brass Pub in Old Belmont Square. The pub had already been well crafted and set on a good course when they purchased it. Don took to the bridge to guide his pub amidst its neighborhood and the people of Portland, with seasoned knowledge from the Mad Hatter and Strawberry Fields and other business ventures. Now he knew much more about the venerable British public house and the beer served there. This pub would be a different ship.

As before, Bill would watch over the business end of the pub as a trusted partner and financial navigator. He would measure depths and provide soundings to help guide the Horse Brass and keep her from running aground. Joellen would watch over the books, give hard-nosed advice and pitch right in and work at the pub as needed. From Jay Brandon, Don inherited a good first mate, Brian Dutch, with his steadying English hand on the helm and on Don's shoulder. Before setting sail and casting off, they gathered to review their provisions, procedures and policies and to set a proper course. Their heading would be: "It's a bit of England where good companionship is the order of the day."

Don thought about what policies he would implement at the pub with regard to what he had seen and learned in England. He discussed these at length with Bill. In the end, they did not deviate much from what Jay Brandon had put in place. They sat down with Brian to discuss how the pub should be run for the benefit of the neighborhood. Don was now the publican with the weighty responsibility of ensuring his pub served the village, with pub before profit well in mind.

Before he left for England, Don had realized that there was something special about the place and had decided not to change anything. But there may have been some residual thoughts in the back of his keen mind about pool tables, television screens, shuffleboard, pinball machines and the like. Such things were common in taverns and bars, things very familiar to Don and Bill. They were comfortable with them as part of the Portland tavern scene. But Don's experience in English pubs now changed his thinking. He firmly laid down his new policies for the pub.

First off, there would be no pool tables. There certainly was nothing wrong with pool. It was an enjoyable game that required considerable skill and had historical ties to billiards back in England. But the clacking of balls and male bravado that sometimes surrounded the green felt tables would not fit a quiet, conversational atmosphere.

Pinball machines, with their garish lights and electronic noises, would also be out of character with the pub. While shuffleboard was quieter, he also thought it would not fit. These familiar entertainment devices would not be part of the Horse Brass. Don personally liked pinball and shuffleboard and was very good at them, but he would find those pleasures elsewhere, as would his patrons.

There would be no television. Sports bars were gaining popularity in Portland. The atmosphere found in such places was exciting, replicating or even exceeding that found in the stadiums of popular sport. Cheering by young men, encouraged by pitchers of beer, likewise would not go well with the quiet nurturing of companionship over a pint of ale. Plus, the sights and sounds of a sporting event would wedge their way into conversations.

But there was a later exception. A large-screen mobile TV was purchased, but only to be used on special occasions appropriate for a British pub. These included European soccer matches between teams well known to the pub's patrons, and the pomp and circumstance surrounding events of the Royal Family, their weddings and funerals. At other times, the lone television remained rolled away in the back room. A large flat-panel, ceiling-mounted TV screen supplemented that one, but remained turned off except for those rare, appropriate occasions. Normally, it was discreetly covered by the British Union Jack or the flag of Saint George's Cross.

Dart Boards? Absolutely! Having been entwined with the public house for centuries, what could be more British? The game of darts went back to the time of King Henry VIII, and well before that with connections to the longbow archers and foot soldiers at the Battle of Agincourt. The game of darts, as experienced by American servicemen stationed in England during World War II, would remain an important part of the Horse Brass.

Don wanted to keep the pub special and unique, but inclusive of England, Wales, Scotland and Ireland, despite the political turbulence in the British Isles over the centuries. Regardless, the public house was a common core of village life in all those regions. Don preferred to speak of his pub as a British pub rather than an English pub. He encouraged his staff to gently correct that perception in discussions at the bar.

Don had some misgivings about the A to Z beer punch cards. The intention was good enough, but he was worried about their administration. Some patrons had lost their cards and there were other minor problems, so he quietly discontinued this promotional program and made restitution to customers with partially-completed cards.

There was another item, a patron's flag. Flags had been around for a very long time, from heraldic banners on ancient battlefields to the national symbols of modern times. Flags adorned the pub, such as the British Union Jack. Don implemented a special policy for his pub: the label on a customer's bottle of beer was that customer's flag. A very key ingredient of the Horse Brass Pub from its very beginning was the wide variety of beer offered there. Beer was imported from abroad, some of it in kegs, but most in bottles. When a bottle of fine Newcastle Brown was set down on a table with its companion glass, its label heralded the discerning taste of the patron. Just a bit of pride was involved, whether the patron realized it or not.

Rules were made for both barmen and wait staff. They were not to remove a beer bottle, even if it were empty, unless replaced by another that had been ordered. Don correctly advised that his customers would feel ill at ease if their flag were removed, let alone feeling that the staff was encouraging them to buy more beer, or leave so that other customers could take their place. Don knew that many restaurants missed this fundamental truth when customers' tables were cleared without their request. He rhetorically asked, "Who has not felt uncomfortable trying to continue conversation over a quickly partially-cleared table?" For the Horse Brass Pub, this would be a violation of the principle of the public house, putting profit before pub.

But Don added another bit of advice so he and his staff could help spread the gospel of beer. This was to be applied when there were other customers seated near a patron being served. Don advised that when setting down a bottle of beer in such circumstances, it be done so that the label, the flag, could be seen by others. A person at an adjacent table, with natural curiosity, could glance at a neighboring flag and proudly order, "A bottle of Newcastle Brown, please, like the gentleman over there."

But what to do when the bottle just happened to be set down by the patron so the flag could not to be seen by a new customer that sat close by? Employees were told not to go about the pub examining, fondling and turning half-full beer bottles. Don would step in. He always genuinely liked talking to his customers. It was part of what made his pub a welcoming home. When he came over to introduce himself as the publican, or to welcome back a contented patron, he would surreptitiously turn the bottle with its flag while speaking. Sometimes he would just pick up the bottle and ask how his patron liked Newcastle Brown. Then he would set the bottle back down with the flag facing other patrons.

Don's business philosophy was simple: never lie and pay your bills. Don could be forgiving and understanding if somebody had a vague, confused recollection of the facts, but to lie outright, never. Once caught in a bold-faced lie, or its close cousin, theft, a person's relationship with Don was permanently changed. At a minimum, their esteem in Don's eyes was held very low to match his mistrust of them. As for paying his bills, Don was reliable, but as to timeliness, less so. With his array of other business ventures and complicated cash flows, paying precisely on time was not always achieved, but in the end, payments were always made.

Don had a personal policy, one that he exercised from the very first day in the pub until his last. He had done the same at the Mad Hatter and Strawberry Fields. That policy was embedded in his character and personality. He walked about the pub, sincerely welcomed people as guests, sat down and talked with them with genuine interest, got to know them and made them feel comfortable in his home. Don's welcoming nature became a signature of the pub. He would casually sit down, beer in one hand, cigarette in the other, and ask, "How are you doing? Is everything OK? Do you like what you ordered?"

He had a great memory for names, and that made his customers feel special. It was not uncommon for Don to stop to converse three or four times on his way from one end of the bar to the other. He never said that he was the owner. Those that became regular patrons would find out soon enough, often to their surprise.

If a patron were an attractive woman, his conversation might lean towards harmless flirtation. While Don would use salty language among men to emphasize a point, he never swore, told dirty jokes or used vulgar language around women. He embarrassed easily around them. Don never married, but he certainly liked and admired women. But his first love was the pub. The first years were the honeymoon, and he remained faithfully married to the Horse Brass.

In those early years, a typical day for Don started around 7 am, working in the kitchen getting ready for the lunch business. He would walk in with a morning coffee and cigarette and finish both at the bar. Then, he was off to the kitchen. When all the food had been prepared, Don sat at the bar, lit up a cigarette, poured another cup of coffee and took a break before the lunch crowd arrived. When that settled down, he would have more coffee, light up and just walk around the place. In the evening, the cup of coffee was exchanged for a pint of beer.

There would be music, some from live entertainers, but mostly from recordings. For the latter, music was selected to accompany and encourage conversation, not to overwhelm it. The type of music had to fit the ambience of the pub, certainly a subjective call. Acid rock, heavy metal or classical symphony music would never do. Soft rock and country folk rock often fit the bill, after Don had listened and approved. The volume of background recorded music was also important. It had to be just right, not too loud to make conversation difficult, but loud enough to help make conversation at a table private. Conversation and background music had to softly meld to encourage companionship.

Overarching his policies for his pub was Don's strongly held philosophy, supported by Bill and Brian, about dealing with the neighborhood—give back to your neighbors. The Horse Brass was not merely within a neighborhood, it was a part of the neighborhood. Like Jay Brandon who had attended neighborhood coffee-and-donuts meetings with Walt Tooze, Don attended neighborhood meetings. If there were a scheduling conflict, he would ask one of his employees to attend. Either way, he kept a close ear to the ground as regards the Horse Brass being part of the village. Don was well aware of the neighborhood stress that had been caused by the Firehouse Tavern. Such meetings had a more formal background as the Portland City Council had recently instituted a neighborhood involvement and feedback system from neighborhood associations. The Sunnyside Neighborhood Association encompassed the Horse Brass, which was only two blocks from the Mount Tabor Neighborhood Association. Evening meetings of these associations were often attended by Don or somebody from the pub. They listened, explained and adapted.

Arthur Hague was born in Leeds, Yorkshire, before World War II. He grew up in a small village in Devonshire and joined the RAF after the war as soon as he was old enough. He served his nation for many years, learning culinary skills to maintain the health and morale of the RAF lads. After leaving the RAF, he worked in food companies in England. After a time, he and his wife decided to emigrate from England and settle in America.

After brief employment in the East, he moved to the West with his culinary background and found employment with a food service company in Portland. A fellow employee overheard his distinctive accent and mentioned that there was a real English pub on Southeast Belmont near Mount Tabor, the Horse Brass Pub. Arthur knew what a horse brass was, and he certainly knew about pubs. He had seen many horse brasses in many a pub back home. He just had to check this out.

Arthur sat at one of the old round pub tables, pint in hand and admired the place. He nodded as he looked about, listening to soft conversation, noting the horse brasses. He smiled and knew he was home, at home in America. That would not be his last visit.

One day, Don overheard Arthur's Yorkshire accent, walked over and introduced himself. There was some discussion about the Horse Brass Pub and pubs in England. Don learned more about Arthur, his English roots and his culinary skills. No sense waiting. Don offered him a job at the Horse Brass. Arthur thought to himself, Why not? He liked the pub and liked its eccentric publican. Thus began a very long and good relationship with Don and the pub. Like Brian, Arthur brought much from England to the table.

Arthur worked at the Horse Brass, in the kitchen, behind the bar, and on the floor waiting on patrons to welcome them as guests in his home. He had to leave Portland and the pub for a time. When he returned, Don learned of it and contacted him straight away, "Arthur, do you need a job again?" More accurately, Don and the pub needed Arthur.

Over the years, working closely with Don at the pub, Arthur synthesized Don's polices into one, overarching view. Arthur spoke of it well. "Greet anyone who comes in, no matter their class, status or anything else, and provide them a damn good beer and a good place to enjoy it." This was Arthur's interpretation of ". . . where good companionship is the order of the day."

Arthur also let it be known that if there were any trouble, he could "take the mickey out of 'em," a quaint expression used in England. If Arthur had any trouble doing that, Brian could "sort 'em out."

Don never ordered Arthur about, but did have a favorite saying to keep him on his toes. One day, Arthur was behind the bar, talking to a patron. Business was slow at the moment. Don walked over, sat down and said, "Arthur, with a little bit of luck, I might actually catch you working."

Over the years, Arthur became the unofficial curator of the Horse Brass museum. It was not a separate adjoining space: it was the pub itself. Jay Brandon had ensured that the walls carried artifacts that spoke to the character of the British public house. They were much more than mere decorations. Basically, nothing was taken down or went on the walls or was hung from the ceiling without Arthur's approval. Every museum needs a strict curator, and the Horse Brass now had one, a good one.

Something was shining down on Don and the Horse Brass. About the time Arthur came aboard, the next member of the ship's crew walked in the door, Clay Connolly. This man loved to cook and had considerable talents in this area. He had lived in Portland, moved to Eugene, Oregon, and returned to Portland with a wife. As luck or destiny would have it, they bought a house a few blocks from the recently-opened Horse Brass Pub. It was certainly a friendly place to meet friends and neighbors. The Horse Brass became his "watering hole," his local, as a Brit would say. At the time, he worked as a bartender at Stanich's, a well-known and long-established sports bar and restaurant in Northeast Portland. While his wife had a day job, she took a part-time job at the Horse Brass as an evening waitress. It was not too long before Don got to know her husband, Clay.

Clay and Don were kindred spirits, internally and externally. From outward appearances, they had been marching to the same beat. Don had his distinctive shoulder-length hair, brown at the time. Clay had shoulder-length hair as well, and a beard, to boot. Over a pint, Clay discussed the Horse Brass with Don. Clay was taken with Don's views and policies for the place, not catering to the rougher crowd that could sometimes frequent a tavern or bar. Despite loving to play pinball, Don told Clay that those brightly lit, noisy machines with a bouncing steel ball did not fit his pub, and that pool tables and TV screens did not fit either, taking away from table conversation. Don said, "Clay, if people want to watch TV, they can buy a six-pack and go home and watch from their easy chair. When people come into my pub, it's for company. They want to talk."

He stressed to Clay that he very much wanted to keep the English theme in the place. He proceeded to tell Clay what he had recently experienced in England. Clay was impressed when Don strongly described that he was not going to provide everything that every possible customer could possibly want.

When Don mentioned the fundamental truth of pub before profits, Clay was intrigued, if not hooked outright. He thought, This *is* a different public place.

The next shoe fell. Clay left Stanich's. Don had been impressed with Clay and immediately offered him a job. Clay's talents and outlook fit the Horse Brass. Clay worked for about a year as a cook in the kitchen, working shoulder-to-shoulder with the wait staff and Joellen, who worked there part time when not behind the desk at the Willamette Trading Company. He got to know the bartending and wait staff very well, and they all got along, the working family of the pub.

Don moved Clay to the bar. He had already had good experience as a bartender, but more importantly, he had the same stuff that Don had seen of barmen in pubs back in England. Clay got to know the patrons and regulars and welcomed them into the pub by name, and he very much enjoyed doing it. He got to know which beer to pour when a patron walked in the door, remembered their birthdays, and listened to their tales of happiness and sorrow.

It was not long before Clay realized that he and Don shared a common love, gambling, primarily blackjack. In those early years, Clay and Don made short trips to Reno, Nevada, three or four times a year. It was not so much for the gambling itself but for the companionship found around the blackjack tables. Sitting for hours, as if in a trance, pulling the handle of a slot machine was not for them. In Reno's casinos, blackjack bore a similar relationship to companionship as did beer at the Horse Brass—plus, they could have a beer at those gaming tables.

Clay had worked at the Horse Brass for a number of years when an apparently better opportunity lured him away. The employees and managers at some of the casinos got to know Don and Clay. One thing led to another, and Clay was offered a management position at a Harrah's casino. Don understood and bade Clay a good farewell and the best of luck.

Don continued his trips to Reno after Clay's departure. While there, he would ring up Clay and soon they were back at the tables together, as friends. Managing a profit center in a casino was a bit different than managing the bar and welcoming customers by name at the Horse Brass. Clay wanted his job back at the pub. And Don welcomed him.

Don now had the core team. A seasoned team to crew a steady ship and keep her on course: Brian, Arthur and Clay, with Bill and Joellen to watch for shoals and financial leaks in the hull. They were to serve together for many years with their shoulders to the helm, through thick and thin. Initially, the profit side of the Horse Brass was thin. Thick would come later. In the early days, cash flows between the Willamette Trading Company and the Horse Brass Pub were not always in the right direction.

There was more discussion among the core team, this time about making the pub a welcoming and safe place for a woman by herself. When a lady was so observed, they made it a policy to ask if she would like to be escorted out to her parked car, whether out back or on the street out front, and do so when requested. This not only made the pub *feel* safe to a woman alone, whether patron or employee, but *made* it so.

Don and the crew put their heads together and established a training policy for the wait staff; know the beers available at the Horse Brass. This went beyond knowing the brand names of beer sold there or whether they were lagers or ales, porters or stouts. They had to know the beers firsthand to be able to describe attributes and recommend a particular one to suit a patron's request, or the best one to go with the food ordered. This didn't happen overnight. The core team set a policy that dovetailed with Don's compensation policy; in addition to pay and tips, a bartender, waitress or waiter could have lunch and a beer each day they worked, on the house. The lunch would be eaten before starting a shift waiting on patrons. Properly, a beer followed the end of the shift. But there was a catch. They could not have the same beer twice until they had had every beer. This was a variation of Jay Brandon's A to Z program, but now applied to the staff. There was a little administrative overhead, an individual checklist, ensuring all beers had been sampled. But before long, employees that served patrons were able to describe or recommended beer from personal experience. Don did not want the waitress or bartender to give a nerdy recital such as, "Sir, that ale is made from Crystal malt and Cascade hops with an original gravity of 1.050 and a terminal gravity of 1.009. It has an International Bitterness Unit measure of 46. The alcohol by volume is 6.01 percent, Trust me, you'll like it."

That could prompt a confused, "Say what?"

The proper information provided would be more like, "It's a hoppy, caramel amber ale; very smooth with a subtle aftertaste. It will go well with your fish and chips."

"Thank you very much. We'll have two pints, please."

A few months after the summer of 1976, Greg Bundy started coming into the pub on a regular basis, usually after work, for a Ploughman's Lunch and a beer. He and his wife had moved a block away. It was all very nice and convenient.

Greg had noticed a different person behind the bar, a tall thin one with long brown hair. It was not long before this gravelly-voiced fellow walked over and introduced himself as the owner of the pub. Don got to know them both.

Greg's wife worked at a nearby machine shop. Wednesday nights soon found Greg's wife, the owners of the machine shop, and Greg all gathered around a table with conversation over pints of beer, often with Don. Greg's wife soon earned Don's trust. To bring in a little extra money, she started working as a waitress on Friday and Saturday nights. At that time, Greg's trade union was preparing to go on strike, so Greg prepared as well. He sat down with Don and asked if he needed extra help in the kitchen on weekend nights. From earlier employment, Greg had his food handler's license. But Don needed more. Don described in detail how he wanted food at the pub prepared. He was very particular. Greg also had Don's trust. So for three months, Greg worked in the kitchen until his union had settled its strike. Greg and his wife were seen in the Horse Brass more and more often. The pub was now more than convenient. It was their home.

In a British public house, it was common to find mugs behind the bar. Beer pulled from the cool cellar could be served in one of the pub's glasses, large enough and so-marked to hold a proper imperial pint. But for the pub's regulars, personal mugs were kept at the ready at the bar by the publican. These were stout containers with a handle so it could be firmly gripped as the evening wore on. The mugs were made of crystal, glass, pottery with a porcelain glaze, or from various malleable metals, like pewter or brass. Some were silver-plated. Such mugs were not provided by the pub. They were brought in by the regulars. The regulars usually had their names etched or engraved on the side of their mugs, or on the mugs' flat undersides. When a regular entered, his personal mug was soon set under the beer engine with its long wooden handle to accept the regular's preferred brew. The regular was welcomed with something like, "Earl, how ya' doin', mate. How's your wife? Young's Bitter comin' right up."

Don Younger noticed this custom at many pubs during his first visit to England. Don thought this was a charming, welcoming custom. Jay Brandon certainly knew it from his time in England decades earlier. Jay's personal mug had hung over the bar at his local, The Star, a 16th century pub in Lidgate. When he entered the pub, the barman would automatically grab it and pour a Black and Tan.

Brian, Arthur and Clay discussed doing the same thing with personal mugs at the Horse Brass. It was an easy sell; mugs it would be. They casually informed their regulars that they would keep their favorite mug on a shelf behind the bar and automatically fill it with their favorite beer when they came in. Soon, patrons started bringing in their favorite mugs and steins. Your own mug at your favorite pub; what could be more British, what could be more hospitable?

For the full-time barmen, like Brian and Clay, which mug belonged to whom, as well as their favorite drink, came naturally. But it drove new part-time evening bartenders crazy. A regular would expect the barman to know his mug, or at least where to find it amongst all those on the shelf. Having to ask, "Which one's yours?" kind of detracted from the familiar homey feeling.

Paula and Gary Snoddy lived not far from Old Belmont Square and had come into the Gaslight Tavern of Belmont and the Firehouse Tavern, the latter only once. A friend had told them that a British pub had opened up where the tavern had been. They went in, and the pub grabbed them—at least once a week. Paula did not know Don but ran into him there after a Portland Timbers soccer game. She was saving seats at a table for her husband and a friend. Don walked over to sit nearby, saw a purse and a jacket on two low stools and said, "Well, I'm not going to sit there."

Paula looked up at this long-haired guy and somewhat rudely said, "Yeah, I know you're not."

He frowned at her, thinking, Who is this woman? A few months later, she learned that Don was the owner of the pub, and she embarrassingly recalled the tone of voice she had used at their first meeting.

In the ladies room one Saturday evening, Paula declared to a waitress, "I spend so much time here, I ought to get paid for it."

The waitress said, "Not the bathroom, I hope."

Paula flushed and replied, "No. I mean the pub."

The waitress suggested, "I'm leaving soon, moving to another city. Why don't you apply for the job?"

Paula did apply and made quite a splash, right in front of Don. She came by during the day. The rear parking lot was full of cars of the tenants and visitors to other businesses in Old Belmont Square. Normally, she and Gary parked there in the evening after the cars had thinned out and came in the back door. Now, she came in through the front door for the first time. It was a bright sunny day and her eyes had not yet adjusted to the darker interior of the pub. She saw Don at the bar talking to somebody. She walked directly towards him, tripped and fell down, rolling to a stop at Don's feet. Don quickly reached down and helped her up, asking, "Did you hurt yourself?"

A little red-faced, she replied, "No, just my pride."

She got the job. She hit all three bases at the pub—waitress out on the floor, kitchen duty, and one day a week behind the bar. Sometimes she did the floor and the kitchen all by herself after every order. Things were not so bustling back then.

As started and fostered by Jay Brandon, the number of Portland's large British expat population that frequented the Horse Brass grew and grew. Don's love and appreciation of British culture and the public house also grew. While the local expats loved America, they missed their pubs, their locals. But now they had the Horse Brass. Soon, every Wednesday at the Horse Brass was hailed as British Pub Night. This was a natural evolution from the sing-alongs started by Jay.

In addition to the traditional fare that included bangers and mash, Cornish pasties, Scotch eggs, scones and similar fare, Don ensured there was plenty of freshly roasted beef for his patrons on British Pub Night.

Before long, a group of creative expats presented well-rehearsed skits at the Horse Brass on British Pub Night. Out back, beyond the shallow drain swale by the door, the players changed into their trademark costumes. On rainy nights when that swale was filled with water, they would advise their compatriots who were not yet initiated to the water hazard to, "Mind the moat."

Knotted white handkerchiefs topped their heads and rolled-up trousers exposed hairy legs. The wife of one would take to the piano and start playing the theme song from the movie *Chariots of Fire*. On this cue, the players would enter the pub with great pomp and circumstance, whereupon they performed their skit followed by rave reviews from all. This continued for a while. Wednesday nights, roast beef, pints of good beer and the *Chariots of Fire* theme from the old piano became expected fixtures at the Horse Brass. When music and song finished late in the evening, the patrons were still wound up tight. To quiet things down, Clay would put on a Roger Whitaker tape. His soothing ballads would calm the excited crowd to more normal levels.

Then, there was the first day after Christmas. For Americans, it was a day to rest after the festivities and write thank-you cards. But in England, it was Boxing Day. The old tradition there was for superiors and employers to give a Christmas box of gifts to servants and tradesmen. This perfectly fit Don's philosophy of social responsibility of giving back to the neighborhood, giving gifts of appreciation. Boxing Day at the Horse Brass was for the children of patrons, regulars and employees. The pub being closed to the public, the kids ran about the large interior, having a grand time. The *Chariots of Fire* crew entertained them with skits and children's games. Songs were sung as one of the British wives played at the piano. Their favorite was "Ring-a-Ring o' Roses." The children held hands while they danced around in a circle, singing the English lyrics found in one of the nursery rhymes in *Mother Goose*, then fell to the floor, laughing, with the last line: We all fall down.

British Pub Nights became exceptionally popular. But even good things can have unintended consequences. This came in the form of the Portland Fire

Department. Safety from fire was paramount in any activity, and overcrowding in public spaces was watched very carefully. Soon, people were standing outside on British Pub Nights, peering in through the windows, waiting to get into a packed space. This was noted by the Fire Department. Don was formally warned. Consequently, on future British Pub Nights, Brian served as a doorman handing out free entry tickets. When the total reached the maximum number of people allowed in the pub, no more were given out, except in direct correlation with the number of patrons leaving. This was tedious and time consuming, but necessary. But another unplanned factor arose to help sort things out, which would remain with the pub for a very long time.

The very popular Wednesday nights continued for almost two years before something interfered. Something gradually got in the way—smoke from burning tobacco. Before long, a mere 10 minutes in the friendly, smoke-filled pub produced clothes that reeked of the smell of tobacco smoke. Often, clothes had to be hung on the porches of homes to air out overnight before being hung in closets.

Don loved a good cigarette; some said he was a heavy smoker. Certainly, smokers were welcomed in the home of this publican, but smoking in the pub was an unintentional filter. It encouraged smokers and discouraged those that did not smoke. As it turned out, many of those attending British Pub Nights, the *Chariots of Fire* performers in particular, did not smoke. After a while, they or their spouses and other British expats stopped going to the Horse Brass and encouraged other nonsmokers to do the same.

Don realized he had a conundrum on his hands. Restricting or preventing smoking was out of the question. So fan-driven filters to extract smoke and clean the air were installed. However, some expats complained that there was a "bloody wind roar" from the machines. The filters detracted from the conversational ambience of the pub. Windows or doors could be opened. This was requested occasionally on smoke-filled Wednesday evenings, but not often done because patrons would complain about sitting in cold drafts. All in all, attendance at British Pub Nights started to fizzle out. Before long, Wednesday evenings became just another good evening at the pub. But at least the Fire Department was not breathing down Don's neck anymore.

As done since the pub first opened, Don continued to fill it with music and song on Friday and Saturday nights, in addition to British Pub Night. A local duo, Pope and Paul (Nat Pope and Paul Sabrowski) would cheer up the throng with banjo, piano and renditions of old favorites like "The Hokey Pokey," "Knees Up Mother Brown," "It's a Long Way to Tipperary," and "Row, Row, Row" from the Broadway show, *Ziegfeld Follies of 1912*. The latter song prompted patrons to sing and make rocking motions and rowing gestures in time to the music. This was not done at pub tables but while sitting on the floor. When "Row, Row, Row" was announced as the next song, an impulsive person would run forward and sit on the floor next to and facing the banjo player, legs straight out. Others moved tables out of the way in anticipation. The cheerful initiator would wave for others to join in. The next person would sit behind and grasp the shoulders of the person in front. Others followed suit, forming a sitting, stationary version of a Cuban conga line. They awaited the first "row" as the musician played the well-known tune. In time with the music and lyrics, the seated line leaned back and forth together, hands pulling on shoulders as imaginary oars, as if they were part of a rowing crew. Reportedly, this floor-polishing activity occasionally netted a few backside splinters. This became a favorite sing-along and everyone got to know each other better. The line of sitting rowers normally extended from the banjo player near the piano on the north wall all the way to the bar. This was a tag-team format. If rowers on the floor got tired or ran into splinters, they could stand up. Other more timid patrons would be encouraged to take their places to continue polishing the floor. On one particularly festive evening there were two lines, one to the bar, and a second, longer one wrapping around the partitioned area all the way past the regulars' table and out to the back door by the moat. There was nary a person sitting at a table when that song began that night. All were merrily rowing the Horse Brass Pub up Belmont Street towards Mount Tabor when a pair of first-time visitors, a man and wife, came in the front door. They stood transfixed not only by the sight of the warm interior of the pub, but also by the cheerfulness of the pub's patrons as they sang and polished the floor. When it was over, the merrymakers all stood up and went back to their tables and pints. The husband leaned over to his wife and whispered, "Honey, this place is different. Let's stay."

Arthur noticed an older couple that had been coming to almost every Saturday sing-along, and they dressed up for it. They would get up and dance to songs like the "Hokey Pokey" and appeared to be thoroughly enjoying themselves. Arthur came over, introduced himself and sat at their table to get to know them a little better. They claimed that they had a connection to this pub longer than anyone. Arthur politely explained that Walter Tooze and Jay Brandon had been responsible for the building and the creation of the pub respectively, and that they were still around. Surely, their connection to the Horse Brass could not precede them. He was wrong. This couple had lived in one of the old homes that had been torn down to make room for Walter Tooze's Building Four. As best they could figure, their favorite table in the upper deck area of the pub was where their living room had been. Arthur had to agree, their roots went far deeper than anybody's, geographically at least. One living room had been replaced by another. The couple enjoyed this living room as much as their earlier one, maybe more. Again, they were home.

More than a bit of England was brought into the Horse Brass by the likes of Robert Lane-Smith, a native of London. Better known as London Bobby, this gent was quite the piano-playing singer and music hall entertainer. Don had run into him where he was performing, and an invitation extended. London Bobby dressed as a Pearly—black pants, coat and jaunty cap all festooned with mother-of-pearl buttons. With a vest and a large necktie with Union Jack patterns and an emphasized Cockney accent, he was a bundle of energy to entertain straight from the heart of London. He brought the Horse Brass piano and the pub to life on many nights as patrons clapped and sang along.

A special group gathered at the East Wall of the pub on Monday nights. They had a shared special interest: sea shanties. Raised pints were swung side to side as all in the pub heard, "To me, way hey, blow the man down." Soon other patrons' heads were nodding and weaving in time to the rhythm, a few raised their pints as well. Another well-known sea shanty was sung by these merry mariners. This shanty rose to a crescendo during Portland's annual Rose Festival Fleet Week in June. The rafters rang with, "What shall we do with a drunken sailor, early in the morning?" Visiting sailors had made their way to the Elephant and Castle near their docked ships. Some even found their way to The Brass and did not leave until early in the morning.

Some quite interesting talent provided entertainment in the pub. Sean Slattery, an Irish folk singer, was one of them. A signature song of Sean's was *The Salvation Army*. Half-way through the song, he would say, "The hell with the Salvation Army," down a bottle of beer and start singing about how men should drink and carouse. It was very "tongue in cheek" with regard to the needed work done by The Salvation Army, but it certainly got people's attention. Then he sincerely asked for donations for this very worthy cause. One of the early regulars, Bob Garnes, was intrigued and entertained by Sean Slattery's seemingly-irreverent words and the resulting hoots and hollers around the pub. The following Sunday, when Sean was slated to perform, Bob came in dressed up as a priest, complete with black flowing robes and white collar. When Sean started his trademark song, unbeknownst to him, Bob Garnes jumped up, downed a pitcher of wine and started singing with him. He stripped off his priestly garments and passed around a tambourine to collect money for the Salvation Army. It was so big a hit that they collaborated and performed the charitable, money-raising skit for many Sundays thereafter. This caught on throughout the city. Sean Slattery would perform. Reverend Bob would show up in the audience. It went so far that Bob started passing out business cards at the Horse Brass to young couples. He dressed as Reverend Bob and his card said that he would perform a marriage that was good for 24 hours. Reverend Bob of the Horse Brass Pub would perform a short *faux* marriage, right at their table, for $5 that would be donated to the Salvation Army. Bob actually fell in love a couple of years later and was married, not in a church, but in a pub. It was a new place in downtown Portland called the Rose and Raindrop. That marriage lasted a bit more than 24 hours — over 30 years.

Music and song at the Horse Brass were nothing if not eclectic, some planned, some not. But the Horse Brass was open to all, and all were welcomed. Word of the place soon reached students attending one of the top liberal arts colleges in the United States, Reed College. It was not too far away in Southeast Portland. It was founded in 1908 as an independent, coeducational, nonsectarian college of the liberal arts and sciences, to provide an intellectually rigorous undergraduate experience. That experience included the study of music and song in the Renaissance and Baroque periods in Europe. To live their education, a college group of madrigal singers was formed. Sing they did, without the accompaniment of musical instruments, as was done in Italy where madrigal singing originated; it had spread to Germany and England in ensuing years. What better place for the Reed College madrigal singers to fill their soul than in the warm, English surroundings of the Horse Brass? While the interior of the pub did not date back to the 1600s, it pointed in that direction. On weekends and during college breaks, the Reed College madrigal singers would carve out a section of the pub for the better part of a day. Sometimes this was the area and table normally used by the pub's regulars. While their song was not as rollicking as the singing found on British Pub Nights or with London Bobby, it did add a certain charm to the Horse Brass on a quiet afternoon. Their appearance was frequent enough to warrant a pub name, the "Reedies," whether they sang or not. This name soon extended from the madrigal singers to other students from the college having a brew at the pub. Don did have a certain affinity for them in one respect — the hair of male students and his hair were about the same length. These students were a well-behaved lot, being serious intellectuals. They did not comport themselves like the proverbial spring break students from party colleges. In fact, the preferred beverage of the madrigal singers was more often free water or coffee, with free refills, than good English beer. They treated the wait staff well enough, but without intention, they occasionally seemed to exude mental superiority when placing their orders. One day, Arthur was behind the bar when some students came in and sat down. He leaned over the bar to the waitress for that section, alerting her, "You've got some Reedies in your section. Good luck."

In keeping with their well-earned reputation as a top center of learning, Reed College had a nuclear reactor on campus. There certainly were many, redundant safeguards for the reactor, but its existence often prompted some friendly humor at the Horse Brass. One of the regulars spotted a group of Reedies at a table across the pub. He picked up his pint and puffed on his pipe as he walked over to where they sat. As he approached, the students looked up and heard, "Hey, you guys have been down in the lab too long. You're starting to glow."

One cold, rainy Saturday during the Christmas holiday school break, the madrigal singers came in and occupied the regulars' area. After a beer or two and many cups of coffee, they broke into Baroque song, quite lovely really. Customers' heads turned and smiled. The singers added to the charm of The Brass, almost like the sound of Scottish bagpipes. Towards the end of the afternoon, regulars started arriving for companionship and some good brews. Their normal area being taken, they soon found themselves sitting at the bar. Finally, when the number of regulars was about the same as the number of madrigal singers, the regulars also broke into song at the same time. Their songs were more of the "Knees Up Mother Brown" variety, not medieval verse. These dueling singers got everyone's attention, even some applause after the first round. That encouraged the regulars to increase their tempo and volume. Finally, the singers from Reed College realized that they had been there for many hours, got the hint and understood that it might be prudent to practice back on campus. As they left, the regulars raised their pints in a toast. Smiles were exchanged. It was all in good fun.

Don made more visits to Britain. After discovering CAMRA, his second visit to England was more focused. Don, with a couple of his friends tagging along, went to the Bass Brewery, a brewery founded in 1777 by one William Bass. At reception, he explained about his Horse Brass Pub in Portland some distance away in Oregon. This caught their interest; their vice president of marketing took the lot out for a good pub lunch. He returned to spend the entire afternoon with them and invited them back the following day. Don smiled internally, recalling Brian's efforts to change his tastes from Blitz to Bass. This was the start of a good, long relationship with Bass.

On his list of things to do on one trip was to visit Watneys, an English brewing company with roots back to the Stag Brewery of the early 19th century in the central London district of Victoria. That brewery later made Watneys Red Barrel. This was a bitter that had traced its origins at Watneys back to the 1930s. By the 1960s, it was very popular in the United Kingdom. Now it was popular at his pub, also.

While not the reason for visiting England again, this trip netted more artifacts and bric-a-brac. Don was impulsive and became compulsive, always keeping an eye out for things to further infuse Britain into The Brass. He could not walk by a collectables shop, junk shop or street fair without netting items to send or bring back home. Most things wound up in his basement, but some wound up on the walls of his pub after being critiqued by Arthur.

Like his first trip, Don visited pubs and conversed with their publicans and regulars, gleaning more of their heritage and tradition. At one pub out in East Anglia, near Cambridge, a publican told Don about a book written by two Yanks who had been stationed in England as United States Air Force officers over 25 years earlier, at about the time that Jay Brandon had lived there. Don was told that the book captured the essence and spirit of an English pub. The book was entitled *English Pubs through American Eyes*. This small, 90-page paperback had a wealth of condensed information and advice for a novice American pub owner, as well as for American patrons of English pubs. The book reinforced what he had already learned on his first trip to England.[11]

Don went to book stores as he travelled around England and bought quite a few copies. When he returned home, he handed them out to current and future employees. It became the Horse Brass training manual, specifically the first five chapters: What Is A Pub?, Pub Protocol, Pub Beverages, Pub Food, and Pub Games. The remaining chapters contained descriptions of recommended pubs in England and where to find them. To help ensure a safe arrival, there was a chapter on driving in England with advice beyond which side of the road was proper. The names of the recommended English pubs were almost poetic, speaking of an England of old: The Eagle and Child, The Oxford Arms, The Crown and Tuns Inn, The White Hart, The Rose and Crown, The George and Dragon, The Studley Priory, The Swan, and Ye Olde Red Lion. Don would visit some of these pubs to experience their full effect and spirit, including the large painted outdoor signs with pictorial images that captured the pubs' names.

The Horse Brass training manual was very important in the early days of the pub. Business was a bit thin in those early days, except for Friday and Saturday nights. For the first few years, there were no full-time cooks. Sometimes, whoever took the order also prepared the food in the kitchen and served it. This made service at the Horse Brass very personal, like that given guests in a one's home. On the busier Friday and Saturday nights, wait staff took turns taking orders and preparing food.

In those lean years, some staff could only be hired part-time. This kind of staffing had the consequence of more frequent turnover. Wait staff stayed with the pub anywhere from two months to two years. Training quickly became important. When each new employee was hired, Don would give them a copy of *English Pubs through American Eyes* and tell them, "Read this. Make that work here."

Certainly, the book did not reveal anything new for Brian or Arthur. But it did help reinforce their explanations of the English public house to new employees — "See, look here, lass. This is what I was tellin' ya 'bout."

The small, thin book from England about English pubs applied to patrons as well as publicans. Dave Krummann was a frequent visitor to the Horse Brass, a regular. He read the little book and asked Don if he could affix a small brass plate with his name engraved on it on his favorite bar stool, a stool at his favorite location. Dave pointed out to Don the section in the book that justified this in Dave's mind. There, one of the two authors of the book, Mr. Henabray, described an event he witnessed in an English pub that involved the other author, Mr. Teeter, when the latter had first come into his local pub shortly after arriving in England:

> "About 7:10 p.m., Cyril arrived. Cyril ordered a pint, and then started looking about. There were two or three other barstools open. One was next to Teeter's, in fact, and there were plenty of other empty chairs and tables. Cyril, however, chose not to sit. Instead, he squirmed about and took nervous swallows of his pint. Teeter could see Cyril was agitated over something. Cyril seemed to know everyone in the pub except Teeter. He spoke, but joined no one. At the time, Teeter took very little notice of Cyril and soon Teeter was engaged in conversation with another patron who suggested they move to a table near the fire. {Newly arrived Yanks tend to be cold.} Teeter had no more than left his barstool when Cyril was seated on it. As they sat down near the fire, Teeter's new friend said to him in a quiet whisper, "I say, you were in Cyril's chair." It seems that practically every night for the last twenty-five years, Cyril had entered the pub at 7:10 p.m., and then sat on that particular barstool. Teeter had been sitting in Cyril's chair and it was upsetting the entire pub. No one was quite sure what to do. Later, Cyril and Teeter became friends and they shared many a pint, but Teeter never again sat in Cyril's chair." [11]

The book described expected behavior by those that come into a pub. Don was already applying the filter of politeness and civility to foster that behavior, helping to mold and form the very nature of the Horse Brass. But on rare occasions, there could be clientele not appreciative of the publican's home, exhibiting rude or boisterous behavior, thereby disrespecting the pub. Don strongly felt that such things would not be tolerated at the Horse Brass Pub. He had not been tolerant of such behavior at his other businesses. But he felt that this was particularly important for his pub. If such behavior were allowed, putting profits before pub, others of that ilk would gravitate to the place and displace his patrons. If allowed to continue, a tipping point would be reached and the very character of the pub would change, and it would cease being a pub. A kind heart sometimes required a strong hand for the good of all. Don had both. There was a legal tool available to all business owners in Oregon. Anyone, whose behavior was deemed by a business owner to be very offensive or even dangerous to others, could be directed to leave and be barred from returning to the premises. In the early days of the pub, this had to be applied on a few occasions by strong verbal directive or by way of legal form.

One evening, Clay was behind the bar. Don was at his favorite spot at the end of the bar. In walked four young men who were full of themselves. They sat down, and the evening waitress took their order. Clay noticed some commotion in that direction. The waitress placed their order for a pitcher of beer and delivered it and four glasses to their table — then, more commotion. Back at the bar, she confided to Clay that these fellows had been verbally abusive by making suggestive comments, but that she could handle the situation. Clay calmly walked over to the table, placed their monetary refund upon it, picked up the pitcher, returned to the bar and ceremoniously poured its contents down the sink. Then he asked them to leave. They took some umbrage at this, saying they would contact the owner the next day and have Clay's job. After they left, Don asked Clay, "Why did that take you so long?" As threatened, the next day Don received a phone call. He was treated to an ignorant summary of how badly the caller and his friends had been treated. The caller demanded that the bartender be fired. Don drew a deep breath, summoned up some fitting vocabulary and let loose a blast that certainly was not misunderstood. This was followed by strong invective to never set foot in his pub again, and if they did, they would be treated to a formal ban and bar order, or worse. Don did not relish the few occasions when this was required, but he took the stewardship of his pub *very* seriously. With the stature of an athlete and the forearms of a professional cricket player, if there were any hint of physical trouble, Brian could sort anyone out. Most often, his mere presence or verbal intrusion into a situation was enough.

The filter that Don had established led to patrons that came into the pub to enjoy companionship over good tasting beer in a comfortable, safe and interesting British environment. Eventually, the need for such filtering dwindled, but the filter was always at the ready. The patrons themselves became filter enough to ensure that people respected their home. That sorting process covered the waitresses, on their behalf. The introductory briefing to a new waitress by Brian, Clay or Don included, "Nobody harasses the staff here but us. If anybody ever touches you and you don't want them to touch you, you come tell me and they will go away."

Some of the rules of this home came from the bartenders and regulars as events and incidents randomly occurred. These rules were neither written down nor discussed. Rather, they evolved as patrons came and went. One such rule was what a customer should call the place. Some first-time customers would look around and say to Clay, "Hey, this is nice bar."

Clay would give a cool, droll reply, "This isn't a bar. It's a pub."

They would ask, "What's the difference?"

Clay would smile and, in jest, would counter with, "If you don't know, leave before we have to hurt you." Of course, that humorous dictum was immediately followed with Clay's invitation, "Please, take a stool. Welcome to the Horse Brass Pub. I'll explain while you enjoy a good beer."

A few new customers came in and asked, "How come it's so smoky in here?"

The tall, thin long-haired man at the bar, Don, would look over while taking a drag on his cigarette, but usually he would not say anything. Sometimes, a smoking regular would lift his head with a slowly drawn-out, pejorative reply, "Because we're *smoh-king*."

A few would ask, "Can you stop?"

This was usually followed by a bone-dry reply, "Why? I've paid for this stool. You haven't even gotten a beer yet."

On occasion, pool playing enthusiasts came in expecting the place to have such tables. Clay and some of the regulars had a short skit they performed when they heard, "You guys got pool tables?"

With a straight face, Clay would direct them, "Yeah, over in that corner there."

The new customers would come walking back to the bar, after a few minutes of scouring the pub for the promised pool tables. They would state, "Hey, man, there's no pool tables over there."

On cue, one of the regulars would stand up, walk over and exclaim, "Hey, Clay, they've stole another one!"

The incredulous customers would say in amazement, "They stole the pool table?!"

Clay would add in, "Damn it, it's the fourth one we've lost this year."

A very few would not get it, at least not right away.

Don had not directed such interactions with new customers and stressed that all were welcome at the Horse Brass, and one should not be rude or flippant. When he overheard some of this dialogue, he often smiled, realizing that this, too, was forming the patronage of the pub.

When Brian was a mere eight years of age back in England, during World War II, he had helped out at the village butcher shop. Many things were strictly rationed in wartime England, including meat, well into the 1950s. The butcher would sometimes have odd scraps of meat. With some ingenuity they became an ingredient for a special wartime sausage. They were mixed with bits of bread and crumbs, fat, water and spices for flavor. The lot was stuffed into natural sausage casings, sold outside the restrictions of wartime rationing. When tossed on a hot skillet, the overabundance of water eventually turned to steam, splitting the casing with a loud pop, or bang. Throughout England these culinary masterpieces became affectionately known as bangers.

Brian remembered the wartime recipe for bangers and offered it to Don. The recipe was tasted and tested; Don nodded in agreement. This would be part of the English menu at the pub, albeit with more meat than used in wartime bangers. It was a secret recipe, a bit spicy for some palates, and it set Brian's bangers apart. He also offered the recipe to an established meat company that serviced the Horse Brass. They quickly adopted it, supplying bangers made to Brian's specifications. In retrospect, a patent would have been prudent, but these were for the Horse Brass and anyone else in Portland. Those bangers became sought-after fare at the Horse Brass; they were a tie to England. Don's early menu did not exactly match that of Jay's, but it included these British items:

Beef with Mushroom Pie
Banger (English Sausage)
Saveloy (Smoked Beef Sausage)
Bridie (Meat and Onion Popover)
Ploughman's Lunch (Cheese, Apple, Garnish, Bread and Butter)
Scotch Egg
Sausage Roll

This menu was later supplemented with a very traditional British fare—Fish and Chips—after the addition of a necessary fryer in the kitchen.

About the time Don and Bill were running the Mad Hatter, another enterprising young man, Bud Clark, was getting started in the tavern business with little else than an honest work ethic and a supportive wife. His first establishment was the Spatenhaus Tavern downtown on Southwest 3rd and Market. The Spatenhaus got in the way of urban renewal and was closed in 1967, making way for the public Keller Fountain Park. He then bought Ann's Tavern in a neighborhood at the foot of Portland's West Hills. There, a century earlier, in early Portland's Tanner Creek Gulch, women raised geese that they let run loose, making short work of neighbors' gardens. Tempers arose, and the police were notified. The chief of police went to the gulch personally to straighten things out. The women who owned the geese did not take kindly to this intrusion. He was set upon by a half-dozen angry women who attacked him with sticks and stones, causing a hasty, tactical retreat. His later attempts to corral the errant geese resulted in similar attacks and retreats. Things eventually sorted themselves out, but history had been made. With sincere regard for the neighborhood and its interesting history, Bud renamed Ann's Tavern the Goose Hollow Inn.[12]

About a decade later, Bud heard about a new and interesting place, an English pub near Mount Tabor. With his conviction that a tavern should be the respectable social center of the neighborhood, he went to check out the place. There, he met a very kindred spirit. Outwardly, his distinctive mustache and beard and Don Younger's shoulder-length hair spoke of men that marched to different drummers. In the coming years, they hoisted pints at the Goose Hollow Inn and the Horse Brass Pub as they discussed that taverns and pubs should more respectable, serving as real social centers, and that people should not be looked down upon if they shared a drink and conversation there. This fit with the vision of the McMenamin brothers. Don and Bud also agreed that business people should be part of their neighborhoods and give back to them, with special attention to those in need.

Bud's schemes to gain attention to raise money and promote worthy causes were varied. One got him a fair bit of notoriety. Bud was quaffing a few beers one night with a neighbor, a photographer. Bud hit upon an idea to help raise money for a worthy social cause. They agreed to do it early the next morning, a quiet Sunday morning in downtown Portland when there would be very few people about. Bud showed up with his bearded smile, wearing a pair of heavy work boots, low black socks, an overcoat and a funny looking hat. His bare legs showed below the hem of his coat, making it appear as if he was wearing nothing underneath. Actually, he was wearing shorts and a t-shirt with words promoting donations to solve a local health issue. Photographs were taken of Bud holding his coat wide open in front of a work of Portland public art downtown, a bronze abstract nude (Norman J. Taylor's statue entitled Kvinneakt, meaning nude woman in Norwegian). Some photographs were taken with the t-shirt showing, some taken from behind. One photograph was judged to be far and away better than the others. It appeared that Kvinneakt and Bud were flashing each other. They managed to get the photograph run in their neighborhood newspaper. They offered a prize to the person that came up with the best caption to be used for a poster to be sold to raise funds for their charitable cause. They received several hundred responses and a couple of Victorian-laced complaints. They selected "expose yourself to art." It was a natural for the poster, and it promoted the arts as well. Bud Clark did march to a different drummer. Don thought Bud's fund raising idea was absolutely great. They shared a few pints and much laughter discussing Bud's famous poster.[13]

Bud did something that publically cemented his business outlook as also being pub before profits. Oregon had implemented the Beverage Container Act in 1972, also known as the bottle deposit law, aimed at reducing litter and increasing recycling. This meant increased costs for those involved in the production and sale of beverages, and this included bottled beer. One of the large breweries, whose beer was being sold in the Goose Hollow Inn, had publically maligned Oregon's deposit law. That was it! Bud publically had the taps for that beer removed from his pub. Don agreed wholeheartedly with that decision, which also gained Bud some notoriety for what was to come next.

Don and Bill sold Strawberry Fields when Don was publican of The Brass. But they always kept their antennae up for other business opportunities. Walter Tooze did also. Walter learned of an opportunity in downtown Portland. The Turquoise Room was a business on the ground floor of the historic Multnomah Hotel. It was up for sale. That was not for Walter, so he told Don about this opportunity. Don and Bill inspected the large space with its fine bar and restaurant, discussed the sale price and lease costs and shook hands with the owner. The Turquoise Room was theirs in 1982. But what should they call it? They could keep the same name, but the spirit of the public house was in their blood now.

They sat at the Horse Brass bar, endeavoring to come up with a good name for their new pub. Many pubs in Britain had paired names, like the Eagle and Child and the Rose and Crown. The first English-style pub in Portland had a paired name, the Elephant and Castle. They kicked a number of names around, but none seemed to fit. Then Bill sat straight up, slapped his hand on the bar and said, "I've got it! We'll call it the Rose and Raindrop."

Don gave Bill a somewhat incredulous look and thought a bit. He quickly realized that this was a perfect name for a pub in the rainy city of Portland, also known as the Rose City. Roses of all varieties grew well and in profusion here. A world-famous festival, the annual Rose Festival, was ingrained into the culture of the city, and raindrops that helped rose bushes grow were not uncommon. It was a perfect name, and it rolled off the tongue with alliterative ease.

At the time, the upper floors of the Multnomah Hotel were being leased by the Federal Government for office space. With those offices came government workers who needed lunches and a place to relax after a hard day. They had been using the Turquoise Room. Now they would gather at the Rose and Raindrop.

One gathering at the new pub was Bob Garne's wedding. The ceremony and reception was held there shortly after it opened. Reverend Bob of Horse Brass fame hired the place and the open bar. Don and Bill cooked the entire dinner for over 100 people and treated the newlyweds like royalty. When the evening was over, Bob asked Don and Bill for the invoice for the reception. They handed him a sealed envelope. On the way to their wedding night hideaway, Bob opened the envelope. He read the note aloud to his bride. "Have a great life. Paid in full." They looked at each other knowing they were part of the real family at The Brass.

Bill and Joellen did the transfer and start-up and managed the Rose and Raindrop. But larger forces were afoot. A new Federal building in Portland was nearing completion. When it was finished, all those government office workers moved there and away from the Rose and Raindrop. There were other customers, to be sure, but the number fell sharply. The cash coming in did not exceed that needed for the overhead. Payments to the landlord could be delayed for only so long. Despite turning some assets into cash and risking the Horse Brass Pub as collateral, the Rose and Raindrop was closed not many months after it had opened. But there would be other opportunities.

The Horse Brass was a good place to play darts from the start. Darts were also played at the Elephant and Castle and many other taverns and bars in Portland. Its popularity was expanding, and a dart league had been formed. Dart teams were sponsored by pubs, taverns and bars. Don sponsored dart teams playing out of his pub. Cheerful, beer drinking dart players filled his pub on mid-week league nights. With four dart boards dedicated to league play on those nights, four teams (two matches) could play there. Soon the pub's walls started filling with engraved plaques of winning Horse Brass dart teams. One by one, the plaques were hung near the dart boards. To even the casual patron, it became obvious that this place was a dart pub. Games were played with the best of order so as not to interfere with other patrons. Darts became another dimension of the pub's companionship.

Don kept up and expanded the soccer tradition at the Horse Brass. The Portland Timbers were now in the blood of its citizens. Bus trips between the pub and the soccer stadium continued as long as there were games to attend. Beer at the departure and return ends of those trips fueled good cheer. They were usually made in a large bus, but sometimes the red double-decker that Jay had used could be rented. Just like darts, Don sponsored men's and women's intermural soccer teams out of the Horse Brass, the Rangers and the Angels. Joellen was a founding member of the Angels. Many of the Rangers drank beer at the pub after their exhausting games; often it was Newcastle Brown. Some laughed and thought that an alternative name for their team could be Newcastle United, owing to the post-game beer they drank. The Angels drank beer, as well, after their games. This made for memorable gatherings at the pub between people with a common interest in soccer: the Rangers, the Angels, and the Portland Timbers.

Don Younger kept the Horse Brass Pub on a proper course; he retained the essence of the British public house and further infused it into the pub. The seas ahead were not anticipated, but there was change in the air. Beer, people, charity, and a London pub would change The Brass, a change for the good, expanding its soul.

SEA CHANGE
(1982 – 1993)

Don came into the Horse Brass one afternoon. He had another relic from England under his arm, one of a few brought back from a recent trip. Brian was behind the bar; Arthur was preparing a food order. Don set the item down in the doorway to the kitchen, asked Arthur what he thought and stepped behind the bar. After hot bangers were delivered to a customer, Brian heard a little hammering. Arthur stood back from the wall and thought his placement was quite good. He wanted Don to see it, just to be sure. He walked around the pub, looking for Don. At the bar, he asked, "Brian, where's Don?"

"He's in the cooler, checking out the beer."

Don walked out, talking as he pushed the thick, heavy cooler door open. "Brian, we're getting a little low on Newcastle Brown, don't you think? The Rangers and Angels will be playing this weekend. Order more."

Arthur interrupted, "Don, you have a good eye. It dates way back. I've put it up. Come an' look."

Don grabbed a bar towel, walked over wiping his hands as he stood in front of this bit of England he had purchased at a village market. It was now on his wall. Don knew that things in his pub added more than just decoration; they spoke to its character and British roots. His patrons would be looking at them while they drank good beer and would feel that heritage. Don nodded in approval. "Looks good, Arthur. I knew if I waited long enough and with a little bit of luck, I'd catch you doing a little work."

With a smile and a chuckle, Don patted Arthur on the back as they headed to the bar. They took two stools, and Brian poured coffee. Clay walked in to start the night shift. Don lit a cigarette, took a long drag and asked, "What do you guys think about this home-brewing thing? You know, it's now legal to brew beer at home. Folks have been doing that before, but now it's legal as long as they don't sell it. Do you think they'll stay home if they can learn to make good beer rather than coming here?"

Arthur and Brian thought for a moment. A sage Brian advised, "It's a good thing. In England, way back, beer was brewed in homes. Some were the homes of publicans, and their brews were their signatures. Of course, things have changed now. Large breweries own most of the pubs as tied houses. For us, the more people understand and appreciate what good beer's all about, the more they'll be coming here, and for more than just beer. They can't find that at home. Plus, some new local breweries are making stuff that Arthur and I might actually drink."

Clay chimed in, "I don't know English pubs like you chaps, but we've got something very special here. I felt it the first time I came in. Oh, people will still be coming here alright. Trust me."

Don said, "Yeah . . . I agree, but we'll have to watch this. We've got some pretty good beer in here already. Any new stuff from new local breweries has to taste good and satisfy our customers. You can't fool them."

Everybody went about their business. Don did not say anything more. He sat through another cigarette with a somewhat distant stare, deep in thought—about beer.

Months later, a bright young man who knew what he was about walked into the Horse Brass and waved to Don. He had been in The Brass before, and they also knew each other from Don's visits to the Produce Row tavern to drink Bass Ale. Mike McMenamin took a stool at the bar, and Don welcomed him. "How're you doing, Mike? How's things been going since you and Brian sold Produce Row?"

Mike replied, "Going good, Don. We learned a lot about beer from that. I'm into the beer distributing business now. Brian has some other irons in the fire, buying unique buildings and making them into interesting pubs like yours."

Don asked, "We really liked Red Hook Ale; what else you got?"

Don and Mike discussed the beers from new breweries that were springing up in the western states. Mike went out back and returned with samples. Don carefully tasted and nodded. These would be added to the expanding number of draught beers on tap at the Horse Brass. Mike went into the cooler, then behind the bar, checking kegs, lines and taps for the beer he had just delivered. He came back over to Don and asked, "Are you going to the grand opening of the Hall Street Bar and Grill in Beaverton?"

"Yeah, they called and invited me. I hear that the shakers and movers of good beer will be there, even an expert from England. I guess they think I'm one of them. Maybe it's because of this place. I've been carrying the new brews when they've been rolled out."

Mike replied, "Brian and I plan to come. We'll see you there. Cheers."

Don went to the grand opening of the Hall Street Bar and Grill in the summer of 1982; those there that day were at the very core of the craft beer revolution.

Don and Bill had maintained vigilance by staying alert for changes surrounding their pub. In response to pressures from the public, laws had been changed to allow people to brew beer at home for personal use. They thought that this development had two aspects: greater interest in beer, and drinking home brews rather than the beer served at their pub. Within just a few years of purchasing the Horse Brass Pub, something was clearly afoot when it came to beer; they could sense it.

Beer aficionados frequented the Horse Brass, drawn not only by the warmth of this British-style public house, but also by the variety of beers available. These people were really into it. As they sampled different beers, they were not content to merely say whether they liked them or not. They used sophisticated beer terms related to taste: brightness, maltiness, strength, and hoppiness. Don talked with them to keep his ear to the rail concerning the future of beer. He was taking it all in.

New brewing companies had been starting up; the wave was starting to swell: Cartwright Brewery, Widmer Brothers Brewing, BridgePort Brewing, all in Portland; and Grant's Brewery Pub in Yakima, Washington.

People that Don knew well were taking on the law that governed the manufacture, distribution and sale of beer in the state. They were spending more time walking the halls of the Oregon State Legislature than at the Horse Brass. Oregon law was changed in the summer of 1985, unleashing the start of a huge industry. More craft beer breweries were started, some became successful, some not—but the growth of this industry would be inexorable. Don had seen this very large wave coming. He would be a part of it, catching and riding the wave of enthusiasm for good beer made locally. In turn, he would help make the wave even larger through his incessant, honest promotion and helping small start-up breweries. New terms entered the lexicon of beer: microbrews, microbreweries, brewpubs, and craft beer. A veritable beer sea change would lift up the Horse Brass and propel her forward; Don would help lead the craft beer revolution from the bridge of his pub.

At the Hall Street Bar and Grill grand opening, Don met its bar manager, a sharp impressive young man who certainly knew about beer. Don struck up a conversation by asking, "What's your name?"

"I'm Rob. Rob Royster."

Rob had been raised in California. He started spending his summers in Oregon as a young teen while his father was studying at the University of Oregon. The family fell in love with Oregon and its beautiful and rugged coast. Their fourth visit was a permanent one, settling in Pacific City, the center of dory-boat fishing. Without a convenient harbor, rugged dory fishermen launched their stout craft right through the surf, which weeded out the casual fishermen. Oregon surf could be nasty and dangerous. Rob was part of the dory fishermen community; this continued for two years after high school. After that, he took a job with a cruise line to see the world. That world included stops in the British Isles and shore excursions that included British pubs. He loved them. With his wanderlust somewhat sated, he attended the University of California at Davis. There his schooling included programs in the fine art of winemaking and brewing. Returning to Oregon, he hired on with a Portland restaurant situated on a bank of the Willamette. Its owners had set their sights much higher. They purchased the Clinkerdagger, a restaurant in nearby Beaverton and remodeled it to include a bar that would carry the finest wines and very best beers. They had renamed it the Hall Street Bar and Grill. It was there that Rob's path crossed that of Don's. Rob knew beer: the drinking, the making, and the management of its selling. Theirs would be a good relationship.

After their first meeting, Don returned to the Hall Street Bar and Grill a few times, just to say hello. They talked and talked, about a lot of things. Then Don made his decision. "Rob, if you're ever looking for a job, come see me."

The lure of the sea beyond the breakers at Pacific City was strong. Rob returned and fished over the summer from a dory launched through the waves. But his income from that was below his expectations. Rob returned to Portland and found a stool at the bar of the Horse Brass, a stool next to Don. He told Don that he was looking to get a job with one of the beer distributors and asked for his advice. Don offered to put Rob to work at his pub until something came through for him. So Rob signed on at the Horse Brass as the lead bartender at night. With a wife and two young children, Rob also worked for the McMenamin brothers during the day. He left both for a try in the beer distributing business, driving truck and making cold sales calls; that did not work out to his liking. Don brought Rob back on to bartend and help manage: payrolls, inventory control, developing lunch and dinner specials, and the like. Management training sessions, Don Younger style, often lasted until 4 am. He gave Rob his basic business philosophy. "Rob, as long as you got more money at the end of the day than what you started with, you're doing some good."

Rob's time was again divided, this time between the Horse Brass and Dick Ponzi's new BridgePort Brewing in Northwest Portland. Then a major beer distributor hired Rob full-time as a manager; he learned the ropes there over a number of years until fate stepped in. An established tavern in Pacific City was up for sale. Still a frequent visitor at the Horse Brass, Rob told Don that he was interested in the place. He had known it as a patron in his younger days and wondered aloud whether it would be a good business opportunity.

Without telling Rob, Don drove down to Pacific City and checked in at the Anchorage Motel, two blocks away from the Sportsman's Pub•N•Grub. He spent a couple of days there, watching, listening to and conversing with patrons and bartenders, all while having a few pints. Back at the Horse Brass, he met with Rob and advised, "You'd better buy it. That place has it going on, the business, the people and more. I can feel it there."

That put Rob back in Pacific City, taking the reins of the pub. That was certainly not the last time the two would cross paths. When Don strode in the door at the Sportsman's Pub•N•Grub, he was usually not alone. His entourage often included some of his regulars, visiting British musicians or regulars from a special pub in London. On such excursions, the next stop south on the Oregon coastal highway was Newport, the home of Rogue Ales.

Sometimes the visits just happened to coincide with the Hooker's Ball at the Sportsman's Pub•N•Grub. This annual event had been started a few years before Rob had purchased the tavern, and he kept it going. In keeping with Don's charitable outlook on life and the events held at the Horse Brass, the Hooker's Ball was held to raise money for charity, while having a good time. People came from far and wide, dressed stereotypically as hookers and pimps. Attendance grew to over 500, and the pub had to expand with tents into the adjacent parking lot. Prizes were given for best costumes and related categories. Some looked very authentic. One year, some people from California were the genuine article.

An Omaha native and gifted professional folk singer and musician, Tom May, walked into the Horse Brass one afternoon at the invitation of Don Younger. Peter Yeates, a veteran singer and guitarist from Ireland, had often played at the pub since making the Pacific Northwest his home. He knew instinctively that the Horse Brass and the folk singer from Nebraska were made for each other. Tom entered the life of the Horse Brass and the life of Don Younger. Tom eventually made his home in southern Washington State and became tightly wrapped up in the family of the pub. He loved the pub and composed "Ballad of the Horse Brass Pub." The resulting synergy and creativity benefited many people well beyond The Brass, among them the Sisters of the Road Café, a very worthy Portland charity that helped the homeless. Tom became involved in two major annual events at the Horse Brass, the Thanksgiving Orphans' Dinner, where he performed his ballad, and a concert called Winterfolk; both are linked with the pub and Sisters of the Road.

The publican of the Goose Hollow Inn, "The Goose" to those with affection for the place, took his views of the hard-working small business owner, and social responsibility, to the next level. Bud Clark made a formal, low-key announcement during the big snow and ice storm of 1983 — he would run for the office of Mayor of Portland. With dangerous, restricted travel throughout the area, people's attention was distracted from this important announcement. Those who would be his competitors paid little attention. How could a tavern owner with little political experience be elected?

With a campaign manager and staff in place, a well-publicized campaign kick-off was planned. Bud had to decide where to hold this important event. In front of City Hall? At a fancy Downtown hotel? In front of the Kvinneakt statue? No, no and, well, no. In early 1984, crowded with well-wishers, reporters and camera crews, Bud Clark held his mayoral campaign kick-off at the Horse Brass Pub with his supporters.

Before people started showing up for the kick-off, a longtime regular walked in. Bud was already there. The regular was met at the door by a lady member of Bud's campaign staff. She asked excitedly, "Are you going to support Bud Clark?"

He responded, "What? Did his lederhosen fall down again?" One of Bud's signature garments was a pair of real German lederhosen that he often wore in public. That set him apart, as did his poster, *expose yourself to art*. The campaign lady did not get this humor and did not smile one bit. Bud overheard and declared, "Not bad, Mike. Not bad." He told the campaign volunteer, "Just leave him alone; he's OK. He's a regular here."

Not long after the campaign kick-off, Bud held a fund raiser at the Horse Brass. There, some of the regulars received his campaign posters that played off the ads of a large American brewing company: "This Bud's for you."

Bud Clark was elected outright in the spring primary balloting with over 50 percent of the vote. His honest views of city governance and community responsibility held sway. However, Don might have thought that the magic of the horse brasses in his pub had rubbed off on Bud and had helped him carry the day.

Bud Clark won the next election as well; he was no "flash in the pan." His grassroots principles had taken hold. He served as Portland's mayor from 1985 to 1992. He led by example and convinced others. A large new building in Old Town, near Portland's old train station, was envisioned by Mayor Bud Clark. It would provide temporary housing and rehabilitative services for vulnerable people experiencing homelessness. It was completed in 2011 and named the Bud Clark Commons.

Mayor Bud Clark never left his roots. He regretted, as mayor, having had to direct the closure of a tavern in another part of town because serious illegal activity had been conducted there. He and the Portland City Council had no choice; crime and social dysfunction were persistent problems in that area. Bud Clark realized that this large area would become a "pub and tavern desert," devoid of places where people could gather, young and old alike, to discuss their neighborhood and its problems.

Bud was also a frequent Sunday visitor at the Horse Brass. As a "hands on" mayor, he often visited the sites of proposed land development, rather than relying only on staff reports before land use issues were brought before the Portland City Council. Getting exercise as well, he often rode his bicycle to the site, walked the property and the surrounding area, and sometimes talked to neighbors. The next stop was often the Horse Brass. There, with a good beer and an order of bangers, he found respite and companionship with Don. At times his visits were very colorful, with Bud wearing his trademark lederhosen, a white shirt, a pair of black suspenders with red rose emblems, and an alpine hat with a large feather. Don realized that his friend, now the Mayor of Portland, deserved and needed some quiet time because of the press of city business and politics. When not sharing a beer by his side at the bar, Don would watch out for overeager patrons. Some thought that they just had to stop and talk to the mayor, using the Horse Brass for lobbying, or to just meet him and say hello. Don often interceded with an outstretched hand and a gruff, firm, "He needs his quiet time. Leave him alone."

On one such Sunday visit, Bud Clark found Don "in his cups" at the bar, looking quite despondent. He asked his friend what was wrong. Apparently, with the juggling of other business ventures, he had gotten quite late with his lease payments for the space occupied by his pub. His payments were almost never on time. But Walter Tooze loved Don and what he and the Horse Brass did for Old Belmont Square and the neighborhood. A few times, Walter had huffed and puffed for effect, just to get Don's attention. Don had been late before, but he and Walter had always worked things out and payments were always made. Walter Tooze had died in 1983, and now the properties of Old Belmont Square were under different management. This time the demand for lease payment was more blunt, enough to convince Don that the Horse Brass would be closed and padlocked if payment were not received by a firmly fixed date. That got Don's attention!

When Bud realized the apparent pressure his close friend was now under, he reached in his pocket, pulled out his personal check book, and wrote Don a check for a considerable amount, a loan to tide him over. With sincere appreciation and relief, Don accepted his check. The funds were now there, just in case. Bud had no doubt that he would be repaid. Things were worked out with the landlord to mutual satisfaction, and the Horse Brass remained open. But in Don's eyes, it was an uncomfortably close call.

Don was planning another trip to England, leading a Horse Brass dart team. He cast about for people who would like to join him. Clay had never been to England. He stepped forward and said he would very much like to go, despite the cost which would stretch his budget some. A couple of weeks before the trip, Don went behind the bar where Clay was working and told him to go to the other side and sit down on a stool. On cue, many regulars and friends came in and gathered around him. They presented Clay with a stack of British pound notes of various denominations. Those that knew and loved this barman had contributed their money to help offset his expenses, and maybe help pay for a pint or two at a British pub. Clay's wife had exchanged the money for British pound notes; she also had them glued together along the short edge so that they could be carried like a book of coupons. At each pub he visited, he was to peel off a pound note and spend it there. He accepted the bundle of paper money with gratitude and a hint of emotion. As he leafed through the stack, he noticed that there was a signature on each note, Don's signature. The money came with strings attached. Don told Clay that he had to keep a journal. In it he was to write down the denomination of the note spent in the pub, the date it was spent, the name of the pub, and the name of its village. The publican or barman was to sign next to each entry, confirming Clay's visit.

To make sure Clay was properly outfitted for travel throughout Britain, Mike McCormick took him to the John Helmer store in downtown Portland. It was a very fine haberdashery, founded in 1921. They were known for quality men's clothing and their collection of classic hats. Clay bought a soft felt hat, a fedora that would travel well, even if it were folded up in Clay's backpack. He wore it into each pub he visited and usually heard, "Hey, mate, nice hat."

Clay had had an absolutely fabulous time traveling from village to village, pub to pub. After his return, it was obvious to his friends that Clay was a happy man. But there was something different about him; he exuded a bit of England. Don readily identified with what he saw in Clay. The same had happened to him. When asked about his trip, Clay described his fondest highlights. He would proudly place his travel journal on the bar to be read. It was like a travelogue. A typical entry was, "10 Pounds, The Chequers, Wickham Bishops, Essex" with the publican's signature and comment, "Cheers, Clay. Nice hat." Clay and his journal brought some more of England into The Brass. He left a bit of himself there, including his hat. The fedora had been tacked to the ceiling of a pub somewhere in England, a conversation piece for its regulars and a remembrance of the cheerful, visiting Yank.

The summer of 1986 was significant for the Horse Brass. There was another trip to England, this one fostered by beer, darts, and an invitation to compete in that most British of sports. Don and his dart team from The Brass, plus a contingent of fans, went to London. It was a first visit for some of them. The day before the dart match, the group had been treated to a daylight pub crawl by Young's Brewery, the sponsor of the London darts tournament. That evening, all of the people from the Horse Brass, including Don, were independently drawn back to a particular pub, the Prince of Wales, located in a southwest borough of London. In the wee hours of the morning, it was twinned with The Brass. True friendships were made and kept, through good times and bad; the twinning became a bonding over the following years, with visits by publicans and regulars in both directions across the Atlantic.

During World War II the RAF and the U.S. Army Air Corps, in addition to helping win the war in Europe, their relationship produced another link between Britain and the Horse Brass Pub. A young lady, a member of the RAF, fell in love with a young man, a member of the U.S. Army Air Corps. She became what was affectionately known as a war bride. After the war, her American husband was redeployed back to the United States. She followed her husband later and arrived in New York City aboard the Cunard Line's RMS Queen Mary. She was among the first of the war brides to come down the gangway. Newspaper reporters had learned of this historic voyage before the ship's arrival. Her picture, with babe in arms, and an article about war brides were featured in a New York newspaper. She and their child rejoined her husband.

To them was born a second daughter two years after the first, Jillian Flynn. Jill was raised in America, but at 19 years of age, with close relatives in North Wales, she went to live there for a time. In that village she was introduced to the public house. Jill felt quite comfortable in them, whether on the lounge side or in the public bar side; for this young woman, they were comfy, cozy, friendly and safe. Jill ended up working in her local pub part time. She tended bar, poured beautiful pints of beer, and otherwise ensured that village people felt at home. She learned firsthand what a pub was all about.

After 10 years in Wales, she returned to the U.S. and ultimately settled down in Portland. To make ends meet, she took a job at the Elephant and Castle. While there, she discovered the Horse Brass Pub. Occasionally, a tall, thin, interesting fellow with shoulder length hair and a beard would come to the Elephant and Castle. With him was a shorter, slightly stouter chap, also sporting a beard. She served and got to know Don and Clay. They, in turn, got to know her views about a proper village public house.

The Elephant and Castle closed earlier in the evening than The Brass. Since her late-evening trip home took her up Belmont and right by this understated pub, she found herself stopping in for a pint of good beer before calling it a day. Jill felt the pull of this pub and immediately recognized the somewhat-mystical allure that she had found in her Welsh local. The frequency of her visits increased, and soon she was sitting at the regulars' table, a part of the family. She already knew Clay, one of the bartenders. With its interior warmth, its employees and the regulars, Jill thought that this pub would be a good place to work.

Downtown Portland had been changing, and the number of patrons at the Elephant and Castle unfortunately declined. Many customers had stopped coming in on their way home after work because parking nearby had become a problem; it had become a hassle to meet friends there for a beer. For a host of other reasons, people did not come downtown as often. Those that wanted the atmosphere of a British-style pub began drifting to The Brass, since by late afternoon there was ample parking behind the pub. Without intention, the Horse Brass had siphoned off pub-loving patrons who lived on the east side of Portland.

With her income based largely on the number of customers served, Jill approached Clay one night at The Brass and asked about employment opportunities. An opening soon arose, but Don would never, ever lure employees away from another bar or tavern. He and Clay went to the Elephant and Castle and asked the manager, Dennis Vigna, about hiring Jill. Don and Dennis were fellow publicans and friends; they frequented each other's pubs. Dennis admitted that his place was making less money now and that Jill, whom he highly recommended, would do better at Don's place. Jill was hired. With that simple gesture of affirmation from Dennis, her 18 years of service at the Horse Brass began. Over those years, she gained a deeper understanding of the silent power within the walls of the pub near Mount Tabor.

Don, Bill and Joellen had frequented Sweet Tibbie Dunbar's, a rather posh Portland pub and restaurant. Its character and charm fit that intended by poet Robert Burns from the first line of one of his renowned poems by that name, "O wilt thou go wi' me, sweet Tibbie Dunbar?" Don was very impressed with the head bartender there. He wore a tuxedo and was friendly, honest and caring. Mel Hickman certainly knew how to make customers feel at home and provide quality service. Don and Mel spoke about a lot of things over the bar, and they became friends. Don liked him instinctively. They both listened to that same distant drummer of life. Without realizing it, they had been interviewing each other, and just in time, because Sweet Tibbie Dunbar's was changing. Mel found himself working for Don at the Horse Brass, sometimes behind the bar, sometimes lending a hand in the management end of things. Mel fit in very well with the family of the Horse Brass Pub, working and offering the perspective he had learned at Sweet Tibbie Dunbar's.

Don had located a tavern business that was for sale in the Raleigh Hills neighborhood. It was at the very complex intersection of Scholls Ferry Road, Oleson Road and Beaverton-Hillsdale Highway in Southwest Portland. Drivers had dubbed it Kamikaze Corner. Don dusted off the beautiful pub name that had been coined by his brother, purchased the business, and opened the second Rose and Raindrop pub at Kamikaze Corner.

Don needed a business manager who could also tend bar and provide good service; he looked to Mel. Don showed him the graphic artist's sketch for a sign with a rose and raindrops on it. Don had given the design to a local sign maker, an artist, who was to make a large, backlit plastic sign to be framed within the small cupola on the roof. Mel agreed to manage Don's pub at that crazy intersection, very much wanting this opportunity. With verbal plans in place, they sealed the deal with raised pints of beer and a handshake. Mel looked a little uncomfortable, nervously squirming on his barstool. Don was a good judge of people and sensed that something was wrong, maybe the financial arrangement was not right or the responsibilities were too much or ill-defined.

While Mel felt he knew Don quite well, he was uncertain of Don's views on social matters. Don never wore his politics on his sleeve or forced them on others, but he was never bashful about voicing a position on the issue of the day. Don did not fit neatly into a political category.

Mel said, "Don, I've got something to tell you."

Looking a little concerned, anticipating a serious family or medical problem, Don inquired, "What's that?"

Mel confided, "I'm gay."

Don raised his eyes and voice at the same time, "Thank God! I thought you we're going to tell me you were a Democrat!"

A smiling Mel walked out of the Horse Brass that day. As he left, Don confided to those sitting close to him at the bar, "I trust that man." Coming from Don, that was not a trivial statement.

Mel was at the helm of the second Rose and Raindrop, but only for a short time, months rather than years. He was doing fine, but as with any new business, it was slow to net sufficient customers to yield a profit. With his pub before profits philosophy, his other side ventures, and the craft beer revolution not yet being up to full speed, Don's financial bottom line was in a bit of a pickle. The landlord at the Rose and Raindrop was not as tolerant as Walter Tooze had been. Don was now a wee bit late with his lease payment for the second Rose and Raindrop. The landlord had other tenant plans for that building, and he used the unpaid payment as justification to shut the business down and ban access. Soon Mel was greeted with a changed lock on the door and a posted eviction notice, matching the legal notices received by Don and his investment partners. With that, Mel was looking for other opportunities.

Jack Joyce, the owner and publican of Rogue Ales Brewery and Public House in Ashland, Oregon, called Don one day. Jack and Don were very good friends; craft beer from Rogue Ales was on tap at the Horse Brass. Jack was in a "spot of bother," as the English would say when faced with a difficult situation. While his ales were catching on quickly, management attention was needed at his public house. Don quickly recommended Mel, who packed up and headed south. For over three years, Mel worked for Jack at his pub in Ashland, famous for its Oregon Shakespeare Festival.

North Dakota, its winters, the incessant wind and the original European settlers of the flat open land produced hearty, hard-working, honest folks. Bumper stickers in that part of the United States proudly claimed, "40 Below Keeps the Riffraff Out." The path of one young man, born and raised in Jamestown, North Dakota, would intersect the path of Don Younger and the Horse Brass Pub. A stint in the U.S. Navy during the Vietnam War lay between Jamestown and Portland. His final assignment was at Naval Air Station Alameda near San Francisco. After the Navy, he returned to Jamestown with the intent to head west where the mountains were higher than a barstool. San Francisco was his destination. A Navy buddy who lived in Portland invited Rick Maine to visit en route. As Rick drove down the Columbia River Gorge, he was captivated by its natural beauty. He thought to himself, This is it. I'm not going any farther!

In Portland, he partnered to form a small, successful construction company that specialized in window installation. There, over the course of 12 years, he garnered a very good understanding of management, bookkeeping and business principles. His business partner lived a few blocks from the Firehouse Tavern on Belmont. Before it was closed down, he and Rick had visited there a few times for a beer after work. After the space was transformed into the Horse Brass Pub, Rick's visits continued on a regular basis. He met a very interesting chap, Jay Brandon, who went to great lengths describing his love of England and pubs. The taste of bangers and a pint of Watneys Red Barrel became firmly

110

embedded in Rick, often prompting him to drive clear across town just for lunch at the pub. Often, by the time he walked to the bar from the front door, a pint of Watneys already awaited him, while Brian nipped off to the kitchen to warm up the expected order of bangers.

Looking for a change from the construction industry, Rick went to a bartending school and became a mixologist. His personality and skills were quickly recognized. Rick was hired to work at the Willamette Valley Country Club, where he learned about customer expectations and service at that lofty level. Later, he hired on as the lounge supervisor at the Thunderbird bar at the Red Lion hotel on the Columbia River. Because of these job changes, it would be almost 10 years before Rick would set foot again in the Horse Brass. But when he did, it was fateful for him and the pub.

Rick was enjoying a Watneys and bangers at the pub, just like earlier times, when an interesting-looking, long-haired dude walked over. Rick had seen him there long ago, but just thought him to be a neighborhood tavern rat. This man looked at Rick's plate of bangers and started talking about cheese plates and the English ploughman's lunch. He walked back into the kitchen. Rick asked Brian, "Who the hell is that?"

Brian flashed a wide grin, and answered, "That's Don Younger. He owns the place."

Rick raised his eyebrows. "Really?"

Don came back out with some samples of cheese and stated, "I'm Don Younger." He asked Rick, "What do you do?"

Rick replied, "I'm Rick, Rick Maine, the lounge supervisor at the Thunderbird bar at the Red Lion."

Don was always on the lookout for good people. A week or so later, an energetic man came into the Thunderbird and ordered a complex drink. Rick mixed it flawlessly and served it up with panache. In the course of casual conversation, the customer reached across the bar and offered his hand with, "Hi. I'm Mel Hickman."

Sometime later, with Mel's scouting report, Don Younger stopped by the Red Lion. Don and Rick got to know each other even better across the bar and in the cooler. Don looked around in there and asked if the Red Lion was thinking of offering craft beers from microbreweries. Don strongly encouraged Rick to do this, but Rick had a complex corporate structure above him.

Rick had seen the technology wave coming. He left the Red Lion and went to college to study computer technology and repair. He needed money to afford school and to house and feed himself. Being from North Dakota and not afraid of hard work, he signed on with a temporary employment agency; it provided bartending for parties and special events.

One day Rick checked in with the agency to see about work. There were no temporary jobs, but he was told that a fellow had called wanting to hire somebody to work at the Horse Brass, a fellow named Don Younger. Rick excitedly replied, "Tell him Rick, Rick from the Red Lion, is interested!"

Rick called Don and some minutes later they met at the Hutch Tavern in Northeast Portland. As luck would have it, Rick had been scheduled for another interview that afternoon, for a management position at the Red Lion. He was dressed for a corporate interview. No surprise, Don was not. They discussed what each was looking for, not only in work but in life. He told Don about the Red Lion interview, not to leverage his position, but to be completely honest, something that Don admired. Don reached in his pocket, pulled out a quarter and slid it across the table saying, "Call and tell them you're not going to be able to make it."

Rick used the quarter and turned down a lucrative corporate package. That deed done, Don took Rick to Mel's Diner. Mel was cleaning up, getting ready to close. He waved to them and said, "Hi, Rick," and took a bottle of vodka out from his desk. He made some strong mixed drinks. Don and Mel welcomed Rick into the fold. Rick, like Mel, knew the hard-liquor end of the tavern business; this fit Don's plans for The Brass — mixed drinks.

Rick chose the work path that offered more freedom. This was the job flexibility he needed to complete his degree in computer technology. Don was agreeable to that. Rick, as Don had done when at Lever Brothers, had opted for a path far different than those found in the corporate world. They had a few more drinks that day at other watering holes around Portland, cementing their mutual expectations. Then the sun came up. Like others before and after, he discovered that it was hard to hang with Don.

Rick worked behind the bar, but he also became an advisor and confidant, as had others who were close to Don. One of the first things Don asked of Rick was to computerize the business records of the pub. In addition to bartending, Rick found himself digging through shoeboxes of records. After some work, he and Don had a better handle on the revenue stream and the expenses of the company. With the data spread before them to analyze, some problems were identified and solutions proposed. Rick's business acumen, gained from running his construction company, was now applied at the Horse Brass. Along with this foundation, there were suggestions to help promote business.

The first was to expand the hours of the pub by extending the closing time to as long as the OLCC rules allowed — 2:30 am. The Brass had been closing around 11 pm; the exact time was more the whim of the evening bartender, depending on the number of customers, as was the case for many other bars and taverns. This was a generally accepted practice at the time. Rick's suggestion was in competition with one from Mel, which was to open earlier to offer breakfast. Considering Mel's experience running his early-opening diner, this was not surprising. There was a lot of heated discussion about the pros and cons. They each had an honest passion for their point of view, intended for the good of the pub. Don sat, listened, drank and puffed on cigarettes, offered his opinions and sometimes served as referee. Rick emphasized that the extended hours would bring in fellow workers from bars and taverns that closed earlier. From a business standpoint, that also meant more employee hours and more overhead. The sharper edges of running a business started to creep in. Don discussed this with longtime regulars of the pub. He said, "I'll have to sleep on this one." A few days later, Don came in, slapped Rick on the back and gave him the simple directive: "Go with it." That opened the door, literally, not only to more people in the immediate neighborhood, but from well beyond.

Another draw would be a discount to these same workers one day a week. The plan was to spread the news during the day that the Horse Brass would be staying open until 2:30 am. Rick and two new bartenders, Greg and Marty, served as early morning Horse Brass roving ambassadors, complete with a stack of business cards to hand out. They traveled about in their off hours and promoted the pub. Along with this, Rick suggested offering discounts one day a week to other workers in the same industry. He had helped institute such a policy when he was at the Red Lion. What went with staying open late, as directed by Don, was that the closing bartender would have to prepare ordered food, like Brian and Arthur had done in the early days of the pub.

A side benefit from the second Rose and Raindrop was Don's hard-liquor license, which he maintained. Mel was certainly trained to deliver quality concoctions of a wide variety, as was Rick. Small, clear valves on the necks of inverted bottles, mounted above the back bar, could dispense hard liquor. Merely pushing the valve up with a glass underneath delivered a precisely-measured amount of whiskey, vodka, rum or gin. These little devices were known as "optics." There was much discussion about serving mixed drinks at the Horse Brass. Rick cautioned about training and quality control for properly mixing more complex drinks. This warranted more thought before making a decision. It was put on hold.

Then there were the craft beers. Rick and Don had had more than a few discussions about them. Don had supported the craft beer revolution from the get-go. He knew the brewers personally as trusted friends, and he knew their beers. But by now things were really accelerating, with more and more microbreweries and brewpubs opening up seemingly by the week. Don expressed some concern that the Horse Brass could be overwhelmed and, ironically, be sidetracked from its fundamental purpose. Above all, he wanted to serve beer brewed from the heart, real beer for real people as he had experienced in England.

There were many things in the pub, beyond craft beer, that people had not learned of by word-of-mouth. Trips and events of various types had been planned. Distinctly British food items from Art's Cupboard were offered. There were the results of pub-sponsored dart and soccer teams, the activities of the *Brass Pegs* cribbage team, parties and gatherings, and the talented musicians that were slated to entertain; the variety went on and on. What to do? Rick suggested a Horse Brass newsletter. Don would have to mull this one over, with a beer and cigarette, of course. A newsletter would have to be written and edited by somebody, printed, and distributed. Rick and Don looked at each other, thinking the other would take on this task. No such luck. Don said, "I know the perfect couple for this — George and Nancy Bieber. They first met at the Rose and Raindrop, met again in here and got married."

George had been coming into the Horse Brass almost as long as Don had been its publican. He certainly knew the pub and was a member of its family. What made this the perfect fit was that George was also a top journalist who worked for KGW TV in Portland. If anybody knew how to write, and write very well, it was George. Plus, George had been recently wed, and Nancy was also a pub regular. Surely, she would lend a hand.

Don was at his favorite spot at the bar. An unsuspecting George and Nancy came in. As they walked to the regulars' table, Don motioned for George to come and join him. By the time George took a stool next to Don, a pint of his favorite beer awaited him. The proposal was made, and George accepted. He would write, publish and distribute a Horse Brass newsletter. George asked, "What should we call it?"

Don just stared at George and asked, "What do you think? You're the writer."

George replied, "You're the publican. It's a newsletter for your pub."

Don discreetly raised two fingers off of the bar, noticed by the barman. Two more pints of good beer were set before them to stimulate thought. They came up with *Brass Tacks*. The logo would be a horse's head within an upturned horseshoe, set between the words *Brass* and *Tacks*. Beneath this front page header, and borrowing from a larger publication, would be printed:

An Authentic Horse Brass Publication

All the News that fits

The first issue rolled off the press in August, 1992; actually, it rolled off of a cheap office copier purchased for this purpose. George did all the layouts, the graphics, most of the writing and all of the editing. Don was very firm that he did not want any "fluff." The *Brass Tacks* would be about the Horse Brass, things that sprang from the pub and things British. There were expenses, such as printer, paper and postage, let alone the time involved. These would be reimbursed by Don. Compensation was pure Horse Brass — free beer for the duration of the publication for George and Nancy. George consumed beer in quantity and ordered beer for many of the regulars, under this provision, in an attempt to roughly balance the cost ledger of the *Brass Tacks*.

At first, stacks of the newsletter were set on the bar or handed out at the regulars' table. Little flyers were also set around the pub, advertising the *Brass Tacks*. One could write down his name and address on the flyer and give it to the bartender. But a patron could not get on the mailing list unless he bought a beer when he turned in a flyer; at least one beer was required to receive free copies of the *Brass Tacks*. From personal friendships among the regulars and the completed flyers, George set up a mailing list. At the Bieber household, publishing went into high gear: printing, folding, sealing the edge, affixing postage, and making trips to the post office with bundles of ever-increasing size. For one issue, during the four-year life of the *Brass Tacks*, distribution topped 900.

Shortly after Rick Maine came onboard, James Macko signed on as a waiter to support his "art habit." This was very familiar territory for James. He was already a member of the family of the pub; his first drink at the Horse Brass had been over a decade earlier.

For his first few visits, he had thought that Brian was the owner, and that the man with long hair at the end of the bar was just an eccentric patron, a leftover hippie from the '60s. Finally, one of the regulars advised him that that person, named Don Younger, just happened to be the owner. James thought, Oh, really? One night early on, he ended up sitting next to Don at the bar. They started talking and drinking, talking and drinking. James felt like he was being interviewed for membership in the human race as they discussed life, death, religion, God, and matters of similar weight. Before long, James became a regular at The Brass, not just by the frequency of his visits, but much more importantly, by joining its family, feeling its spirit, knowing it was his home.

James Macko had moved with his family from the state of his birth, New Jersey, to the Pacific Northwest. They wound up in Walla Walla, Washington. James later graduated from Walla Walla University, with majors in Theology and French and a minor in Biblical Languages. Before the year of his graduation, he spent a summer in France as part of a concentrated language course at La Seminaire Adventist du Saleve. Before and after that course, just like other young men seeking to know themselves, James traveled throughout Europe. He absorbed its art and sampled beers and wines in the process.

After graduation with a Bachelor of Arts degree *cum laude*, he moved to Portland, taking a job for two years as an intern pastor at a church in Southwest Portland. But something internal guided him to leave the ministry and pursue a career in art.

James had not taken any formal art courses but had shown a real, natural talent from a young age. He sketched, drew and painted as he grew up. Teachers and friends noted that he was able to really capture perspective and the human face, well beyond mechanical replication. A close friend, with a degree in Art History, looked at James' work and said, "I have people coming to me all the time and asking if they should market their art work. I usually tell them no, but you haven't asked me. I'm telling you—Do it!"

James began producing art that people admired and wanted. His works started showing up in many galleries in and around Portland. He would eventually sell over 400 paintings during his career in art. To support his early art habit, between sales of paintings or the commissions to do them, James took on every other job known to man, in his own mind. Starting in 1993, one of those jobs was working for Don by waiting on patrons at the Horse Brass Pub.

When Don first met James, he knew that he was speaking with a true artist, one with a deep theological background. After many pints over the following years, James convinced Don that his art and theology were closely entwined. They were not paintings of Biblical scenes or the legendary people and saints of religious history. They were of people and their surroundings, intended to stimulate viewers to think outside of denominational boundaries, to think about existential reality outside of their complacent views of life, to think about their personal relationship with the created cosmos. Don felt that these views and his pub were somehow connected.

Not long after James came onboard, Rick left for England as directed by Don. James went "from the frying pan into the fire," as he had to fill in for Rick, including some management responsibilities. While certainly capable of working behind the bar, waiting on tables was his best fit. James fostered the welcoming feeling of the English public house, as Don required. It came naturally to him, and he took great satisfaction from serving people up close and personal at their table, rather than from the pulpit. While waiting tables, he would never, ever bring his beliefs or his theology and philosophies into the conversation; patrons felt it through his interactions with them.

One night after closing time, James sat down at the bar. Don asked, "How'd things go tonight?"

James replied, "Great. Really good people come into your pub. But they've done more for me than I've done for them."

Don had to ask, "What do you mean?"

With rock-solid sincerity, James explained, "I feel that I've touched more people here over the last two years than I ever did as a pastor."

Don replied, "Yeah . . . this *is* a church—you know, a church with levers."

James' close association with the pub as a regular and a waiter actually put him at the right place, at the right time, for the events that lay ahead.

Rick had come aboard a few years after the Horse Brass had been twinned with the Prince of Wales pub in England. At The Brass, he met a contingent of regulars from there at one of their many exchange visits. Among them were the publican of the Prince of Wales and his wife, Terry and Debbie. They said a group of three young lads from their pub would be coming over in a few months to tour the United States for the first time, a circumnavigation of what should have been British colonies. The Horse Brass would be their first stop.

Rick hit it off well with the English visitors, being a good host and assisting where needed. After an evening of over-celebration at The Brass, Rick assisted Terry back to Don's house a few blocks away, since Terry and Debbie were staying with Don as invited guests. Rather than taking Terry to the front door and depositing him inside the house, Terry was left on the front porch steps. In the mild summer morning air, Watney's Red Barrel and Terry decided to take a brief nap together, curled up on the porch. Don woke up later that morning and tried to leave, almost tripping over his sleeping guest. He pulled Terry into the house and onto the couch to sleep on something more appropriate. Apparently, Rick had violated some quaint English social norm and had become a "right bastard" for leaving Terry defenseless on the porch. Rick was informed by Debbie that "right" in British slang meant that he was really good at it.

One day during the visit, Rick took Debbie to dinner, thinking he would be done by the time of his evening shift. Somehow, she convinced Rick that it would be OK to be a little late, maybe even missing it altogether, that Don and Terry would cover for him. The shift was covered, but Terry added to Rick's English nickname; Rick now answered to "unreliable right bastard."

Sometime later, as forecast by Terry and Debbie, the English lads arrived at the Horse Brass, all eager to see the colonies. This was during the year of Rick's 40th birthday, graduation from college, and his plans to visit family back in Jamestown. Rick's status at the Horse Brass was in considerable flux during this time. He went from part-time bartender and management assistant to an employee on an indefinite sabbatical, as approved by a growling Don, followed by full-time work as a working manager upon his return.

Rick's sabbatical from the Horse Brass was accompanied by the three blokes from England. They set out together in a big Cadillac, headed to Jamestown with more than a few stops en route. That trip set many things in motion.

The Horse Brass had weathered a veritable sea change. Important things had taken place in and around the pub: the beginning of the craft beer revolution, the writing and singing of the "Ballad of the Horse Brass Pub," the starting of the Thanksgiving Orphans' Dinner, the twinning with the Prince of Wales, and the strengthening of the crew and the family of the pub to keep the ship on course. Now the publican and his crew would be tested—Don would lose some of those closest to him, fierce winds would blow and the seas would rise.

Heavy Seas — Steady as She Goes
(1993 – 2001)

Since the Horse Brass had first opened in 1976, profits had been somewhat thin. This unintentionally fit Don's adopted vision of pub before profits. The Horse Brass had been nudged along by puffs of wind, British Pub Nights and weekend nights when it was filled with music and song. But more often than not, there were periods when the good ship had been financially becalmed. Then, the regulars took to the oars and their pints to keep her moving. After a number of years, the regulars were firmly established. Beyond the regulars, there were the employees and entertainers that were part of this close-knit family. The early years were the golden years, years when the pub was a real home for its family without the distraction of a pub packed to the brim with people.

The stars used for navigation were changing, not the least of which was Oregon's craft beer revolution — the number of taps for craft beers at the Horse Brass had started to increase markedly. People who loved different beers were attracted to The Brass; craft beer fit the British soul of the pub. Word was also spreading that the pub was a gentle, authentic British place where young and old alike would find companionship in a relaxing atmosphere. Energetic, keen business management was added to the mix. All of these combined to move the ship ever faster with some unintended consequences. The Horse Brass grew into something bigger than a traditional public house in Britain.

Like Don, Bill loved to cook, both having learned early in their mother's kitchen. Their skills and supervision of cooking staff were quite evident in their taverns and restaurants. Yet Bill wanted to take his cooking skills to the next level and well beyond. He enrolled in Portland's eminent Le Cordon Bleu College of Culinary Arts. While attending this very challenging school, he had opened his own hamburger joint, Billy Burger. Don and Bill's younger sister, Sue, worked at Billy Burger to help out. Sue knew her way around a kitchen; she, too, had grown up at her mother's side. A pressure fryer, known by the brand name Broaster, was used by Bill and Sue to cook burgers and chicken. It was a commercial cooker which combined pressure cooking and oil frying to cook food faster.

As graduation from Le Cordon Bleu approached, Billy Burger was shut down. Bill installed his Broaster in the kitchen of the Horse Brass. Before this, prepared foods had been heated upon order. Until the Broaster arrived, a rather common fare known throughout the British Isles had not been offered at the pub. Don had wanted for a long time to expand his British menu to include fish and chips. He started out slowly with due regard to the quality of food offered to his patrons. The training of the kitchen staff in the art of fried food was neither simple nor inexpensive. There was a larger margin for error in keeping the quality of such food consistent. This paralleled the complexities of making consistently good craft beer. But preparing deep fried and grilled food had to be done much faster, from receiving the order to its being served. Fish and chips were initially served only on Friday nights. This expanded to more nights as the popularity of this British fare grew. Eventually, fryers and a grill were added to the kitchen. Don could often be seen strolling about amongst his patrons asking for feedback on their meals, especially the fish and chips; he insisted on using halibut rather than cod.

Bill graduated from Le Cordon Bleu, their hard-earned certificate held proudly in his hands. There was some close brother-to-brother talk at Don's favorite spot at the bar. Don toasted Bill's graduation with a special bitter, cask-conditioned and developed specifically for the Horse Brass by Rogue Ales. The Horse Brass was on the rise and becoming the epicenter of Oregon's growing craft beer industry. All this, and a brother with a Le Cordon Bleu certificate—life was good!

Clay had been checking out airfares to Reno, Nevada, when he came across some very inexpensive roundtrip airline tickets to Boise. This was definitely not Reno; it did not have casinos. But considering the price of the tickets and that there were two breweries in this fair Idaho city, a group excursion to Boise was planned. Don and Rick had been visiting new microbreweries in Oregon, many by invitation. Consequently, breweries in Boise were a natural extension, and they had a chance to sample and possibly order new brews for the Horse Brass. A group of six beer-loving, adventurous folks was formed. Bill drove Don, Clay and Rick to the airport mid-week. They would meet the rest of the gang there. On the following Friday, Bill drove up to the airport arrivals area and found the smiling trio. Bill had a serious cough and was apparently quite congested. The next stop was at the Horse Brass for trip stories over pints. Bill usually joined in to hear tales of life on the road, but he dropped them off at the pub and said, "Don, I'm not feeling so good. I'm going home."

Don stepped out of the car and leaned back in to say, "I hope you feel better. Take care of yourself, brother." On Sunday, Don received a phone call from Bill's daughter. She had been trying to contact her father and was quite concerned. She had gone over to Bill's house over the weekend. He lived alone at the time. Despite her knocks and a few shouts, there had been no response. Now, Don was concerned.

He drove over to Bill's place, unlocked the door, walked in asking, "Bill, Bill? Are you home?" There was no answer. Don walked into Bill's bedroom.

Over the weekend of May 22, 1993, William Younger had died. It was an unabated shock to his family, those at the Horse Brass, and especially to Don. He was absolutely devastated.

They held a memorial gathering at the pub, attended by many people. They crowded slowly around the regulars' table with hugs, tears and words of sympathy. Beer was served, including the one that had recently been rolled out at the pub from Rogue Ales. Finally, Don quieted the assembly. The wake and testimonies began. One by one, people poured out their feelings with stories of Bill and their tributes to him. Don was the last to speak. The pub turned stone silent. With barely controlled emotion, Don spoke of their years growing up together in Gresham, their first tavern, the Mad Hatter, and all their other ventures leading to the pub within which all were now standing. Then Don held up his pint of the new special bitter brewed just for the pub, held it high for all to see. Don turned slowly, sweeping it across the pub, and with tears of emotion, he gave the familiar toast, "To the caveman!"

Those at the wake responded in unison, "To the caveman!" This toast had been created and made often by Bill in tribute to those cavemen and cavewomen everywhere, throughout time, who had suffered through the early, wild world with short, hard lives. Bill had often said that if it were not for them and their tenacity, we would not be sitting here today and drinking beer in a friendly pub.

The pub's house beer had arrived just before Bill's death by sheer coincidence; others at the wake thought otherwise. The beer used at the wake to toast Bill and the caveman was later named in Bill's honor.

As the wake eventually thinned, Don went over and stood briefly in the lane of Dart Board One, stared at and lightly touched the barrelhead on the wall, the same barrelhead he had knocked on when he had first brought Bill into the Horse Brass Pub, the barrelhead with the painted words, William Younger's Tartan Bitter.

At Bill's home, family members had found the familiar light tan overcoat that he wore almost all the time. It looked very much like the crumpled one worn by Peter Falk in the 1970s TV series *Columbo*. Also, there was Bill's tan cap with Mad Hatter embroidered on it. One of the regulars, Mike McCormick, stepped forward and requested that they be allowed to fasten both hat and coat on a post at the pub, a post with horse brasses, a post close to the regulars' table. There they remain, right by the plaque in Bill's memory.

The shock of Bill's death was still raw in the hearts of his siblings, parents and pub family. A large wave had crashed over the decks of the Horse Brass. But life moved on and so did the pub. Business and service still had to be tended to. With Sue's experience at Billy Burger, Don asked her to come onboard and manage the kitchen. Quality food from the Broaster, deep fryers and grill needed Sue's hand. She took the helm of the kitchen and successfully steered that important part of the Horse Brass ship, its galley, for over seven years.

After Bill's death, Don wanted another trip to England. This time, he would celebrate New Year's Eve with his mates at the Prince of Wales. Don called back to the Horse Brass after midnight and ordered Rick to visit England and sample her pubs, like he had done nearly 20 years before. The three Brits who had visited America could not stop talking about North Dakota and of Rick's shepherding them around.

Rick saluted smartly and later spent six weeks in the general vicinity of the Prince of Wales pub. He visited over 100 pubs and sampled beer with many regulars and publicans. This was post-graduate pub management work, hands-in British style. Rick did well and returned with enthusiasm and ideas. He was met with 13 days of long shifts, with only one day off, because of an unavoidable turnover in staff that had occurred while he was away.

Rick found the time to give Don, Brian and Arthur a trip report, complete with new suggestions to increase the business of the pub. The reins of management were soon turned over to Rick, but with Don's hand firmly on the tiller. Rick would manage, but Don was the publican. He now knew what a proper public house was, and he was enthused to transfer his perspectives and ideas to all who worked at The Brass. Rick had appreciated the mindset of Brian and Arthur before his trip, but now he understood it internally. He had lived it. He saw how neighbors met, conversed and entertained each other at their local; it was part of the social glue that bound the village together. The Horse Brass was similarly embedded, but its patronage was expanding from well beyond its neighborhood.

Things at Jack Joyce's Rogue Ales Brewery and Public House in Ashland settled down and smoothed out with Mel's help. Jack soon opened a second brewpub on Oregon's coast in Newport and moved his brewery operations there. Mel turned his eyes north for possible business opportunities back in Portland.

After some discussion with Don and a little financial support, Mel bought the Eastside Café in Southeast Portland. It was a breakfast and lunch place in an industrial area, catering to daytime workers' schedules. It was open from 6 am to 2 pm, only on weekdays. Everybody at the Horse Brass referred to it as Mel's place, so he changed the name to Mel's Diner.

Paula Snoddy learned of Mel's Dinner, signed on and worked there as a waitress. She had had considerable experience at the Horse Brass and brought some of that to Mel's place. At first, she thought that Mel was very hard to work for and could not figure him out. Another waitress told her that he was a really nice man, but that he had been coming in a little under the weather each morning because of some English visitors staying at his house. The visitors were from the Prince of Wales. When his house guests returned to England, his imbibing returned to normal. Soon his true colors as a wonderful boss and giving person were evident.

As Don's dear father aged, Don ensured that he always had transportation to his local lodge of the Benevolent and Protective Order of Elks and, of course, the Horse Brass Pub. His visits to the pub became less frequent, and he eventually succumbed to failing health on February 9, 1995. A few days later, on the date of the arranged funeral, a severe snow and ice storm hit Portland, much like the one back on December 24, 1983. The funeral was cancelled, but not everyone got the word. Some had braved slippery roads and made it to a very quiet funeral home. The funeral was rescheduled, but it was not as large as the one Don's father had desired. Regardless, his wake was held at the Horse Brass. Don spoke as did his mother and many others. His father had a good and proper send off.

Don was not one to knee-jerk at the first suggestion flung at him by Rick. Steering the Horse Brass, keeping her on the proper course, was always his top priority. He knew that the best ideas were not forced; they needed time to ferment. When staff, patrons or those promoting craft beers met with Don and offered suggestions, they were usually met with, "Slow down, slow down. Let's have a pint and think about this." This was normally followed by a few days of reflection after Don's, "Let's sleep on it." Don also had a simple philosophy about business, especially when it was his. He often voiced it to those closest to him when discussing changes and the future of the Horse Brass, "If it ain't broke, don't fix it."

123

Rick had considerable experience as a certified mixologist, having done very well at the Willamette Valley Country Club and the Red Lion. However, Rick advised Don that to train the current bar staff and new bartenders as mixologists would be a bit daunting. It would be required for consistency of not only drink quality, but for the sizes of shots used. He suggested that Don use optics. He had seen them in the pubs he had visited in England, but Don already knew of them. The devices were British, the result of the 1963 Weights and Measures Act of Parliament. These ensured that a patron received a standard, known measure of alcohol. Both barman and patron could also see the liquor filling a shot glass. The precise amounts used in different pubs were randomly checked by serious government blokes. The size of the shot could not be subject to the skill or financial whim of a barman or publican. Rick had witnessed some unsmiling lads from the weight and measures side of British government, confirming that the optics were calibrated and they functioned as required by law. Rick noted that each optic had a little loop of wire and tag with a government stamp. Rick watched the inspectors cut the wire, do a precise measure of the spirit delivered, and if accurate, install another wire with a new regal certification stamp. This was right in line with a measured pint. Rick had noted a small mark at the top of beer glasses. Beer had to measure up to that line, with the bottom of the foamy head above it, or the pint would not be a proper pint.

Rick commented to one barman, "You guys take this pretty seriously, don't you?"

The immediate response was, "Haven't you been paying attention to our prime minister?!"

"Well, no, I haven't," Rick answered sheepishly. "What does he have to do with it?"

The barman explained, "That was one of his campaign promises, a pint in every glass."

Rick chuckled, knowing of an early 20th century presidential candidate in the U.S. who had promised, "A chicken in every pot."

Rick suggested to Don that only basic mixed drinks, such as rum and coke or gin and tonic, be served using optics, as well as straight whiskey. Beer, especially craft beer, was firmly in the blood stream of the Horse Brass. Now, Don wanted to introduce hard liquor at the pub to better serve the tastes of his patrons. Like many of his course-changing decisions, he bounced this idea off of his unofficial board of advisors at the regulars' table. "Hey, what do you guys think of putting hard liquor in here?"

The beer was great, but the almost unanimous response was, "Oh, yeah!"

Don already had a few of the British-made optics in the basement where he lived; Rick remembered seeing them when he had helped Don move. The optics had been the result of Don's earlier visits to England. These optics had been used at the second Rose and Raindrop. Mel researched and found an American manufacturer and also dug into all the legalities and health requirements. Under Rick's management, optics connected to inverted liquor bottles were added to the back bar of the Horse Brass. But there was a condition about which Rick was adamant; single malt Scotch whiskey must be offered. He had seen how a good Scotch and a good cigar went together when he was a bartender at posh bars. Somebody also suggested Tequila, but that one did not make the initial cut.

The Horse Brass Pub was becoming well known for many good reasons. The number of taps of local and regional craft beers at The Brass continued to grow. Rick and Don discussed craft beer and the Horse Brass at length. Actually, they discussed everything at length, almost daily. Each other's thoughts and ideas were shared, discussed, discarded or implemented. Even after the tragic passing of his brother, Don included some of Bill's ideas. It was a vibrant, exciting, yet tragic time. Don could not forget Bill.

The sea change of craft beer was now a heavy sea, stirred up by the rapidly increasing number of microbreweries and brewpubs. Don had incessantly supported the craft beer revolution ever since he carried the first beer from the Cartwright Brewing Company in Portland in 1980. Back then, he had known the brewers personally, knew their motivations, knew their breweries. Now it was hard to keep track of the new faces in the industry. Rick helped convince Don that now was the time to renew, to reenergize.

Soon, they were making beer road trips, visiting breweries and brewpubs just about everywhere in Oregon and Washington. Don was meeting and listening to new brewers to understand both the motivations as well the processes for making good beer. Don thought back to the first beer road trip he had made with Tom May to Bert Grant's new brewery and brewpub in Yakima, Washington. While Don appreciated the entrepreneurial profit motive, he looked for beer made from the heart. He attended grand openings and offered to carry good new brews at the Horse Brass. Before long, Don was the invited guest of honor at brewery openings and beer events. But the seas got a bit rough. Not all beer was good; making consistently good beer was difficult. Some beer tap names at the Horse Brass had to be removed. There were a few cases when the decision to carry a beer had been premature, when enthusiasm had preceded reality and tasting. But that soon settled down. If the breweries and their brews met Horse Brass standards, Don would roll them out with fanfare and honest promotion and add them to the pub's *Guest Beers on Tap* menu. For a start-up microbrewery, the honor of being rolled out at The Brass, getting a beer tap, and being added to the guest beer menu became a *big* deal, as was being associated with its publican.

By this time, Rick had transferred his vision and enthusiasm to the staff. They knew that they were going to get slammed with business, and they welcomed this. Everything was coming together, and the team had to have a coordinated way to handle the increased business. The focus shifted to smoothing out the operation to give employees more time to sell; sell the pub, sell the product, sell the service, sell themselves. Rick instilled that if you did these things, customers would return. Rick wanted to provide people with the experience of a British public house. Of course, there was also the unique experience of the Horse Brass itself—and of Don, its eccentric publican.

On many early mornings after the pub closed, hot wash meetings were held at the regulars' table between Rick and the evening staff. If something had gone wrong, they collaborated on how to correct it. When things had gone right, they came up with ideas and worked to make things even better. After one of these meetings, Rick remarked, "We're working towards being like Ivory soap, 99.99 percent pure." Above all, there was real pride in serving many customers well, making them feel at home, all while keeping the Horse Brass a British public house; it was a difficult balance.

Horse Brass advertisements appeared in newspapers and beer-related publications, but Rick also enlisted the employees to become active ambassadors for the pub. He encouraged them to spread the word about what could be found in the Horse Brass beyond the beer and food. Rick ensured that every employee knew the history of the pub and every story that Don allowed them to tell. If a patron asked a question about The Brass, a barman or server could usually answer it. They were able to talk to people on every aspect of the pub, including the array of craft beers offered, and took pride in being able to do this.

Everything started coming together, business-wise, during the late 1990s. The gross revenues for the Horse Brass increased significantly. Don, Rick and the employees were all deserving of the benefit of the increased business. There were times during these heady years when people were lined up outside, down the block, waiting for room to be let in. This had occurred in the past for special events, but now it was becoming more frequent. Some drove in from the hinterlands; some made it part of their vacation plans. The Horse Brass was becoming more of a destination than the lounge of a village. Don may have viewed the expanding business as a way of sharing the spirit of a British pub with more folks—by expanding the village. This fit his view regarding new businesses that would compete with the Horse Brass. He spoke about this, stating, "Don't worry about your slice of the pie; make the pie bigger."

Those in the craft beer, pub and tavern trades, and his regulars, absolutely loved Don. Yet not many gave him high marks as a steely-eyed, sharp-penciled businessman. He left that to others at the pub and back at the Willamette Trading Company. As Don pointed to the horizon from the bridge of his ship, his crew was busy: taking soundings, warning of shoals, scraping barnacles, and caulking leaks. His vision had a different kind of accounting. "Don't count the money in the till. Count the smiles of those who enter. If the people are satisfied, the register will take care of itself." [14]

Those closest to Don had often discussed the success of the Horse Brass as a business and as a home. Like the business conundrum of putting pub before profit, others had posed another — that the Horse Brass was successful because of Don, *and* in spite of Don. It depended on which facet of the pub was viewed. For the human spirit, they all knew which was the most important. Don sometimes punctuated their thoughts when he said, "Hell, I'm a drinkin' man, not a business man."

As the Horse Brass rose to the next level, the philosophy of pub *before* profit morphed into pub *and* profit. There was natural tension between these poles, but they came into a balance that Rick helped Don achieve; profit to sustain the pub, pub to sustain the spirit.

Through all this, Don was ever watchful for trends and attitudes. He sensed pushback from some of the regulars, those that were among the early family of the pub. He overheard some complaints that the pub was just not like it was in the old days. Those cozy, quiet days were also the financially-thin days when the pub was supported largely by the devoted regulars. That had formed a strong bond. There was still conversation and companionship, to be sure. But private conversations rose almost to a din on some nights. The hours of evening quiet time around the regulars' table were shrinking.

It became harder to provide the personal touch found in a small English pub, with a larger number of people regularly frequenting the place. Knowing people by name, their birthdays, and where to find their personal mug behind the bar became increasingly difficult, especially for new bartenders and wait staff. The number of mugs kept for regulars had peaked at over 170. At this level, many patrons had to point out their mug, or otherwise help the bartender find it. It was hard, if not impossible, to maintain the feel of a cozy, small British pub at this scale of operations. The decision was made; personal mugs would be returned to their owners. The transition to a mug-free pub proved a bit awkward, but understandably necessary. Some regulars took a little umbrage when their mug was handed back to them. This was an indication of the delicate balance that lay ahead, of a cozy pub where they knew your name and personal mug versus a pub with an expanding business that crowded its space.

During this decade the Horse Brass became something different, a hyper-pub, a large, very charming space, one with regulars and many customers and a large number of taps of craft beer, but one that also clung to its history and the British public house, keeping its very soul.

Portland was changing as well during this time. Young people from all parts of the country were pouring into the city, attracted by the surrounding natural beauty, its unique life style and progressive, liberal politics. Many were referred to as yuppies, young urban professionals, using a term coined in the 1980s. With this influx, the land in the morning shadow of Mount Tabor was changing, expanding. Newcomers to Portland were swept into the Horse Brass. They, too, felt its spirit and thought it was a wonderful place to meet with friends.

The Horse Brass was operating on a different level. The ship now had to be guided through heavy seas at exhilarating speed, while remembering "It's a bit of England where good companionship is the order of the day." The crew watched the compass and made necessary corrections to maintain that course. The standing order to the helm was: "Steady as she goes, mates. Steady as she goes."

Like most things in life, balance was needed. Don had felt he might have to "tap the brakes." He sat down with George Bieber and discussed the *Brass Tacks*. Don and George had similar views about beating a dead horse: stop beating it. Certainly, the newsletter was anything but a dead horse. It had very much met its intended purpose. And the amount of beer consumed under the *Brass Tacks* agreement and other costs helped sway the decision; both agreed, and the last issue was published four years after the first. Don gave George a hearty, gravelly, "Thanks."

George sighed as he swung his head side to side, thinking, No more free beer.

But there entered another into the story of the Horse Brass Pub. A new-fangled thing called the Internet was growing even faster than the pub. Rick and other "techies" at the Horse Brass convinced Don that money spent on developing something called a website would be a good thing. Don slept on it and gave his permission. Now, the most-modern of technologies was mated with something quite old.

As with urban planning, Don Younger realized that patron growth and overcrowding could overwhelm the very things that made his pub special.

What to do? Don had had a number of ideas that he had occasionally run by his unofficial board of advisors.

He had talked about an outside seating area where his customers could enjoy fine weather, when it occurred, an outside garden patio like the very nice one at the Prince of Wales. The weather in Portland and England were about the same, so why not? But available real estate put a dent in that plan. Also, Don had seen microbreweries within the ever-increasing number of brewpubs. He carried craft beers from many of them. Maybe the Horse Brass could be expanded to make room for a microbewery. His brief daydream envisioned a window through which equipment could be seen brewing a special beer for his pub, a house beer brewed on the premises. But with minimum space requirements for brewing equipment, offices immediately overhead, and the gauntlet of building permit dictums, brewing beer at the Horse Brass was not quite feasible. These ideas for changing the pub remained just that, ideas at the bar that were nice to think about.

Video poker machines were also in Don's sights. At the very beginning, he had wrestled with the idea of pool tables and pinball machines, but they were never part of his pub. He realized that they did not fit. He liked playing video poker, as he liked playing blackjack in Reno or Las Vegas. Quieter, smaller video poker machines would not be as intrusive as pools tables or pinball machines, and they would be hidden away, as required, in a separate little enclave of the pub. Don certainly did not want to take advantage of his customers, but the machines were profitable. He did want to provide them as entertainment. There really was no space for the machines unless he removed a couple of dart boards and took over the floor areas of the throwing lanes. Remove dart boards?! That was out of the question.

In the southwest corner of Building Four of Old Belmont Square were two small offices leased by other businesses. Don had had an eye on them for some time since they dovetailed with some of his plans. Those offices were on the other side of the interior southern wall of the Horse Brass, at the southwest corner. The leased office and storage space for the Horse Brass was located across the tunneled pedestrian plaza. Rick frequently walked across this plaza and could see into the other two offices. Normally, at least one of them had always been occupied. One day Rick noticed that both offices were vacant. Considering the growth of the pub's business, now was the time to act. He suggested to Don that these spaces could be used to expand the seating area of the pub to keep up with business and help relieve the press of new customers. They were frankly discussing this over pints of beer after the pub had closed, after an especially busy day. At 4 am, Rick dragged Don into the walkway, pointed to the empty office spaces saying, "Listen to me. We need this. We need this now!"

The following day, Don approached the landlord of Building Four of Old Belmont Square about expanding the Horse Brass into the office space behind his pub. A lease was signed, and Don called a longtime regular who was also a degreed, certified architect. Detailed plans were drawn up and submitted to the City of Portland. The building permit was approved. Don contracted the right man for the job, Jeff Robinson. He had signed on with Walter Tooze and had been in charge of building maintenance at Old Belmont Square when the Firehouse Tavern was opened. He had been coming into The Brass nearly every weekday for lunch for over 20 years; he had also become a remodeling contractor along the way. What better person to put hammer to nail? The separating wall was ripped out, and floor-to-ceiling window panes installed next to the tunneled plaza. The extended interior walls were plastered with a texture to match the original pub, the bar extended to the south, wooden features relocated and new wooden edges tinted with the familiar brown-black color. The two dart boards at the west end of the pub were relocated to the south wall of the new space. The previous wall upon which the boards had been fastened was transitioned into the Guinness Wall, owing to future displayed items from that well-known beer company. Many things related to that famous brew were soon mounted where the dart boards had been. The freshly plastered and painted snow-white walls started to pick up the soft brown tint of tobacco smoke, but very slowly; they were many shades lighter than the walls in the rest of the pub, which had had a 20-year head start. Items related to the manufacture and sale of beer, photographs and things tied to England eventually adorned the new walls under Arthur's watchful eye.

A low, head-high wall wrapped around a small area in the southeast corner of the new space. The entry into this corner niche was through swinging wood doors, like the front entry of a saloon in the Old West. A few brightly-lit, quiet video poker machines were installed. This was the least intrusive place in consideration of the rest of the pub. Patrons had to walk by to notice them, and the staff did not promote their presence, but word got out. Video poker had arrived. Don felt uneasy about the intrusion of soft gambling via modern electronics. But on his recent trips to England, he had seen the British equivalent in their pubs, so-called "fruit machines," attracting customers. Don and Arthur were the first to christen video poker at the Horse Brass. Some of their trips to England were partially funded by some good fortune behind the swinging doors.

There were some growing pains with the expansion. A veneer was affixed to the top of the new extended bar. For a while, the pungent, vaporous glue left patrons with a special buzz. The cavernous, sterile interior echoed in response to conversation. Despite everything done to integrate the new space into the charm of the Horse Brass, it seemed vacant and empty by comparison.

One of the longtime regulars, a large, muscular man called Grizz, did not like the expansion one bit. He predicted that the cozy charm found in the west side of the pub would be irretrievably lost. For him, it was. He strongly thought that it would not be like the pub he had come to know and love. To cement his statement, he firmly announced that he would never go into the new space, nor ever go past the large ceremonial brass "key to the city" that hung near the entry steps down to the bar. For him, the new area and the adjacent part of the pub did not exist. Grizz lived up to his proclamation. He died having never set foot past the brass key after the pub had been expanded.

Employees of the Horse Brass had informally given names to different areas of the pub. Wait staff were assigned accordingly. "Sara, you've got the zoo tonight; James, you take the mids and regs." Some names for the new space were suggested at the regulars' table, for Don's approval. There was a wide range of possible names, some very imaginative. Grizz had a suggestion, indelicate in intent. "Hey, Don, why don't you call it the prancing pony and paint it pink with purple beams?"

Don just gave him a hoarse, "Harrumph."

Another suggested it be called Horse Brass 2.0, in deference to a software version in the new computer age. Don had not made a decision when fate stepped in. The yellow ribbon barricade was simply removed; it was just quietly opened and patrons drifted in. A larger Horse Brass Pub had opened without ceremony. It was a soft opening like Jay Brandon's had been, over 20 years earlier. Many had seen and heard the construction going on and had smelled it; there had been an expectation of its opening. When the main areas started to fill up, customers noticed the previously empty area in the rear, complete with large round tables and well-lit dart boards, but the area was somewhat devoid of English artifacts.

One of the top waitresses, Sara Kickham, was assigned to the new area that night. She would be the one to christen it with her work. Rick was behind the bar. A relatively rare event occurred, first-time patrons who did not have proper respect for the pub. A youthful group sat down around one of the round tables. They were trying to impress their dates who giggled at their rude, immature behavior. Sara bore the brunt of their remarks and suggestive comments. As she came to the bar with their drink orders, she stated with earned frustration that those customers were real assholes, but that she could handle them. Sara just wanted to make this known to Rick. He reached over to the corner of the bar where the light switches had been installed for the new area and pretended to toggle them. He told Sara that he had programmed those customers to be assholes, as could be done on the holodeck of the Starship Enterprise. In that space of the fictitious spaceship, people were simulated as holographic images. Rick further explained, "Sara, you were interacting with my holograph of asshole customers in the pub's holodeck. I was operating it in subjective mode." Rick and Sara were well versed with *Star Trek* and the science-fictional operation of the holodeck. When people in the famous holodeck were able to interact with its programed characters, it was being operated in so-called subjective mode.

Sara sighed and feigned relief, "Thank God! For a while there I thought they really were assholes."

In the following days, wait staff assignments were made to that area, referring to it as the holodeck. Don overheard this new moniker and not so gently asked, "Holodeck? What the hell?!"

Don wanted to change the name to something more British, but a suitable one had not yet been suggested. To the regulars and wait staff, the large room echoed and was a bit noisy when filled with people. It had snow-white walls and was relatively empty of charm. To them, it seemed like a large hollow space as compared with the cozier areas of the pub. The elevated area of the pub was already known to employees as the upper deck. Some suggested that the new space be called the hollow deck.

Discussion of the hollow room as the hollow deck intersected the discussion of Rick's reported operation of the holodeck in subjective mode. A few more nights without an alternative name for the new space and, too late, holodeck stuck forever more.

Grizz chuckled, with some satisfaction, that the name did not seem to have much connection with an English public house. Another long-time regular, a science fiction aficionado, had built a model of the Starship Enterprise and given it to Don. This model matched that in a *Star Trek* feature where the science-fictional USS Enterprise had a holodeck. Don grumbled, took the irreverent gift and had it hung from the ceiling. Later, at the regulars' table, Grizz just had to comment, "Hey, Don. That model should go well in there. Just pretend that the Scottish engineer is aboard the Starship Enterprise. You can beam Scotty down with a bottle of Macallan 12."

A year later, the same model-building regular built another. This time it was of *Star Trek*'s Starship Voyager. It, too, would grace the holodeck—which then had its own Starfleet.

After the holodeck opened, Don was often seen pushing through the swinging doors to relieve the State of Oregon of some funds through the Oregon Lottery Commission's video poker machines. This was also an almost-private place to catch a few winks in the shank of the evening. On occasion, a concerned patron would speak to the bartender, "Sir, there's a homeless person asleep back there, leaning on a poker machine."

The bartender would just smile and reply, "It's just the owner. Let him snooze. I'll wake him in 10 minutes."

After a short while, a refreshed Don would take his favorite place back at the bar. He often took Sir Winston Churchill's quote to heart — "I leave when the pub closes."

Across the Atlantic, threat and tragedy added turbulence to these exhilarating times. The old British brewery that owned the Prince of Wales had decided to sell that pub — to be torn down and replaced by an automobile dealership. Don and the regulars interceded and helped turn that decision around.

A few months later, Princess Diana, having divorced the Prince of Wales of the Royal Family a year earlier, was killed in a tragic, high-speed car crash in Paris. Don and his regulars reached out with compassion again to their twinned pub. Leadership in that same British brewery changed that pub's name to the Princess of Wales, with a new pub sign showing a large white rose.

Don was not particularly happy that employees and regulars referred to the pub's expanded space as the holodeck. And there was another term that grated on his sensibilities. Around the regulars' table, Don had first overheard, "The Brass is my favorite place."

Don quickly admonished, "Hey, there . . . this is the *Horse . . . Brass . . . Pub.* And don't you forget it."

This verbal shorthand, The Brass, was not used casually or with any irreverence. It was used with sincere affection among those who loved the place, but never in front of Don. When directing newcomers to the pub or describing it to them, they certainly used its proper name. But when setting a date to meet there, the comfortable, quick reference was used. It rolled off the tongue with greater ease — "I'll see you at The Brass tonight," or "Next week's dart match is at The Brass." People still lovingly call it The Brass.

The sea under the ships timbers was changing, and the crew could feel the roll from the swells. The regulars and those who had been with the pub since the early days certainly felt the steep ramp-up in business. In the course of four years, gross revenues increased significantly. The place was crowded more often than not. But there was some solace for the regulars. Outside of the holodeck, the physical pub had not changed, and despite the crowds, nor had its soul.

The crowded Horse Brass had become more than a neighborhood pub. The regulars discussed this with Don at their table one evening. They were concerned that the business growth would inadvertently put profit before pub, and the pub they loved would drift away. Don strongly disagreed. He reassured them that his watchful eye would keep the British soul of the pub as it rose to another level. "I'm just expanding the village. I'm allowing people to experience a British pub without having to travel there."

Jack Joyce, the founder of Rogue Ales, learned of a pub business on the ground floor of an old historic building not too far from the Horse Brass, Digger O'Dells. In its distant past, this building had housed a mortuary with a crematorium in the basement. The name of the pub had seemed intentionally appropriate. The business was up for sale, and the owners of the building let Jack know about it. He had recently opened other Rogue Ales pubs in Oregon, some in Portland, and had moved the Rogue Ales brewery and headquarters to Newport, Oregon. Jack passed up buying Digger O'Dells since it did not fit with his expansion plans. So he told Don about it. Don seized this opportunity and discussed it with Mel, who sold his diner so he could manage the third Rose and Raindrop. Like the Horse Brass, the Rose and Raindrop was a warm and inviting place; it was successful. Some years later, a serious illness befell Mel and management of the Rose and Raindrop was transferred to others.

Mel died from his illness, another tragedy, and it shook Don to his core. The memory of his brother's death had not faded. There was a wake for Mel at the Rose and Raindrop, but another wake for those closest to him was held at the Horse Brass. Not only had Mel fit in very well with the family of The Brass, he had also been part of the family at the twinned pub, the Princess of Wales. A short time after Mel's funeral, Don was again winging his way to the Princess of Wales. This would be Mel's last trip. Don carried another bundle for Britain, Mel's ashes, to be buried behind the pub in British soil under an English rose.

Rick was very much a working manager at the Horse Brass, a hands-on manager out in the middle of the action. From there, he could observe the things he had established and lead the efficient staff. He was not one to lead from an office from behind a desk. He managed and led from behind his stand-up desk, the Horse Brass bar. Rick was quite proud of helping Don take the pub to a higher level of revenue, while keeping its soul.

Rick was behind the bar one busy evening, working hard to serve patrons quickly and well. A waitress noticed him clenching his fists and rubbing his knuckles, as if to warm them. There was pain and stiffness in his hands. Maybe it was the weather. But the pain increased in the following days. Soon, it was time to see a doctor. The news was not so good. He had a chronic and debilitating ailment, rheumatoid arthritis. Eventually, working behind the bar was out of the question and so was working from behind his office desk. He talked it over with Don and transitioned from working manager to a seat at the regulars' table, advising and assisting Don and caring for himself.

Joellen had been involved with the pub, helping from behind the scenes as she had done for many years. Don asked her to assume the full responsibilities of pub management. She had been with Don from the very beginning as an office manager, administrator and bookkeeper at the Willamette Trading Company. She had helped Don at various times at the Horse Brass, so she knew the pub and its business and his other ventures. Like Rick, she had her own ideas of customer service and running the business. She oversaw the implementation of a computerized point-of-sale system that helped keep track of things, but more importantly, it enabled the staff to better serve customers when the pub was packed. Don valued her loyalty and trusted her. Beyond that, Don's quick mind, entrepreneurial tendencies, and overall cash flows outside of the pub itself needed the hand he had come to know and trust. Don had also become part owner of Lompoc Brewing in Portland with good friend and fellow publican, Jerry Fechter.[15]

In addition to increased business, employee training and turnover at The Brass, there were also the third Rose and Raindrop and another tavern on the southern Oregon coast. And if all this were not enough, there was Belmont Station.

Across the pedestrian walkway, in the northeast corner of Building Three of Old Belmont Square, there was opportunity—a vacant space ready for leasing. Up to that time, Arthur had been importing England into Portland, bit by tasty bit: HP Sauce, Mushy Peas, Weetabix, Ribena, Colman's Mustard, Devon Cream, Yorkie Bars, and Kipper Fillets, to name just a few bits. These were displayed in Art's Cupboard, the locked glassed-in shelves in the main entryway. The stocks were in the back reaches of the Horse Brass. Patrons coming and going could not help but see and be drawn to these British food items. They and their prices were listed in the *Brass Tacks*. Word of mouth was an even better advertisement. Patrons that came in for a bit of England could take some bits home with them. This had caught on and needed space for expansion.

With all his other chestnuts in the fire, he partnered financially with Joy Campbell, Don's dear friend. The space was leased, and Belmont Station was created. Arthur's bits of England went on sale there, but the offerings were supplemented with beers on tap and bottled beers from just about everywhere. It became a beer store cum café, where packaged items from England and prepared food could be purchased. Beer accessories were added to the mix: beer mats, special beer glasses, bar towels, and similar items. Somewhat coincidentally, beer tastings and other events were held there in concert with happenings at the Horse Brass across the breezeway.

Belmont Station Logo
Courtesy of Lisa Morrison

Belmont Station outgrew the corner space in Old Belmont Square and moved just a few blocks due north into new digs on Southeast Stark. Their business continued to grow, and they opened an adjacent Biercafé in the building. It had many beer offerings and locally-sourced cuisine. It featured a beer engine to pour cask-conditioned beer, and taps that served a wide variety of beer on a rotating basis. Initially, British food items were in the bottled beer shop, but these gave way to more beers; the shop eventually offered over 1,200 varieties and brands. But Belmont Station carried something else, the spirit of the Horse Brass Pub.

With outdoor seating out front and a covered seating area out back, it also carried the spirit of the Princess of Wales pub in London. Belmont Station became a comfortable neighborhood gathering place, for young and old alike, where good companionship was still the order of the day.

The 25th anniversary of Don and Bill Younger's purchase of the Horse Brass Pub was upon them. This would mark 25 years with Don as publican and chief steward. A celebration was planned. One day would not be enough. It would take 12 days, centered on the November 1st anniversary date, for the notables of Oregon's craft beer industry to pay proper tribute by brewers, brewmasters and beer writers. Of course, other publicans and the family of the Horse Brass would be part of the festivities. Each night for 10 straight days, beers specially made for the event were tapped at the Horse Brass; they had been made by the most legendary Oregon brewers in the industry. Don received a certificate of appreciation from the Oregon Brewers Guild, in honor of his being the first retail member.

Music filled the place. Captain Black and Company from London and Hard Day's Knights, a Beatles tribute band, were among the groups that played by the old piano. The eccentric Don Younger, long gray hair and beard, classic cowboy attire, turquoise and silver rings, and rodeo style belt buckle, was in his element.[16]

Don's close friends at the twinned pub in London made sure that this anniversary was commemorated good and proper. As in days of old, a foundry man filled a hand-crafted mold with molten brass. Horse Brass Pub Silver Jubilee horse brasses were cast in England. This hefty package of horse brasses was securely lugged by hand by Martin Weller and his Crush UK British pop-rock band. Included in the package was a goodly amount of Anchor Butter, Don's favorite which was not available in America. This was just a few weeks after the 9/11 terrorist attack on the United States. Getting metal horse brasses and butter through airport security offered a special challenge to the British lads. There was some good-natured bitching and moaning to the regulars at the pub about the weight of the brasses, and clearing bloody customs at the airport. A few pints smoothed things over, with gratitude. Martin and his mates played at the pub, as they had done at the Prince of Wales when it had been rechristened as the Princess of Wales.

25th Anniversary Horse Brass
Courtesy of Dick Kaiser

The very special anniversary horse brasses were each personally given out with love by Don to those closest to him, his Horse Brass Pub family. Rob Royster had come up from Pacific City to help celebrate. When he returned to his Sportsman's Pub•N•Grub, a Silver Jubilee Horse Brass was hung above its bar.

The Horse Brass ship had sailed far since Don Younger had taken the helm. The course had been maintained, but the voyage had not always been easy. The loss of close family and friends, conflicts of ideas, and difficult decisions made to maintain the Horse Brass as a British public house during accelerated business had all put stress on its publican and crew. Now it was: "Steady as she goes, mates. Steady as she goes." After 25 years, it was time to take the good ship's bearings.

BEARINGS
(2001 – 2011)

After a long time at sea, a good captain will take bearings and not rely on dead reckoning to determine position. Don Younger, his crew and the family of the pub would meet to take stock of their voyage. Their collective memory was the ship's log. The bearings to other ships and landmarks and the condition of the ship would determine their heading.

Brian, Clay and Rick, an interesting part of the crew, were sitting at the Horse Brass bar one afternoon. After a few pints, they began reminiscing about one thing or another. They found themselves discussing what it had been like working for Don. They agreed on one thing—running the pub had not always been smooth. There had been push and pull, stress and tension when these compassionate people disagreed about something they cared deeply about, the Horse Brass Pub. Sometimes that passion was at odds with Don's views.

Each recounted times when Don had summarily fired them in the heat of the moment, usually over a relatively trivial matter, upon later reflection. In such circumstances, the aggrieved parties, Don among them, would just show up at work the next day. Nothing about the earlier debate and resulting firing would be mentioned. Each just went about the business of the day and let the matter die. They knew that when not viewed through the veil of too many pints of beer, in the heat of the moment, things usually looked different.

The discussion around the table turned into a competition. Who had been fired and re-hired by Don the most times? Recalled incidents were summed up as best as their memories could recall. Rick recounted how tensions arose right along with the increase in business in the late '90s, the tension between profit and keeping the Horse Brass a British public house. Rick punctuated his claim to the dubious title with his description of his trip with the English lads to Jamestown, North Dakota, a trip when a two-week vacation turned into a two-week notice, and oscillated back and forth a few times, before settling down into an indefinite sabbatical. Rick claimed the title for himself.

Brian and Clay did not agree as they made their own claims, recounting vivid instances from the past. The disagreement over who had earned the dubious title was settled Horse Brass style; they ordered another round of beer.

One of the founding fathers of the craft beer revolution walked into the Horse Brass one afternoon. He had been there many times before. He and Don knew each other very well—it was Fred Eckhardt. He came up to the bar and very comfortably sat next to Don. Very soon, two more pints of Younger's Special Bitter were set before them. Knowing that Fred's influence regarding almost anything to do with beer had reached far and wide, Don welcomed him with, "Hi Fred. What brings you to the Horse Brass Pub?"

Fred replied, "Oh, I'm working up something for the *Celebrator*. I'd like your perspective on a few things."

Don trusted Fred implicitly. "Sure, what would you like to know?"

Fred knew how Don had found and purchased the Horse Brass, but probed further, "When did it start working for you?"

Don rolled his eyes and recounted, "Twenty-five years ago there was no justification for this place. It was a struggle for 20 years. I almost sold it. It wasn't until '94 that we actually saw the light, when I thought we could make some money."

Fred looked amazed and asked, "Really? I would think it should have picked up sooner than that, what with the new beer revolution."

A little exasperated, Don explained, "People don't understand how hard it is. It looks so easy now, with hindsight, but those early years were really tough."

Fred continued, "I know that for some time you really wanted to have a brewery."

Don did a double-take, and had to catch the cigarette that fell from his open mouth. He emphatically replied, "No."

Astonished, Fred said, "Really? I had the feeling you wanted to do something like that."

Don launched into his deeply-held beliefs. "My single mind is not about pubs, bars, not even about beer. It's about the preservation of the neighborhood tavern, or pub, and that's why I am so adamant about this," as he pointed to his lit cigarette sitting in an ashtray, its smoke curling up right in front of them. After a pause, taking a long drag on that cigarette, Don continued. "It's the destruction of the neighborhood pub that concerns me more than anything. I'm wanting to stop the sterilization of the neighborhood bar. Some of these new places are not pubs or taverns. They're filling stations. They do serve a necessary thing in life for people who want a drink and food. They have nothing to do with taverns or pubs. Pubs do not serve food and drink. They serve atmosphere, with food and drink."

Fred jotted down some notes and asked Don to please continue.

"My first concern is the ambience or feeling of the place. You can get the same drink, the same food in a grocery store for about a third the price. That's not why they come here. They come here to experience whatever it is they take out of the place. It may be hanging with friends, meeting new friends, or getting lucky." Don swept his hand over the pub and went on. "You go to a place like this not specifically for the drinks and food, you go there for the atmosphere to consume the drink and food. That's where I come from."

Fred nodded and nudged Don back to the topic of beer.

"Fred, from day one I had a number of chances to get involved with these new breweries. I've never brewed beer, but I've been to more breweries than just about anyone. My interest in beer starts right at the end of that spout," as Don pointed to where their Younger's Special Bitter had just flowed by hand pump.

Fred mentioned that he knew of Don's recently getting involved with a brewing operation, a silent partner at arm's length.

Don replied, "Yes, that's right. Most people wouldn't understand. Most people in the microbrew business, especially outside of the Northwest, they don't have a clue as to what it's about. They actually think it's about good beer. It's *not* about good beer, but rather it's the perception of good beer. Because they use the word 'good' you could get into all sorts or arguments."

Don took a drag on his cigarette, and continued. "Our brewers and our market grew together. In other parts of the country, what you have is a bunch of young pups who are obsessed with winning some sort of medal. They're so obsessed with impressing everybody that they are back there brewing, fresh out of the University of California at Davis or the Siebel Institute of Technology, with some kitchen manager out front who's just out of a culinary school. They're saying to the people who come into their bar, 'We're serving you the best beer and all this.' And the people are going, 'I don't think so. I think I'll go get a Pabst Blue Ribbon and a corn dog.' They don't understand that 'good' means satisfying your market. We've forgotten about the people who brought us to the dance, and we've forgotten to bring some beer down there for them."

Fred asked if we have lost our way.

Don easily answered, "Yes, we've got the best beer in the world, but the average bar-stool guy doesn't give a shit. He wants a glass of what he thinks is good and that satisfies whatever he's there for. There's the mistake that any burgeoning industry does. They get too full of themselves."

Fred pushed a little, asking what Don meant by that.

Don was on a roll by this time, explaining, "The people that come here are like diner's going out to dinner. They are going out for beer, but they have the very same beer in the refrigerator, a fridge full of the stuff. That's only one-third of the equation, but there are times when they need the other two-thirds.

That's what I do. I provide the rest of it. I'm in the hospitality business, not the food and beer business."

Then Don explained his core philosophy: "People have three places in life. They have their personal life, they have their working life, or whatever you want to call that, and may have their third place. We have all kinds of third places; could be a church, could be the Elks, could be a folk dancing group, could be a bar—could be, could be—it could be just about anything these days."

Don looked squarely at Fred, enunciating carefully, as if bringing home an epiphany, "Society has crossed the line, we're over-regulating; we're starting to encroach on people's lives. What scares me about the bar preservation is that we're losing the third place. If that happens, you've got a society with real problems."

Fred agreed. "Yes, and that's what happened in Prohibition. They outlawed drinking, but what was so damaging is that they removed the third place. The result is that they destroyed our respect for law and order."

They were connecting, and Don added, "Our third place might be the Horse Brass. It might be a bowling alley. People don't understand what these government regulations are doing. It's the interruption of life. For smokers, it's altering their place beyond belief. And it's accomplishing very little. Restricting alcohol is somehow the same thing."

Fred had his own thoughts on this. "The average duff goes to his local and enjoys himself, but there aren't enough bar denizens to make more Don Youngers."

Don disagreed. "I'm saying they're out there. I could make a parallel. The bars haven't risen as fast as the brews have. I call that upside down marketing. Marketing is usually driven from the top down, but this entire craft brewing industry has been driven from the bottom up. It's driven from the barstool. Some brewers can't figure out where they're coming from. They are constantly waffling, and their beer and sales are suffering." Don summarized, "It's not about the beer. It's not about the bar. It's not about the people. It's about all of them put together. They're inseparable. When you take or separate one part away, the rest of them are not going to function. It's not about the beer; it's about John's beer. It's the beer of the guy sitting next to you."

Fred admitted, "I don't come here to find a famous beer. I come here for the atmosphere and if I find a famous good beer, I try it."

Don raised his glass as did Fred. When their rims touched with a crisp clink, Don said simply, "Thank you." [8, 9]

The family of the pub and those that were close friends of Don knew his views on social freedom and self-reliance. Some had summarized them as, "Socially he's liberal; fiscally he's conservative." But that was far too simple. Don was as complex as he was eccentric and intelligent. For sure, Don did not fit neatly into a political category, but his discussions seemed to lean in the conservative direction regarding individual liberty and choice, that is, the government should stay out of it. His considerable ire was directed at the government, working to enact laws that would prohibit smoking in the Horse Brass Pub. But he had supported government legislation that freed publican brewers to sell their own beer on their own premises which resulted in many craft beers and the individual freedom to choose.

Don's suspected political affiliation was sometimes a topic at the regulars' table. Some thought Don's feigned relief that Mel was gay and not a Democrat was fodder to support the contention that he was a Republican. Many pints of good beer had been used to fuel these idle, inconsequential debates. Finally, a regular at the table declared, "Well, 'pub' and 'publican' are in Republican. If he were a Republican, he'd make sure 'pub' was in their party platform."

Jill came into the pub early one afternoon. She took her favorite spot at the southeast corner of the bar near the kitchen and the regulars' table. Before long she was engrossed in a book, as usual. After being a waitress for many years at the Horse Brass, she regularly came to this spot for relaxation and reflection. The pub was her home. The regulars and employees were very used to seeing her there in the afternoon when the pub was relatively quiet.

A regular came in and tapped her lightly on the shoulder, "Hi, Jill. How're you doing?"

"Oh, I'm OK. How about you?"

He took a seat at the bar next to her. They talked about a few things. He turned the topic to the Horse Brass. She had lived in Wales for 10 years, worked there at pubs in a small village, worked at the Elephant and Castle for seven years, and at the Horse Brass for over 18 years. She had earned the credentials to speak about the soul of The Brass.

He broached the subject, "Jill, what makes this pub what it is?"

She thought for a moment, turned and answered with excitement in her eyes, "There's something in the walls that made this, and it is still making it."

Her friend cocked his head and stared, "Come again?"

The cadence of her response slowed with emphasis on key words to make sure he understood. "There's a certain essence that builds up in this building, the essence of people enjoying themselves. People who are sensitive to this essence notice and respect it. Those that do not understand it certainly do not feel it."

He placed his hand on her shoulder and just nodded in agreement.

143

She continued, "I believe that people leave a little bit of the spirit of themselves in the essence of the pub. Some people have come in and disrespected our home here over the years. You can't prevent that altogether, despite the horse brasses. Those that have caused trouble here — rarely, thankfully — have done so because they don't understand the place. There's something here that absorbs. You can't say it's the walls, but there must be something physical that holds it. Many have felt it when they walked in here for the first time. I felt it."

He chuckled and replied, "Well, the walls have certainly absorbed a lot of smoke. Just look at them. When this place was transformed into the Horse Brass Pub, the walls were snow-white. Look up there where the wooden letters for the Rangers were."

She did not laugh and took on a more serious tone. "Let me give you an example to help you understand where I'm coming from. It's like when you're looking for a house to buy or an apartment to rent. It has nothing to do with the décor, how it's painted or the furniture. You walk in and feel that there is something in the rooms, and you say to yourself, 'Oh, my God! This just feels right.' I don't know what it is. For me to make sense of it, I just say the walls absorb — the walls absorb."

His voice now turned more serious, "I agree, Jill. I felt the same sort of thing the first time I walked in here. I hope that what's here, in the walls, stays here."

James Macko had contributed much to the Horse Brass, his friendship, his love, his spirit. He also contributed his natural talent as an artist. At first, some of that talent showed up as humorous caricatures in the *Brass Tacks*. Without being able to explain just how, James was able to capture the personality and essence of a person, from photographs, no less.

A Portland jazz great, Monte Ballou, had sung and played his banjo many times with his Castle Jazz Band at The Brass, New Orleans style. Shortly following Monte Ballou's last Friday night performance at the Horse Brass in 1991, James took Monte's photograph and created an oil under-painting of him. Sadly, Monte died before the under-painting was dry. When it was, James presented it as a gift to the Horse Brass in memory of Monte, as *The Ghost of Monte Ballou*.

After Princess Diana was killed in that horrific traffic accident in Paris, Don asked James to do an oil portrait of her. It became the centerpiece of a large fund-raising event at the Horse Brass for charities supported by the late Princess. The painting was given to John Young of Young's Brewery, owner of the Prince of Wales pub in England. This beautiful painting was part of a ceremony when the Prince of Wales was renamed the *Princess* of Wales. It hung in that pub for over 12 years, before being retrieved as a precaution when the owning brewery merged with another. It was brought back to hang on the East Wall of the Horse Brass.

A few days after the London pub's renaming ceremony, Don, Arthur and James were at another pub in that great city. Early in the morning, Don was in his cups, looking very pensive with a distant stare. James recognized this as a moment of history — and art. He took Don's picture from across the table. Two years later, back in Portland, James was rummaging through photographs of his trip to the Prince of Wales pub where he had presented his painting of Princess Diana. Deep in the stack, there was the photograph of a pensive Don at a pub somewhere in London. It reached out and touched James again like the real scene had done back in London. He transformed it into an oil painting on canvas. It was framed and hung on the East Wall.

Also, there was Grizzly Bear; he was Grizz to Don and the regulars. He was a huge, muscular hulk of a man with a large, kind heart to match. He was a close member of the pub's family. Sadly, well before his time, Grizz succumbed to multiple sclerosis. Before his death, James and Grizz's wife, Lisa, visited the dying man. Horse Brass pub love was at work. She was there to give Grizz his requested "buzz cut" to help ease his self-care. He had very distinctive long hair and a Foo Manchu mustache. James photographed Grizz before the hair cutting began, capturing his character in his final days. After Grizz died, James used that photograph to make a pen and ink drawing for the cover of the funeral announcement. Constrained by the amount of remaining unused space on the East Wall, James later made a photo-reduction of the original pen and ink, framed it, and presented it to Don to be hung on the wall that by now commemorated many people that had been part of the Horse Brass. Grizz was in good company.

Arthur had added another photograph to the wall, this one of the Queen Mother, Elizabeth, mother of Queen Elizabeth II, affectionately known as the Queen Mum to her subjects. She had died at 101 years of age. Don and the family of the pub had gathered at the Horse Brass in sympathy for their mates in England. The photograph was of her at a Young's pub in London, pulling a pint of Young's Bitter. It now rested on the East Wall alongside James' painting of Princess Diana.

One evening, James Macko was sitting at the regulars' table. Don came over to join him. He looked briefly at the East Wall right behind James as he sat down. Don started the conversation, "Hi, Jimmy. Say, I'm not sure I like pictures and paintings of dead people on that wall. I've spoken to Arthur about it."

Puzzled, James asked, "What do you mean?"

"The Horse Brass is about life. We should be celebrating life."

James countered, "Don, these people have had a connection with the pub, and not all have died. Look at those photos of Terry and Debbie sitting in front of the Princess of Wales, and of Brian over there as a young cricket player in England."

"Yeah, yeah, I know. But it bothers me. And another thing, when you've painted them, they've died, or were about to. Look at Monte over there," pointing to the wall by the piano.

James replied, "Don, you asked me to paint a portrait of Princess Diana when she was killed in that terrible car accident in Paris. What better way is there for us to keep the spirit alive of those we've loved?"

Don flicked his hand towards the East Wall, towards James' oil painting of him in his cups and sort of laughed, "That damn painting may be my death sentence."

James lamented a bit. "People right here at this table keep bringing up that my works will be worth something after I'm gone. How do you think that makes me feel? They're worth something now, beyond mere monitory value."

Don thought for a moment, then said, "OK, OK, whatever," and raised his glass towards James.

Don had been sailing the brass horse, or more precisely, guiding and nurturing the Horse Brass Pub for over 25 years as its publican and chief steward. One quiet weekend afternoon, James Macko walked in to refresh his soul in Don's church. Patrons and a few regulars were scattered about the pub.

Don looked over. Their eyes met in familiarity. No request was needed. Soon pints of their favorite bitter were on the bar in front of them as they sat side by side at Don's favorite corner. They had discussed many topics in similar settings over the course of their friendship. But that day the center of the discussion was the Horse Brass itself.

James took a sip, looked at Don, raised and swept his hand around the pub as he pointedly asked, "Don, look at this place. What happened?"

Don just stared straight ahead, "Jimmy, I don't really know. It just did."

James quickly replied, "Come on Don. You've been at the center of all this for many years. You've got to have some perspective on how this all came about."

With that, Don reflected silently for what seemed like a long time. He turned toward James, looked at him very directly and philosophized, "You've studied theology, the divinity of the universe. Hell, you were a minister for a while. I know about the Holy Trinity. That's part of what's going on here. It's also about people." Don continued, "First, we have the management of the place. No, Jimmy, that's too sterile. It was the overall guiding hand of Bill and I, and the managers along the way. My employees are the second leg of my trinity. Whether waiting on patrons, cooking in the kitchen or tending the bar, this place couldn't be what it is without them. I talked a lot with them, interviewed them, I guess, before and after hiring. I had to know in my heart that they had the attitude and appreciation that fits the British public house."

James just stared at Don, then interrupted, "Don, that's very good. That's a heavy interpretation that parallels what I've been thinking about the Horse Brass Pub. OK, what's the third part of your trinity?"

Without hesitation, Don replied, "My people, my patrons and the regulars. They're much more than customers. They're the family of this place."

"Does that sum it up?" asked James.

Don threw up both hands, saying, "Hell, no! There's stuff going on here I don't understand. Take beer. That's always been a central part of the pub. Visionary local brewers, microbreweries and craft beers came on the scene and got added to the mix. Before that, we had to rely on imports to keep real beer in the place. It's complex, very complex. There was no real plan. There were motivated people, and it just happened. The people of Portland, the people of Oregon, made it happen. My neighbors made it happen. The pub's family made it happen."

James questioned, "Is that it?"

With that familiar hoarse, gravelly voice, Don continued with a long, drawn-out, "Nah, there's other things that have happened. The twinning with the Prince of Wales in London, now the Princess of Wales, was a big part of the Horse Brass Pub—the exchange visits, the real friendships, sticking together through ups and downs on both side of the Atlantic. That's had a lot to do with who we are today. My God, Jimmy, just look at what you've done!"

James' eyebrows arched. "What?"

Don lowered his voice almost to a whisper, leaned close and explained, "Jimmy, you've got God-given talent. Your art has a spiritual dimension. You know that. Just look at your painting of Princess Diana, the one of me in my cups at a pub in London, and for sure, *The Ghost of Monte Ballou.* They've brought something very different and special into the Horse Brass Pub. Speaking of

Mind the Moat sign
Courtesy of Author

147

Monte's ghost, one day I looked up and I'd swear I saw my brother in here. For God's sake, there's water, who-knows-what kind of water from deep down, running right under the regulars' table to the moat out back."

Don stopped for a moment to collect his thoughts, took another sip of bitter, took a deep breath and allowed that the place had been off to the right start when he and Bill had bought it. "As you know, Jimmy, much of this stuff, some of the furniture and things on the wall, came from England. The place was built out and remodeled with an English pub in mind by Jay Brandon who'd lived in England and loved their public houses. Those horse brasses were his. That's all part of the complexity going on here."

James took all this in, nodded with hand on chin, and very seriously added, "Don, you and the people you've mentioned have all been on a voyage together in this ship. People on a long voyage get real close to each other. This has required human communication, honesty and the very real vulnerability that comes with it. They know how to interpret the Horse Brass Pub, even though it's difficult for them to explain. They instinctively know that the pub is their home. They're able to *understand what they see.* This is quite apart from others who are complacent and only *see what they understand.* Don, you know that. You've promoted that."

Don put his arm over James' shoulder, an artist's shoulder, and summed it up. "Jimmy, this place is my canvas. It's *my* art. It's *my* painting. Everybody's contributing to it, and everybody's interpreting it. Like a real work of art, it stops being the artist's work at a certain point and becomes the work of those who look at it. It's now well beyond me. It's now the viewers' responsibility to figure out what it means. Everybody who's part of the core group here is involved in that. Everything basically boils down to human relationships. It's about how people relate to one another. That's hard to put into words, but you've gotta try, Jimmy, because that's all we've got." Don looked down at his pub's *Guest Beers on Tap* menu, lying on the bar next to him. He held it up and whispered, as if it were a state secret, "Jimmy, it's about the *beer*, and it's *not* about the beer—it's about *more* than the beer."

The 30th anniversary of Don as the publican rolled around. This called for another large celebration, to put it mildly. Many people came from many places and walks of life from different corners of the Globe, including England. Don was surrounded by those that loved him and respected what he had done for the craft beer industry; but more importantly, what he had done for their lives though the Horse Brass Pub. The tribute spanned over a week. The Rogue Ales' brewmaster, John Maier, made a special brew just for the occasion, Imperial

Younger's Special Bitter Ale, the "big brother" variant of the now legendary Younger's Special Bitter.

The cover of *Celebrator* magazine headlined "Thirty Years Younger." The entire cover of the magazine showed Don, with his distinctive long white hair and beard and mustache, at a softly-worn wooden table at the Horse Brass. He was sitting on an old church pew from England, close to a window facing Belmont. A lit, half-finished cigarette was between the fingers of his left hand. He held the Imperial bottle in his right hand, with a full pint of Imperial Younger's Special Bitter Ale set in front of him. It was pure Don Younger, pure Horse Brass.

A couple of months later, Don was enjoying a relaxing afternoon at the Horse Brass. A cigarette and a pint of the pub's special bitter smoothed his time alone with his thoughts. Before him on the bar was the December 2006/ January 2007 issue of *Celebrator* magazine with its photo of him on the cover. He looked at James' painting of Monte Ballou and thought about the family of the pub being on a voyage together.

The patrons were few that afternoon. Only quiet conversation could be heard from a far corner of the regulars' area. A customer walked in, a tall, clean cut young man in a knitted wool cap. Don had not seen him before, but he seemed to be comfortable with the place. He confidently took a seat on the old English church pew at the table by the north window, near the painting of Monte. He took off his cap, revealing a perfectly bald head, and flipped open his laptop computer. His fingers soon began dancing across its keyboard in earnest. Tony had journeyed far to reach the Horse Brass, from Oregon to Albania and back. Any number of places could have been better suited for a theology student working on a scholarly paper: a study hall, a library, or a quiet chapel. Maybe he had felt the soul of this church with levers.

Tony had been very well-grounded in Christianity and his faith. Something had pulled him to a country where Islam had dominated the culture for centuries. Now he was in Portland, working to further fasten the corners of his faith at a Portland seminary not far from the pub.

Don watched as one of the regulars, a young bearded one, walked over and engaged Tony in apparently serious conversation. Ironically, this regular's pub handle was Pope. Don was to later learn that Pope and Tony had already sparred over issues of faith. This pleased Don. He relished such human dialogue at the bar or at a table over a pint. It fit. This was the Horse Brass Pub.

Pope reached over the table and tapped Tony's chest, over his heart. Don could not hear. There were more words with serious faces. Then Pope crushed out his cigarette in the table's ashtray, stood up, and started to walk back to the regulars' table. He stopped, turned around, and Don heard, "Oh, and don't quit."

Tony watched Pope all the way back to the regulars' table. A few minutes later, Tony walked over to the bar with, "Hi, Dennis."

The day bartender turned while polishing a gleaming pint glass. "Hi, Tony. Nice seeing you again. What can I get for you?" Don watched this short human exchange and saw that this young man was at home here.

Tony returned with his drink to the church pew and his table by the window. Later, an older woman walked in. She appeared to be about Don's age, with little makeup, and long white hair almost like his. Her long, flowing flowered skirt and colorful silken scarf spoke of a free spirit from an earlier era, an era with which Don was familiar. It was evident that this was her first time in the Horse Brass. She looked around at walls, ceiling and bar, almost gawking. She was trying to absorb in an instant what the pub had absorbed over the years. She spotted Tony and walked over so gracefully that she appeared to float across the floor and down the steps. As she sat down, Don overheard her say, "This place is wonderful."

Don moved, hopefully unobserved, closer to where they were sitting. The *Celebrator* was still in his hand. He was not trying to intrude on the content of their conversation. Don was observing the unfolding fundamentals of the village public house and loving it. He lit up another cigarette and cocked an ear in their direction. Their private conversation was of no interest to him, but their words that described the Horse Brass Pub, their feelings within its walls, were of supreme interest.

As they spoke, Don studied the cover of his treasured *Celebrator*, glancing a few times at the magazine and then at Tony. He was sitting where Don had sat when the *Celebrator* cover photograph had been taken. The same window, walls, table and pew had framed Don. Now it framed Tony. Don thought this might not be coincidence.

Many people over many years had described to Don what the pub meant to them, how they felt about it, its meaning, even how it had changed their lives. Now, Don heard two simple words that confirmed to him that he had properly captained the ship for over 30 years. Don watched as Tony cast his hand in a slow, wide arc across the Horse Brass, as he said simply, "It works." [17]

In Don's mind, a Sword of Damocles hung by a thin thread over the Horse Brass. It had been hung there by the Oregon State Legislature in the summer of 2007. The sharp end of that sword would cut into a pillar of the pub—tobacco smoke. With each tick of the clock towards January 1, 2009,

Don's mood darkened. On that date, smoking would be banned in all public establishments across the state, and that included the Horse Brass.

Don was a heavy smoker, and he welcomed smokers to his pub. The Horse Brass was most definitely a smoky place; the formerly snow-white plaster walls stood in silent testimony to that. They now enveloped the pub in a soft, warm golden-brown. Don considered smoking such a fundamental freedom of the pub, he thought that surely the smoking ban would hurt business and change the very character of his pub. Conversation and companionship without a cigarette, cigar or pipe? Not being able to smoke in one's own home, his pub? It was all too horrible to imagine. From the pit of despair at the bar one night, Don was overheard, "I'm going to leave it all behind!"

From the apex of the celebration of 30 years as the publican of the Horse Brass to this impending doom, for Don the descent was steep and dark. But the regulars would try to add a little mirth to cheer up their beloved publican. Three days before the law was to take effect, they arranged the tables next to the East Wall and staged themselves. They posed in close replication of a painting, *The Last Supper*. In the center, sitting at the table, was Don. With his esteemed position as Horse Brass publican and his shoulder length hair, he was type-cast for the part.

A regular who was an expert photographer, Aaron Barnard, took a few photographs. One became *The Last Smoker*. It was featured in brewery magazines and went viral on the Internet. New Year's Day had come and gone. The smoking ban was in place and being observed, for the most part. The general patronage did somewhat change. Some hard-core smokers tended to their pleasures in the parking lot after crossing the moat, Don often among them. He was with his family. Back at the bar inside, Don counted the smiles of those who entered. Some that came in the door were different, but as in the past, they had Horse Brass smiles. There was no need to count the money in the till. Don's spirits rose a bit. Months later, he was heard to admit, "Who knew?"

Aaron's wife, Diana, had worked at the Horse Brass in the early '80s, served in the U.S. Army for eight years, and returned to Portland. Upon her return, she walked in the front door of the Horse Brass wearing a backpack. Brian looked up and properly welcomed her back, "Bloody hell! Look who's here!" He stepped out from behind the bar and gave her a big cricket-player's hug. Almost as important to her as a seat with the regulars, was for her to find a place to live close enough to the pub so she could stagger home in three-inch heels.

She had met Aaron at the third Rose and Raindrop, and they had been married in the Horse Brass. Don had walked her down the aisle.

Aaron and Diana went to the Goose Hollow Inn one evening. There, they said hello to Bud Clark and noticed a poor quality picture of *The Last Smoker* hanging on the wall. Somebody had taken a cell phone photo and had sent it out into the electronic cloud for all to see. An enlarged, poor-quality photograph had been made from that digital image. Aaron and Diana told Bud that they could get him a much better picture. Rather than merely giving it to him, they negotiated a trade, *The Last Supper* for a signed poster of *expose yourself to art*. A handshake and a beer sealed the deal. Diana took this opportunity to tell Bud how she had gotten into trouble because of his famous poster. While in the Army in Europe, she took leave and visited Munich. She was poking around through shops near the city's beautiful English Gardens. As she flipped through a stack of posters, she spotted *expose yourself to art*. Being a highly-trained linguist, Diane excitedly said, "*Der Mann, das ist mein Bürgermeister!*" (The man, that is my mayor!)

Confused, the German clerk asked, "*Was?*" (What?)

Excitedly, Diana exclaimed, "*Stimmt genau! Das is mein Burgermeister!*" (That's right! That is my mayor!)

She told Bud that she had tried and tried to explain to the German woman that the poster was indeed a picture of the man who became the Mayor of Portland, Oregon, in the U.S. Apparently, this was too much for her; she thought Diana was an unstable, deranged American. With a pained, puzzled expression, the clerk said, "*Wir sind jetzt geschlossen.*" (We're closing now.) It was only mid-afternoon. As Diana left, the woman hastily locked the door and peered out at her suspiciously, probably wondering whether she should call the *Polizei*. (police)

Bud let out a good belly laugh, pleased that his charitable effort was still affecting people's lives.

Reporters and journalists, many of them, had visited the Horse Brass Pub as its well-deserved reputation grew. Some came and went clandestinely and reported on what they saw and experienced. One reported to *Esquire* magazine. An employee at the Horse Brass just happened to have a friend who worked for this upscale men's magazine. He confided that something about the Horse Brass would be in the June, 2009 issue. This was passed to Joellen. She said to keep this quiet since they had no idea of what it was going to be about. When it hit the streets, she immediately went to a bookstore to see how the pub was featured, to see if it was a good article and to brace herself and others if it were not. A quick review and she thought to herself, Outstanding! She bought as many copies as the store had.

Don was unaware of the national notoriety his pub was about to receive, not that it needed any more. Right after the publication of that issue of *Esquire*, Don attended Fred Fest. This was an annual event celebrating Fred Eckhardt's birthday, the iconic, local, renowned beer writer. Fred Fest was always held at the Hair of the Dog brewery in Portland. Many who loved beer, or had anything to do with the craft beer revolution in Oregon, would be there if they possibly could. Of course, among them would be John Foyston, longtime beer writer for *The Oregonian*, to cover and report on Fred's brewery-centered birthday party. Attendees had to pay to get in, but all proceeds went to a charity selected by Fred. Don loved this about Fred.

At an appropriate time in the celebration, Joellen surprised Don with a copy of *Esquire*, telling him there was something about the Horse Brass inside. Don quickly leafed past photos of elegant female models to the section titled, "The Best Bars in America 2009." He scanned the article, absorbed it quickly and called out, "Hey, Fred, take a look at this!"

There it was; a list of the top bars in America in 2009, determined by *Esquire*'s secret investigation and seasoned judgment. The only photograph, in color, embedded in the center of the introductory first page was of the bar and the warm, inviting interior of the Horse Brass. The introduction included ". . . our ever growing list of harmonious and radiant places where the bartenders are generous, the taps are clean, and the conversation is at least mildly amusing." If *Esquire*'s undercover reporter had sat at the regulars' table, that last bit would have been an understatement.

The introductory commentary was followed by the reporter's short characterization of the Horse Brass: "A German beer hall dressed up as an English country pub, this pillar of Portland drinking has to be the biggest serious beer joint I've ever been to. It's also one of the best, with a poleaxing selection of local microbrews, many cask-conditioned (which means they're aged in a cask, not in a bottle), and carefully curated imports on tap." [18]

John Foyston took a picture of Don and Joellen holding *Esquire* open to the page featuring the pub. It would appear with an *Oregonian* article about *Esquire*'s designation of the Horse Brass as one of the best bars in America, topping the list. During John's interview, Joellen admitted that the apparent designation as being number one was a fluke of the geographical layout of the listed bars; the list started in the West and worked its way towards the Atlantic. But she added, "What the heck. They've got the lede and the photo at the top of the column and that counts."

Joellen emphasized that the people working at the Horse Brass, even more than the beer, were very important to this public house. "That's testament to our crew. The writer didn't get treated differently than any other Horse Brass customer, and that says a lot about our great crew . . ."[19]

The Horse Brass had appeared in other publications, beer publications that listed the best places to have a beer, or one of the top places to have a beer before you die. However, being described in *Esquire* as one of the best bars in America was especially satisfying to Don and the people of his pub. Back at the Horse Brass, Don reflected on how he had made the voyage to this point in time. He had never made beer himself; the Horse Brass was not a brewpub. He had been transformed over the course of 34 years, from being happy with just a six-pack of Blitz to being considered by many in the industry, and beer lovers in general, as the archbishop of craft beer in Oregon, serving it in the cathedral of craft beer, the Horse Brass Pub.

December, 2010 brought Bud Clark to the Horse Brass to see his old friend on a Sunday. Like Bud had done when he was the Mayor of Portland, he parked his bicycle outside, came in, and sat down at the bar where he had sat many times in the past. Don was sitting at his favorite spot, enjoying a pint of Younger's Special Bitter. The shot glass of Macallan 12 on the bar was a more recent addition, noted Bud. Don came over and joined his old friend as Bud ordered his favorite beer and bangers, as in the old days. These two old rogues had been through a lot since their first meeting. Bud asked how Don was doing and said it was good to see him again. Don set his pint down and said, "It's good to see you, too, Bud. How're things going at The Goose?"

Bud affirmed that things were going well in Goose Hollow, with neighbors coming in to have a beer and to talk, making the place feel like the Horse Brass.

Don continued, "That's good, that's good. We had another great Thanksgiving Orphans' Dinner last month. I was feeling a little under the weather. Tom May was there. You know, the folk singer. He sang the ballad he wrote about this place, like he usually does. That cheered me right up. Say, do you remember that big check you wrote me when you were mayor, and I was in a bind?"

Bud thought a bit, then feigned forgetfulness.

Don recounted, "Well, I was really in bad financial trouble, too many irons in the fire. My brother and I managed to sort things out, but it was good to know I had your check, just in case. I never cashed it. It's in my collection of memorable things, a personal check from the Mayor of Portland, as a friend and fellow publican."

Bud was pleased to hear this.

Don admitted, "I'm so appreciative of Walter Tooze. In the early days after I bought the pub, business was not good. Anybody else would have shut me down."

After talking and enjoying each other's company for a while, Bud said, "Boy, those bangers were really good, the beer too. Well, I've got to be going. Stop by The Goose. Take care of yourself, Don."

Don watched Bud walk out, raised his glass, and gave him a small wave through the window as Bud took to his bicycle.

Bud headed back down Belmont and across the river to his neighborhood and his Goose Hollow Inn. As the Horse Brass and Don distanced behind him, Bud did not realize that this would be the last time he would sit down with Don at the bar and talk, over bangers and beer.

Don turned back to the bar, now lost in his thoughts. A lot had happened since he had returned from his first visit to England. A lot of water had flowed under the regulars' table to the moat. He missed those early years when he had strolled comfortably about his pub, really knowing his patrons, his regulars, his pub family. Those were memorable years despite the thin profits, maybe because of them.

He looked down at the model lifeboat from the RNLI mounted on the wooden base of the beer engine levers from Manchester. The little boat had collected donations from many patrons over many years; now it held little matchboxes. He had always felt pride when he wrote the checks and mailed them to that noble British life-saving organization. Just maybe, those donations had helped secure or maintain equipment that saved lives along the British coastline.

Don took considerable satisfaction in that he had held the course through the heady times: the ubiquity of craft beer, the Oregon Brewers Festival, Winterfolk, Younger's Special Bitter, helping to save the Prince of Wales, honoring Princess Diana, his pub's rise to a level of significant prominence, and, dare he think it, profit.

There were sad times as well. He glanced at the East Wall and realized that the number of those that he knew closely as true friends were fewer now. Time had taken its toll. Some now had their framed images and likenesses on that wall. Others had drifted away after the smoking ban. That prohibition changed the pub, for better or for worse, depending on individual perspective. For Don, it was for worse. When he could not smoke in his own front room, some wind had been taken out of his sails; the glint in his eyes diminished some. But he and the Horse Brass were known well beyond Portland and the shores of America. Don was proud of that and took satisfaction that complete strangers came to his pub because it was a well-known destination. Some even came to see *him*, the iconic, eccentric publican. A few came to the Horse Brass drawn only by its reputation, without knowing anything of the publican.

Don stared down into his half-full glass. Life had now come full circle, confirmed a minute later when a young couple walked into the pub, apparently for the first time as they hesitated and looked around. They sat down at one of the small round tables that had once been in an English pub. Pretending not to, Don overheard, "Honey, look at this place. It's just like they said. Shhhh . . . over there, look. See that interesting, long-haired man at the bar? I'll bet he lives in the neighborhod and comes here often."

That entry and reaction could have taken place years earlier—and it had, many times.

Things of life did not always conspire for good, but conspire they did. An unseen object, maybe a misjudged step at his home, brought Don down. In pain, he got up with a broken shoulder and was hurried off to the nearest hospital. After a few days, he was allowed to go home. Unforeseen complications required a trip back to the hospital. Things turned tragically from bad to worse. At 69 years of age, the publican of the Horse Brass died in the early morning hours of January 31, 2011. Unexpectedly, suddenly, just like that, the archbishop of the cathedral of craft beer was gone.

The publican of the Horse Brass had moved on, leaving the crew to manage in his wake. The shock was felt around the world, especially at the Prince of Wales pub in England and by its retired publican and his wife in Christchurch, New Zealand.

There had been a vigil at the Horse Brass during his passing. The spectrum of human emotions was there that evening: quiet sorrow, grief, disbelief, hope, despair, and open anger at the inevitable flow of life. Then, the wake was held.

Don had designated and documented that others take the helm of the Horse Brass should the unthinkable happen. The ship had now been rocked by the heaviest of seas, but bearings had been taken and her position fixed. In the following months, the new captains maintained the direction set initially by Jay Brandon—a course continued, strengthened and refined by Don Younger, in both gentle airs and strong winds through heavy seas. The standing order of the day was: "Steady as she goes, mates. Steady as she goes." They maintained their heading: "It's a bit of England where good companionship is the order of the day."

PART IV

Stout Keel
and
Strong Ribs

IT's About the Beer

Humankind has had a special relationship with brewing and beer for some time, back to when our ancient ancestors began to collect in villages, towns and cities for mutual benefit. Beer and bread vie with each other as to which came first. Both contain many of the same ingredients but with quite different methods used to make them. From very basic beginnings evolved different beers based not only on things naturally and locally available, but from cultural tradition and the art of the brewer as well. The variety of ingredients (water, grain, yeast), their proportions, the variety of the processes (malting, mashing, fermentation) and the temperature and duration of each, added flavorings (hops, fruits, berries), storing, and aging made the number of possible beers and tastes, if not infinite, certainly very large. Coupled with the human variable, perceived taste, the motivation for development and testing to make the "perfect brew" was strong and continues to this day.[20]

From a few simple hues of oil paints or water colors, artists can make virtually an infinite variety of paintings to satisfy the eye and influence the mind. In the skilled hands of chemical artisans, a wide variety of beers can be made to fit human tastes, moods and social environments. A brewmaster is almost an alchemist, turning common ingredients into the liquid gold of sight, smell and taste.

The sight of pints of beer—clear yellow and honey-brown ales, rich opaque stouts, all topped with white heads of foam—set down at a table amidst friends added something very special to a gathering. It was hard to define, but there was expectation beyond the soothing balm of the alcohol within. Beautiful pints raised and viewed against the light, clinked together in a toast as their aromas slowly spread softly across the table, were great catalysts. The rich flavors and slight warming afterglow added to discussions of the day, announcements of happy events, or problems solved. The publicans and patrons of British pubs knew this magic.

From the start, a very key decision for the Horse Brass Pub, as for any pub or tavern or bar, was what type and variety of beer to offer. Availability, cost and profit had to be considered from a business perspective. However, just like a British pub, the beers offered at the Horse Brass were very important because they spoke to the soul and character of the pub. Real ale was and remains a central ingredient of a traditional British pub. This ancient beverage was an enabling catalyst that softened the corners of the heart, soothed the weary spirit, and fostered conversation and companionship.

The Horse Brass Pub grew within a beer culture that went back to the middle of the 19th century. European cultural traditions and beer-making knowledge were firmly planted in the Pacific Northwest with the arrival of Henry Saxer and Henry Weinhard, and later, Arnold Blitz. Other immigrants brought with them the tradition of the German *biergarten*, a place where family and friends came together, not unlike the British public house.

Like all good things, beer should have been enjoyed in moderation. But in some quarters of Portland, beer had been used for more than cultivating good conversation and warm friendships. Abuse of the foamy malt beverage had led to problems. One indication that things had gotten out of hand was Henry Weinhard's offer to city leaders, around 1886, to provide free beer from his brewery through a mile-long fire hose, so that Portland's citizens could have free beer flowing from a public fountain, the new Skidmore Fountain.[21]

The offer was understandably turned down as being undignified. Simon Benson helped set the stage for what was to come. He was a very successful Oregon pioneer and philanthropist, and strict teetotaler. Simon provided money to the City of Portland to install his namesake fountains, Benson Bubblers, to discourage his workers from drinking alcoholic beverages in the middle of the day, to drink water instead.

But alcohol had done more than interfere with work since mankind first learned to make it. When not consumed in rational moderation, marriages suffered, lives were lost and the burden on societies rose to intolerable levels. In response to such problems in the early 1900s, church ministers, civic leaders and ladies of good intent created a dead-serious temperance movement. All this eventually led to the prohibition of the manufacture, sale and consumption of alcoholic beverages in Oregon, a full five years before Prohibition became Federal law under the 18th Amendment to the U.S. Constitution in 1920.

Under Prohibition, it was illegal to make, transport or sell alcoholic beverages. Beer from other sources, well-hidden sources, certainly existed during this great experiment, making some entrepreneurial, unsavory types quite wealthy, if not infamous. Unfortunately, under the 18th Amendment, it also became illegal to make beer and wine at home, even for private consumption. Some felt alcohol was evil, whether purchased from a store, or at a bar, or made in the home. No doubt, beer continued to be brewed in secretive corners and basements of private homes. Making beer went underground.

Finally, the Federal Government felt the pressure from its citizens and also realized that the intended gain was not worth the pain of unintended consequences, the rise of organized crime and the loss of tax revenue during the depths of the Great Depression. Prohibition was repealed in 1933 by the 21st Amendment to the U.S. Constitution. However, to get enough states to agree, the amendment also banned the importation of alcohol in violation of state laws. Not wanting to go back to the "good old days," Oregon and a number of other states established liquor control commissions and laws to regulate the distribution and sale of alcoholic beverages to meet public demand in "a socially responsible manner."

After the repeal, a few breweries were resurrected; beer making and drinking beer in public establishments returned to Portland. There were some difficulties and scuffles between breweries and the union truck drivers who had traditionally delivered beer to regional markets. To sort things out, laws were enacted that forced bar and tavern owners to purchase beer only through licensed distributors.

The brewing hiatus during Prohibition had another downside; large commercial brewers had lost sight of fuller-flavored beers. Instead, they now offered beers with limited variety and taste, hoping that most customers had forgotten what good beer really tasted like. The "bean counters," the administrative backroom boys with green eyeshades and spreadsheets and adding machines, were ascendant following Prohibition. Their natural motivation was to minimize the costs associated with equipment, production, distribution and advertising, and to maximize production volume — all done to offer the public beer on a price-competitive basis, not a flavor-competitive one. Taken to its logical conclusion, beer was produced that attempted to appeal to everybody and offend nobody. This resulted in the great blanding of beer.

A U.S. Marine who had fought in two wars, Fred Eckhardt from Washington State, settled in Portland. Having tasted good beer abroad, he was somewhat frustrated at the overall brewing state of affairs. So Fred focused on the craft of making good beer in one's own home. In 1969, he wrote and published *A Treatise on Lager Beers: How to Make Good Beer at Home.* This was at a time when it was still technically illegal to home brew beer. A clerical error in the language of the 21st Amendment allowed the making of wine at home, but not beer.[22]

Despite this administrative oversight, Fred Eckhardt's very popular book promoted home brewing. Even though technically illegal, there were basements, kitchens and garages in Portland where the soul of full-flavored beer had been kept alive.

Don had become a true believer after his guided tour by Jay Brandon through the Norfolk Broads in East Anglia, an area well-populated with pubs stocked with rich, cellar-temperature, cask-conditioned ales and bitters. But to get good-tasting beer, the Horse Brass Pub, as well as McMenamins' Produce Row, had to rely primarily on imported brands.

A beer distributor serving the Pacific Northwest specialized in imported beers. This served the Horse Brass very well, and it started to change the beer tastes and expectations of the public. Foreign bottled beers could be purchased at the Horse Brass. Guinness in bottles was soon supplemented by Guinness in kegs on tap; the Horse Brass was reportedly the first pub in Portland to offer Guinness served this way. Then followed beers from British breweries: Bass, Newcastle, Watney's, and Young's.

Most taverns and bars in Portland at that time normally carried a more limited variety of less expensive beers, those made by large breweries. Their beers were rather bland and weaker-flavored as compared to German pilsners and lagers and English ales, stouts and bitters. In the early days of the Horse Brass, it was prudent to appeal to a wide variety of tastes. Whitbread Pale Ale on tap, and Whitbread Brown Ale and Newcastle Brown Ale in bottles were balanced by more familiar beers from the Budweiser, Olympia and Blitz-Weinhard brewing companies.

There was another dimension to selling beer, "beer-to-go" in a container brought in by a customer. That tradition went back to the 19th century in the U.S., briefly interrupted by Prohibition. Containers that did not exceed two gallons and that could be sealed were filled at the Horse Brass. An innovative bartender came up with the idea of the Horse Brass Beer Buddy, a plastic container sold at the bar for beer carry-out service, suitable for reuse. The Beer Buddy did not last long. Why encourage selling beer to take home? When patrons came into the Horse Brass Pub, they *were* home.

Finally, the government realized that the clerical error in the 21st Amendment was making a lot of basement and garage beer criminals. Senator Alan Cranston from California introduced a bill in the U.S. Senate to make the home brewing of beer legal, and exempting it from taxation if brewed for personal or family use. His bill was passed by the U.S. Congress, and President Jimmy Carter signed it in 1978. It went into effect February, 1979, and it became legal to brew beer at home.

Now, home brewers could come out of their secretive corners to publically find like-minded souls devoted to the brewing of good beer at home. They realized there were many such souls in and around Portland. Clubs were formed to exchange notes and methods and to test results. Beer entrepreneurs emerged from this grassroots movement. Companies sprang up to sell home brewing equipment and beer-making ingredients.

Just three weeks after President Carter signed the bill legalizing the making of beer at home, the American Homebrewers Association was formed in Boulder, Colorado, by home-brewing pioneers Charlie Papazian and Charlie Matzen.

A group of inspired home-brewing aficionados formed the Oregon Brew Crew in the summer of 1980, but there were meetings of the founders as far back as 1978 in front rooms, backyards and probably at the Horse Brass. The Oregon Brew Crew was basically a brewers' club. Like skilled tradesmen in Europe had, they considered themselves to be a guild, a beer brewers' guild.

The Cartwright Brewing Company was opened in Portland by winemaker Chuck Coury in 1980. It was the first brewery of its kind in Oregon. The floor space of his brewery and the size of the equipment were much smaller in comparison to that of the large, established brewing companies. A term was coined for it—microbrewery.[21]

Despite some problems with brewing consistency, the initial response to this brewery demonstrated that the beer-drinking public was ready for a beer made locally, one that was not bland. He inspired others to join the movement and more microbreweries soon followed, and with them more taps. Before this, a person could travel far and wide and find only Budweiser, Blitz or Olympia, and almost never a place with even two of them on tap at the same time.

When the Cartwright Brewing Company opened, it was a top priority for a visit by the Oregon Brew Crew in July, 1980 for their first meeting. They were not only rewarded with insights into the ingredients and methods used by Chuck, but also with samplings. At this scale, like home-brewed beer, they saw beer brewed from the heart as a craft.

Mike McMenamin saw this growing enthusiasm and got a license to distribute beer. He would focus on distributing beers from the new microbreweries. Soon he was setting up taps at the Horse Brass. At his pub, Don boldly stepped forward and carried beer from Cartwright Brewing Company. To better serve his patrons and to accommodate this growing industry, the number of taps at the Horse Brass started to increase. The diminutive term, microbrewery, was initially not thought to be a good one. At a public venue, Chuck Coury was heard to have said that his brewery made craft beer, a new moniker that stuck.

The Oregon Brew Crew and other lovers of good-tasting beer were motivated to participate in the revolution of craft beer. Some members of the Oregon Brew Crew and other beer aficionados frequented the Horse Brass, drawn by the variety of beers available there. Don realized that these people were really serious about their beer. As they sampled beers in the Horse Brass, they were not content to merely say whether they liked them or not. They used sophisticated beer terms related to sight, smell and taste, such as: brightness, aroma, maltiness, hoppiness, bitterness, and balance. He discussed with them what made a beer good. Don listened intently, very intently. Something new was happening.

Newspaper articles started to focus on the increasing interest in beer made in the Pacific Northwest. An interesting fellow in Yakima, Washington, with deep technical underpinnings, was making a splash very much worth noting. He opened the Yakima Brewing and Malting Company in May of 1982, brewing Scottish ale and a stout in the British tradition. Bert Grant was a craft-brewing pioneer in the truest sense of the word. His brewery had a tasting room open to the public, and together they formed what was to become common — a brewpub.

There were considerable craft beer rumblings and the beginnings of a huge groundswell. On the other side of the Continental Divide, the first Great American Beer Festival created by Charlie Papazian was held in 1982 in Boulder, Colorado. That festival was patterned along the lines of CAMRA's Great British Beer Festival, although that older festival only permitted cask-conditioned real ale to be served at the event.

Ever alert, Don saw something coming and correctly sensed that he and the Horse Brass were perfectly positioned to be a part of it, positioned to influence and help the craft beer revolution. He felt in his heart, instinctively, that this was right — not for himself, but for the citizens of Oregon.

In the summer of 1982, Don was invited to attended the grand opening of the Hall Street Bar and Grill in Beaverton, Oregon. But this was much more than the grand opening of a fine, upscale restaurant and bar; the event marked the formal and very public introduction and rollout of craft beers. Attendees were the "who's who" of beer. Among them were: Michael Jackson (legendary English beer writer, journalist and publisher); Fred Eckhardt; Mike and Brian McMenamin; Charles Finkel (importer and national promoter of world-class beers); Rob and Kurt Widmer; Dick Ponzi of Ponzi Vineyards; executives from Portland Distributing; and regional craft-beer brewers, including Bert Grant, Paul Shipman and Chuck McEveley (brewmaster) of the Redhook Ale Brewery in Seattle, Washington, and Ken Grossman and Paul Camusi of the Sierra Nevada Brewing Company in Chico, California. These were truly founding fathers of the craft beer movement, all gathered together in one bar, sampling beer, exchanging ideas and discussing the future of craft beer.

Don certainly felt the gravity of that gathering; he knew that something very important was taking place.[23]

Mike and Brian McMenamin started purchasing unique buildings and converting them to pubs, each with its own interesting character. They wanted to be able to brew and serve their beer in the same place. Dick and Nancy Ponzi felt the same way. As announced and promised at the Hall Street Bar and Grill grand opening, two new breweries opened in Portland in 1984, the BridgePort Brewing Company, founded by the Ponzis, in a 100-year-old building where rope for sailing ships had been made, followed nearby and shortly after with Widmer Brothers Brewing, founded by Rob and Kurt Widmer. Jim Goodwin, Fred Bowman and Art Larrance stepped forward and founded the Portland Brewing Company two years later.

Despite the pioneers' enthusiasm, there was still bland-beer inertia and public perception to overcome. Most taverns were selling domestic beers from the major breweries. The Widmer brothers discovered that the vast majority of tavern and bar owners had never heard of anybody starting a small brewery. To market their wares, they would bring in a small keg for "wet sampling," so that owners and bartenders could taste their beer. They were under 30 years of age, "young whippersnappers" in the view of old tavern rats, and this did not immediately instill confidence. Some thought that their wet sampling was illegal or could even make them sick. Rather than taking a chance, most said that if their customers started asking for Widmer beers, only then would they carry them. Not many wanted to be out front, taking a risk with a new type of beer, especially since these beers were more expensive. Were they worth the cost? Most were taking a wait-and-see attitude. The beer wholesalers took this approach as well. "When the taverns start asking for it, we'll carry it."

There was much work ahead to smooth out the bumps on the road for craft beers. But there were an early handful of supportive owners, pioneers, Don Younger certainly among them. They called upon Don at the Horse Brass, and soon Widmer Altbier was on tap, followed by Widmer Hefeweizen. BridgePort Ale was on tap at the Horse Brass as well. Don was one of only a few publicans and tavern owners who took an early chance on these beers. Don did not carelessly take risks; he had a vision of what was coming.

Don fondly remembered his first taste of cask-conditioned beer in England. An avid reader and book collector, he had acquired a book published by CAMRA, *Cellarmanship*. He conspired with a brewer in Washington State, Mike Hale, about making cask beer and lent him the CAMRA book. Mike affirmed that he could make cask beer, but mentioned that Don would need a hand pump at the Horse Brass. Don had gotten one from somewhere, perhaps on an earlier trip to England. They fished around Don's basement, found it, and Mike took it home to try it out with a cask of unpressurized beer. A few weeks later, Mike came in the back door of the Horse Brass with a wide smile, a cask of his beer and a working hand pump. After some drilling and installing, the Horse Brass became probably the first anywhere in the country to serve cask-conditioned beer. Patrons at the pub loved it, as Don had that first time in England.[23]

One fine day in 1984, Tom May, the celebrated professional folk singer, was at the Horse Brass Pub, resting over a pint. He would be performing his folk music there. He had just driven out from Omaha in his new Dodge Colt Vista station wagon. While small, it had room in the back to haul Tom's musical equipment. Tom announced, "Hey, Don, I've got a new car."

Don said, "Let's take a look."

Out back, Don looked it over with particular interest as he peered in through the rear window. Don suggested, "Let's take a trip up to Yakima in your new rig and go visit Bert Grant and his new brewpub."

As always, Don put Tom up at his place, music equipment and all, leaving the back of the car empty for a little luggage and other things they might bring back. Don called Bert; they had hit it off at the grand opening of the Hall Street Bar and Grill. Don said that he and Tom would be driving up to Yakima to visit Bert's brewery and brewpub and to taste the beers there. Bert had heard good things about the Horse Brass from friends and beer drinkers and was eager to have him visit. They shared similar visions. Don and Tom took a nice drive up the Columbia River Gorge, through the open prairie leading to Yakima. As they neared the city, Don noticed fields and fields of very tall leafy vines growing up high post-and-wire trellises. Don smiled and nodded. Hops were everywhere; hops were certainly used in Yakima. The area was considered to be one of the most prolific hop-growing regions in the country, supplying many large breweries.

They drove into the center of town and found the Yakima Brewing and Malting Company and Grant's Brewery Pub. It was wonderfully nestled in an old two-story brick and stone opera house across the street from the train station. The building had a beer birthright. Operatic interest had waned around the turn of the century, and the North Yakima Brewing and Malting Company moved in. With all the hops in the surrounding fields, things were going pretty well, only to be stopped when the citizens of the state voted to prohibit anything to do with alcohol. Like their neighbors in Oregon had done, they did this a couple of years before Prohibition became the law across the land. A transfer and storage company turned that space into a warehouse. As in other cities, the intersection of train tracks and warehouses became somewhat seedy. Along the way, a pool hall and a bordello became next door neighbors. What better place for Bert Grant and some investors to start up a brewery?

Bert Grant was a brewer apart. Born in Dundee, Scotland, he grew up in Canada near the Great Lakes. He was something of a child prodigy. By age 10 he had two main interests, serious chemistry and beer; his father let him "taste" beer at home out of already-open bottles. While doing college-level chemistry, he was able to graduate from high school six months early and take a job as a chemical analyst for a large Canadian brewery. Bert moved around in the beer-brewing industry in Canada and the United States, speaking his mind but feeling stifled by bean-counting managers that did not know one whit about beer that tasted good. The chemistry of beer, brewing methods, testing, and tasting were his life. He bucked the trends afoot at the time, trends to make beer in economically large bulk, beer that attempted to satisfy most everyone. Bland beer fit that bill.

Bert added a special touch to his brewery, some bar stools and a wooden counter top in the entryway. But he had to overcome resistant bureaucracy in Olympia, Washington's capital. Bert's attorney friend waded through the laws governing alcohol. Buried in the arcane text, he discovered that a brewery could operate one tavern. For Bert, that tavern would be in the same building as the brewery. So Bert Grant opened the first brewpub in the United States since the end of Prohibition.[24]

Don signed in at a nearby motel. Being a musician, used to traveling and living on the road frugally, Tom was grateful to spend the night on a mattress on the floor of a spare room in Bert's home. Bert, Tom and Don hit it off very well and thoroughly sampled the brewery's beer that night and the next day. After quaffing a few pints, Don was reminded of his first trip to England and the Artichoke pub in Norwich on a Sunday. This was real beer, ale and stout, right here in America!

On the return trip to Portland, the back of the little station wagon carried some white plastic bottles with wide-mouth screw-on lids. Bert had two brews at that time, Grant's Scottish Ale and Grant's Imperial Stout. Don convinced Bert to sell him some of both to take back to the Horse Brass. Cradled in the back of Tom's small vehicle were Bert's brews, discreetly covered with a blanket. Don continued to sample Bert's ale and stout from two bottles set on the floor between his feet; Tom abstained since he was at the wheel.

Don realized that importing beer across state lines under a blanket in the back of Tom's car was unlikely to tickle the OLCC's funny bone. But he did not intend to sell these samples. Instead, they went into the cooler at the Horse Brass, to be handed out to regulars for their at-home sampling pleasure. Don wanted feedback only. At the time, there was no better craft-beer focus group than the Horse Brass regulars. Tasting reports made their way back to Don, not only how they liked Bert's brews, but whether they would buy them if served at the Horse Brass. Don called Bert and passed on the results of his taste test as good news. This was a big help to Bert back in Yakima. This also helped set the course for planning and decisions, some made at The Brass.

Another beer pioneer, Jim Kennedy, founded Admiralty Beverage in 1983. Jim imported and introduced many of the world's great beers to enthusiasts in the Pacific Northwest. That included the Horse Brass Pub and Don Younger. Don and Jim became more than close business associates; they became close friends. Don admired Jim's honest "hands on" approach. If a new tap was needed for a new beer, Jim was there with his tools and knowledge, doing the installation and adding the needed drain. When a new beer was ordered, Jim insisted that only he touch the draught setups at the Horse Brass. That continued until Jim's death in 2002.

Liquor control laws in a number of states, formed after the repeal of Prohibition in 1933, did not permit self-brewed, self-sold or self-distributed malt beverages. This was clearly an impediment to the creation of brewpubs. Out of the grassroots interest in good beer, a core group of pioneers formed: Dick Ponzi, Mike and Brian McMenamin, Rob and Kurt Widmer, Art Larrance, Fred Bowman, and Fred Eckhardt. A few others would assist and advise, Don Younger among them.

Out of this core, a citizens lobbying triad was formed: Dick, Mike, and Kurt. They plotted and planned; their intention was more honest and noble than how such groups are normally viewed by the public, other so-called special interest groups. This group would give lobbying a good name. Their interest *was* special—the interest in seeing craft beers available from an array of brewpubs and microbreweries across Oregon, for the benefit of the public.

Influencing legislation was new territory for the group, except for Dick Ponzi. He had been down this trail some 15 years earlier when he had walked the same halls in Oregon's capital, Salem, petitioning on behalf of Oregon wineries. Dick had helped change laws that governed the making and selling of wine. The result of changes in those laws allowed wine-tasting rooms on the premises of Oregon wineries, and they could do their own distribution. Dick was quick to cite the growth and success of Oregon's wine industry to legislators because of those changes.

Dick Ponzi detailed his success and inspired the group. They realized that the same could be done for breweries—importantly, for craft beer microbreweries that would be part of local public houses. Beer could then be brewed in the backrooms and cellars of pubs, sold across their bars and possibly distributed directly to other pubs and taverns.

The citizen lobbyists started meeting at McMenamins Greenway Pub to plot a rough game plan. They knew what they wanted to accomplish, but changing the laws of the state was a tricky business. After each planning meeting, they would jump in Dick's car and head to Salem to walk the halls leading to the offices of elected legislators, sometimes buttonholing them right in the hallway. More often, they presented their views at committee meetings, where they ran head-on into unfriendly lobbyists representing large breweries and beer distributors, who were comfortable with existing laws that favored centralization and controlled distribution to retailers. Money, and the thought of losing it, were good motivators. These forces felt very threatened and did their best to derail the craft beer revolution. They needed to be convinced that this was in their long term best interests, and that they needed to cut craft brewing a little slack.

A few meetings were held at the Horse Brass. Don sat in on them, listened carefully and advised. His experience in Yakima at Grant's Brewery Pub and the results of his local market research were discussed. A lot was at stake. Part of the overall plan, in addition to convincing the Oregon Legislature, was to also get the support of local people who really had a desire for craft beer. The beer revolution team met with local home brewing guilds and amateur brewers, those who made beer as a group and those who supported each other in this endeavor. They were asked to support the efforts to change the law governing the brewing and selling of beer in Oregon, and to support the results of such a change. Their support was necessary; once craft beers from brewpubs started to be produced, community support would be needed to help spread the word to the beer-drinking public at large.

Beer-tasting rooms at big breweries were one thing. But pubs and brewpubs would help get the craft beer industry really started, leveraging the knowledge and enthusiasm of the brewers' guilds and home brewers. If the law could be changed to not only allow microbreweries to sell on premises, but to also allow distribution to other pubs, the fledgling industry could take wing faster. The variety of beers would certainly increase. Extended tasting rooms, other than the brewpub of origin, were needed to introduce the beer-drinking public to craft beer and fundamentally change tastes and expectations. Dick Ponzi advised the group that craft beers should not be rolled out and introduced indiscriminately. The atmosphere, the feel of the places serving these beers, should match their taste. There were only a few such places in Portland at the time, pubs with patrons well-educated in good-tasting beers from Europe.

Among them were the Vat and Tonsure, the Elephant and Castle and, of course, the Horse Brass Pub.

During his early visits to The Brass, Dick Ponzi described the lobbying effort, its progress and the legislative status. Fred Eckhardt and other beer pioneers visited the Horse Brass on occasion to discuss the future and how to mold it. Anticipating the coming beer sea change, Dick Ponzi asked Don for advice about running a pub, including food, at the BridgePort brewery. Dick also knew that the Horse Brass would be a necessary part of educating the beer-drinking public with honest marketing through tasting. Don understood the difference of craft beers, and that what they offered justified the higher price. Don had been hearing from the craft beer pioneers and kept track of what was happening as reported by John Foyston in *The Oregonian*. John was a beer columnist, and his timely articles served to not only bring together the beer pioneers, but also to educate and enthuse the general public.

In the course of one conversation, Dick looked Don squarely in the eye and asked if he would carry the new craft beers from small start-up brewpubs and microbreweries. Don put down his cigarette, lifted his pint towards Dick and answered, "Sure." Don's support of microbreweries and craft beers would be the natural, continued extension of helping others and his love of beer. As he had done with Bert Grant's brews, as well as those from Chuck Coury, Rob and Kurt Widmer, and Dick and Nancy Ponzi, an *a priori* quality tasting by Don would be inserted in the process, of course. Brian and Arthur also threw in their tuppence-worth of advice. What better sources to help guide what beers would be allowed in their pub?

Now, all that had to be done was to convince elected representatives to change the law for the greater good of the people of Oregon. The craft beer pioneers set out to do just that. Trips to Salem increased, as did frustration. In addition to large breweries and beer distributors, the existing laws were also favored by those who still had a bit of the spirit of Prohibition in their blood. There was a learning curve on both sides of the fence. Legislators had changed over the course of 15 years. Meetings with lawmakers in the capital were steep learning experiences; at first, the lobbying beer activists felt like they had had their backsides handed to them. But they persisted; education, reason, and the force of political will were brought to Salem and the Legislature. It was a slow, frustrating process. Just as things seemed to be going well, there would be setbacks. The focused team met often to review the status of their efforts, sometimes with Don at The Brass. The political process formed in backrooms, pushed and pulled by competing interests, could drain enthusiasm from the weak-of-heart. But this team had heart to spare.

CAMRA had earlier come to the rescue in Britain. Its descriptive slogan said it all: "Campaigning for real ale, pubs & drinkers' rights since 1971." Drinkers' rights? What a concept! It was a philosophy that influenced the thoughts of the founding fathers of the Oregon craft beer industry, to take form in Oregon law.

There was finally a breakthrough. Common sense prevailed in Salem. Things took shape in the form of House Bill 2284, the so-called Brewpub Bill. There was no opposition in the House of Representatives. It was approved there on March 4, 1985, 56 to 0; a rare unanimous vote. It was then sent to the Senate. With that legislative momentum, what could go wrong?

As is often said, timing is everything. Unfortunately for House Bill 2284, an out-of-state major beer manufacturer, Coors, had been lobbying to get their unpasteurized, albeit filtered, beer sold in the state. About this time, a member of the Coors family reportedly made a statement during a speech to the Salem Chamber of Commerce that the Brewpub Bill was the legislative vehicle he would use to get unpasteurized Coors sold in Oregon.[25]

Before, unpasteurized Coors could not be sold or distributed in the state. The only way it was found in Oregon refrigerators was when it was privately purchased out-of-state and hauled back in coolers in private vehicles. The Brewpub Bill did not require brewpubs to pasteurize beer made on premises.

There may have been some confusion, not unheard of amongst elected officials. Another bill was winding its way through the Legislature, Senate Bill 45, also known as the Coors Bill. This bill had two major features; it would allow unpasteurized beer to be sold in Oregon and allow breweries to open taverns on their premises.[26]

House Bill 2284 began looking to some interests like a Trojan Horse, with the out-of-state beer maker hidden inside. If unpasteurized craft beer could be sold in Oregon, so could unpasteurized Coors.

But the real "stick in the spokes" came from labor interests in Oregon. The relationship between Coors and its workers was at the core of discontent and active opposition to what was happening on the other side of the Continental Divide. Strikes and unionization were brewing at the home of Coors. Those that favored unions in Oregon, and supported their cause, naturally did not favor the brewery back in Colorado or its beer. Pro-labor union forces in Oregon sharply focused legislative opposition in the Senate, and the innocent Brewpub Bill suffered collateral damage. The clean message in the bill got muddled up with other interests. Suddenly, some state senators moved to table the Brewpub Bill indefinitely, a mortal blow in reality. Dick Ponzi and crew could only scratch their heads in disbelief. "What the hell does that mean?!"

Phone lines burned, as did the tires of Dick's car on the interstate highway to Salem. Finally, there occurred more-reasoned discussions. Groups of moderate state senators from both political parties met to discuss the merits of the Brewpub Bill, to clear away the emotion and politics of the side issue. They considered the businesses and jobs that would be created, as well as the provision of good beer to Oregonians.

With reasons unknown to the craft beer industry's founding fathers, an apparent miracle took place. A Senate bill arose from the political ashes from behind closed doors. This bill closely resembled House Bill 2284. Many, including the Governor of the State of Oregon, thought this well-crafted legislation to be a clean bill with a clear message, that is, one without obtuse riders and entanglements that had nothing to do with its main intent.

Senate Bill 813 was passed and signed into Oregon Law as AN ACT by Governor Victor Atiyeh on July 13, 1985: *Relating to alcoholic liquor; creating new provisions; amending ORS 471.290; and declaring an emergency.* The law enabled the start of a revolution in Oregon; July 13th of 1985 was the July 4th of 1776 for the craft beer revolution. The key provisions were spelled out in the first part of the fourth section:

> "SECTION 4. (1) A brewery-public house license shall allow the licensee:
>
> (a) To manufacture annually on the licensed premises, store, transport, sell to wholesale malt beverage and wine licensees of the commission and export no more than 10,000 barrels of malt beverages containing not more than eight percent alcohol by weight;
>
> (b) To sell malt beverages manufactured on or off the licensed premises at retail for consumption on the premises;
>
> (c) To sell malt beverages in brewery-sealed packages at retail directly to the consumer for consumption off the premises;
>
> (d) To sell on the licensed premises at retail malt beverages manufactured on the licensed premises in unpasteurized form directly to the consumer for consumption off the premises, delivery of which may be made in a container supplied by the consumer; and
>
> (e) To conduct the activities described in paragraphs (b) to (d) of this subsection at one location other than the premises where the manufacturing occurs."

Maybe without realizing it, the legislators took some language from English law, "public house," and modified it to "brewery-public house." The brewpub was born in Oregon.

Limited distribution was an apparent concession to the large breweries and beer distributors in order to bring the bill to a vote; they had a powerful lobby which was not exactly pleased about losing control. A compromise had been struck.

The normal wheels of legal administration were far too slow for Governor Atiyeh, especially after the political wrangling, confusion and unnecessary shelving of a well-written bill that had been unanimously approved by Oregon's House of Representatives. Rather than wait the normal time for a law to take effect after signing, Governor Atiyeh directed the insertion of a final section in Senate Bill 813. This standard legal language, the Emergency Clause, was routinely added to all budget bills at the time, for speed and efficiency when handling state funds. This was *not* a budget bill, but one to unleash the creativity of craft beer makers for the benefit of Oregonians. This final section put the new law into an interesting, if unintentional, light:

> "SECTION 5. This Act being necessary for the immediate preservation of the public peace, health and safety, an emergency is declared to exist, and this Act takes effect on its passage."

With the Brewpub Bill now law, Don readily owned up to his promise to Dick Ponzi. The Horse Brass was one of *the* first pubs in Portland, if not the first, to serve a craft beer from a brewpub microbrewery after the Brewpub Bill was signed into law. The McMenamins' Hillsdale Brewery and Public House in Southwest Portland was the first brewpub in Oregon since Prohibition. On the same day that Governor Atiyeh signed the bill, they sold their own beer brewed on their own premises over their own bar.

As with any new industry, it was hard to know which came first, investment in brewery equipment and the resulting product to change consumers' tastes, or consumers' changing tastes to promote investment in a microbrewery or a brewpub. In any event, Don and The Brass were always there, continually supporting both counts. Originally a six-pack Blitz guy, Don would now be promoting craft beers and helping start-up microbreweries and brewpubs. A lot had happened since Don and Bill had purchased the Horse Brass Pub.

The craft beer explosion did not happen overnight. There would be successes and failures, trial and error. Making beer, good beer, was a bit trickier than making good wine. The process was more sensitive due to a number of variables.

But overall, growth was steady. Through the initial years, the number of taps at the Horse Brass grew and grew. There was certainly a slowly-changing main beverage menu at the Horse Brass, as there was in the beginning with the likes of Guinness and Whitbread on draught and an array of imported bottled beers. With the new law in place, Don started his *Guest Beers on Tap* menu. This gave small, startup brewers the opportunity to present their brews to a sophisticated beer drinking public at an iconic British pub. Soon, he was invited to the openings of new craft breweries and brewpubs. He tasted, listened, learned and offered help and sound advice — always. A new brewpub was never viewed as a competitor, but as an overall ally and partner.

Dick Ponzi had led the way, and Don now knew the way to Salem and the corners of power found there. As with the actual implementation of any law that governed a new, growing industry, there were always a few lobbyists and a couple of legislators who felt like mucking about, tweaking regulations here and there for some perceived financial advantage. Whether from a large national brewery, or from a small local brewpub, the transportation and distribution of beer could be complex and frustrating. But the experience of having that intelligent, long-haired, bearded, gruff-speaking chap from Portland on the other side of their desks was a memorable experience for some elected officials.

In the decade following the Brewpub Bill, Oregon witnessed the creation of dozens of craft beer breweries. As the original team knew and stressed, there were two focus points, brewing the beer and the environment where the beer was first consumed. It was important to have one's beer sold in a comfortable environment, a place that was part of a community. As Dick Ponzi knew, if a pub were not there for its community, it would not do very well. Don certainly knew and understood that fundamental principle. The Horse Brass Pub was a key part of the introduction of new craft beers to Portland.

But bar and tavern owners had to be convinced to give them a try. The founding fathers promoted gatherings at bars and taverns with bartenders and owners; they introduced them to craft beers. Many bartenders became designated tasters. Dynamic, knowledgeable, enthusiastic men of beer such as Fred Bowman, co-founder of the Portland Brewing Company, and Karl Ockert, founding brewmaster at the BridgePort Brewing Company with a fresh degree in Fermentation Science, joined the ranks of the movement. Karl summed up the essence of craft beer brewing as a "combination of science, engineering and art."

But the word had to be spread. Who better than Fred Eckhardt? His 1969 book on home brewing was catalytic to the craft beer revolution. Fred's articles about beer appeared in a wide array of publications, including his own quarterly publications, *Listen to Your Beer* and *Amateur Brewer*. Twenty years after his first book, he published another that was to become the bible of beer — *The Essentials of Beer Style: A Catalogue of Classic Beer Styles for Brewers and Beer Enthusiasts.* Fred Eckhardt kept the faithful informed and drew in new believers. He had real depth of understanding, from the complex details of brewing itself, to the larger picture of beer as a part of life. "You don't have to drink it because it's there, you can also enjoy it. And you don't have to drink it because it has alcohol, you can also enjoy the taste of the stuff." John Foyston and Russell Sadler, two excellent journalistic reporters and writers, followed the trail of the craft beer revolution for *The Oregonian.* Their articles, along with the writings of Fred Eckhardt, literally covered the gamut of craft beer in Oregon and the Pacific Northwest. Readers followed along; many became converts.

It did not take very long for Portland to have a beer festival. It was held in the summer of 1988 in a large waterfront park on the Willamette River. Among the festival's organizers was one of the early pioneers, Art Larrance. The festival actually got its start the previous year at the first annual Portland Blues Festival, where craft beers were served — the amount of beer served there was ten times more than anticipated. The following year it was a festival of its very own, the Oregon Brewers Festival. The founding fathers of the craft beer revolution and a growing cadre of beer aficionados got their heads together and made it a great success. Don was among them. They had been inspired by the annual Great American Beer Festival in Denver. The focus was showcasing Oregon beers, but they made special note that this was to be a festival for brewers and anything to do with brewing, beyond the beers themselves. Hop growers, merchants of home brewing equipment and supplies, and collectors of just about anything to do with brewing were welcomed and part of the festivities. Don encouraged them to increase the length of the festival to five full days. The festival's attendance grew and grew, attracting people from all over the country and different parts of the world, with attendance eventually exceeding over 80,000.

Don went to beer festivals across the nation, but he was not normally found under the tents. He and others would somehow find an iconic brewpub in the festival city. For the Great American Beer Festival in Denver, the Falling Rock Tap House was his watering hole. When they came to the Oregon Brewers Festival, the gathering place was the Horse Brass, of course. Over the coming years, with more beer festivals and more brewpubs around the country, Don had informally formed a real fraternity of those that loved and made craft beer.

Far to the south of the Horse Brass, three years after the signing of the Brewpub Bill, another would make his mark on the craft beer industry. Jack

175

Joyce opened the Rogue Ales Brewery and Public House in Ashland, Oregon. A wild river flowed near there with a name bestowed on it by French fur trappers with regard to the local Native Americans; the trappers thought them to be rogues. Jack was not one to run with the pack and considered himself to be a rogue. The name he gave his brewery also fit his philosophy of brewing craft beers—"Variety is the spice of life".

He relished a persona that hinted at being a rascal, a rascally knave in the expanding craft beer industry. Jack used an unpasteurized process with no preservatives, proprietary yeast, and natural ingredients, including malts and hops entirely from the Pacific Northwest, often from their own fields. He added new, interesting flavors to some brews. Rogue Ales would produce a wide variety of distinctly-flavored beers.

In the winter of 1988, Jack Joyce walked into The Brass and introduced himself to Don Younger. His purpose was to convince Don to sell Rogue beers at the Horse Brass, which Don did. The two hit it off famously right from the start. They both were good judges of character, and they knew they were both rogues at heart, marching to different drummers. In 1989, the Horse Brass was Rogue Ales' first account in Portland. The friendship and trust between these two rogues grew. On a trip together to San Francisco, Don showed Jack where his parents had met. He pointed to an apartment nearby and said, "Jack, that's where I was conceived."

Don had very much wanted a "house beer" to be served only at the Horse Brass public house, but only if it were a distinctly British-tasting beer. Don asked Jack if Rogue Ales could craft a beer for the Horse Brass along those lines. After shaking hands on it, they had to determine what kind of beer it should be. How should it taste? The voyage to creating a house beer for The Brass had begun.

John Maier, the Rogue Ales brewmaster, was the perfect man to create a great beer. He was a graduate of the Siebel Institute of Technology in Chicago. But his roots were also firmly planted amongst home brewers. Like them, John brewed from the heart, much like Don guided his beloved Horse Brass.

Don and the regulars of the Horse Brass had frequently visited their sister pub, the Prince of Wales, near the ancient Ram Brewery. With Don, John made the visit twice as part of the project to make Don's house beer. They were sitting at the bar of the Prince of Wales enjoying beers from Young's Brewery. A few pints into the evening, Don took a long sip from a freshly-poured pint of Young's Bitter and held it up to the light in front of John; he asked in his gravelly voice, "John, can you make something like this?"

John inhaled deeply over the brew and took a long investigative sip, swirling the bitter around in his well-seasoned mouth. There was some general discussion about the contents, what ingredients went into its making, the hops, the grain, the yeast. Terry and Debbie, the publican and his wife, and some regulars claimed to know something about Young's beers and offered their opinions. However, John's calibrated nose and seasoned palate narrowed the possibilities.

John took Don's request to task when he returned to the Rogue Ales brewery, by this time having been relocated to Newport, Oregon. Much skill and expertise were applied, the use of a special variety of hops grown only by Rogue Ales, the barley grown in the eastern parts of Oregon and Washington, and a special secret brewing yeast to get the flavor just right. Don approved of the slight deviation from the English bitter of his liking.

Many batches and tastings later by John Maier, Jack Joyce, Don and a few others, including Brian and Arthur, and a very special bitter was born. It was rolled out at the Horse Brass in 1993. It was offered under pressure, on tap, and, of course, cask-conditioned.

Tragically, Don's brother Bill passed away shortly after the special beer had been introduced. In his memory, the bitter was served at his wake at the pub, but remained unnamed. A few weeks after the wake, the regulars and Don were sitting around their table. Don was distraught, still in deep sorrow, and the family of the pub was reaching out to him. The topic of what to name the special house beer was brought up. A number of names were tossed around, but none seemed to fit the Horse Brass, especially in this period of mourning. Some of the suggested names sounded too regal or pretentious. As Don had intended, the beer associated with his pub would be simply honest and good tasting.

Rick Maine looked over to the barrelheads hanging on the wall next to Dart Board One. He stared at the image of the elderly gentleman with a beard and a pint on the barrelhead that Don had gifted to his now-departed brother some 17 years earlier, wrapped in the Horse Brass Pub. He pointed to the barrelhead and said, "There's a name to consider."

The portal behind that barrelhead opened again, as it had when Bill had first walked in and Don had knocked on it. Again, the past reached forward, and a name arose from those around the table, "William E. Younger's Special Bitter."

Somebody who knew about beer in Britain suggested they prudently ask Scottish and Newcastle Brewery for permission.

Puzzled heads looked up, "Scottish and Newcastle? Why?"

He explained, "Because once it had been Younger's Brewery in Scotland, since the late 18th century. Now it's Scottish and Newcastle."

The regulars took to researching Younger's Brewery, to help Don out. Just maybe, Don and Bill Younger were related to the founders of that Scottish brewery. They found that the brewery had been started in Edinburgh. It later merged with McEwan's Brewery in Edinburgh, forming Scottish Brewers, which later merged with Newcastle Breweries to form Scottish and Newcastle.

Apparently, one William Younger had headed off to Edinburgh to seek his fortune and was thought to have started working in a brewery near there at a tender age. But he did not continue in that profession. His son, William Younger II, started William Younger & Company, East India, Pale, and Strong Ale Brewers. In due course, they produced a special bitter, with due regard for the founder and the family tartan, William Younger's Tartan Bitter, as painted on the old barrelhead in the Horse Brass Pub.[27]

Not wanting to tempt fate, or the long reach of a Scottish solicitor, Don jotted off a request. The proposed name was approved for the special bitter created by John Maier. However, documented blood ties to William Younger II were not found, as had been hoped.

The regulars bestowed a fitting pub name to the new bitter, Billy Beer. It would not be its advertised name. For those that knew and understood, an order of Billy Beer at the Horse Brass would result in a pint of very fine, award-winning British-styled beer. The glass would hold William E. Younger's Special Bitter—YSB for short, Billy Beer for memory. YSB that was not cask-conditioned was also served, but the taste was slightly different. YSB had become the house beer of The Brass; it would only be served there and at Rogue Ales public houses. YSB went on to win many top medals, at the World Beer Championships and other regional beer tasting competitions.

By the turn of the 21st century, the revolutionary part of the craft beer industry in Oregon had met its objectives, and then some. The Oregon Brewers Guild, founded in 1992, was one of the oldest craft brewers' associations in the United States. The "who's who" of Oregon craft beers could be found in the Board of Directors, Associate Members and Brewery Members lists. Their mission centered on promoting great beer and beer styles and providing a vehicle for networking between brewers, their suppliers and retailers, and with beer enthusiasts worldwide, with a goal of quality products made with integrity.[28]

Now, craft beer was an established industry in the state serving sophisticated palates. The movement had had allies across the Columbia River in Washington State. A free-lance writer there, Alan Moen, covered the world of beer, wine and spirits. He traveled extensively throughout the United States and Europe. Many writers search for the perfect sentence. In his travels, Alan was also looking for the perfect pint. In this quest, Alan managed an audience with Don Younger, hoping that this sage of craft beer could point him in the right direction. Maybe the perfect pint had been poured and savored at the Horse Brass. If not the elusive perfect pint, he found something close—the perfect philosophy about good beer.

Referring to some of the latecomers to the craft beer revolution, to the public house, to the brewpub, those without the proper motivation, Don firmly explained to Alan: "I think the people that are opening and closing don't understand what it's about. They're trying to catch a wave. They're not beer people. The places I've visited — plastic pubs with plastic beer — yeah, they're brewing on premise, but there's no heart and soul in the beer, there's simply a consortium of investors, and the public won't be fooled. This is a bar stool revolution, and it's driven from the bottom. It's not what I like, it's what they like. I respond to my customers." [23]

On the 25th anniversary of Don Younger as publican of the Horse Brass, he received a certificate of appreciation from the Oregon Brewers Guild that summarized his involvement and that of his pub in the craft beer revolution: "This certificate is awarded to Don Younger, Horse Brass Pub, In recognition of his 25 years as Oregon's premier publican, in appreciation for his support of the Oregon brewing community and the Oregon Brewers Guild and in honor of his being the first Retail Member of the Oregon Brewers Guild. Happy 25th Anniversary, Nov. 1, 2001." That certificate hangs on a wall of the pub.

Some nine years later, a large framed print in black and white of the front exterior of the pub arrived. It was a formal designation by the importers of Bass Ale. Under the elegant depiction of the pub's entry was: "Horse Brass, Certified Proper Pint Establishment." If not perfect pints, proper pints were served at the pub. Joellen asked Arthur to hang it on a wall of the pub. The next day, they asked Don to come over to that part of the pub because they had something to show him; it was a surprise. Don was proud. Brian later saw it and took particular satisfaction in that formal designation, remembering that it took his considerable encouragement years and years earlier to get Don to even try Bass Ale. That first tasting by Don, behind the bar at the Horse Brass late one night, may well have been the turning point in the history of the pub that led to its now being recognized as a "proper pint establishment."

The Horse Brass and Don had become the unofficial epicenter of the craft beer industry in Oregon and those that swirled about it beyond the state's border. His tireless dedication to promote locally-sourced craft beer was well known. Don had visited new microbreweries, giving sound advice and strong encouragement. It was not long before he would be invited to microbrewery openings and beer-centered events in Oregon and across the Pacific Northwest. To be listed on Don's *Guest Beers on Tap* menu became enormously significant.

One evening, he was engaged in serious discussion at his favorite spot at the bar with a YSB in hand. The talk revolved around craft beers and how he felt about their impact on Oregon, let alone the Horse Brass. He was having a little trouble getting his thoughts understood by those with less appreciation for good beer. Don leaned back, held up his pint and pronounced, "It's not about the beer. It's about the *beer*." He emphasized the last word strongly and drew it out to make his point. This statement became a canon for beer drinkers at the pub. Don smiled inwardly at his statement, recalling that he had been a firmly-entrenched Blitz six-pack man when he had purchased the Horse Brass.

There had been forerunners of this beer revolution, across the Pond. Those that had formed CAMRA knew it was about the beer, a type of beer—ale. As their name defined, this movement was created to save another part of British heritage, real ale. The 1971 movement was enormously successful. Its membership exceeded 130,000 when Don died in 2011. While CAMRA focused its efforts on the number and quality of breweries to make real ale, that emphasis closely overlapped their Local Pubs Campaign in that pubs and ale were closely entwined and had been so for centuries. CAMRA defined its philosophy, one that Don whole-heartedly agreed with: "Well-run pubs play an invaluable role at the heart of their local communities, providing a safe, regulated and sociable environment in which people can enjoy a drink responsibly and interact with people from different backgrounds. CAMRA's own research shows that 84% of people believe that a pub is as essential to community life as a shop or post office." [29]

Don Younger had the same passion and leadership when it came to locally brewing good craft beer—it was about the *beer*. After the first successful Oregon Beer Week, officially proclaimed by Governor Kulongoski and celebrated the last week of July, 2005, Don had led the creation of Oregon Craft Beer Month in July, 2006. Many events were held that month that centered on craft brewing, capped off by the Oregon Brewers Festival in Portland's Governor Tom McCall Waterfront Park. The festival had become the largest all-craft beer festival in the United States. Don Younger was a big part of its success.

Don had spoken often about the craft beer revolution and its positive impact on the state economy: Oregon jobs, Oregon money, and Oregon hops. This became Don's mission. The July, 2006 issue of *Portland Monthly* magazine captured this: "Younger is referring to his part in the promotion of Oregon Craft Beer Month (that would be July), a grassroots movement that encourages Oregonians to reach for local brews rather than out-of-state options. It's also a reminder to area brewers—especially the big boys—to make use of those regional ingredients. 'Some of these brewers have gotten too big for their britches,' Younger growls. 'You're supposed to leave the dance with the one who brought you.' And Don Younger's been to his share of dances." [30]

The article also captured how fellow publicans felt about Don. "He's a great character," Mike McMenamin says. "He's the classic publican." [30]

The fall of 2006 approached following the Oregon Brewers Festival that year. With it came the 30th anniversary of Don Younger as owner and publican of the Horse Brass Pub. This was to be a big event. London regulars from the renamed Princess of Wales flew over to help celebrate. Others from different corners of the Earth came as well, such as the North Wales Formation Drinking Team.

Some breweries and brewers' guilds made special beers just for this event, which would last more than a few days. Absolutely, Jack Joyce of Rogue Ales would do something quite special. John Maier, the renowned Rogue Ales brewmaster, crafted a strong smooth special brew for this anniversary. This imperial ale came in an imperial bottle. It was emblazoned with a caricature of Don, holding high a pint, riding a horse that is leaping through an upturned horseshoe, with XXX in red, denoting 30 years. Below was the name of the special brew, Imperial Younger's Special Bitter Ale, with the words 30 Years & Holding. The emblem fit perfectly.

Imperial Younger's Special Bitter Ale, 30th Anniversary Commemorative Bottle Courtesy of Rogue Ales and John Maier

On the reverse of the bottles, above the listed ingredients, was printed the perfect memorial toast—To THE CAVEMAN. Imperial YSB had just a wee bit more alcohol than Billy Beer. Don drank more than a few pints of this celebratory bitter and accurately commented on its smoothness and alcohol content. "Unnoticeable until the morning after."

YSB and Imperial YSB Ale were true and fitting legacies of Rogue Ales, Jack Joyce, John Maier, Don and Bill Younger and the Horse Brass Pub. Bill Younger would have been quite proud of Billy Beer and its Imperial cousin.

The Mayor of Portland, 2005–2009, Tom Potter, led a parade from the Rogue Ales Public House to the Portland waterfront to open the 2007 Oregon Brewers Festival. After a pint of one of Oregon's finest craft beers, he waxed eloquently about Portland's affectionate name amongst the brewing faithful. "To me, Beervana is a nice summer day with maybe 80, 82 degrees, sitting here on the grass at Waterfront Park, listening to really good music, and having some of the world's best beer. That's Beervana." For sure, Don Younger was there. Like always, he had something insightful to say—"It's not just because the beer's good, it's because it's ours. We know the people that make our beer. We all know each other. That makes our product taste so much better."[31]

In addition to the 2009 article in *Esquire*, recognition of the Horse Brass Pub went far beyond Portland and the Pacific Northwest. *Draft Magazine* listed the pub among the 150 best beer bars in America in 2010: "This iconic bar has been at the epicenter of one of America's beeriest cities for more than a quarter century, and it still quietly sets itself apart. Unabashedly English, the food ranges from fish and chips to steak and kidney pie, while the beer's an unparalleled selection of more than 50 taps highlighting local favorites and the best of craft here and abroad. There's also hand-pumped cask ale, of course; three rotating selections round out the beer menu for an authentic British experience." This was one of very many articles in many venues that had been and would be written about Don Younger and the Horse Brass Pub.[32]

After this well-deserved rise to prominence, somewhat surprisingly Don Younger was not known to all in the beer business or to all those who loved beer. At an Oregon Brewers Festival, a visiting brewmaster from Pennsylvania sat down at a table with a full pint in hand. To the person across the table, the visitor started raving about the Horse Brass Pub he had discovered and about YSB, Younger's Special Bitter. He excitedly explained everything as Don just sat and listened. He recommended that Don go and visit the pub. Don smiled and nodded in agreement. Finally, the visitor from Pennsylvania asked who his festival beer-drinking table buddy was. Don chuckled a little and dryly replied, "I'm 'Y'—for the 'Y' in YSB."

Some learned of the inevitable before it came, and they held vigil at the Horse Brass. Then the news spread, a wave of shock and disbelief—Don Younger had died in the early morning hours of January 31, 2011. The outpouring of grief and testimony was absolutely enormous, using virtually all forms of human communication from Portland's citizens and from the many corners of the world that had been touched by the Horse Brass Pub and Don's hand. Among them were tributes from those that had been part of the bar stool revolution for craft beer—those who made it, those who enjoyed life more because of it. At the wake, the pioneers and captains of the craft beer revolution stepped forward with their stories of Don, what he and the Horse Brass Pub had done for their industry.

It would be hard to overestimate the influence that Don Younger and the Horse Brass Pub had on the craft beer and microbrewery industry. Don had been part of a revolution that resulted in Portland having more breweries than any other city in the world. If one considered the entire state, Oregon ranked near the top of the list of the number of breweries per capita. Portland became the real nirvana of craft beer. If there was a beer heaven on Earth, Portland was it and Don had helped make it so. If there is a Beer Heaven, Don will certainly be sitting at its bar, conversing with its Publican and asking for a perfect pint.

The legacy of Don Younger at the helm of his Horse Brass Pub and his influence on the craft beer revolution lived on in the hearts of beer lovers. *Draft Magazine* continued its annual evaluation and recognition of America's 100 best beer bars. Their inclusion of the Horse Brass Pub in a list of "bars" can be forgiven, as their 2012 write-up captured the essence of the pub well beyond the beer served there. "When founder Don Younger, who passed away last year, claimed, 'If it were any more authentic, you'd need a passport,' he wasn't kidding: Bric-a-brac adorns the nicotine-stained walls (from the old smoking days) of this dimly lit, wood-paneled pub, perfectly re-creating the neighborhood haunts of England. Horse Brass has championed the craft beer movement since 1976, and with its legacy still intact as perhaps the best bar in the nation, it isn't just a destination in Portland, but a bucket-list item for any beer lover." [33]

Lompoc Brewing of Portland rolled out a special barley wine brew in tribute to Don. It had been brewed some 14 months before Don's passing. It was aged in Heaven Hill Bourbon barrels for 10 months and cellared for another 13 months before its release party at the Lompoc Sidebar in November, 2011. They named it Old Tavern Rat. Fittingly, the flyers for this brew had the image of James Macko's painting of Don, in the early hours at an unknown London pub.[34]

On the first anniversary of Don Younger's death, the Horse Brass was crowded with regulars and many from the craft beer industry. To memorialize Don, an oil painting had been done by John Foyston, longtime beer reporter and writer for *The Oregonian*. In addition to excellent writing skills, John was also an artist. It was absolutely appropriate, a painting of a famous image of Don with smiling eyes, holding a cigarette and a pint, sitting at an outdoor table at a local craft brewery. It had appeared on the cover of *Beeradvocate* magazine and had captured Don's essence and spirit. It was unveiled in the pub by John Foyston, followed by testimonials and toasts. Of course, one toast was

"To the caveman." One patron had learned of the event and milled about in the throng. To somebody in the crowd he innocently suggested, "I guess this place and Don Younger were important to the craft beer industry."

The owner of one of the successful local craft breweries overheard this uninformed and naïve statement, spun around, pint in hand, and declared, "This is the cathedral of craft beer, and Don was the archbishop! Don't you know that? It's about the *beer!*"

Don Younger
Courtesy of Lisa Morrison and *Beeradvocate* magazine

THANKSGIVING ORPHANS' DINNER

It was that time of year again, Thanksgiving. The new cook, Clay, was a well-trained and accomplished chef, now turned bartender at the Horse Brass. He absolutely loved this holiday. Newly married, he moved into a house just a few blocks from the pub. His first Thanksgiving, after his move to Portland, was at his mother-in-law's house. Her idea of a Thanksgiving turkey was a pressed roll of turkey meat parts. This was surely not his idea of the main course for this traditional national holiday. With "never again" firmly, but carefully, lodged with his beloved, he hosted the following Thanksgiving at their home. He prepared and cooked everything. This impressed everyone. His new in-laws now thought Clay was a very welcome addition to the family.

At the following Thanksgiving, he planned to do the same. By this time he had gotten to know the other employees and regulars at the Horse Brass. He knew that some would be home alone on Thanksgiving, their family members being distant. He overheard some regulars bemoaning the fact that they would be spending this holiday by themselves. People in such circumstances were dubbed Thanksgiving orphans. This caring bartender and sometime-cook at the Horse Brass, and his wife, invited all these Thanksgiving orphans to their home, free to come and go as they pleased. Over 20 people came to that warm, love-filled home, including a folk musician from Omaha, Nebraska, that was having a gig at the pub.

Clay called this first gathering The Orphings. Clay cooked a couple of turkeys, and his guests brought appetizers and side dishes. It was wonderful and certainly in keeping with the real meaning of this holiday. Clay continued this for the next two years, three Orphings' Dinners in a row. Attendance reached well over 30 people, filling their house to the brim. This included Mike McCormick, one of the early regulars at the Horse Brass. Don Younger would usually stop by, balancing his time with his family, siblings and parents.

When Clay took a job in Reno, the fledgling tradition was at risk. Mike stepped forward and held the next dinner, now called the Thanksgiving Orphans' Dinner, at his home. That gathering was even larger.

During these times, some other forces were at work. Don, Bill and their parents were always invited to Thanksgiving dinner at one of their sisters' homes. This was in addition to his sisters' children and extended family. Don, being a very caring man, often showed up with friends or acquaintances, more than just a few, who were also Thanksgiving orphans. Some may have been just picked up at Clay's or Mike's home.

The ladies of the Younger family prepared the traditional meal for many. They were left to clean up, as was the male tradition back then. Finally, an exasperated sister took Don aside with a firm, "Don, you do something about this!" Don was at some risk of becoming a Thanksgiving orphan himself.

The next month, nature stepped in and changed everything. A severe winter blizzard struck the Pacific Northwest on December 24, 1983. Snow and ice covered the roads in Portland and the Willamette Valley. People were correctly advised to stay home and not risk travel on dangerous highways for holiday family gatherings. "The National Weather Service warned motorists of extremely dangerous road conditions and predicted snow and freezing rain over much of Oregon on Christmas Day . . . Snow and blowing snow will make travel extremely dangerous over the mountains and in most of the state." [35]

This produced holiday orphans, this time it was Christmas orphans. Clay had returned to Portland and back into the fold of the Horse Brass by this time. Some of the regulars and Clay had prepared Christmas dinners for friends and relatives at their homes. But dangerous, icy travel conditions prevented Christmas gatherings. Don quickly realized that the social center of the village, his pub, should be used to bring people together on this holiday, despite the weather. He started calling around the neighborhood to regulars and employees within walking distance. With his gruff voice, they heard, "Hey . . . what're you guys doin'?"

The answer from most was basically the same, "We're just sitting here drowning our sorrows because nobody's gonna be able to show up and eat our turkey and fixin's."

Don offered, "Yup, we've got a whole bunch of people in the neighborhood in the same boat. If you've got a ham or turkey, bring it down and a side dish or two. We'll have a Christmas potluck at the Horse Brass."

The front door of the pub stayed open that day, but the bar was closed for business. Clay brought some savory food. He also fixed hot soup and coffee for anyone just passing by. Neighborhood people trudged by in boots or slid by on skis. They peered in through the open door. Some kicked snow from their boots and came in. Those contacted by Don started showing up at the back door. They were careful to mind the moat, now covered with snow and ice. Over 30 Christmas orphans came to the Horse Brass Pub that day. Sharing and companionship for the neighborhood village was the order of the day.

As Thanksgiving rolled around the next year, Don started thinking about his holiday relationship with his sisters and the overcrowded dinners at Clay's and Mike's homes. With the experience of the potluck gathering at the Horse Brass on that icy Christmas, Don thought that he would solve the problem of too many people at two different homes. He was well aware and appreciative of the Thanksgiving Orphans' Dinners hosted by Clay and Mike. He approached them and described his sisters' tales of overburdened woe and the flak he was getting from them. He said he fully understood that their homes were getting quite cramped. Don had a solution. "Let's hold it at the biggest house we can."

Mike said, "We're not going to hold it at your place. Your apartment's dinky."

Don replied, "No. I mean the pub." Don offered to close the pub and turn it over to host Thanksgiving dinner for the seasonal orphans. Don said that he would provide the turkeys. He insisted that Clay did not have to do all the cooking, but that he could supervise and assist. It would again be a pot luck affair. Clay and Mike agreed. Don would invite many of his immediate family, his sisters included. What better way to mend the old fences of their overcrowded dinners?

The Horse Brass was closed for normal business and came to life, shutting the cold and rain outside. It was a family gathering, people that worked there and patrons who called the place home. Like the very first Thanksgiving in America, people brought things to share, food and themselves.

The cash register stayed closed as Don directed. He said there would be no business conducted there that day; no money was to cross the bar. Employees were not to work behind the bar, either. Patrons and regulars took turns serving pub employees and each other.

Don was charitable; the beer taps were opened and brews flowed. One orphan placed an empty beer pitcher on the bar and suggested people should voluntarily toss in a few bucks to help defray the expenses of their publican. Considering all the costs that day, the donations exceeded Don's expenses, actually netting a profit. Don thought that this would never do. In keeping with his philosophy of giving back to the community, he made a donation to a local charity on behalf of the Horse Brass Pub. He most definitely put the pub, and the village, before profits.

The next Thanksgiving, Don placed a pitcher on the bar and announced that the money would again go to a local charity, and that his brews would flow freely to stimulate charitable giving. He tossed in a significant sum of paper money. That was Don Younger, the Don Younger behind the seemingly rough exterior. The spirit of that empty chair at his mother's dinner table was there at the pub. The annual Horse Brass Pub Thanksgiving Orphans' Dinner was now in place.

There was a next time, the next Thanksgiving, and every Thanksgiving thereafter. It became tradition, with a locked front door and an unlocked, inviting back door. Credentials and identification were not required. If a pub patron invited a friend, or a lonely neighbor had just heard of the event, all were welcome. Don would buy five or six turkeys, hand them out at the Horse Brass the night before to some of the orphans, instructing them to bring back cooked turkeys the next day. Some regular guests at these Thanksgiving dinners became turkey carvers. One regular with a special carving prowess earned a pub handle, Frank the Knife. Another became the source of sought-after rolls, better known as Bundy's Buns. Many eagerly awaited Mike McCormick's specially cured and cooked hams. Some became bartenders, and all helped clean up.

The memorable part of these holiday feasts was when Don raised his hand, quieting the pub, getting people's attention by tapping a knife on an empty pint glass. Don's words varied somewhat year to year, but he generally led off with, "I'd like to thank everybody for coming and welcome our new friends. It's been a great year." With a raised pint of his favorite beer, he'd say, "I'd like to raise a glass to old friends that have moved away, and especially those who have passed on this last year." What followed was Don's verbatim toast. He gazed across those gathered, which included his brother. After a long pause with glass held high, he proclaimed, "To the caveman!"

The guests stood and raised their pints and responded in unison, "To the caveman!" This toast later took on a solemn tone, done not only for ancient cavemen, but in remembrance of Bill following his unexpected, tragic death.

Charitable giving was also a welcome guest at the following Thanksgiving Orphans' Dinners. From the beginning, Don had donated to various local charities. Eventually, Sisters of the Road Café became his favorite charity, associated with the Thanksgiving Orphans' Dinner. He had learned that they also helped orphans, the orphans of society, not just on one day but throughout the year.

Sisters of the Road Café was a well-known, well-run, very effective local charity. Two women had opened the café in 1979, just a few years after the Horse Brass Pub was born. They opened the place with $10 cash and bartered for the rent. But they and the volunteer directors at the new establishment had their sights set higher, a different outreach to help people. Booklets could be purchased and its coupons given to people in need, redeemed for food at the café. They later proposed being able to accept U.S. Government Food Stamps from those experiencing homelessness in exchange for the meals prepared there. It was endorsed by Oregon's Senator Mark Hatfield, but the proposal was rejected the first time around by those in the Federal Government. The bureaucrats in charge of the Food Stamp program and legislators needed to be convinced, and convinced they were. Under pressure from Senator Hatfield and a committee in the House of Representatives, a law was passed that homeless people could use their Food Stamps to purchase meals from non-profit restaurants that cared for the less fortunate. The Sisters of the Road Café was the first such facility in the entire nation to implement the new law.

Their focus, creating community-driven, non-violent solutions to the calamities of homelessness and poverty, struck a resonant chord with Don and the family of the Horse Brass. Their Thanksgiving Orphans' Dinners were unique, like the outreach practiced at the Sisters of the Road Café. The family of the Horse Brass was thankful and shared with others through the Sisters of the Road. Some people would have dinners well after Thanksgiving, thanks to Don and the Horse Brass regulars.

The spirit of the Thanksgiving Orphans' Dinner was catching on. Rob Royster experienced the dinners first hand. Rob had been the general manager and head barman of the Horse Brass for a while. With Don's encouragement, Rob went on to take ownership of the Sportsman's Pub•N•Grub on the coast in Pacific City, Oregon. For a short time, he managed both places, then moved to where the salt air was fresh and the people hard-working and honest, like those around the Horse Brass Pub. Following the very good example and mentorship of Don, he decided to do a similar orphans' event on Thanksgiving, for his community. Just as Don had required for Thanksgiving dinners at the Horse Brass, nobody paid a dime for food and friendship at the Sportsman's Pub•N•Grub, stimulating charitable giving. The spirit of Don and his pub had spread.

One of the first Thanksgiving orphans was a balladeer from the heartland of America. Tom May was an Omaha native, a gifted folk singer and musician. His considerable talent had been recognized by Gordon Lightfoot, who achieved international fame and success as a folk, folk-rock and country singer. Tom had been part of Gordon's team and opened for him on tour more than 25 times at the height of Gordon's popularity in the early '70s.

Musicians and singers hung out together and stayed in touch. Theirs was a unique profession. Tom's agent was a good friend of an accomplished Irish balladeer who had performed at the Horse Brass, Peter Yeates. The agent got the phone number from Peter and cold-called Don, touting Tom's talents. He tried mightily to convince Don that he would be a very good fit for the pub. Don did not take kindly to being solicited by a distant stranger over the phone. The agent received an abrupt reply before Don hung up. "I really don't like music much; don't have music here much at the pub."

But there was persistence. Don received Tom's first album in the mail, released by Capital Records of Canada. Don was not overly fond of folk music, probably because it was not like that spun by his favorite disc jockey years earlier, Wolfman Jack. But Don played the album, listened intently, nodding in time to the music; he agreed with the lyrics. There was something about Tom's music and song that Don really liked—they had real meaning and genuine honesty. So in April, 1982, Tom May opened at the Horse Brass.

Portland was familiar to Tom before the Horse Brass was born. Ten years earlier, he had attended the University of Portland for a couple of semesters on a full music scholarship. Tom had played many gigs in many venues since then, but his introduction to Don and his pub were different and unforgettable.

On a Saturday afternoon, he walked into the Horse Brass for the first time, a day before he was scheduled to perform. The place was calm and quiet. Clay was behind the bar, a few patrons were conversing over a pint. Don was at his usual spot at the far end of the bar. Before being introduced, Tom soaked in what he saw. He knew instinctively that he and his music would be in harmony with this place. Without knowing why at the time, he also sensed that his life was changing when he walked into the Horse Brass that day.

Eight hours, much conversation and many pints later, he and Don strolled with a hint of stagger to Don's home that was close by. Tom had reached his limit, not only for driving, but for walking. They had impressed each other very much. Their views of life were congruent. Don put Tom up for the night. This was repeated in subsequent years. Don opened his home to Tom, three or four times a year, when his ballads filled the pub. Much more than a repeat entertainer, Tom was becoming part of the family of the pub. He did not realize it at the time, but as for so many others, an irrevocable life change was taking place. Tom thought that for a pub and its publican to have that effect on people was immensely powerful, and good.

Tom was a real student of Irish and English culture, which gave real depth to his works. Over the years when staying at Don's house, he noted with admiration that Don held to the tradition found in those cultures regarding drinking. Don never drank at home and never had drinks in the refrigerator. As in England or Ireland, he drank at the pub, the social place to have a drink. The drink of choice at home for Don was Classic Coke over ice, with a good book, in front of a good television show, or with a good friend.

Following his 1982 debut, Tom was again at the Horse Brass that following November, playing at other places in the Pacific Northwest, as well. He was on a tight schedule. A professional musician's life on the road could be draining. His newborn son and wife were back in Omaha. He missed them both terribly. He was playing at the Horse Brass when Thanksgiving rolled around. His schedule prevented him from getting back to Omaha to his family. Tom was a true Thanksgiving orphan that year and found himself invited to Clay's house for dinner, only a block away. The house was warmly crowded with friends, the smell of Clay's wonderful cooking, some orphans and some of the family of the pub. Don was there, too, at that first Thanksgiving Orphans' Dinner.

On repeat engagements at the Horse Brass, Don would take Tom to other pubs and warm neighborhood taverns, to help him get a real sense of Portland. Sometimes that included places with old rock and roll music, revealing Don's very esoteric tastes in music. Of course, Tom got to know the regulars at The Brass. From then on, Tom plotted and planned to get back to the Pacific Northwest, to Portland, permanently. Don encouraged this, offering engagements at the pub, and his home to help him get established—real friendship. Tom finally moved out west in 1996.

Tom continued to play at the Horse Brass from time to time, and he always attended the Thanksgiving Orphans' Dinner if he were in town. Don and his pub meant very much to him. With heart, he composed a ballad about the pub in 1987, outlining a positive fulcrum of change for people. The following, with permission, is Tom May's "Ballad of the Horse Brass Pub" (from the CD *Blue Northern*), October 1988, words and music by Tom May, copyright 1989, Blue Vignette Music, ASCAP:

> 1. If you're ever in Portland with the old Hangtown Blues
> Your pockets as lowdown as a bum's pair of shoes
> Cross the Morrison Bridge, head up Belmont Way
> There's a Horse, with a collar, on a sign that will say;
>
> Chorus (after each verse)
> Have a Grant's beer for me, at least two or three
> Beneath the soccer flags waving from the ceiling up above
> You're a stranger no more, when you walk through that door
> You'll find what you're after at last
> A drink and a smile at the old Horse Brass
>
> 2. After one beer you'll find, that the bartender's kind,
> But don't play him in cribbage or darts all the same
> For you'll find that if you do, he's better than you
> And you'll have only your bad luck, and the good beer to blame.
>
> 3. From a ship at the pier, came a sailor for beer
> Birmingham seemed such a long ways away
> Then he walked in the Horse Brass, sat and ordered a Bass
> Now he's drinking there nightly, till this very day

4. Don is at the bar, that Brian is behind
Marge serves the brew with some mischief in mind
Howard moves his pegs, Mike smokes his pipe
Here at the Horse Brass, it'll be a good night

5. Now I've traveled this country from pillar to post
There's weak beer and strangers from coast to coast
But there's a bit of old England, kind faces to be found
In the Oregon rain, of old Portland town.

It would be hard to tell who had the bigger heart, Don or Tom. Back in 1988, before Tom moved to the area, he started a folk concert-based charitable movement. It was born in the Horse Brass, nurtured by its spirit and the spirit of the Thanksgiving Orphans' Dinner.

An avid Portland fan of Tom's music and song invited him to fly out from Omaha for an impromptu concert as part of her 40th birthday celebration in late January. The concert would be at the pub. It was well attended. She and Don decided they would walk around the pub while Tom was singing and take up a collection for a good cause, people experiencing homelessness. The collection was generous and went to a private, non-profit charitable organization that had an office in Old Belmont Square, a good neighbor of the Horse Brass.

This impromptu winter folk concert was so successful that it was repeated in the following years at the Horse Brass. It was always held on a Sunday in January. In the years before Tom moved to the Pacific Northwest, he would fly out, stay at Don's house, organize other musicians to get involved, and set up the microphone and speaker system at The Brass. He and other musicians would play from noon until late into the evening. There was a cover charge that totally went to charity, but people often gave more when the spirit of the Horse Brass and Tom's songs moved them. Tom eventually named the event Winterfolk.

As with the Thanksgiving Orphans' Dinners, the recipient of Winterfolk's charity became the Sisters of the Road Café. They partnered with them in 1990. When Winterfolk outgrew the size of the pub, larger venues were found, first at Kells Irish Restaurant and Pub. In 1994, its permanent home became the much larger Aladdin Theater. It was a block from where Bill and Don had owned the Mad Hatter, which later became the Bear Paw Inn. The first Saturday in February became the recurring date of Winterfolk, with an impressive array of performers including, of course, Tom May. Winterfolk became a sold-out affair, netting a significant sum for the Sisters of the Road

Café. Tom and Don were very proud that something born at the Horse Brass Pub was helping make a real difference in people's lives.

For Don, the publican, there would be a last Thanksgiving Orphans' Dinner. As always, the pub was filled with family and orphans. And as always, there was a tremendous jovial nature flowing through the throngs of people. Despite being in the second year of a state-wide smoking ban, with the front door closed to the public this became a private affair; the family of the Horse Brass could have a pint and smoke, as in earlier times. Don was at his usual spot at the bar. Naturally, Tom was there.

With alarm, Tom sensed something was wrong. He had not yet sung the "Ballad of the Horse Brass Pub" when Don got up, put on his jacket and headed slowly towards the back door. Tom rushed over and asked, "Don, you're not going to leave yet, are you? I haven't played the ballad yet."

With a hint of the future, Don simply replied in his distinctive voice, "Aw . . . I'm not feelin' very good. I think I'm goin' home."

Tom quietly pleaded with his dear friend to stay just a little longer, that he would sing the ballad right now. He got his guitar out, and Don came over to him. Tom started singing in the center of the family. They all chimed in, sang along, double-clapped and double-stomped at the end of each chorus. This was the spiritual elixir and tonic that Don had needed. When the singing ended, he went back to his favorite spot at the bar and sat down in the center of his home.

A half-hour later, he was still there. Concerned, Tom asked Don if he needed a ride. With now-elevated spirits, Don answered, "Nah, I'm havin' a good time now, fuck off." Tom knew his old friend was joking. They sat and talked privately at the bar for quite some time, Tom's hand on Don's shoulder. Don admitted to Tom that until the ballad had been sung and his family of the pub had joined in, he had not felt very good, but that now he was feeling better.

An hour later, Tom got up to leave. He made his way towards the back door and the moat after bidding farewell to all. As he was leaving, Tom stopped, looked around and saw what would become for him a poignant scene—Don Younger sitting at his favorite spot, cigarette in hand, a pint of Younger's Special Bitter and a shot of Macallan 12 on the bar, all framed by his pub and his people at his last Thanksgiving Orphans' Dinner.

THE TWINNING

A decade after the opening of the Horse Brass Pub, its people crossed paths with people from another public house, the Prince of Wales in London, England. This intersection had not been planned. It resulted from serendipitous events centered on darts and beer, beer made in Britain by a company founded over 150 years earlier, beer made in a brewery that had been doing so continuously for nearly 500 years. This mingling of people with the same views of the village public house, despite being separated by thousands of miles, resulted in these two pubs becoming sister pubs.

Twinning across international borders was nothing new. Cities had become sister cities with formalities and proclamations signed by their mayors. American taverns, German *Gasthäuser* and British pubs had been informally twinned by correspondence and exchange visits, usually following vacation travel when relationships with friendly people had been formed.

The twinning between the Horse Brass Pub and the Prince of Wales pub in the southwest London borough of Merton became a solid bond through many exchange visits, as well as shared happiness and tribulation. Well beyond that, that part of London, the Prince of Wales pub and the beer served there, have historical heft that deserves to be told. They are integral to the story of the Horse Brass Pub.

The Navy Chancellor laid the parchment on the large oak table before the English king of considerable stature and power. Carefully written with inked quill, the top of the official document read: "Places where provisions of beer shall be made." Beneath was a list of villages where beer was made. Some were near the Thames River, where ships tugged at ropes tied to London docks. On the list was the village of Wandsworth. It was less than a mile by horse-drawn beer wagon to the moored vessels of war. King Henry VIII signed the Royal Order in February, 1512.[36]

The Navy Royal protected and extended Henry's Tudor dynasty with power at sea. That navy would become a national institution, the Royal Navy, global in reach, extending power across an empire upon which later "the sun would never set." With yet another disagreement with those across the English

Channel, preparations for war were underway that chilly February day in 1512, and that included beer.

Provisions for a man-o'-war contained more than gun powder, shot and hard tack. Beer was fit to drink longer than water when stored in barrels aboard ship, an important consideration for prolonged voyages. The sailors needed beer not only to prepare for battle at sea, but also to provide a brief respite after. Beer at sea was rationed, a gallon a day. This was the forerunner of the daily ration of rum, a well-known tradition in today's Royal Navy.

The name of the brewery in Wandsworth was not listed in that 1512 document, just the village. The number of breweries in a small village with a good reputation and sufficient capacity to supply King Henry's Navy Royal was likely very few, probably just one. Beer had certainly been produced in that village before then and served in public houses. If not, there would not have been a provisioning order for King Henry VIII to sign that included the village's name. Why risk the executioner's axe by recommending a beer of poor quality or a brewery that could not sufficiently supply?

During the reign of Queen Elizabeth I, in records dated 1581, prominent commercial brewing is mentioned as being at the sign of the Ram in Wandsworth since 1533. Later historical records confirm that the Ram Brewery was in constant operation into the 21st century, making it the oldest, continuously-operating brewery in all of Britain.

While its operation was continuous, the ownership of the Ram Brewery did vary over the centuries owing to many factors: the retirement of its owners, inheritance after death, the taking of profits from the sale of land and brewery, and the stresses of finance. In the early 19th century, ownership of the Ram Brewery stabilized. Young and Company Brewery was formed by a partnership between Charles Young and Anthony Bainbridge in 1831. Young's purchased the Ram Brewery, and the sale included 80 public houses in and around London.

Purchasing a public house could be "a bit dear," expensive, in English parlance. If a pub were owned outright by its publican, it was called a free house, wherein the publican was free to sell beers of his choosing. Free houses were a small minority among pubs in England; there would not have been a sufficient number of them to sell the large quantities of beer brewed and demanded by the public. The solution was for large breweries to purchase or build their own pubs, wherein the publican was either a tenant or a manager that worked directly for the brewery. The vast majority of pubs had tenant publicans. Even though owned by a brewery, a pub would still be the publican's home, with his private living quarters most often upstairs.

Young's was quite successful, owning many pubs in and around London, over 220 eventually. Some were purchased, those that had been transformed from carriage houses and inns some centuries before. Others were designed and built to be public houses. Young's became a British pub chain, as well as an exporter of fine beer.

In the early 19th century, a building designed to be a pub was built on a turnpike road in Merton, not far from Wimbledon. The land for this development was purchased in 1824 at public auction, with the Prince of Wales pub rising on it a few years later. The property first appeared as a public house in local records in 1870. The Prince of Wales became a Young's leasehold (rented) pub in 1876. Young's bought the freehold in 1919 and purchased the adjacent land in 1949, the houses upon it having been bombed out during World War II.[37]

This pub was within walking distance to the Ram Brewery in Wandsworth. From the pub's beginning, draught horses did not have to go far to reach the pub, pulling a wagon loaded with beer barrels.

For Americans not yet Anglophiles, a freehold in England is the legal ownership of indeterminate duration of real property that is immobile, like a pub and the land upon which it stands. For perspective, the purchase of this piece of English real estate in 1824 was a mere 20 years after Lewis and Clark headed out to the Oregon Territory, and 27 years before Portland, Oregon, became an incorporated city. During this period, the land upon which the Horse Brass Pub would rest was treed, green and vacant of settlers.

Young's founders also realized that this pub was more than a nice public house in the center of a nice village just southwest of London's center. It had been built on, or very near, land steeped in the history of England. An old Roman road, from London to Chichester on the English Channel, passed not far from the Prince of Wales pub.[38]

Over 1,400 years after the Romans, Admiral Horatio Lord Nelson came to live in Merton in 1801. It was a village of around 800 people. Nelson would later become famous on October 21, 1805. He bravely led the Royal Navy to victory over Napoleon's larger, combined Spanish and French fleet off a little-known cape in Southwest Spain—Trafalgar. Admiral Nelson was killed aboard *HMS Victory* during that epic sea battle, cementing forever a place of highest honor in the history of England. An almost sacred plot of land a few hundred yards from the pub had been part of Lord Nelson's estate. It was sold in 1823 and has been known ever since as Nelson's Fields.

Another famous English patriot had a great impact on the history of England and an indirect impact on pubs. The First Duke of Wellington, Field Marshal Arthur Wellesley, after his victory at Waterloo over Napoleon, introduced the

Beerhouse Act as Prime Minister in 1830, and Parliament approved it. The Act was designed to lower beer prices by increasing competition among brewers and entice people away from the demonstrated evils of strong drink, most notably cheap gin. This was a follow-up to the Sale of Spirits Act of 1750, also known as the Gin Act of 1751. Since its introduction in England in the late 1600s, the population had been weathering and suffering a "gin craze." The intention of the Act was to reduce the consumption of strong spirits, chiefly gin, thought to be one of the primary causes of crime in London. Through Wellington's Act, Parliament further restricted the selling of gin and increased fees on legal sales.

Rather than accentuating the negative, the Beerhouse Act encouraged the positive, a beverage with lower alcohol content, beer. For a small license fee (about $3.00 in today's currency) essentially anyone could legally brew and sell beer. Many did from the first floors of their homes. Many beerhouses became public houses, and their owners became publicans. The 1830 legislation may well have been the stimulus for the entrepreneurial formation of Young's Brewery in 1831.

The Prince of Wales pub grew and flourished in that environment, as many people changed their tastes from addictive gin to affordable beer. This was similar to how the 1985 Brewpub Bill in the State of Oregon allowed and stimulated brewpubs. Like the Prince of Wales, the Horse Brass Pub flourished in Oregon's craft beer environment, fostered by legislation over a century and a half after the 1830 initiative of the First Duke of Wellington.

The Prince of Wales was a fine Victorian building. Within, a patron found a warm public bar and an adjacent large comfortable salon with a fireplace. Out back, for use in the drier warmth of summer, was a pleasant courtyard-style garden with a roofed area. Upstairs was the residence for the publican. A true English pub had been born next to the old Roman road and Nelson's Fields, not far from the old Ram Brewery. Young and Company's Brewery now had this jewel.

Adjacent to the Prince of Wales, the land under the village homes that had been destroyed during World War II was purchased and turned into a car park for the pub. Before then, automobiles were not yet ubiquitous. Over 50 years later, the car park and the land under the pub became attractive for a different commercial enterprise. Business interests sought to have the pub destroyed. If bombs could not destroy the pub, land development planning could.

Young's Brewery went from strength to strength, expanding into foreign markets. Young's had gone on a major campaign to introduce their bottled beers into the United States. Their minions, some related to the Chairman of Young's Brewery, John Young, spread across the land seeking the "perfect pub" in America for the introduction of Young's bottled products. At first, the Elephant and Castle was thought to be the place, but its publican recommended that the Young's representative go and see the Horse Brass Pub. He did and called back to John Young, "I think we've found the perfect place."

Young's had reached across the Atlantic and into the Horse Brass Pub with the help of Jim Kennedy, founder of Admiralty Beverage, a beer pioneer in the Pacific Northwest. Young's Bitter and Young's Special would become available to the citizens of Portland through him and the Horse Brass Pub.

The big roll out was scheduled for Young's bottled beers at the Horse Brass. Dan Kopman, Young's export manager, returned for the festivities. Earlier, Young's had thought that the publican, Don Younger, would take about 20 cases each of the bottled brews. Don was contacted to confirm the order to be delivered through Jim Kennedy. Don called Jim regarding his order for Young's beers and said, "I want everything you've got."

So the Horse Brass ended up with about 100 cases of Young's beer in the cooler and another 200 cases in a refrigerated truck in the parking lot. The grand opening of Young's beer at the pub was well advertised, and there was a very big crowd. Don decided to keep the profit mark-up on the beer very modest. The grand opening of Young's beer in Portland was a huge success, even if not very profitable for Don. After two more days, all 300 cases of beer had been sold to satisfied customers. This was reported back to John Young in England, who was so impressed that he wanted to give the Horse Brass, through Don, a large bonus to help compensate for the thin profit margin. However, there were some legal entanglements due to laws that governed the sale of beer in Oregon.

During the evening of the roll out of Young's beer, an impromptu dart tournament had been set up in the Horse Brass. Dan Kopman was fairly familiar with the game, so he entered. Unfortunately for Dan, he was knocked out early. It was rumored that the regulars had encouraged Dan to over-sample the beers at The Brass.

To celebrate the success of Young's beer introduction, Jim Kennedy and his wife, Bobbie, invited Dan Kopman and Don Younger to a party at their home. Horse Brass regulars and Portland brewers and beer aficionados attended as well, among them Rob and Kurt Widmer. Jim also distributed Widmer Brothers beer and a couple of kegs of their beer were at the party.[39]

Don and Dan had a great time. They chatted about Don's trips to England, beer, and that English game of mutual interest, darts. Widmer beer was skillfully drawn by Don from the kegs. Somehow, Dan never had an empty pint in his hand. Dan quaffed another pint, and Widmer's beer kicked-in, nudging the hand of fate. The intended bonus from Young's had been blocked. Instead, Dan announced that Young's would sponsor five of the top dart players from the Pacific Northwest to compete as a team against a pub team sponsored by Young's. Airfare and hotel accommodations in London would be covered by them. These men of beer sealed the deal with a handshake and a toast with another pint of Widmer Brothers beer. Game on!

For weeks, Don organized dart match playoffs at different bars, taverns and pubs in Oregon and Washington State. Through a series of elimination playoffs, the teams were winnowed down to the best Oregon team pitted against the best from Washington. A bus load of Oregon dart players and supporting fans headed to Seattle, where the final match would be played. With a designated professional driver, the group became exuberant with the help of liquid refreshment. They even changed the route name on the front of the bus from "Portland to Seattle" to "Portland to London." Leaving as little to chance as possible, Don had scoured the local dart scene and put together the very best players, most having played out of his Horse Brass Pub. The team from Oregon was victorious!

A few weeks later Don, as captain, and four players from the Horse Brass, backup players and supporting fans were winging their way to London: Don, Clay, Bill, Lori, Kathy, Art, Gene, and Duane — their beer-drinking cheering section. The team would compete against the best players from one of Young's London pubs.

That first night, they all stayed in a hotel near the Thames River, but only after wandering around London, sampling pubs and beer. Jet lag be dammed, this was London! For one in the visiting group, this turned out to be more exciting than planned. He stepped off a curb to cross a busy London street and, like most first-time American visitors, looked the wrong way. He was hard of hearing, to boot. A black London cab nicked him and knocked him down. This was not realized by the driver, who merely sped on. Fortunately, there were no serious injuries other than some tread marks on his pants, showing that he had been duly christened by a London cab.

Dan Kopman and John Young met them at their hotel the next day. As good hosts for Young's, they had arranged a bus tour of some of their pubs in London, the ones of which they were most proud. This was a daylight pub crawl for the visiting Yanks. They had a smashing good time, spending enough time at each pub to get to know the publican, get the feel of the place, to sample Young's beers and to play some friendly darts. The old Ram Brewery, still producing beer, was part of the pub crawl. The visitors were treated to a tour back in time to 1512 and 1831. There, over pints of Young's Bitter, and such addictive fare as scones and clotted cream, Don got to know John Young.

They hit it off very well right from the start. While from very different walks of life, they were kindred spirits at heart.

One pub stood out for these Americans, most of them first-time visitors to England—the Prince of Wales on Morden Road in Merton. The friendly proprietors, Terry and Debbie Urwin, were new to the pub. They hailed from a far reach of the British Commonwealth, New Zealand. With them were their two large, friendly boxers, dogs being a rather common adornment in many pubs. With pints in hand, the Yanks strolled about as Terry and Debbie proudly explained their pub and its history. They pointed to Nelson's Fields near Morden Road, casually mentioning that the road had been built by Romans.

Don and his crew were impressed. During the tour of the pub, a few of the Horse Brass regulars chuckled and pointed at the framed "Rules of the Inn" that had been established in 1786 for another public house somewhere in London.

> NO THIEVES, FAKIRS, ROGUES or TINKERS
> NO SKULKING LOAFERS or FLEA-BITTEN TRAMPS
> NO 'SLAP an' TICKLE O' THE WENCHES
> NO BANGING O' TANKARDS on the TABLES
> NO DOGS ALLOWED IN THE KITCHEN
> NO COCKFIGHTING
> FLINTLOCKS, CUDGELS, DAGGERS and SWORDS
> TO be handed to the INNKEEPER for safe-keeping
> Bed for the Night . . . . . 1 Shilling
> Stable for Horse . . . . . . 4 pence

After nearly an hour at the Prince of Wales, they moved on to the next pub, and the next. At the end of the day, with Don and his crew aboard, the bus pulled up outside their hotel. Dan told everyone that this was a free night, free to do whatever they wanted. The scheduled dart match would be the following day.

The visitors from The Brass went back to their rooms, rested a little and freshened up with no group plans for dinner or the evening. Nothing had been discussed or coordinated. Some went out in pairs, others by themselves to further enjoy London. There certainly were many pubs to see for the first time, and they certainly did sample them. Remarkably, later that evening, all in the group started showing up back at the Prince of Wales, a considerable distance from their hotel. At first, two or three just happened to meet at the Tube stop near the pub and walked in the front door together. From behind the bar, Terry looked over with his big Kiwi smile. "Well, what are you blokes doing here? You should be knackered from the long flight and the pub tour."

"We had such a good time with the people here, we came back."

Later, one by one, Don Younger and all the others came through that same door. Just like first time visitors to the Horse Brass Pub, everybody felt something special when they had first walked into the Prince of Wales that afternoon. Something drew them back. Without speaking it, they knew—they were *home*.

Deep into the early hours, the pub worked its magic—the old Roman road, Nelson's Fields, the Ram Brewery, Young's Bitter, and especially Terry and Debbie and the regulars. Everyone hit it off. Lori Christal had an interesting discussion with an elderly pub regular who thought it not proper for a lady to come into a pub before 7 pm, as she had done earlier that day. She politely disagreed and explained what was proper for a lady in America. She may not have changed his mind, but they got along fine for the rest of the evening. There was considerable conversation that night as everyone got to know each other. It was like long-lost family members had come together without having met before. Their common bond was their membership in the family of companionship found only in a real public house. There was no signed document, no public ceremony. But late that night, the Horse Brass Pub in Portland and the Prince of Wales in Merton were twinned.

The next day, the lads from Portland played a dart team from a pub owned by Young's. With over 220 Young's pubs in London, they picked a *very* good team. While the America players were quite good, they were playing darts in the country where darts had been born before King Henry VIII. They came up against some very skilled chaps, probably having played since they were old enough to enter a pub and hold a dart at their father's knee. While Don and his team did not win at darts, they won friendships. Their new mates from the Prince of Wales came to cheer them on and to invite them back to their pub.

On the last night of their stay, after 11 days in England, all the Americans chose to come back again to the Prince of Wales. The captain of the pub's dart team, Vino, had a special trophy made earlier that day. A match that night between the two teams would determine which pub would get to display the trophy. While the Horse Brass team lost that last night, all had a great time. Don turned to Terry, a fellow publican, and issued a challenge for their team to come to the Horse Brass for a re-match for the trophy. Pints were raised, the challenge was accepted. Game on!

Back at the Horse Brass, Don recounted his time in London to Brian, Arthur and the regulars. He excitedly told of his time at the Prince of Wales and his visit to the oldest, continuously-run brewery in all of Britain, the Ram

Brewery. Brian and Arthur looked at each other and smiled. They knew of the magic Don had encountered in their home country. Brian had seen the same excitement in Don's eyes when he had returned from his first trip to England. They sensed that this encounter with Terry and Debbie and the pub regulars would be significant and lasting. It certainly was.

Brian had close relatives in England, an aunt and uncle that lived not far from Wandsworth. He and his wife visited them the following year. Certainly, after Don's stories, they just had to visit the Prince of Wales and the Ram Brewery. The pub was great, as was the hospitality and friendship of Terry and Debbie and the regulars. They toured the old brewery and learned its history and were escorted into the brewery's hospitality room to taste the fruits of the brewmaster's labor. A workman happened in with four large horseshoes to show the visitors. One of the brewery's draught horses had just been reshod. With new shoes, that horse would team to pull a Young's beer wagon through the streets of Wandsworth. Young's beer had been transported over roads from the Ram Brewery in wagons pulled by heavy black Shires, large beautiful steeds with white-haired lower legs. On their leather harnesses were horse brasses. These brasses were like those seen in the pubs that served their beer. Powerful lorries now transported the beer, so these Shires were stabled at the Ram Brewery to maintain traditions.

Brian hefted one of the horseshoes and quickly thought, Don needs to have one of these. He was quick to arrange possession of these four large horseshoes. Two went to his aunt and uncle, he kept two. Back in Portland, Brian gave one to Don, who had it gold-plated and hung above the back bar at his Horse Brass. It was fastened with ends up to catch good luck, to help the pub's horse brasses in that endeavor, near Don's favorite spot at the bar. When having a pint at the Horse Brass, Don would look up at the horseshoe—from a black Shire of Young's Ram Brewery—in his pub!

John Young was a steady champion of the black Shires. There was a time when he had stabled 24 of the beautiful steeds in the Victorian stables at the Ram Brewery. Since 1998, a six-horse team of Young's Shires has pulled the coach holding the Lord Mayor of London on his annual procession through the streets of the city. [40]

Trips began, pub to pub. Groups from the Horse Brass made their way back to England and the Prince of Wales, Don Younger almost always among them. Regulars from the Prince of Wales returned the favor with frequent visits to the Horse Brass, often with Terry and Debbie. As with the original twinning, the magic happened again and again, in both pubs.

One of the hallmarks of these visits was a dart match for the trophy Vino had made. The winner proudly tried to display the trophy at their pub, until the next time. But Debbie added something different to the traveling-trophy dart matches. Both pubs had locked glass display cases to show things of significant historical importance to their pubs. The first match at the Horse Brass was won by the Yanks and the trophy proudly locked in the pub's display case at the front entry. But somewhere between then and when the Brits left for England, Debbie somehow "nicked" the trophy. Later, it was learned that it just happened to be on display at the Prince of Wales. Now the matches not only required good darts, but also cleverly hiding the trophy. It became tradition to abscond with the trophy. Game on, indeed!

For the Horse Brass Pub, these cross-Atlantic visits were important injections of England, cross-pollinations continuing those very first ones between Jay Brandon and his family in Norwich. There was a byproduct of these cross-Atlantic visits, not surprisingly. A few English-American marriages of regulars resulted, a further twinning of people with similar shared views on pubs.

Visits from the Prince of Wales soon included bus excursions down the beautiful Oregon coastline as arranged by Don. There they found refreshing ocean air and warm friendships at the Sportsman's Pub•N•Grub in Pacific City, owned by Don's close friend and former employee, Rob Royster. The spirit of the Horse Brass was certainly there. After a couple of days, Don pried them lose from the grip of Pacific City, the Sportsman's Pub•N•Grub and the nearby Anchorage Motel run by a British expat. Then it was down the scenic Pacific Coast Highway to see Jack Joyce and John Maier. Rogue Ales brews were sampled in earnest in the brewery's hospitality room, which had the genuine feel of a public house. With all this, walking barefoot on the beach at the edge of the surf, or sitting in the dunes watching spectacular sunsets, visits to the Horse Brass were quite memorable.

For a few visiting Brits, a quick trip to an area just south of Portland became a must-do. The name of this unincorporated area, also on a sign attached to a saloon and café, prompted knee-slapping laughter. Photographs of the visitors standing next to signs with this name were shown to their mates back home with the same result. The first part of the name just happened to match an offensive term of English origin, Wankers Corner.

On a subsequent visit to America, Don and another publican, Dennis Vigna of the Elephant and Castle, escorted a group of Prince of Wales Brits to Reno. Don told them he had been there before. This was confirmed when one of the blackjack dealers welcomed them to his table with, "Hi Don. Where's Clay?"

One visit to England by Don, Clay and a couple of others from the Horse Brass tested the twinning, and the friendship and understanding of Terry and Debbie. Like the hospitality shown to Prince of Wales visitors at the Horse Brass, the Yanks were lodged upstairs. A sofa hide-a-bed and a couple of cots made for a cozy bedchamber. Of course, this bedchamber was very handy, should too much Young's Bitter affect one's ability to walk. A slow crawl up a staircase was a good last resort in case one was unable to navigate a public sidewalk. This option was exercised one night, way after closing time. Twinned friendships had been refreshed and refreshed and, well, refreshed. At differing stages of sobriety and at varying times, the visitors ascended the stairs, some as a literal vertical pub crawl. Finally, to the last celebrant still at the bar, Terry said that he would have to open the pub in a few hours and if he did not mind very much it may be a good idea to get some sleep. Internally, in his mind, he was being blunt, but outwardly he spoke with gentlemanly English understatement.

The last American up just had to have a before-bed smoke, and thought he would just lie down to enjoy it while he stared up at the old plastered ceiling, since standing or sitting had become a chore. The smoker fell asleep very soon. About an hour's worth of smoldering minutes later, a fuming mattress filled the room with heavy smoke that seeped into other rooms. Fortunately, Terry and Debbie were either light sleepers or had sensitive noses. Maybe one of their pub dogs, Bruno, had been alerted and had wakened them. One of them threw open the door to the visitors' bedchamber shouting, "Fire! Fire! Fire!" The other rang up the nearby Wimbledon Fire Brigade. Like a jerky scene from an old silent Keystone Cops movie, the smoldering mattress was dragged out and thrown through a window onto the sidewalk of Morden Road. The others stumbled out of the room, out a window onto the flat deck above the salon, then down the outdoor steps to safety in the rear garden area of the pub. All of this was set to the background music of the siren of the fire truck fast approaching. The firemen doused the mattress and clambered up the stairs to make sure the building was safe. Declaring it so, the firemen left and things finally settled down. Windows were shut after the smoke had vented out. They returned to the visitors' bedchamber, only to find one of them had slept through it all—Don. When he awoke, they told him what had happened while he had dozed peacefully. Very sincere apologies were offered. Terry and Debbie took it all in good stride, stiff upper lip and all that. "What's a little fire among real friends, as long as you don't bloody well burn my pub to the ground?!"

First thing, Don went to a furnishings store, purchased a new mattress and had it delivered to the upstairs bedchamber. That evening, the regulars came in for companionship with their American friends. They did not have to search very far for a topic of conversation. They, too, had heard the fire brigade. "*You blokes did that!?*"

Human nature is not perfect, nor is the human judgment of it. A pub is open to all, a welcoming place, as long as public behavior is appropriate. There were avid readers at both pubs. A regular at the Horse Brass, Ian Griffiths, happened upon a particularly interesting paperback containing a nonfictional account of terrorist training and planning. Earlier, three terrorists had been arrested for the attempted murder of the Israeli Ambassador to the United Kingdom. A public trial followed at the Old Bailey; for centuries it had been London's Central Criminal Court, referred to by the name of its street. As one of the suspects stood in the dock, his questioning and testimony were noted intently and recorded. He had lived in a suburb of London, having quietly attended colleges there for a couple of years. He had been trained to melt into the community, to be part of it, until called upon to act. Becoming a resident in a town near Heathrow International Airport had been desired, where clandestine packages and communications could be sent and received. A location was selected — Merton.

During the testimony at the Old Baily, it became apparent that he enjoyed the good life in England, despite plotting against her allies. He spent time in pubs where he met fellow students and compatriots and discussed world politics, their similar beliefs and darker subjects. He was especially fond of a pub near the South Wimbledon stop of the London Underground, the Prince of Wales. [41]

Regulars at the Prince of Wales learned of this intrigue in their newspapers before those at the Horse Brass Pub. Heads shook in disbelief. How could this have happened with nobody the wiser? As pints were finished, a regular at the Prince of Wales philosophized, "Mates, this proves that a good pub is open and welcoming to anyone, no matter where you're from."

A Prince of Wales group came over for the 20th anniversary of the Horse Brass Pub in 1996; Debbie, JC, Damien, Raz, Tim, Lee, Carol, Steve, Paul and Ap. This large lively group was met by an equally lively group from the Horse Brass at the Portland International Airport. The days that followed and the anniversary celebration were again quite memorable at this family reunion. But this close pub family would be stressed the following year.

It was a dark year. Storm clouds rolled in as they had back in the mid-'70s when some breweries in England had sought to modernize their pubs. A part of the soul of Britain was saved and that misguided effort turned around. But one should never let one's guard down. People with a shallow understanding of history, with lives overwhelmed by the concept of profit, will always be lurking just around the corner. Such forces hovered like a darkening cloud over the Prince of Wales pub in Merton, unbeknownst to those inside.

The office of the Merton Council received a planning report and an application for planning permission for a Young's freehold, the building known as the Prince of Wales public house and the land upon which it sat, including the adjoining car park. The clerk had handled many such planning applications in the course of governance for the public good. He stamped it: date valid 18 April 1997. He glanced over it before sending it into the wheels of motion of Merton Council administration. Eyes widened; eyebrows shot up. The planning report called for the destruction of the public house. Destroy the Prince of Wales pub?!

The plot of land purchased in 1824 for the purpose of a public house was now thought by some business types to be just perfect for a new car showroom and a vehicle repair shop. The business model that had influenced breweries to modernize their English pubs some 20 years earlier had lodged in the management echelons of Young's, the owner of the Prince of Wales freehold. Sadly, the old admonition to publicans everywhere of pub before profits was being ignored in deference to the bottom line of beer sales. But a brewery's pubs cannot be operated at a loss with declining beer sales forever, even with the absolute best of tenants and village-serving publicans.

Terry and Debbie were tending to the pub and its patrons one afternoon when a representative from Young's walked in. They quickly recognized him. His face spoke of unhappy matters as he asked to speak to them in a more private section of the pub. The decision to sell and the plans of the buyer were told to them. This unexpected, unhappy "bolt from the blue" came as a shock. This would change many things for many people; it would change them, their regulars and their village. The executives at Young's had kept the possible sale of the Prince of Wales a secret. Now the proverbial cat was out of the bag.

Coincidentally, Don and a few regulars from the Horse Brass were in England on a visit to the Prince of Wales that had been planned months before. A week after Don's arrival, he invited Terry to have dinner with him and his mates at the White Horse Pub near Parson's Green Park in London. A bartender at the Horse Brass had also worked at the White Horse and had suggested Don have a pint there. It was across the Thames from the Prince of Wales.

Terry appeared somewhat nervous and his voice became very serious. He leaned over the table and announced the demise of the Prince of Wales.

Don exclaimed, "What?!"

Back at the pub, Terry and Debbie informed the regulars as they served them over the bar that evening. One wondered aloud, with little in way of understatement, "Why, on God's good green Earth would anybody request the destruction of a fine English pub built next to a Roman road, near Nelson's Fields, one that served beer from the oldest continuously-run brewery in Britain?!"

At the pub late one evening, Don picked up a handy copy of *London Drinker* published by CAMRA. In it he found the phone number of a CAMRA branch contact, one Martin Butler, and called him at home. They had met briefly on an earlier visit; Martin was a regular at the Prince of Wales. This was the first that Martin heard of this. He, too, was shocked. They met at the pub the next day with Terry and Debbie and many of the regulars.

The Prince of Wales regulars sounded the call to arms; the battle to save the pub was joined. That started the neighbors thinking of ways to increase patronage and profit. But first, the pub's destruction had to be stopped. They handed the Merton Council a petition signed by many that lived on or around Nelson's Fields, to save their pub. It was the opposite of what had happened around the Firehouse Tavern in Portland.

Don, Rick and regulars of the Prince of Wales and Horse Brass Pub soon found themselves in newspaper photographs standing in the car park outside the pub. A Prince of Wales regular was quoted in a British newspaper: "The battle has begun. The Prince of Wales is an institution. It's been our local. We do not want to see a car showroom take its place." [42]

An American stepped forward and spoke, a publican, Don Younger. "I bring people from America over here just to visit this pub, which is twinned with mine. We'll all be heartbroken—it's like family to us. The pub brings people over to this country who would never have the opportunity to visit it otherwise. The sistership between us is very strong." [42]

One newspaper headline put the battle for the pub into the proper context: "Right royal ruck over Prince of Wales' future."

Just in case members of the Merton Council did not read newspapers, or the executives at Young's were not paying attention, Don wrote a pointed letter to them both. Over a good pint of bitter, ironically Young's Bitter, while sitting at the bar of the pub, he drafted a letter, making some edits here and there. Satisfied, Don asked where he could get it typed up. Debbie stepped forward without hesitation.

On May 2, 1997, Don signed two identical letters addressed "To Whom It May Concern," to Young's and the Merton Council, and posted them in a red box of the Royal Mail. In them, Don emphasized the closely intertwined comradeship between friends at the Prince of Wales and the Horse Brass Pub for over a decade. In the letter, he confirmed how sad he and the people of the Horse Brass Pub were to learn of the possible destruction of the Prince of Wales to make way for a retail establishment, and that this would be a tremendous loss personally and to the community. Just in case those at Young's and the Merton Council had forgotten just what a British pub was, Don summarized the Prince of Wales for them—a welcome, safe and relaxing place to bring families and enjoy excellent companionship and good cheer; it was a decent, quiet, well-managed neighborhood pub with real hospitality that served the community as a second home.

Even the actors of the long-running, popular television police drama, *The Bill*, got in on the battle to save the pub. Episodes had been filmed near the Prince of Wales, sometimes in it, and they frequented the pub often between or after takes. They, too, voiced their displeasure very publically in the press over the proposed destruction of their favorite pub, one they considered to be one of Young's best pubs.

Pressure was also brought to bear by CAMRA, that large grassroots movement begun in Britain in 1971. A detailed, blunt description of the threat to close and demolish the Prince of Wales appeared in a CAMRA publication to sound the alarm. It got people's attention. "Merton Council has received an application for outline planning permission for the demolition of the pub and its replacement by a car showroom and vehicle repair workshop . . . The Prince of Wales remains a fine example of a community pub. Indeed I would suggest one of the best in London." [43]

The petition, newspaper coverage, intercession by CAMRA and Don Younger's letter caused people to stop and ponder the weight of their decision. John Young certainly felt the truth and conviction in the petition, the CAMRA article and Don's letter, and so did those on the Merton Council.

A Young's management spokesman released a statement to the British press: "We are selling because it's losing money and the trade has gone down progressively over a number of years. We could have spent thousands of pounds on revamping it but we were not convinced there was trade in the area. We are very sad about it." [44]

Revamp an old English pub? It was those modernization lads at it again, or at least somebody with that same thinking. But Young's did have a point. The amount of private housing near the pub had dwindled over the years, owing to conversion of some land to light industrial and commercial use. Land use planning over the years, approved by the Merton Council, did have unintended consequences. The number of people living around the pub had dwindled as industry and commercialization crept in. But there were no imaginative alternatives presented as to how to increase patronage at the pub. Surely, there must be a way.

There was considerable discussion at the pub, not only regarding how to prevent its sale and destruction, but also how to draw more attention to it and increase patronage and, dare they say it, profits sufficient to take if off of the management chopping block at Young's. Don, Rick and Debbie were sitting at the pub's bar engaged in a pint-fueled brainstorming session — how to revitalize and save the pub? Many ideas were brought up.

At the time, an estranged previous member of the Royal Family was most certainly in the news. Until August 28, 1996, Princess Diana had been married to the Prince of Wales, Prince Charles. Before the divorce, she was an eminent celebrity well known for her fund-raising support of charities around the world. After the divorce, she received much more attention being hounded by the paparazzi and tabloid press. All this was not well received at Buckingham Palace. A thought just popped into Rick's head. He showed his well-known wry smile and suggested, "Why don't you change the name of the pub to the Princess of Wales?"

What a thought! Terry, tending bar, overheard the conversation and the suggestion. He offered that Debbie and he would suggest that to the representative from Young's. Terry said, "Mate, you never know."

Don and the Horse Brass contingent departed for America, leaving behind a fateful decision not yet made. Two months after the planning application was received by the Merton Council clerk, it lay before a public meeting of the Merton Council Planning Applications Sub-Committee. There was much public discussion, some of it quite heated, even above English standards of public decorum. As the dust settled and the beams quit shaking, that planning application was refused "on officers' advice." This news flashed around to those at the Prince of Wales and the Horse Brass Pub. Don stood by the regulars' table at the Horse Brass, informed all of the news that the pub had been saved and raised a pint of Younger's Special Bitter. Disaster had been averted. "Well done!"

Then, life and coldest irony diverted attention. Absolute tragedy of Shakespearian dimension occurred on August 31, 1997 — Princess Diana was killed in a high-speed car crash in Paris. The people of the United Kingdom, the Commonwealth and the whole world mourned her death. Certainly, those at the Horse Brass Pub sat in sorrow.

As had happened at the twinning, one by one, without planning or invitation, regulars came into The Brass when they heard the terrible news. Where else would they gather? They raised sympathetic pints to the Princess and her sons. They talked about her life and about the Prince of Wales pub. Horse Brass regulars who had visited their twinned English pub offered more insight and feeling on this news. Quite fitting was the spontaneous wake for Princess Diana held at the Horse Brass. Don called Terry and Debbie and conveyed condolences to them and their regulars on behalf of his pub. But out of the ashes of this tragedy came an even stronger bonding between the sister pubs.

The Brass regulars learned that in the wake of the death of Princess Diana, Young's was going to change the name of their pub in Merton from Prince of Wales to Princess of Wales. Rick was sitting at the regulars' table when that news was announced. He could only smile with satisfaction. His suggestion, likely fostered by Terry and Debbie, had possibly convinced those at Young's to make the change. Whether the decision was made before or after the death of Princess Diana was not revealed.

With a professional talented artist in their midst, James Macko, the regulars gathered with Don and suggested that James do a painting of the Princess, to be presented to Debbie and Terry to hang in their pub. To change the name of an old pub was rare stuff in traditional England. This would be quite a well-publicized event. James was asked, and he readily agreed to accept this honorable commission.

He set to the task of finding a photograph of the Princess in a pose suitable to memorialize her on canvas. He sorted through some old newspaper and magazine articles. A member of the Royal Order of Saint George stepped forward, Arthur Hague. This very distinguished organization was founded in 1726 to provide for a means of honoring the nobility and recognizing distinguished civil and military service. By virtue of his membership, Arthur had obtained the complete bound photo album of the Royal Wedding of Princess Diana and Prince Charles. He handed the album to James. Within, James found a picture that he felt captured the spirit of the Princess. From his other research, he learned that this was her favorite photograph of herself. This was it! This pose would be immortalized in oils by his skilled hand.

Don announced that a fund raiser would be held at the Horse Brass for donation to charities that had been supported by the Princess. Having hailed from England, Arthur and Brian stepped right up to organize the event. They felt it was appropriate to do so.

Princess Diana was patroness of charities and organizations all over the globe that worked with the homeless, youth, drug addiction and the elderly. This fitted in very well with the generous spirit embedded in the pub, exemplified by the Thanksgiving Orphans' Dinner and Winterfolk. The date for the fund raiser was set. The painting of Princess Diana would be unveiled there.

With the temperament of an artist, James struggled internally to get her pose outlined just right on the canvas. The date for the painting's unveiling approached. Two days out, that stark truth resulted in a near-continuous effort with no sleep to complete the portrait. Time was running short.

Portrait of Princess Diana
by James Macko
Courtesy of James Macko

Many attended the fund raiser. To add to the enthusiasm, a drawing was held for two donated, round-trip tickets to London. The framed painting, not yet dry, was covered and set on an easel in the area near the pub's piano, where another painting by James Macko hung on the wall, *The Ghost of Monte Ballou*. When the portrait of Princess Diana was unveiled, there was a soft gasp from the crowd. In life, and in the painting, she was beautiful! The Princess was set elegantly and regally within a dark background. It was presented to Don to be presented at the to-be-named Princess of Wales pub. The drawing determined who would receive the airline tickets; a mother and daughter won. Amid the celebration, Don placed a significant sum in the collection pitcher and encouraged all to give from their hearts for worthwhile charities. When the donations were counted, the sum was the largest ever collected at the Horse Brass.

Don, Arthur, James, the winners of the drawing and others from the Horse Brass, ten in all, flew to England to present the painting. They and many others gathered at the Prince of Wales on Friday, December 5, 1997. The British press was there as well. John Young and executives from Young's arrived.

Don spoke as he presented the painting inside the pub. John Young responded with kind words of appreciation on behalf of Young's and the pub. Terry and Debbie said thankful words as well. Photographs were taken of the event, one with James Macko and John Young behind the bar holding either side of the painting. The painting was hung with ceremony in a place of prominence in the Prince of Wales. Then all moved outside and gathered around the tall, stout post next to the low brick wall at the edge of the car park. The post held the elevated pub sign. It was veiled with a white cloth waiting to be removed in front of the many onlookers, including newspaper reporters and the contingent from the Horse Brass. Holding a pint of Young's Bitter, John Young stepped atop a hydraulic lift platform with Debbie. Around them were Terry and his regulars and the American publican, Don Younger, and his regulars from the Horse Brass Pub. The lift was slowly elevated above all to the level of the sign. John Young raised his pint and christened the pub the Princess of Wales public

James Macko and John Young
with the portrait of Princess Diana
Courtesy of James Macko

house as Debbie removed the covering. On the sign, Princess of Wales was lettered beneath a picture of a large white rose. At the top of the new pub sign was the name Youngs under the logo of the Ram Brewery. White roses and white lilies were reported to have been the favorite flowers of the Princess. John Young selected the white rose. He personally knew that it was her most favorite flower.

A public relations manager from Young's told a newspaper reporter, "The brewery was actually thinking of renaming one of our pubs after the Princess of Wales, so when we received the suggestion from the Prince of Wales' regulars the pub seemed the obvious choice." [45]

From the proposed destruction to make way for a car showroom to a Young's pub with a new name christened by the chairman of Young's Brewery in honor of Princess Diana, all in less than a year, the emotional ride that year had been a rollercoaster. Now the pub had considerable notoriety, a new lease on life, and more patrons to show for it. It would take a disastrous bottom line to close a pub so publically christened. The twinning was now even stronger, a real bond between the Princess of Wales and the Horse Brass Pub.

After the unveiling and all the photographs, everyone adjourned into the newly-christened pub to celebrate. Inside, John Young made a solemn pronouncement to fit the occasion, short and straight to the point—"Let's have a few drinks."

Don spoke at length with John Young about the Princess of Wales pub and his Horse Brass Pub. Since 1831, when Young and Company's Brewery was formed, their number of tied pubs had increased from 80 to over 220. Don described his first expansion attempts, the first Rose and Raindrop in downtown Portland and the second at Kamikaze Corner, and mused about why they had not succeeded. John Young listened intently. John offered some advice and commented on what a wonderful name that was for Portland, the Rose and Raindrop. Don affirmed that he would be keeping an eye out for an opportunity to open another Rose and Raindrop pub. John Young told Don of his appreciation of the painting of Princess Diana, commenting that he personally knew her and had worked closely with her, supporting her favorite charities.

For the pub's christening, music and song were provided inside by the pop-rock Frampton Weller band. They had just released their first record earlier that year. Don and Martin Weller struck up a conversation, and a chord of friendship was struck straight away. Don purchased a few copies of their recording and brought them back to Portland to a friend who owned a couple of record stores and a record distribution company. Don also invited Martin to come and play at the Horse Brass Pub, which he did a number of times over the coming years, after he had formed his new band, Crush UK.

The next day the Americans from the Horse Brass had dinner at Young's Brewery at the personal invitation of John Young. Next to James at the dinner table, John said, "I am so impressed with the painting you did of Princess Diana. I knew her personally. How did you capture her presence?"

James replied, "Sir, I can't really explain that."

John gave James the highest compliment an artist can receive for a portrait. "I don't know how you did that, because you didn't know her and I did. When I look at it, she's in there." With that, John said, "I want to share something with you. My family has collected paintings for centuries. Come with me." James followed him into his private office and adjacent rooms. John showed James his art collection on the brewery premises and told him that the family collection included more such paintings at his home. Regardless, the collection at Young's was impressive: original paintings by Picasso, Manet, Degas, and other famous artists.

While taking in the rare paintings, they were interrupted by one of John Young's brewery lieutenants who hurriedly came in and advised, "Sir, we have the proof of the Young's Brewery Christmas card with your photograph we're going to send out. It is ready for your review."

They all adjourned into John's office, including James. There they were shown a picture of a team of black Shires hitched to an old Young's beer wagon loaded with wooden beer barrels, in commemoration of earlier times. In the photograph, John Young was standing next to the regal horses, but not so regally attired in a Father Christmas costume. John laughed when he looked at it, and said, "I feel kind of stupid." He put James on the spot by asking, "What do you think?"

James squirmed a bit. But not one to mince his words, he honestly said, "I think you look compromised, Sir."

John replied, "Great! Honesty! Everybody else says I look good. I look stupid, don't I?"

James continued, "Well, Sir, you don't look that great in the photograph. It doesn't capture your majesty."

John filled the room with laughter and commanded, "We're going to change it. Schedule another photographer. We're going to redo this thing."

The visit to Young's was followed by another pub crawl through London by the Yanks on their own. That weekend, Don met with James and Arthur and said, "Michael wants us to come up to Islington to have drinks with him."

Michael Kahn was a very accomplished acoustic guitarist and was well known in the music and art communities. He had played at the Horse Brass a number of times during tours through the United States. At this time, Michael made his home in London. They knew each other, and Don had contacted him. Now this Horse Brass trio would be his invited guests in a posh area of London. Michael met them at the Tube stop in Islington. From there they went to a local pub, Michael's local, had a few drinks and refreshed their friendships. The group's happiness increased. They laced their drinks discreetly under the table with hard stuff from miniature liquor bottles, like those used aboard commercial aircraft. Someone in their group had a pocket full of them.

Michael told them, "I know a place that will show you what true English society is outside of the highly-marketed tourist area of London. I don't think an American has been in there for at least a year." The group walked down dark, wet streets in Islington that night. They stopped at a quiet street corner in the light rain. Above a pub's entry was the name King of Denmark. Michael opened its door. They went in and were greeted by a brightly lit, rollicking scene. The place was packed. The pub was having a knees-up sing-along, with respect to the old favorite, "Knees Up Mother Brown." A lively player sat at an old upright piano, fingers dancing across the keys. People were dressed in 1940s garb as if this were a Saturday night out during the war.

The group pushed their way through and bellied up to the bar, ordered drinks and found a table in the throng of merriment. Michael almost had to shout to be heard. They sat for a while and just watched and absorbed the atmosphere. People were taking turns at a microphone and encouraging everyone to follow along. This very much reminded Don of British Pub Night back at the Horse Brass when British expats did the same.

People there recognized Michael. Introductions were made to those at neighboring tables and conversations soon started. Those at Michael's table were invited to sing. Michael, being a professional musician and singer, wowed the group with "Unchained Melody." Arthur, feeling quite at home in a pub in his native country, was next. Having served in the RAF, he sang "Kiss Me Goodnight, Sergeant Major." That brought more than a few hoots. As Arthur sat back down, he poked Don in the ribs. "I've done it. Now get your arse up there."

Don shook his head. He would wait. James went to the microphone. He did not sing, but spoke of the renaming of the twinned pub, that his painting of Princess Diana now hung there and what all this meant to him. He was greeted with clapping and nodding heads. When he sat down, he nudged Don and pointed to the microphone. The number of drinks accumulated to that point in the evening finally pushed away Don's inhibition, and he agreed. James and Arthur looked at each other wondering if Don's coarse voice was meant for public song. They had never heard Don sing.

Don rose slowly and said, "Aw . . . OK" and went to the microphone. The gathering quieted. He introduced himself and stated that he was the owner of the Horse Brass Pub in Portland, Oregon, in the United States, a sister pub of the Princess of Wales pub in Merton. With his accent, he confirmed that he was a Yank, alright. Don then turned to the piano player and requested, "It's a Long Way to Tipperary."

With a flourish, the pianist played the introduction. Don started to sing. He sang with emotion and did a great job, by James' and Arthur's measure and judging by the measure of all in the pub. When he finished, applause erupted, some people stood up. Don smiled in acknowledgement. He held up his pint as if making a toast to them and gazed about the pub and at all those welcoming people. Don was comfortable in this pub. He was home.

Michael told his group about a retirement party for a fellow musician at an after-hours bar not far away. They waved farewell to the patrons of the King of Denmark and made their way to the more clandestine affair. In the wee hours of the morning, Don hunched over their table and took on a somewhat pensive look, helped by being a bit in his cups. With a seasoned artist's eye, James seized the moment. He snuck his camera just above the edge of the table and captured a facet of Don's eccentric personality. Later, James would use that photograph to make an oil painting, a gift for Don to remember their early morning pub crawl through London.

They left there after 3 am and made their way to Michael's flat where he prepared some food to balance things a bit. When they awoke a few hours later, they made their way back to the Princess of Wales on the Tube during morning rush hour. Terry saw them come up the stairs, "Bloody hell, you're a knackered-looking lot."

Just before another planned trip to the Princess of Wales, Don and Arthur nipped down to Las Vegas to enjoy a bit of gambling offered on The Strip. Luck was with them; the blackjack tables netted them some serious money. Don and Arthur were not ones to hoard their good fortune. So they purchased 20 cartons of cigarettes for their mates at the Princess of Wales, the price of cigarettes being high in England. The booty was stowed away in their luggage. There was a hurdle, however—Her Majesty's customs agents at Heathrow International Airport. Not all the passengers' luggage was inspected. The agents just kept a watchful eye out for suspicious types. To them, Don and Arthur were an "interesting lot." The luck bestowed back in Las Vegas ran out in the customs line at the airport. They were stiffly and properly advised that only a limited amount of cigarettes could be brought into the country. They were relieved of their cigarette stash. Their tale of customs woe was told over a good pint at the Princess of Wales, and a toast was raised. "Thanks for the thought, mates."

The following day, Don was at the bar of the Princess of Wales, enjoying a pint of Young's Bitter and conversation with Debbie and Terry. A small group of people entered the pub. Who should be among them? John Young. They joined Don and welcomed all to England and their pub. Don very much enjoyed speaking to this noble English gentleman with whom he shared common interests. Don told John that he was planning to open a third Rose and Raindrop pub in Portland. John took this all in and thought a proper English pub sign could help things along.

John Young would meet Don again, this time in the Horse Brass Pub that he had heard so much about. He was en route to Seattle to visit family. Of course, he just had to stop and visit the Horse Brass. He walked in carrying a large, flat square item wrapped in plain paper. He set the package down as Don walked up to welcome him to the Horse Brass Pub. There was a handshake and a brief, sincere man-hug with hands on shoulders. John looked around the pub and soaked it all in and nodded his approval. Then it was to the bar, to Don's favorite spot, for some pints of Younger's Special Bitter. Arthur was there as well and warmly greeted this fellow Englishman. John leaned the package on a barstool as pints were drawn by hand pump.

John held up and examined the pint of Younger's Special Bitter, cask-conditioned, sipped, and let the flavors settle across his seasoned palate. Again, he nodded his approval. He told Don that he was very happy to see that Don and the Horse Brass had somebody from Yorkshire. The two Englishmen laughed as they looked at each other in mutual understanding of the old stereotypes that existed between North and South back home; Londoners were assumed to be educated and smart, while a person that hailed from Yorkshire was thought to be a right twit.

Don and Arthur could not help but notice the wrapped package, but thought it impolite to ask about it. Finally, John reached down, lifted it up and presented it to Don. "I brought over a little something you may find useful."

Don was caught by surprise. He peeled off and tossed the wrapping aside. Don held up a wooden, two-sided pub sign just like the kind that would have hung from a British pub. Don struggled to hold back emotion. There, carefully lettered, was "YOUNGS ALES" at the top and "Younger's Rose and Raindrop" in elegant script at the bottom. Between them, over a deep blue background, was a large red rose in full bloom on a multi-leafed stem with thorns, which also supported a rose bud among falling raindrops. With more than thanks, Don promised that the sign would hang in a place of honor at his third Rose and Raindrop.

A few years later, Mel Hickman died. Don's close friend had passed much before his time. Don and a cadre from the Horse Brass escorted the memory of Mel, and his ashes, to the Princess of Wales. It would be Mel's last visit. Mel had been there before. He was a regular in the truest sense of the word, on both sides of the Atlantic.

Don and others discussed with Terry and Debbie good ways to remember their departed friend. They were sitting out back in the pub's courtyard garden. That was to be Mel's final resting place, in the soil. There was an open spot near the high wooden fence, a small place that was also just right for a rosebush. After all, Mel had lived many years in Portland, the City of Roses, and had managed two of Don's public establishments, both named the Rose and Raindrop. Terry and Debbie purchased a red rosebush. To ensure that Mel's spirit continued to bloom, his ashes were mixed with the soil surrounding the roots of the rosebush. People spoke in Mel's memory as it was planted. Mel was finally at rest. Don spoke last and made this toast with a pint of Young's Bitter: "To the caveman!"

Don lingered by the rosebush alone as the others drifted back into the pub. He again raised his glass, poured a little on the earth that had been mixed with

Mel's ashes and took a sip himself. "Farewell, Mel. It was a pleasure to have sailed with you."

Deep red roses would bloom there each spring. Debbie would tend the memorial rosebush. Its dark red blooms would appear each year. Mel would provide the roses, England the raindrops.

The annual Craft Brewers Conference was being held in the epicenter of craft beer, Portland, Oregon. The conference brought John Young again into the cathedral of craft beer. John Young was to be the guest speaker at the conference the next day.

There was a vast array of mind-numbing flip charts and much beer-marketing jargon at the conference. John Young took to the stage and podium. He spoke from the heart, without charts, providing a ceaseless flow of beer anecdotes and jokes. The huge conference room changed into a pub regulars' table. Many in the crowd laughed, looked at each other and remembered just why they had become brewers. Don just smiled and nodded. [46]

In the spring of 2006, Don led another group from the Horse Brass Pub to the Princess of Wales to help Terry and Debbie to celebrate their 20 years at the helm of the pub. They had come aboard at the Prince of Wales just a few months before the twinning took place. This spoke volumes as to the sincerity of their purpose to maintain the pub as a home for the citizens of Merton. They had taken over the reins of the pub quickly. Their honest, welcoming demeanor had drawn Don and his regulars back to the Prince of Wales on their very first visit there in 1986.

John Young was there, shaking hands, posing with Terry and Debbie with a pint of Young's beer in hand. John Young had been the Managing Director since 1955 and Chairman of Young's Brewery since 1962. John Young was the great-great-grandson of Charles Young, one of two business partners who had formed Young and Company's Brewery and purchased the Ram Brewery in 1831. John Young had also been a Spitfire pilot with distinguished service in World

John Young with Terry and Debbie Urwin
at the Princess of Wales pub
Courtesy of *London Drinker*

221

War II in the Fleet Air Arm. He had also been recognized as John Young, Commander, The Most Excellent Order of the British Empire.

John Young, Terry and Debbie were featured on the cover of CAMRA's *London Drinker*, they behind the bar, he in front holding a pint of Young's Bitter. The accompanying article cited the visitor from the Horse Brass: "Also present were Don Younger, who runs the pub's twinned pub, the Horse Brass, Portland, Oregon, and six of his customers who had made the trip especially for the anniversary."[47]

Six months later, two eras came to an end. John Young died at 85 years of age, September 17, 2006. Shortly afterwards, Young's sold the Ram Brewery and the land beneath it to a property developer and entered into a joint venture with Charles Wells Brewery, creating Wells & Young's Brewing Company, Ltd. The commercial production of beer at the Ram Brewery in Wandsworth would come to an end, but not the making of beer at the ancient site. The candle flame of the spirit of brewing good beer still flickered in the winds of modernization and change. With the new owner's permission, a small, private operation by dedicated brewers, members of CAMRA, continued brewing at the old Ram Brewery, but the site and the beer now brewed there were not available to the public. Brewing beer under the sign of the Ram since at least 1512 would continue without interruption.

Back at the Horse Brass, Don was reading through a British newspaper, *The Independent*, sent to him by his mates at the Princess of Wales. Don had read many such newspapers during his visits to that beloved land. But this one had special meaning; it contained the obituary of John Young. By the fate of birth and circumstance, Don Younger and John Young came from different points of life's compass. Don took a long drag on a cigarette and nodded as he read some heretofore unknown cameos of John Young's life. John had visited a brewery owned by a Trappist monastery in Belgium. In it he had read a plaque that he disagreed with. "In Heaven, there is no beer, so we drink it here." John was reported to have said, "No beer in Heaven?! Surely, God would not create such a place." As John Young knowingly approached death's door, he reportedly bullied his physician into estimating the exact date of his passing. When that date arrived, he wrote in his diary, "Today I die." He confided to those around his bedside that it was a poor show when his Maker did not appear. Don laughed out loud when he read this. There was a lot that these two had in common, their views of life and beer.[46]

A major CAMRA publication is the annual *Good Beer Guide* that lists many pubs throughout the UK. As in years past, the Princess of Wales was listed in an edition of the *Good Beer Guide*, in the *Guide*'s defined area of South

Wimbledon, Greater London (South-West), England. The beers listed for the Princess of Wales were Young's Bitter, Young's Special and seasonal beers.

On a visit to the Princess of Wales, Don Younger met again with Martin Butler. Martin handed Don a copy of the 2007 *Good Beer Guide*, sat back as Don leafed through it to the page that listed the Princess of Wales. Don read the entry and smiled broadly. His pub was listed there. "Twinned with the Horse Brass pub in Portland, Oregon, patrons make occasional exchange visits." Don was exceedingly proud of this. His was the only American pub listed in the CAMRA *Good Beer Guide*! Don was not entirely surprised. Earlier, another CAMRA publication, *Fifty Great Pub Crawls*, described the Prince of Wales pub in Merton and added, "It is twinned with the Horse Brass pub in Portland, Oregon."

Don knew that Terry and Debbie were planning retirement. He suggested that the rosebush be transplanted to the garden behind Martin Butler's house to ensure that it would be properly cared for after they left. Martin did a bit of horticultural research and was advised to not move the rosebush, but that if it must be moved, do so only during the season when it is dormant. Debbie and Martin together advised Don that Mel's rosebush not be moved, so as not to stress the bush and put it at risk. Martin volunteered to keep an eye on it after the new publican took over.

The retirement that Terry and Debbie had planned finally arrived. They were recognized by the London South-West branch of CAMRA for their years of dedicated service at the pub. Martin Butler presented them with a framed CAMRA certificate that read: "Presented to Terry and Debbie Urwin of the Princess of Wales with grateful thanks for over twenty years of good beer in a good local pub."

Their retirement plans included a return to New Zealand to live in Christchurch. Considering that there was new management at the helm of Wells & Young's, and that they were soon departing for New Zealand, Terry and Debbie were concerned about the control of the commemorative gift from the Horse Brass Pub, James Macko's portrait of Princess Diana. The next publican would likely keep the painting in the pub, but this could not be absolutely guaranteed. This concern was telephoned to Don Younger.

In response, Don, Arthur and some regulars made another visit to England to rescue the Princess. The painting was reverently taken down, carefully wrapped, and hand-carried by Arthur back to Portland where it was hung on the East Wall. The portrait of Princess Diana had adorned the Princess of Wales for over 12 years. Now it was in its final place of honor, on the wall alongside a photograph of the mother of Queen Elizabeth II, the Queen Mum.

Shortly after Debbie and Terry left England for New Zealand, they learned that the management of the newly-formed brewing company somehow thought it best to change the pub's name back to its original name, Prince of Wales. This may have had something to do with historical tradition. While this may have been sound from a marketing perspective, the regulars and the villagers of Merton thought it strange. It was apparent that memories did fade with time. This confirmed to Don, Terry and Debbie that retrieving the painting of Princess Diana had been prudent, as her painting would seem out of place in the renamed Prince of Wales.

Over pints of good beer, Martin noticed that Mel's rosebush was being neglected. So he told the new publican the history of the rosebush and offered to look after it. This provided a new pub experience for Martin, coming in for a good pint while toting a set of pruning clippers, gardening gloves, trowel, insecticide spray, rosebush feed, and compost.

A trip, a fall, a broken shoulder, and then complications closed the book of life for the publican of their twinned pub. The news spread. Phone calls, e-mails and letters from England and beyond made their way to his Horse Brass Pub in sad response. When Don's wake was held, Terry and Debbie in New Zealand and the regulars at the Prince of Wales made the same toast at 3 pm, local time: "To the caveman!" Don's death was further eulogized in *London Drinker*. [48]

Before Don died, regulars from the Prince of Wales had planned to come to the Horse Brass Pub to celebrate Don's 70th birthday. Martin Butler and regulars kept that commitment and came to the Horse Brass on July 11th and toasted Don at the regulars' table, to complete the wake in person in Don's pub.

Later that same year, an American visitor and his wife came into the Prince of Wales for the first time and met with Martin Butler, their host. He had met Martin at the Horse Brass Pub when Martin was there with other English regulars on that visit in memory of Don.

The Americans walked about the Prince of Wales and took photographs of the bar, the salon with its fireplace, the pub sign outside, and the courtyard garden out back. A tall rosebush was in the courtyard against a wooden fence. It had only two deep red blooms. Martin and the visitors thought that was very fitting, one for Mel and one for Don. The visitors asked about the stairs to the living quarters and were shown to the bottom of the steps. They looked up, smiled, but did not ask to go up, not wanting to intrude. They knew that Don Younger and many Horse Brass regulars had slept up there, Rick for six weeks. They also knew of the smoking mattress and early morning arrival of the Wimbledon Fire Brigade and tried to picture the scene that night. They all returned to the table and the visitors asked more questions and took more notes for a book being written about the Horse Brass Pub.

The London South West branch of CAMRA marked 500 years of continuous brewing at the Ram Brewery in Wandsworth at the February 2012 Battersea Beer Festival. This huge annual event was held in a vast London hall and was opened by a Member of Parliament. The 500th anniversary of brewing at Wandwsworth was prominently shown in the logo for the festival: "Celebrating 500 years of beer in South West London."

Other forces were at work influencing land planning in the London borough of Wandsworth. Plans for regenerating Wandsworth Town Centre included a high-rise residence, apartments, shops, cafes, bars and restaurants, a residential car park, bicycle parking, open areas for recreation and wildlife preservation. But what about the brewery?

Earlier, the Ram (Young's Brewery Complex) on the Wandsworth High Street had been officially listed as a Grade II heritage building; a building of special historic interest at a national level. With this historic designation and protection well in mind, the planning application included restoration of the listed brewery buildings on the development site — as a working microbrewery and brewery museum. Beer will continue to be made without interruption at the old Ram Brewery.

The Prince of Wales pub changed hands, March, 2013. It was purchased by a private citizen, not a brewery. This occurred after three decades of decline in the number of pubs in the UK; more than a fourth of them had gone out of business during this period. The decline was understood, for a host of reasons, but not accepted. In response, a new phenomenon was being observed across Britain. People from villages and neighborhoods stepped forward to save their pubs. They formed business associations and consortiums, purchased shares and bought their beloved pubs. This groundswell was certainly not driven by the dream of financial profits. As the members of CAMRA knew, the regulars knew what their pub meant to the life of their village.

The Star pub at Lidgate, with over 500 years of history, had been Jay Brandon's local nearly 60 years earlier. It had been at risk of closing, and the people of Lidgate village stepped forward. They now own the pub as a free house.

The Prince of Wales became a free house, free to serve beer of the publican's choosing, where good companionship had always been the order of the day.

GOOD ARROWS, MATE

In the minds of many, there is a game inextricably tied to Britain and her public houses. That game is darts: the board, the darts, the game, their history, and the quiet sportsmanship of play. Almost as common as horse brasses, dartboards are found in virtually every pub in the British Isles. A first time visitor to a pub need only lay his darts on the bar to soon hear, "Care for a game, mate?" For many of those who have lived in Britain, very little was better than a friendly game of darts on a cold, rainy winter night in a warm, cozy pub, sipping on a pint of ale between throws. American servicemen discovered this magic while stationed there during World War II.

Jay Brandon and Don Younger certainly understood this. They also knew that dartboards brought a different, welcoming form of companionship into a pub. Darts were an intentional part of the Horse Brass Pub from its inception. The game brought a sense of community through casual competition at pubs and neighborhood taverns in Portland and through the dart league teams sponsored by them.

When Don and his friends first toured the pubs of East Anglia, led by Jay Brandon, they learned about the public house and different beers, but they also learned about darts. Most of the pubs visited had a dart board, a few more than one. They watched games being played, listened, asked questions and even gave it a try. In keeping with the social atmosphere in a pub, Don saw that darts were played in a gentlemanly manner. There was no cheering, bragging, denigrating or rudely distracting an opponent.

At one pub, Don may have watched an amusing first-time encounter with a dart board, one that had been witnessed by another while assigned to RAF Mildenhall. An American came into the pub. The young man ordered a beer and seemed to be staring at the unoccupied dart board by the end of the bar. The publican tending the bar placed a set of the pub's darts in front of him and offered, "Here ya go, mate. You can use these."

The young man picked up the darts, stepped up to the throwing line marked on the floor, studied the board, and asked with honest naiveté, "Are you sure this is the right distance? This seems way too close. I think I should be standing farther away."

The publican smiled knowingly at this fresh Yank and said, "Give 'er a go."
I think ya'll find it 'ard enough."

At a number of pubs, Don asked about the history and origin of darts. The
information received seemed to vary from pub to pub. At one, the publican
said, "You don't want to get into a discussion about the origin of darts. You can
get into a right argument about that."

Regardless, Don picked up very interesting bits and pieces about the game.
He thought some just had to be true. He learned that the game had very old, if
somewhat uncertain, roots.

One belief was that English archers threw arrows at the ends of wooden
barrels to hone their eye when not on the battlefield. For fun and relaxation
indoors, at the village inn or pub, they may have used cut-down, shortened
arrows. That seemed credible—that archers in olden times hand-threw
shortened arrows into a barrelhead for practice. Watching a dart game at a
village pub, Don witnessed a particularly good throw of three darts, all touching
each other and all in the intended scoring target. Alluding to the archers of
old, the player's opponent took it in good stride and said, "Good arrows, mate."

From a dart player at another pub, Don was told that darts were derived
from an English battlefield weapon of the Middle Ages, a short wooden
spear with a pointed metal shaft at the front, and feathers at the back to
accurately guide its flight in battle. The player said that there was even some
archeological evidence that darts may have descended from the Roman pilum,
or short throwing spear. The barman interrupted with a grin and advised that
the Romans had visited the British Isles for a while, and that Viking warriors
also used throwing spears of various lengths. As he polished a pint glass, he
continued, "Mates, the Romans and Vikings had a wee bit to do with our
history. It's in our blood."

In any event, the game of darts had a history hundreds of years old. English
history documented that Anne Boleyn gave King Henry VIII a set of jeweled
darts in 1530, reportedly made in Paris.

Don and his traveling companions heard many interesting facts and much
lore regarding the evolution of the game—the size and layout of the board,
its height above the floor, and the throwing distance. One speculation on
board layout suggested that it came from how English soldiers practiced with
short throwing spears or hand-thrown arrows back at camp, using the cut-off
end of a log with targets determined by its natural pattern of tree rings and
dried radial cracks. As soldiers were wont to do, practice probably turned into
challenges of skill and eventually into scoring games that found their way into
inns and public houses, where darts combined with pints of the local brew to
make a cheerful mix.

Then, there were those dratted wires. The wire lattice mounted on the surface of a dartboard, with wires directly over or embedded in the edges between scoring areas, has been the bane of many a dart player. Sometimes, at the worst possible moment in a dart match, a well-thrown dart will strike the wire precisely on its front edge, resulting in the dart's bouncing out, landing on the floor, all followed by salty language. The dart is lost for that turn, and such is the risk for both players. But wires are necessary to determine in which scoring areas darts land, to speed the game along and maintain civility in the pub.

A long time ago, some non-players thought that darts was a game of chance. For the beginning player, that may be closer to the truth than would be admitted. But for the seasoned player, the chance part of the game shrinks closer to zero. At one time, in the 1800s, games of chance were frowned upon. Some well-meaning types sought to ban darts from pubs since they thought it was a form of gambling. In any event, skill won out in the hallowed halls of Parliament. A very seasoned chap with considerable dart skill from a small village demonstrated that chance had nothing to do with his game. Members of Parliament called out small areas of the board to hit, as Big Ben announced the time outside. They were impressed and agreed that darts was surely a game of skill.

Back home at the Horse Brass, Don learned that the game of darts likely first came to America in the hands of British and Irish immigrants. Some thought darts could have come over with the Pilgrims. But they were a straight-laced lot and not taken to such frivolity. Others suggested that the game came over on earlier sailing ships from England, around the time of the American Revolution, played by red-coated soldiers.

American servicemen in England during World War II visited a pub or two in nearby villages when off duty. Jay Brandon certainly had. They brought the game to America in earnest. Darts spread throughout the country making their way to Portland, its bars and taverns, into the Elephant and Castle, and into the Horse Brass Pub. This matched Jay Brandon's dream of making his pub a reflection of an old English pub, as if you had walked into it during the Second World War. This had been a commitment made to the neighbors around Old Belmont Square before The Brass was born.

Before the Horse Brass was opened for business, darts were played at a number of establishments in Portland, certainly at the Elephant and Castle. It could not have claimed to be the first genuine English pub in Portland without having darts. As back in England, Jay Brandon again saw the proper marriage between darts and a pub when he tended bar at the Elephant and Castle. Without any doubt whatsoever, darts would be in the Horse Brass — four boards. Importantly, the dart boards in the Horse Brass would be so-called steel-tip boards, referring to the darts used, not the board. The thin steel shaft, sharpened and protruding from the front of the dart body is commonly made of steel. This is the traditional dart for the true dart aficionado, but more significantly, it was the type of dart used in most pubs in England. Consequently, when Jay Brandon decided to have darts in his pub, it would be steel tip darts like he had seen in England and had been played at the Elephant and Castle.

Owing to computer chips and modern electronics, so-called soft tip darts were later played at many bars and taverns in Portland. The tips of these lighter darts were made of plastic to embed in tiny holes in a plastic dart board, triggering sensors behind for automatic scoring by an electronic game machine. Like pay pool tables, these machines yawned for your coins. Coins were not required to play steel tip darts; the accompanying pints of beer to calm the nerves made up for that. The required skill to play good soft tip darts was every bit as demanding as for steel tip darts. But soft tip darts in a British pub? No offense intended, but Don knew that that would never do.

Darts had really caught on in Portland and the Pacific Northwest before the Horse Brass came on the scene. Jay Brandon discovered, to his delight, that Portland was home to a large British expat population who knew a thing or two about darts. In addition to servicemen returning home from England after World War II, these people were born and bred around English pubs, with their steel tip dart boards, and they certainly brought their love of the game to Portland. They helped spread the game into taverns, bars and pubs, depending on the willingness of their owners. The game grew and spread so far and so rapidly that administration and organization were required.

Over tables at the Elephant and Castle, the Portland Area Dart Association (PADA) was formed. It did not start from scratch. It grew out of the Portland Dart Club that had been around for a number of years. At first, teams that were categorized at various levels of skill played out of eight downtown establishments. More were to follow. There was a motivated, enthusiastic hard-working core of dart players that made PADA a great success, Roger and Lori Christal among them. For a time, despite his wall-kicking habit, Roger was a nationally-ranked dart player. He had played in a number of U.S. Open dart tournaments and did quite well.

Leagues were formed, playing out of taverns and pubs with at least two dart boards. More teams playing out of the same pub was the result of leagues formed according to level of play, from raw beginners to near-professionals at the top level. Supporting PADA teams meant that on certain evenings, mid-week, the pub's boards were dedicated to league play.

Out of the Elephant and Castle, PADA organized the Annual Oregon Open steel-tip dart tournament. It was first held in 1970 in Portland—not in a pub, but in a larger venue. This drew players from San Diego to Vancouver BC, from Yakima to Boise. PADA was a good host. It became the longest continuously-held open dart tournament in the United States. This tournament, like most dart tournaments, added the spice and stress of money to see who really had nerves of steel. There was an entry fee for the offered categories of competition: Mixed Doubles Cricket, Mens' Singles 501, Women's Singles Cricket, and a number of others. Money was won depending on the place of finish. First place netted a tidy profit. Lower-place finishes returned lesser amounts, stair-stepping down to getting some of one's money back, but hopefully having fun in the process. Cricket and 501 were the standard games (these are left for the reader to research as their explanation can be tedious for the uninitiated).

The epicenter of darts migrated to the Horse Brass Pub. Whether for league nights, or friendly but serious play, dart players from all around the city were drawn to the Horse Brass. Considering its roots and ambience, the pub's English embrace provided that extra level of enjoyment. In testimony to darts at the Horse Brass, many league trophy plaques soon adorned the high walls of the pub near the dart boards. The Horse Brass became *the* place for darts. Don worked hard to ensure that there were a minimum of four league teams playing out of The Brass at any time.

At Dart Board One, by the William Younger's Tartan Bitter barrelhead, other items of pub dart history were added. There was framed advice that helped set the required social climate, "DARTS—It is a social game, for acceptance. Darts is an activity truly native in the Horse Brass Pub for the enjoyment of the family, of which you can be a member if you wish." Then there was the playing. If your arithmetic was a little weak and you did not know your "outs," a tabular aid was posted near this board. In league play, if you threw 180, a "Ton-80" in English darts parlance (that is, all three darts in the small triple-twenty area with a single trip to the line), your name was added to a public list of those so gifted. At one time, there had been three such long, narrow lists of names hanging on the wall as Ton-80 skill increased. Eventually, one framed list was retained, for historical purposes. But Dart Board One had later, deeper attributes and soul. A small engraved plaque high above the board cited an oft-used remark by a dart-playing regular who has since passed: "Sum'bitch Closed!" Near that, on the East Wall was a framed tribute to another deceased dart player, complete with three darts stuck vertically into the top of the wooden frame of his photograph.

Under the board on the wall, near the floor, a stout board is affixed. It covers a shoe-sized hole Roger Christal had kicked in the wall. When having a beer at the Elephant and Castle, Don had witnessed and admired Roger's dart skill. But he noted some wall damage beneath their boards when control was lost after a throw that was not up to Roger's rigorous standards. At the Horse Brass, Don had seen Roger kick the wall as he withdrew his darts from the board in frustration, after having missed a key target "by a wire." Roger came in the next day, very apologetic, telling Don, "I'll fix it. I'll fix it."

Roger did fix it by covering it with a thick, stout wood board. It could withstand kicks from Roger and any other dart players so inclined. Whether in casual play or a league match, a particularly frustrated dart player sometimes kicks the plate and says, "Thank you, Roger."

The Horse Brass drew people from all walks of life. William "Bill" Laimbeer, Junior, the 6-foot 11-inch Center for the Detroit Pistons of the National Basketball Association was one of them. He would drop into the pub the night before the Pistons were scheduled to play the Portland Trail Blazers. Bill loved the Horse Brass, and he was also a dart player of top rank. He could have had a professional dart career if not for that round bouncing ball and that hoop with a net. Dart players at the pub thought he had an unfair advantage. At Dart Board One, he had to bend down a little to avoid a cross beam above the throwing line. His forward lean and reach did not leave much distance between his darts and the board. Not only was Bill Laimbeer a superb dart player, he was a friendlier, more-genteel person off the basketball court. He fit in very well at the Horse Brass.

One time the Detroit Pistons were slated to play the Trail Blazers on a Friday. That put Bill at the Horse Brass on a Thursday evening. Being league night, all the boards were taken by the home and visiting dart teams. He was disappointed, but understood, satisfied to watch while sipping good beer. But fate and fortune smiled on Bill and the visiting dart team from a Gresham tavern. Unfortunately for them, they were one player short. Fortunately for them, all agreed that Bill could be a substitute, according to their beer-fogged interpretation of PADA rules. What could be the harm? Well, the visiting team won handily, with Bill never losing a single match. In gratitude for being allowed to play, he handed out front row passes to the visiting dart team for the next day's basketball game. He inadvertently overlooked the losing team from The Brass — or maybe just ran out of the passes he always carried with him.

Just before another game with the Trail Blazers, Bill came into the pub. He wanted challenging dart games. Some of the better local players were there. In keeping with true English tradition, the games were friendly, but very serious. He lost nary a game. As he was about to leave, some of the regulars invited him over to their table. Stories of his basketball career and of how he got started in darts flowed across the table. They kept him there very late. Finally, the barman called for a taxi as Bill had asked. He left with a cheery farewell, to earn God's good grace.

God had other plans the next day, or at least was not paying attention to the game as the Trail Blazers won over the Pistons by a wide margin. Sports commentators mused that Bill Laimbeer was off his game under the basket, missing shots and letting players get around him or not effectively blocking shots. But that is life in the sports world — after visiting the Horse Brass.

Following that game, regulars at the pub were taking credit for the Trail Blazers' win. One suggested calling the team's head office and asking for front row passes in return for their play, off the court, at their table at the Horse Brass. One of the regulars went up to Dart Board One where he had played darts against Bill Laimbeer two days earlier and had lost. He lined up and effortlessly threw a dead-center bullseye, followed by two darts almost in the center. From somewhere at the regulars' table was heard, "Good arrows, mate."

April, 1989 approached. Some of the top dart players of the Horse Brass were at the pub practicing in great earnest. Some of them had been on the 1986 pub team that had competed against a dart team from one of Young's pubs in London. That visit had led to the twinning with the Prince of Wales pub and the start of a wonderful cross-Atlantic friendship.

Regulars from the Prince of Wales had been to the Horse Brass the year before. Now it was time for the Horse Brass to reciprocate and participate in a dart match. A traveling Horse Brass dart team was formed: George, Leslie, Alan, Gary, and Clay.

George Bieber, publisher of the *Brass Tacks* pub newsletter, in preparation for the trip, ran blind-draw doubles tournaments on Sundays. Part of the money collected was set aside for celebration and good cheer at the Prince of Wales. Two of every five dollars collected for entry fees went into the pot for planned merriment in the London borough of Merton.

Of course, Don Younger would accompany the team, as chaperone and all-around English pub and beer guide. Others would come, to watch and drink real ale, not necessarily in that order. In total, some 15 Horse Brass regulars made that journey to London. Some planned to stay longer than others, Don, Arthur and Clay among them, and Clay was wearing his fedora.

The wife of the publican of the Prince of Wales, Debbie, met them at Heathrow International Airport and escorted them back to the pub and otherwise warmly welcomed them to England. Some of those that had been on the earlier twinning visit would sleep in the upstairs living area of the pub, while others were taken care of by Prince of Wales regulars. That evening, Young's Bitter awaited to help sort out any jet lag before they took to their beds for some much-needed sleep.

They were up and at 'em early in the morning for a walking tour around London, even a boat ride on the Thames. While roaming about, one of the Horse Brass group noticed Hampton Court Palace that had belonged to King Henry VIII, situated on the Thames. Expressing an interest in history, he broke off in that direction and said that he would see them back at the pub. But between river and palace, there was a pub that nabbed Gary for most of the day.

The dart match had been scheduled for the afternoon of the following day. The Horse Brass team was told that they would compete against the winning team of the large annual dart tournament, held for all of Young's pubs. The Prince of Wales hosts escorted all of the Horse Brass players and visitors to where the match would be played; none of them knew exactly where they were. They had just expected to play at the pub of the winning team. They were led into a building that looked nothing at all like a pub. The match venue was a large, regal-looking hall. It was filled with cheering dart fans, sitting at tables with ample pints. There were handheld signs with "180" printed on them, apparently for waving when a competitor made that top score. At one end of the hall was an elevated stage, complete with a normal dart board setup. Alongside, for all to see, was a very large replica of a dart board with small lights in each scoring section that were to be turned on by a close observer as each dart landed. This was needed so that all the people in the hall could follow what was happening on the stage. A tuxedoed man stood by the real dart board with a microphone to announce dart scores. The Horse Brass team discovered that he did so with greater enunciated relish, the higher the score, topping out at "one hundred and *aay*-tee!"

The winning pub team had been determined earlier. The Horse Brass team was to play against them on the stage in front of the large crowd, which now included the Prince of Wales regulars and its publican. Eric Bristow was there to hand out awards, lend a professional air, and to hold court. Eric had reigned as the number-one-ranked player in the world. He had recently and narrowly been dethroned, but Eric was still one of the world's top dart players. Some from the Horse Brass immediately recognized him. The large hall, the stage, the lights, the announcer in a tuxedo, the crowd, and Eric Bristow—one of the Horse Brass players exclaimed, "What the hell is going on?!"

It turned out that Terry and the clever lads at the Prince of Wales had conspired with Young's and had arranged for the team from The Brass to play the winning team in the very same hall where the tournament had been held. They were somewhat nervous as they ascended the steps to the stage, especially when they heard over the loudspeakers, "From America, the dart team from the Horse Brass Pub." The resulting cheers made the visitors more than a bit on edge. It was as if a guillotine awaited them. In a way, it did.

One of the Horse Brass dart players had a very unorthodox throwing style. He held the dart high above the center of his forehead, waved his arm around in a small circular motion, cocked it rearward, and with an ax-chopping forward arc, the dart was released for its trajectory to the board. The form looked very strange, but it was effective; he was one of the better players at The Brass. He demonstrated his form to the curious crowd with a few more warmups. In the unexpected environment, he was very nervous. On one of his practice throws, he was over-energized on his backstroke, and the dart left his grip and headed in the opposite direction from the dart board. Thankfully, it landed on the stage and missed those in the audience below. There was a hushed "oooh" from the crowd and some muffled laughter. But he recovered and went on to make a good showing.

The Yanks continued to warm up. Soon the announcer calmed the crowd with, "Best of order, please," followed by, "Horse Brass to throw first. Game on!" The legs of the match were friendly but dead-serious, with quite proper dart etiquette, British-style. The Horse Brass team did not win the match, but they did win a few legs, even garnering an occasional "Good arrows, mate" and cheers from the crowd.

To show his prowess, Eric Bristow played a final match with the top player from the Young's pub tournament, who was an excellent player. But Eric was a top-rated professional darter. The match was apparently close, getting down to the required double-out. It was Eric's turn; he had to shoot a double-16 for the win. Rather than performing a merciful *coup de grace*, Eric asked to use one of his opponent's darts. His opponent agreed, and he knew there was something coming. Eric *knelt* down at the line, arched his single throw upward and directly into the center of the double-16. A bit cheeky, that, but Eric was the Crafty Cockney. The winning Young's team, the Horse Brass contingent and Eric retired to the hospitality room normally reserved for England's top dart players. Eric, still a bit cheeky, signed photographs and posed for pictures with the Yanks from Portland's Horse Brass Pub.

On the last night for most of the visitors, the match for the twinned pubs' dart trophy was held. Regardless of who won, Don and crew set out to find and "nick" it, as had become the tradition. To repay Terry for the pub's superb hospitality, and for the on-stage dart match, Don pushed a cream pie in Terry's face. What better way to end a dart game and a visit?!

With the history of darts in England, in Portland and in the Horse Brass Pub, camaraderie at both pubs was promoted by simple, honest praise for well-thrown darts: "Good arrows, mate."

THE TRAPPINGS

The Horse Brass Pub has trappings—the artifacts, décor and bric-a-brac affixed to its walls, posts, beams and ceiling. They are more than mere decorations. For the pub, they are adornments and symbols that speak to its history, character and very soul. Bare walls do not have character; such walls would make a sterile ambience. But those things that are in the Horse Brass are more than just something to look at while conversing with friends, although they perform that duty very well. Horse brasses are also known as trappings, ornaments on the ceremonial harness of a horse. So it is more than fitting to call the décor inside the Horse Brass Pub "trappings."

Things hung on walls make a house a home. They portray the history and essence of the family that lives within: the old clock bought at a rummage sale with children in tow; the sepia-toned photograph above the piano of the great-grandfather who emigrated from Europe; the banner from the son's championship high school football game; the parents' wedding picture; the photograph of the family reunion taken on the front porch; and the photograph of an uncle in uniform who was killed in World War II. For the family in that home, all these trappings are there to remind and remember; for visitors, they evoke the character of the home and of those who live within its walls.

Like the rooms of a home, the Horse Brass has separate areas that wrap around the bar. Some are divided by paneled low railings, each area with its own décor as Jay Brandon had designed. In the early, financially-thin days of The Brass, before the expansion of the pub's floor space, the wait staff divided the pub into two areas they called the zoo, in the west side, and the regulars area, to the east. As business and the number of waiters and waitresses increased, so did their naming convention for smaller sections of the pub. The area with the regulars' table stayed, not surprisingly, the regulars' area. Patrons who came in through the front door entered the elevated area, separated from the lower area around the bar by the wooden railings. The railings had three wide walkthroughs with shallow steps to the lower floor. The staff called the elevated area the upper deck, sometimes the high deck, which was further divided for work assignments into the regs (for the upper area in the regulars' side of the pub) and mids (for the upper area in middle of the pub). The lower area directly in front of the bar, with church pews against the mids' railings, was the Brits' area, harkening back to when British expats frequently occupied it. When the large new space was added, to the south of the zoo, it became known as the holodeck, for the reasons described earlier. Besides the kitchen, the walk-in cooler, the rear hallways, the restrooms and the area of the bar itself, these are the rooms of the Horse Brass home.

As the pub aged, along with its family, some of the walls were given proper names: the East Wall in the regulars' area, the Guinness Wall on the west side between the zoo and the holodeck, and the Rogue Wall on the east side of the holodeck.

When Jay Brandon first built out and filled the cavernous interior left by the Firehouse Tavern, he decorated it with many artifacts, including horse brasses, painted barrelheads, many World War II black and white photographs from *The Times* of London, framed prints depicting life in old England, an artist's rendition of the *Charge of the Light Brigade*, a stained wood engraving for Brandon Travel at the front entry, and the small wooden boat for donations to the RNLI, mounted in front of the beer levers from Manchester in the center of the bar.

Over the years the trappings of the Horse Brass evolved and reflected the people of the pub—its patrons, its regulars, its employees and certainly its publican, Don Younger. On his many trips to England, he always made time to stroll through antique shops and village markets, picking up things that spoke to him: "I belong in your pub." Hand-carried or shipped back, they made their way to The Brass.

The odd purveyor of good beer or whiskey had made contributions as well. Salesmen and representatives of beer and whiskey companies had often donated framed advertisements of their companies and their beverage products. Their intent was to have them hung on the walls, a latter day version of the hand-painted barrelheads that hang near Dart Board One. As the reputation of the Horse Brass grew, more and more companies wanted their advertisements hung in the pub. Many such advertisements have been hung throughout the pub, intermixed with its visible history on the walls.

Whether beer advertisements or English artifacts, all this was not done willy-nilly without control. There was oversight by somebody who knew a thing or two about the British public house—Arthur, Don's curator of the Horse Brass "museum." Like museums all over the world, many Horse Brass artifacts are in storage, and the displayed items are not static. Items on the walls have changed as things have been brought out from storage and others put back. The interior decoration of the Horse Brass is a living environment.

By the time the following is read, the trappings may have changed a little, but not the character of the pub.

Those entering from the rear parking lot, over the shallow moat, are greeted by a Mind the Moat sign on the inside of the rear door, white letters printed on a blue bar encompassed with a red circle, the well-known logo of the London Underground, the Tube. The rear door entrant is then greeted with a black and white reprint of an early work of William Powell Frith, *Coming of Age in the Olden Times, 1849*, showing a large English crowd gathered as a young man of nobility descends the stairs of a manor house. Next is a print of William Hogarth's *Evening*, showing a scene in the village of Sadler's Wells. These first-encountered trappings merely whet the appetite for what lies ahead.

On the left, as one enters, are two large wall maps. These are an above-ground street map and a map of the London Underground. Both are bordered with post cards from many patrons sent while traveling in the UK. Beneath the lot are the London Underground sign for the Oxford Circus stop and a long railroad sign for the Bournemouth — Manchester line.

On the right of the hallway, one brushes against a bit of tongue-in-cheek history in a frame, as told by the makers of Newcastle Brown Ale, The Byker ClooTY Mat. Byker (from the Norse, for a settlement near a church) was a Viking settlement near the coastline of the North Sea, the center of what is now Newcastle upon Tyne. Displayed are 12 sepia-toned postcard size prints of supposed early Norse life in Byker. The designs at the top and bottom borders of each print are identical, as if each scene were taken from adjoining sections of a long strip of cloth. The Scots call a short piece of cloth used in the making of rugs a "clootie mat." They resemble the famous Bayeux Tapestry which describes the Norman conquest of England at the Battle of Hastings. The styles of the depicted scenes appear as if the same artist had done both. Each scene is described and translated. On one, a bottle is held to the lips of a prostrate Viking, with the words "VIKING BROWT ROOND AGYEN WI NEWCASSEL BROWN." Below these words is the description: "Here the essential life giving qualities of Brown Ale are demonstrated upon the unfortunate castaway. The inscription means, literally, 'Scandinavian visitor is brought back to life again with that famous product of S & N Breweries, Newcastle Brown Ale'." S & N stands for Scottish & Newcastle, the result of a merger in 1960. The patron that takes the time to look over and read the Byker scenes might feel the urge to order a Newcastle Brown Ale. Next, Queen Victoria, 1819-1901 are printed along with her image in golden paint on a framed mirror. Alongside the entryway to the bar, is an old Watney painted-wood pub sign for The Dickens Tavern, showing a corner store with the name THE OLD CURIOUSITY SHOP and the names Pickwick and Twist. These detailed descriptions are just a small sampling of what is within the pub.

A patron who minds the moat and enters from the back door is well-wrapped in the history and spirit of Britain even before getting to the bar and tables of The Brass. Posters of Irish literary history adhere to both sides of the short double doors above the kitchen's food service counter. On the inside, facing the kitchen are posters of James Joyce and Oscar Wilde. When the doors are opened wide to use the counter, the images of these Irish writers are seen from the regulars' area. When the doors are closed, posters of Samuel Becket and Brendon Behan greet patrons.

Along the south wall that holds the kitchen's serving doors, to the right of the throwing lane for the dart board, are five barrelheads from old pubs in England—Watneys Red Barrel, Guinness (with their Toucan in flight balancing two pints of their dark brew on its beak), William Younger's Tartan Bitter, Guinness (in rough shape with a slat missing), and Red Lion. Sometimes a dart player who knows the history of the pub will tap the face of the William Younger's barrelhead while stepping past it to retrieve darts from the board, for better luck on the next throw, or in thanks for "Good arrows, mate."

Near the dart board are many plaques of league awards won by pub teams. Many more surround the other dart boards in the holodeck. They speak to hours and hours of steel tip darts thrown into the pub's bristle boards. Not quite in keeping with the British tradition of darts as a gentleman's game is a small engraved plaque high above Dart Board One, quoting a departed regular that often commented at the appropriate moment in a particular dart game, "Sum'bitch Closed!"

Competition in the Horse Brass had taken other forms. In the regulars' area rests a small photograph of the North Wales Formation Drinking Team with Don Younger holding a pint with them, taken at Rogue Ales brewery in Newport, Oregon. They had earlier run into Don and Arthur in England and accepted the invitation to compete in their specialty at the Horse Brass. Judging by their girth and cheery red cheeks, they were a team to be reckoned with. The Horse Brass regulars did try, with the bartenders acting as referees, keeping score by the pint.

Then there is the revered East Wall. It did not start out that way. Early in the life of the pub, that wall had been called the Rangers' Corner. All things to do with soccer and the pub had adorned that wall, the names and artifacts of the Rangers, as well as the Angels and the Portland Timbers. But as people close to the pub died, their images were hung on that wall after their wakes in the regulars' area, displacing the things of soccer. But the image of the Rangers remains. The plaster underneath, where the large wooden letters RANGERS'

CORNER had been mounted, stands out in white relief against the golden-brown wall permeated by years of tobacco smoke.

Many, but not all, of those depicted on that wall have died; the number of departed images on the East Wall has inexorably increased. Most prominent and most appropriate is a large oil painting of Don Younger in his famous "cigarette and pint of beer" pose, one in each hand at an outdoor table at a local craft brewery. The artist, John Foyston, had written about beer, the Horse Brass and Don Younger in *The Oregonian* for many years. This time, he wrote with paint and published on canvas and donated it to the pub on the first anniversary of Don's death. A smaller oil painting on the wall shows Don in his cups in a London pub, painted by James

Painting of Don Younger
in a London pub
by James Macko
Courtesy of James Macko

Macko who was there and clandestinely photographed the scene. Keeping company with Don on that wall are paintings, drawings and photographs: memorials to Bill Younger, Grizz, Krissie, Mel, Princess Diana, and the Queen Mum. More recently, a round, raised-relief name of a new brewery in Bend, Oregon, Boneyard Beer, was placed among those who have passed on. It was in keeping with Don's eccentric sense of humor, with its skull and crossbones logo.

Opposite the East Wall, above the end of the bar is a row of empty boxes that had once held bottles of Macallan 12. These had held only a few of the bottles used for the toast in memory of Don at his wake.

On a post in the corner of the regulars' area hangs the cap and overcoat of Bill Younger, fastened there after his wake. On that same post is a plaque with a bas-relief brass Marine Corps emblem and a brass plaque with the engraving:

William E. Younger
1943 – 1993

On the ceiling are many soccer pennants of teams that that have played against the Portland Timbers. They commemorate the many bus roundtrips from the Horse Brass to the soccer stadium.

241

In and around the regulars' area, on the cross beams near the ceiling, are an array of hats made of aluminum foil. These are more recent additions to the pub. They are the result of Tin Foil Hat Night held on the birthday of a regular, Rick Maine.

On the ceiling, in the regulars' and adjacent areas, are the official flags of armed forces of the United States (Army, Marine Corps, Navy, Air Force and Coast Guard) surrounding the American flag. These were donated over the years by pub regulars who had served in those branches of the service. The RAF flag hangs among them, a flag not easily obtained. Arthur, having proudly served in the RAF, had to formally apply to receive that flag. Other flags hang from the ceiling over other areas of the pub with regard to the personal heritage or birthplace of their donors: Michigan, Ohio, Italy, Wales, and Australia. Each hung and watched over stories, celebrations and toasts below. The Fédération Internationale de Football Association (FIFA) flag for the 2010 World Cup, held in South Africa, hangs over the zoo. That is where British soccer teams were watched on the large TV screen used only for such things, among them, events of the Royal Family.

Significant items hang in the regulars' area upper deck. World War II-era photographs obtained by Jay Brandon are there. A regular, also an artist, donated a framed painting of bottles of imported beer, darts set in an empty wine glass, a clear glass mug and small flags with the British Red Lion and Welsh Red Dragon, all in front of a softly folded British Union Jack. It captures some of the spirit of the pub and rests next to the large framed photograph of Bernard Law Montgomery, 1st Viscount Montgomery, standing proudly next to a painting of himself in uniform.

Down the wall, next to the large framed photograph of Winston Churchill, are testaments to Scottish bagpipes having been played in the pub. There is a photograph of the Portland Police Highland Guard pipe and drum band, fully outfitted in kilted uniforms. Next to that is an emblematic plaque from the Calgary City Police Pipe Band set on their tartan. Above hangs a print of an artist's pen and ink of the scene of the North Prospect of *The City of Edinburgh* that had been presented To Her Most Sacred Majesty Queen Anne who reigned 1702-1714.

To the east, at the back of the lane of Dart Board Two, hang framed items of considerable significance, given to the pub by a regular since passed. This man's father had served with aviation pioneer and World War II hero, General Jimmy Doolittle. Among the framed letter of commendation from General Bradley, and a biography, are photographs of General Doolittle meeting King George VI and Queen Elizabeth during the war and participating in a military awards ceremony. Directly above that is a picture of Big Chief Waistgunner,

Sergeant Gilbert Eaglefeather of Rosebud, South Dakota, manning the waist machine gun of a B-17 Flying Fortress and documenting credit for the downing of a German ME-110 fighter. Between the frames of history is a tall, narrow frame containing embroidered-cloth badges of British Regiments, among them The Royal Sussex Regiment, Grenadier Guards, Royal Horse Guards, Royal Engineers, Royal Welsh Fusiliers, Royal Corps of Transport and Royal West Kent Regiment. These family heirlooms had meant very much to this regular, but the pub had also meant very much to him. Arthur personally hung them so that all may see that history.

On either side of the lane for Dart Board Two, near the board, hang the handicrafts of a lady regular. She had considerable talent creating leaded glassworks of art. On the window facing Belmont hangs a framed leaded glasswork of the British Union Jack, with the word PUB beneath. Between a table and the dart lane is a built-in blue leaded glasswork showing a horseshoe and a horse's head within, and the words Horse Brass Pub below. With these, she left a part of herself in the pub, just after Arthur had hired on.

Above that table is a framed poem written by Ed Meyo, a regular and an employee of the Horse Brass: "The Pickling of Joe McGee." His dedication at the end speaks for every regular of the pub: "To the Younger Man—Thanks for The Brass, a home and family of choice for all of us."

The main entryway represents the history of the pub from its beginning. Patrons entering from the sidewalk out front cross under the hanging wooden Horse Brass sign on the exterior of Building Four of Old Belmont Square; it is certainly the main trapping of the pub. Those that enter through the front door on Belmont are greeted with the newer history of the Horse Brass Pub, items in a glass case. In there, set against a large Union Jack flag, are t-shirts, a cap, paintings, magazines and a light blue pack of Natural American Spirit cigarettes (Don's favorite). There are also special commemorative beer bottles: a bottle of William E. Younger's Special Bitter, with a likeness of Bill Younger on the label; a bottle of Terry's Bitter, with the likenesses of Terry and Debbie on the label, commemorating 21 years of twinning; and bottles commemorating Don Younger's 25th and 30th anniversaries as the Horse Brass publican. Not to be outdone by the Welsh lads, there is a photograph of the Oregon Formation Drinking Team, with Don and Arthur as members. There is the personalized milk carton that was created after Don had received fake rubber buttocks from his pub family. Just like the missing persons ads on real milk cartons, there is a photograph of Don's very loose-fitting, jeans-clad, buttock-deficient backside, asking "HAVE YOU SEEN ME?" Listed among the particulars was, "LAST SEEN: On a barstool at the Space Room," which was a Portland lounge Don frequented.

243

Across the entryway, high above an announcements bulletin board is the engraved wooden sign, Courtesy of Brandon Travel, complete with its address and old phone number.

Heading towards the steps down to the bar, on an overhead beam, hangs an embroidery, red letters on a once-white cloth, WELCOME YANKS. It had once greeted American servicemen in a pub in England during the war. On the post by the steps is fastened a large brass key to an unnamed city, with the word Integrity engraved on its handle.

Lest anyone forget, on the way out by the glass case above the door, is a photograph of RAF fighter pilots with Winston Churchill's famous quote: "Never was so much owed by so many to so few." Next to this, and the city's required maximum occupancy sign, is a metal sign from a regular who had been a serviceman in Germany after the war. The sign has a small Union Jack above the warning, End of British Sector, Do Not Pass This Point/*Ende Des Britischen Sektors, Vor Dem Weitergehen, Wird Gewarnt.*

In the upper deck mids, a patron is surrounded by World War II-era photographs obtained by Jay Brandon from London's *The Times.* Among them is a particularly significant framed welcome to the Yanks during WWII. Beneath an image of Edinburgh are the words: "Foreword by The Rt. Hon. Sir William Y. Darling, C.B.E., M.C., Lord Provost of the City of Edinburgh." What follows is his warm welcome to Edinburgh for U.S. servicemen. If one substitutes Don Younger for Sir William Darling and the Horse Brass Pub for the City of Edinburgh, the words fit the welcome Don extended to his patrons.

There is an upright piano on the lower floor in the zoo. The piano is much more than an artifact. Under skilled hands, it has poured out entertainment and enjoyment for those that have filled the Horse Brass. While not a piano player, a banjo-playing jazz musician performed at the pub many times with a member of his jazz band at the piano. That was Monte Ballou. On the wall by the piano under an old light fixture is an unfinished painting of him with an engraved plate above it, *The Ghost of Monte Ballou* by James Macko. The preparatory underpainting had been drying when Monte died. It was not finished, but presented as it was, when the jazz great died and departed the Horse Brass family.

Above the painting of Monte is a color photograph of a horse-drawn Steward and Patteson beer wagon. That brewery had been founded in 1793 in Norwich, the city where Jay Brandon had fallen in love with pubs and the lady who would become his wife.

By a window facing the street is a framed World War I poster showing the personifications of the United States of America and of Great Britain; Uncle Sam, holding a sword, is linked arm-in arm with Britannia, who is holding her shield and a three-pronged trident. By each, standing on the ground, are their respective national symbols, a bald eagle with outstretched wings and a male lion. Below are the words: "Britain's Day Dec. 7th 1918."

The zoo could well be confused for a section of a London art gallery. Therein a patron will find six framed prints of the paintings of Francis Wheatley, the *Cries of London*, done between 1792 and 1795. The prints of these famous paintings, of street sellers and hawkers where Wheatley grew up, were first hung in the pub by Jay Brandon. The titles speak to London street life in the 18th century:

New Mackerel, New Mackerel
Strawberries, Scarlet Strawberries
Do you want any Matches?
Knives, Scissors and Razors to Grind
Hot Spice Gingerbread, Smoking Hot
Milk Below Maids

A Pears print, *Tempted But Shy*, hangs amongst the *Cries of London*, as does the *Charge of the Light Brigade*, the latter begged from Jay Brandon's barber. Regarding a more sober aspect of old London life, there is also a large print of a 1597 to-scale drawing of the Tower of London. Many other framed prints of various sizes adorn the walls of the zoo, including one of Her Majesty, Queen Elizabeth II. On the same wall is one of the royal yacht, *Britannia*, with Queen Elizabeth II aboard reviewing ships of the Royal Navy near the harbor of Portsmouth, England.

A plaster of Paris bust of William Shakespeare has had a home in the pub from its earliest days. He is mounted up in a far corner of the zoo to watch over things. Scholars of English literature have tried to make the case for Shakespeare's love of good ale. In *Henry IV*, Shakespeare has Prince Henry ask, "Doth it not show vilely in me to desire small beer?" In Shakespeare's *Two Gentlemen of Verona*, one of the main characters speaks of the virtues of a woman, "She brews good ale" and the other responds, "And thereof comes the proverb: Blessing of your heart, you brew good ale." In *Henry V* a boy proclaims, "Would I were in an alehouse in London! I would give all my fame for a pot of ale . . ." The bust of Shakespeare may have smiled when Bass Ale was ordered in the zoo, or had first been drunk by Don. Krissie, a wonderful Horse Brass regular, passed on in her prime years. After the wake, her cap was placed on Shakespeare's head by Mike McCormick, her husband. Krissie had liked good ale, just like William. Their spirits unite there.

South, towards the holodeck, a post carries a large pewter emblem of the United States Marine Corps affixed to the hilt of a large wooden sword, made and donated by a regular. Above that, probably speaking of a celebration in the pub of the Marine Corps birthday, is fastened a faux pint of Bass Ale that the bust of Shakespeare can see.

The west wall, where two dart boards had been, was renamed the Guinness Wall after the holodeck was opened. The dart boards were relocated to the new space, and all things Guinness were hung on the old wall between the zoo and the holodeck. One of Don's proudest displays is the complete set of 12 colored drawings of each basic step of the process to make Guinness Dry Stout, for which they are quite famous. The drawings are mounted at seated eye level, across the north-south breadth of the wall above the tables and chairs found there. They depict the beer-making steps using humorous cartoon-like characters and equipment. The risk of divulging Guinness' brewing secrets is scant. Ostensibly, the only other complete set of these drawings is at the home of Guinness in Dublin, Ireland. Guinness' advertising posters occupy the remainder of the wall. Some of their slogans are: My Goodness—My Guinness, Guinness for Strength, Lovely Day for a Guinness, and My Goodness—Where's the Guinness? One of the longtime regulars was a genuine Guinness drinker; that's all he drank. He arranged for a sketched caricature of Don, sitting on a low chair, and framed it as a gift. He entitled it: *Don Drinks that Beer*! It shows Don drinking from a beer can with Guinness written on it. The thought balloon from Don has him musing, "Can't think of anything I like better." When received, Don exclaimed, "This *has* to go on the Guinness Wall." Don did like Guinness. This caricature of Don was mounted in a prominent place, between two Guinness toucans, each with two pints of the brew on their bills. Right beneath is a certificate confirming a tour of the Guinness brewery in Ireland, 29th Day of March, 2001, by a Horse Brass regular. On the south edge of the Guinness Wall hangs a Certificate of Appreciation awarded to Don Younger from the Oregon Brewers Guild on the 25th anniversary of his being the publican of the Horse Brass Pub.

Around the corner, in the holodeck, hangs a large framed poster: Bass Ale, History in the making. Not to be outdone by the likes of Guinness, the poster is a chronicle of Bass from its founding in 1777. To add a little more historical substance, it cites that the monks of Burton Abbey were the first to realize that the properties of Burton well water gave their fine ale a heavenly quality—in 1002.

Next, prints of William Hogarth engravings hang, *Morning* and *Noon*, both depicting poverty and immorality in London in the 1700s, fueled in part by gin.

Framed under glass, is a deed made out to Donald Younger, Proprietor, Horse Brass Pub. It is for the conveyance of one square foot of land in the Peak District in the County of Derby, England, dated December 26, 1995. Don's land lies north of Batham Gate in the Parish of Tideswell as part of a field that is numbered 8 on Ordnance Survey Map 1921, Sheet IX 16, Plot AG-2 square.

On the south wall of the holodeck are two dart boards. Surrounding them are framed photographs from around the British Isles: a sheep and her lamb on the coast at Neiss Point, Isle of Skye; the coastline of Mull of Oa, Isle of Islay; a bridge over the Thames near the tower of Big Ben and Parliament; the Saint Mary Abbots Football Club, 1st Team, 1897-8; and an unidentified waterway before an unidentified stately home.

From the ceiling in the holodeck hang two models, one of the Starship Enterprise, another of the Starship Voyager, made famous in the TV series *Star Trek*. These had been constructed by a Horse Brass regular and donated for that area because the name given it matched a special place on the starships. Hanging from other areas of the pub are models of actual aircraft, those that had been used in World War II, also made and donated by regulars of the pub.

Quietly concealed as part of the holodeck are the video poker machines. But even these modern electronic devices have framed history in their midst. In that space, separated from the holodeck by a low wall, a patron will find a framed photograph of the Westminster Hospital Rugby Football Club of the 1937-1938 Season and an old advertisement poster by Newcastle Breweries, Ltd.—"Simply Splendid for the Simple Life." To keep up with advertisements from across the Atlantic, there is a framed print of a view of San Francisco, 1846-7, with logos of the beers from Anchor Brewing Company. And to remind patrons of the tie with Portland's soccer team, the green Timbers' jersey showing Day 5, for Graham Day, is framed and hangs on the wall. His soccer retirement party was held at the Horse Brass. Don had hired a Rolls Royce to bring Graham Day to the pub.

Finally, there is the Rogue Wall of the holodeck. In keeping with the smoking tradition of the pub, there hangs a framed Wills's Cigarettes poster with 25 small, color prints of famous actors and actresses of the early days of cinema, such as Mae West, Cary Grant, Ida Lupino and Randolph Scott.

Two things on the wall commemorate the 25th anniversary of Don as publican of the Horse Brass Pub. There is a framed article written by Tom Dalldorf that appeared in the December 2001/January 2002 issue of the *Celebrator*: "Portland's Horse Brass Pub Celebrates 25th Anniversary, Don Younger Honored by Beer Industry." Another Silver Jubilee tribute hangs nearby. It is from the New Old Lompoc Brewery of Portland and replicates James Macko's painting of Don Younger in his cups. Old Tavern Rat, a barley wine made by the brewery, is named underneath this image of James Macko's painting of Don.

Nearby hangs a memorial photograph of a young Pacific Northwest brewer, Glen Hay Falconer, holding a pint of his beer and wearing a tall green hat that looks like a hops seed cone. He was killed in a tragic accident in the prime of his life. Mentored by his close friend, John Maier, Glen became the brewmaster of Wild Duck Brewery in Eugene, Oregon, which produced award-winning beers, Sasquatch Strong Ale among them. The Glen Hay Falconer Foundation was formed in his memory and offers scholarships to prestigious brewing schools. The annual Sasquatch BrewAm golf tournament is held in his honor during the Oregon Brewers Festival in Portland.

High above Glen Falconer's photograph is an old painted-wood sign that advertises Youngers Scotch Bitter, Est 1749, Cast Conditioned. This sign is a close brother to the painted round barrelhead by Dart Board One. To maintain a proper balance, a modern wood barrelhead is mounted next to it, announcing Deschutes Brewery of Bend, Oregon. Beneath hangs a painted metal sign for the Fort George Brewery and Public House in Astoria, Oregon. Beneath that is a large framed document from Import Brands Alliance, certifying the Horse Brass as a Proper Pint Establishment. Above the certification is an elegant black and white image of the entry of the pub and its famous pub sign.

The wall is finished off with a deep-set display box from Rogue Ales, with the words: For Bill and Don Younger, Two of the Original Rogues. Inside is a bottle of Younger's Special Bitter. Hung around the bottle are award ribbons, with medals attached, won by Younger's Special Bitter at regional, North American and world beer competitions. To the left side of the bottle is a photograph of Don Younger holding a bottle of this brew, while drinking its contents from a pint-sized glass. In the photograph, the many awards hang around Don's neck. To the right side of the bottle, on wood panels, is an image of Bill Younger within a horseshoe, inscribed with: *Quae Mira Diu Experti Sumus*. Below his image are the words: Rogue, William E Younger, Special Bitter, Oregon Brewed.

To complete the museum of the Horse Brass, next to the Rogue Wall is the west-facing back bar. High above its center is a gold-plated horseshoe that had been worn by a black Shire draught horse in the stables of the oldest continuously-operating brewery in the United Kingdom, the Ram Brewery.

Below, on a glass shelf in front of the mirror, Don's ashes rest inside a small wooden box. On top of it is a pack of Natural American Spirit cigarettes, with one cigarette missing. Also, there is a small, curved Glencairn glass that Don used to use. Empty the Glencairn is not, with a bit of Macallan 12 always in it.

The artifacts in the Horse Brass Pub are much more than mere décor. They are museum pieces that are at the soul of the pub. These trappings are absolutely part of what makes the Horse Brass what it is.

THE REGULARS

What is a regular? A dictionary definition may be of some assistance: reg•u•lar [reg-y*uh*-ler], noun — a long-standing or habitual customer.

The formal definition of a regular may apply to some public, commercial establishments in general, but it misses the mark, except for "long-standing," when applied to the regulars of a British public house and especially to the regulars of the Horse Brass Pub. Some have ventured their own definition of what it means to be a regular: "Somebody who visits the pub at least four times a week." Such a description is more befitting a commercial business model and does not fit the Horse Brass.

For a pub, understanding and clarity of what it means to be a regular is helped a bit by an inverse definition. In British parlance, the pub frequently visited by someone as their third place, often the only one visited, is called that person's local. He or she has found a public house in the village and has adopted that place as a home away from home, to meet with friends and enjoy their company. "Local" and "regular" are inextricably connected; they are terms not casually tossed about in Britain. They carry deep, readily-understood meaning — "The White Hart is my local" or "She's a regular at the Fox and Hound."

At the Horse Brass, regulars were most definitely people that frequented the place, but they did so primarily because it was their *home*. The frequency of visits was irrelevant. As with any real home, some regulars congealed and became part of a closer-knit family that contributed to that home beyond the purchase of a good pint and quiet conversation. They nourished it, protected it, and above all, they deeply cared for each other and the pub. This became the family of regulars, the family of the pub.

The Horse Brass grew into a real community public house. This had been fostered by Jay Brandon and continued and strengthened by Don Younger. Jay and Don loved the warm, welcoming atmosphere found in English pubs. Like Jay, Don very much wanted the Horse Brass to be that way, reflecting what he had discovered and felt on his first trip to England.

When Jay Brandon was its first publican, the Horse Brass attracted people from the neighborhood within walking distance from the pub. Some started coming into the pub with regularity. Some had to be convinced that it was not the same as the previous Firehouse Tavern. Others just strolled in and out with their own curiosity. Some came from beyond the immediate neighborhood, a few early ones from the East Precinct of the Portland Police Bureau. For these, and many more to come, the horse brasses worked their magic, helped along a bit by the authentic English artifacts and the people who worked there and those who managed and led the pub.

Attracting people continued after Don took the helm. As Jay had done, Don personally welcomed customers and made them feel right at home. But Don went beyond that, in keeping with his unique personality. He moved easily about the pub, asking patrons if the food and beer was to their liking. He often sat down and just visited with them. Don helped personalize a person's Horse Brass experience. It was not false; it fit his personality. This was certainly an expected occurrence in a British public house. Don liked to talk to people. Being rather eccentric, to say the least, a visit by Don Younger at the bar or at your table was hard to forget and brought people back.

There was a young couple, both Anglophiles, who had moved into the neighborhood, Richard and Rosa Houseman. Their anecdotal story had been repeated many times for many others, each in a slightly different context but with the same central theme. One of their co-workers learned of the location of their recently-purchased house near Mount Tabor and suggested they visit the nearby Horse Brass Pub. They started coming there in the fall of 1979. It was love at first sight as they felt the warmth of a British pub when they first walked in. They sat at one of the old round tables on old chairs and ordered some English beer, Bass Ale. They vowed to return. They had not yet met the owner.

The Christmas season was soon upon everyone. One evening they stopped in for two pints of Bass Ale and a bit of Christmas cheer, English style. In a corner of the pub was a Christmas tree, but it was without decoration. Some wooly-looking guy, in their view, came right up to their table with a bowl of popcorn, needles and thread. They had seen him there before but thought that he was just another interesting neighborhood patron. He set the bowl on the table and said they could string popcorn and help to decorate the tree. As they put needle and thread to work for a few minutes, they asked where he lived and how long he had been coming to the Horse Brass. They saw a smile and heard a low chuckle as they learned it was his pub, that he was the publican.

They became regulars. On occasion, they sat with the family of the pub at the regulars' table, but they were usually quite content to enjoy the pub with pints of Bass Ale in their cozy niche in the upper deck and wave a greeting to their friends at the table across the way. They became part of the continuum of regulars at the Horse Brass, as did many others.

On one occasion, Don sat down with Rick and Rosa and said that his pub was different things to different people. To make his point, he suggested they look about the pub as he described what they saw. There were groups, couples and individuals. In different corners of the pub, there were a solitary man reading, another just relaxing, some quiet conversation, some brief laughter, a discussion of the day's events, some planning for the future, and people playing cribbage, chess or darts.

Like others before and after them, there was an indication that they were now regulars. They came in one night and headed for their usual spot. They saw a couple of pints of beer on the table. Thinking it was occupied, they turned to find another. The waiter said those were their two Bass Ales. He had seen them drive up and had everything set up by the time they walked in. They were family; this was their home. They even became part of the lore of the pub. After attending a very formal garden party somewhere, they stepped over the moat out back, came in fully attired in a black tuxedo and black evening dress. Two of the regulars immediately dropped to the floor and bowed humbly, out of respect for the "royal" couple.

Quite a few of the regulars did not have extended families locally. Some were single or did not have significant others. They naturally adopted the Horse Brass as their home, their other living room, a third place besides work and the house or apartment where they lived. Don encouraged this and welcomed all of them.

Like-minded people were drawn to the warm, eclectic British surroundings where Don, Brian, Arthur and Clay could be found, as well as companionship and beer. Soon, very good friends were made there as well. For some, the Horse Brass meant even more and they were drawn to each other, pulled together by the same interests. Some found themselves routinely sitting in the area next to the east end of the bar. People that sat at that table had a sense of ownership of the pub and a sense of responsibility. Greg Bundy and Mike McCormick were among the first. Mike's sense of ownership extended to inviting people to the pub, welcoming them, showing them around, introducing them to Don and having them sit at the regulars' table. Those that sat around the regulars' table became a close-knit family. Their table was not an exclusive domain. As with the Horse Brass itself, all were welcome to join their table and conversation.

There was a different dynamic afoot at the Horse Brass from the start. While it had the soul of a British public house, root and branch, it was larger and more active than what would be found in a small English village pub. It started with events promoted by Jay Brandon that drew people together: trips to Portland Timbers' soccer matches on an English double-decker bus, the Morgan sports car club, and, of course, darts. Don Younger continued and expanded pub-centered activities, aided and abetted by the growing family of the Horse Brass: miniature golf, regular golf, men's and woman's intramural soccer teams, league dart teams at various skill levels, bus tours of the Oregon coast, canoe trips, and other assorted group functions.

From these activities, regulars with compatible outlooks on life started to coalesce, a kind of sub-set of the pub's regulars. They began naturally collecting and socializing on the low padded stools around three square tables pushed together. Without fanfare or formal declaration, the resulting long, rectangular table evolved into the regulars' table, located in what naturally became known to the wait staff as the regulars' area.

With regulars gathering frequently at the same table, with the same basic feelings about the pub and companionship, marriages resulted — not surprisingly. Some weddings took place right in the Horse Brass. Don escorted some brides past the bar and down an arranged aisle in the zoo to their future husbands. These weddings included Grizz and Lisa, Jon and Katina, and Aaron and Diana.

Grizz and Lisa planned to do it up right, on New Year's Day. The pub would be filled with regulars and recovering merrymakers. Their wedding would add to the friendly atmosphere. Invitations had been sent out, written and verbal. For others who just happened to stroll in, the erasable beer specials' menu board was used to announce the wedding. At the top of the board, the name of a beer had been erased and the announcement written in its place. But the price of the beer had inadvertently not been erased. For those entering that evening, they read, "Wedding, Grizz and Lisa, $5.95." A regular went up to Don and protested, "I'm not paying $5.95 to watch Grizz and Lisa get married."

Grizz and Lisa came in dressed for the occasion, along with their minster. The ceremony was performed and the celebration continued until well after "Last orders, please."

Don liked to joke and flirt, and did so with lady regulars he knew as friends. This included Diana. She was certainly a regular and had been a trusted employee as well. At the bar or at the regulars' table, he would jokingly compliment her with, "When am I going to get you? When am I going to get you, girl?"

With her experience at the Horse Brass, and eight years in the U.S. Army, she knew how to handle herself and joked in return, "You, my darling, are greying up, and I'm a hearty girl. I will kill you if I ever take you to bed. I tell you what. To assuage my guilt for your death, you'll have to sign the pub over to me first."

Don's reply was, "Aw," followed by a hearty, gruff laugh.

This became a running joke over the years, before, during and after Diana's marriage to Aaron, until Don's death. Don would feign his proposal and Diana would simply reply, "Sign the pub over, sign the pub over." Then both would laugh.

Don was very happy when he learned of Aaron and Diana's wedding plans and that they wanted to be married in his pub. He was having a smoke out back and gave Aaron some fatherly advice. "Diana is an interesting, intelligent woman. Not too many people understand her, but you do. Good job, mate, and all the best for you both."

Don walked Diana down the Horse Brass aisle, past the bar into the zoo where Aaron awaited. Even then, the joke continued. Don whispered in her ear, "It's not too late, you know."

She just patted his hand as she held his arm and whispered her standard reply, "Sign the pub over, sign the pub over," and added, "There's no *Primae Noctis* in this pub."

Many other marriages had been initiated at the Horse Brass. Formal proposals had been made either in a private nook of the pub, or very publically at the regulars' table. With the joy of weddings came the sorrow of departed friends. Many wakes had been held at the Horse Brass in the regulars' area. With these weddings and wakes, the regulars' area and its central regulars' table became the hallowed area of the Horse Brass.

Certainly, the pub's regulars had sat in other, individually favorite areas or at the bar. But those that frequented the regulars' table unofficially adopted the Horse Brass and its publican. Soon they organized more outings and activities, like campouts, group attendance at the Scottish Highland Games and neighborhood hayrides, all supported and encouraged by Don. Organized indoor activities helped fill any voids of interest. There was the Brass Pegs cribbage team and a bowling team. Soon, chess and mahjong pieces were regularly seen on Horse Brass tables.

Rick and Todd, early regulars who were also machinists, contributed their talent and love to the Brass Pegs and the Horse Brass. They had modified the beer pump handles brought in from Manchester by Jay Brandon. Later, they created a beautiful wooden cribbage board for the pub with brass inlays. They turned out the brass pegs on a lathe in their nearby machine shop.

There was always friendly banter and some verbal jousting between employees and regulars. Arthur would usually tend bar on Sundays. Some regulars even came in then just to soak up his knowledge of England and her pubs. On some Sundays, the Brass Pegs cribbage team would carve out a niche at the Horse Brass for themselves and their opponents from another pub or tavern. As the Brass Pegs team members started collecting and ordering beers, Arthur would usually comment, "Oh, can't you guys come in on a different day when I'm not working? It was nice and quiet until you came in."

One of the longtime regulars, a Brass Peg member, would usually just reply, "And the top of the evening to you, too, Arthur. I'll have a Newcastle Brown, if you don't mind."

There is a special social dynamic that occurs among close friends that frequent a public house. This is the giving of a pub handle, not the kind one holds, but the kind one bestows. These monikers are used in lieu of a person's given or preferred name. They are nicknames, used at the pub, based on any number of factors: personality, profession, an event, a skill, or no particular reason that can be remembered in the sober light of the following day. For the most part, they are given, not requested, sometimes over the objections of the so-named. Not every regular has a pub handle, usually to that person's relief.

Many pub handles have been used at the Horse Brass regulars' table. They collectively speak to the character and personality of the group. People around this table have been known by the following pub handles (some have had more than one at the same time). For a few regulars, their handles were noble titles that befitted their pub circumstances, and "The" was an oft-used necessary prefix. The following list, while not complete, includes some names of visitors from the Prince of Wales pub:

Ap	Maid Marian
The Archbishop	Meatloaf Bob
Bam Bam	The Mayor
Bronco	The Monarch
Brown Bear	Munchkin
Bubba	Old Curmudgeon
Bubble and Squeak	The Professor
Buzzerelly	Rabbit
Don Bob	Raz
The Elderly Brothers	Red Bear
The Emperor	Santi
Frank the Knife	Sarge
Grizz (aka Grizzly Bear)	Shorty
The Hawk	The Tavern Rat
Hambone	Vino
Ice Tea Dave	White Bear
JC	

The Mayor had lobbied for a new pub handle, The Professor, owing to his knowledge of the pub and the beer it served. Much discussion ensued over the regulars' table. Many felt that The Mayor was a better fit, but how to decide? A game of darts would appropriately settle the issue. With a win, The Mayor would become The Professor; with a loss, not. The Mayor was good at the game, but on this occasion not good enough. So The Mayor remained his pub name, engraved in time. And by accepted inference, The Professor fell to the winner of the dart match.

Phil and Don Everly were an immensely popular, guitar-playing singing rock and roll group, The Everly Brothers. Don loved them. When Don was at the bar, in his cups for one reason or another, Phil Bourbeau would come up, wrap an arm around him, and say, "Hi, I'm Phil, you're Don, we're the Elderly Brothers." Then they would launch into a few bars of an Everly Brothers song, such as "All I Have To Do Is Dream" or "Cathy's Clown," futilely attempting to replicate their famous harmony. That brought either a standing ovation from those around the regulars' table, or some sitting boos and hand waves.

The family of the pub was an interesting and creative lot. A fund-raising venture grew out of an evening session around the regulars' table. Money was needed to get into the newly-started Dragon Boat Races on the Willamette River, part of the annual Rose Festival. They decided to take photographs in and around the pub to make a calendar to sell: *Men of the Horse Brass*. One of the photographs submitted to the selection committee, which included Don, was of a lady regular in front of The Brass, back to camera, wearing a man's hat and a trench coat opened wide, similar to Bud Clark's *expose yourself to art* poster. In the photograph, a surprised Professor stands in the pub's doorway in front of this apparent lady flasher— he was shocked, shocked that such a thing could happen at Don's place.

The Horse Brass was not a biker bar, but some of the regulars did ride motorcycles. Three regulars that were close buddies rode motorcycles together, and they found their home at the Horse Brass. They had biker handles that soon became their pub handles. They were the Three Bears—Grizzly Bear, White Bear and Brown Bear. Grizzly Bear, Grizz for short, fit that image. He was a large, powerful but gentle man, a blacksmith and steelworker by trade. He not only adopted the pub as his home, but took protective charge of it when there. Infrequently, folks with improper behavior made it past the mythical protection of the horse brasses. One look at Grizz, or one look *by* Grizz, and proper pub etiquette and behavior were observed.

A fair number of regulars had military service under their belts or were still serving in the Oregon Air National Guard or Air Force Reserve at Portland

International Airport. Some had been stationed in England or had served in the RAF, Royal Australian Air Force or Royal Canadian Air Force. For them, the Horse Brass brought back fond memories of pubs in their home countries, plus they brought something special into the Horse Brass. When a Pararescue Jumper (PJ) assigned to the local Air Force Reserve rescue squadron died, his wake was held at the pub.

At the behest of Santi, and other proud Marines who were regulars at the pub, the birthday of the United States Marine Corps, November 10, 1775, was often celebrated in the Horse Brass. Santi was from the Philippines, but claimed Portland as home. He had served as a Marine in Vietnam in the most dangerous of military specialties, a "tunnel rat." Don's brother, Bill, was a Marine who had also served in Vietnam. Celebrating the Marine Corps' birthday in the Horse Brass Pub was significant and more than appropriate, since the Marine Corps had held its first recruitment drive, during the American Revolution, at Tun Tavern, in Philadelphia, the birthplace of the Corps.

The proud connection between the Horse Brass and military service was soon easily seen by simply looking up. Service flags hung from the ceiling, each officially obtained, brought in and fastened there by a regular who had served in that military service component.

The Horse Brass had been around for about 15 years when Phil Bourbeau walked in late one night. He had taken a job in Portland, but had not yet found a house. Phil had been staying with a friend who lived on the shoulder of Mount Tabor. Phil was working late hours, and, when driving by, he had noticed the understated brick building with the black wooden sign of a horse's head out front. Through the paned windows, the interior had looked warm and inviting. One night, the Horse Brass and his curiosity drew him there. Phil parked out front on the street, went in, and was struck by the welcoming warmth of the place. After soaking in this experience for a few seconds, he walked down to the bar and noticed some signs for XXXX beer, pronounced "four-ex". This was familiar. Back home in Eugene, Oregon, he had lived near Australian expats, and he had become fond of their distinctive accents and beer imported from Down Under. He ordered one. It was set in front of him by the bartender, who hailed from Australia, with a strongly accented, "Bloody 'ell, let's go, mate."

That set things in motion. Phil was hooked: more visits, shared interests, warm introductions, and more four-ex beer. The Horse Brass became more than an evening watering hole. For Phil, it became his home. He was soon wrapped in its welcoming family with a place at their table. With the twists and turns of life, he soon realized that these people were more than just mere acquaintances — they sincerely *cared* for one another, in good times and in bad. As a professional psychologist, he thought that this was human love in the fullest sense. At the regulars' table one night, he coined a term for what he had come to know at the Horse Brass: pub love.

One rainy afternoon he saw pub love in action. By now he had learned to park out back, as most regulars did, and to step over the shallow moat. As he parked he noticed a man, a black man, sitting by himself in the car parked next to his. This man had his head down, almost motionless, staring at his thoughts. A few moments passed. As if from a mutual command, both opened their car doors at the same time and they stepped into the evening rain. Phil said to this stranger, "Hey there, how're you doing?"

The stranger replied, pointing to the back door of the pub, "Hey, you know . . . whatever. I need to go back in there and own up, to face what I'm supposed to face."

Phil heard tension in that voice. To break the apparent stress, he said as they headed towards the moat, "It's a great place."

As they opened the back door and stepped over the shallow water, Phil heard him respond, "I know, I know. It's a great place, with great people."

As they walked into the regulars' area, all heads around the table looked up as conversation abruptly ceased. Somewhat surprised, The Mayor asked, "Do you two know each other?"

"I'm kind of just getting to know him," Phil replied.

In unison, all at the table stood up, came over and hugged the man, a group hug with hands patting his back and cradling his head. Nothing was said as they rocked back and forth in unison, as the pub's family forgave some undisclosed serious transgression. All sat down as pints of beer were ordered. When brought to the table, The Mayor stood and proposed a simple toast that spoke volumes about this apparent prodigal son, "Welcome back." As the glasses were raised, some tears flowed. Everybody knew what was taking place — pub love.

There were other regulars at the Horse Brass, those that made the place a welcoming home by working there. They were pub regulars as much as anyone, maybe more so. These regulars were the cooks, the bartenders, and the waiters and waitresses. Most often, they knew the people they served by name, knew their personalities and their preferences for food and beer. Don Younger had formed such relationships with the patrons of his pub from the very beginning. He fostered that environment and encouraged those that worked for him to do the same, often citing his training manual, *English Pubs Through American Eyes*. At his pub, his employees were more regulars than workers; they were part of the family of the pub. They felt that the pub was more than a place to work, that it was a special place and they were fortunate to be part of it, to have had the privilege of working at the Horse Brass. There was also beneficial cross-pollination between the regulars' table and the employees; some regulars at the table became employees, some employees became regulars. As a result, the family around the regulars' table became more aware of the running of the pub, and they served as an honest sounding board for Don. They became the pub's unofficial board of advisors; they often provided advice whether asked for or not.

The regulars' table became a human resources center for Don. Often, he would hire somebody that sat at that table because of the person, not their experience. Some were hired without any experience whatsoever in a kitchen, behind a bar, or waiting on tables and serving. It was more important that someone fit the pub in character. That was usually determined over some beers at the Horse Brass or at another pub or tavern.

There had been an eager waitress in the pub's early years. She loved the pub and worked hard to make its customers feel welcome. She kept asking Don, "Am I Horse Brass yet? Am I Horse Brass yet?" Don tried to explain to her that a minimum amount of time, frequency of visits, or number of work shifts did not make a customer or an employee a regular. Some never become a regular, even if coming into the pub seven days a week. Others become regulars shortly after their first visit. He told her that it was an attitude, a state of mind, a heartfelt interest in others that made an employee a regular in his pub. They know that they are at home, and they will work hard to make others feel at home. With that, she smiled and relaxed, knowing that she was already "Horse Brass."

One waitress was a part-time employee for many years, yet a full-time regular all the while, Theresa McAreavy. She lived a mere three blocks from the pub. She let Brian know she was looking for work and asked for a job application. It was a simple form, a blank piece of paper upon which to write only name and phone number. She received a phone call to come in for an interview. It was not held in a private office with some personnel manager; it was with Don at a table. He asked, "What would you like to drink?"

She wanted to make a good first impression and answered, "I'll have a Coke."

Don looked at her kind of funny. Brian served Don a beer and Theresa a nice cold Coke over ice. She had waitress experience, but Don's questions seemed to probe into her personality and philosophy. He wanted to know whether she was a good fit for the Horse Brass. She was.

On her very first shift, Clay was explaining things to her, what his expectations were, and he finished up with, "OK. You get a free shift beer."

Theresa had acquired a taste for good beer early in life. She misheard Clay and thought he had left the "f" out of "shift." She replied, "Does that mean I get a . . . ," referring to the comparatively bland beer from one of the large beer companies.

Clay replied, "No, you get a real beer."

Theresa worked primarily Monday and Saturday nights, but filled in other days, sometimes in the kitchen. Theresa especially liked preparing and serving a full breakfast, better known as a Full English (bacon, sausages, eggs, fried tomatoes and fried bread). Bangers and a Ploughman's Lunch were also in her repertoire and on the menu. Like the other wait staff and bartenders, she knew patrons by name and their beer and food likes.

Theresa received her college degree and got a full-time job as a counseling social worker, a month after starting work at the Horse Brass. She loved both jobs and stayed on part-time at the pub for over 15 years. Actually, her career work meshed with serving people at the pub, especially if they appeared stressed.

A regular at the pub was also an artist, a natural one, James Macko, but the revenue from paintings was neither steady nor assured. Working in the pub he loved would help cover the necessary expenses of life. Don and James knew each other well. James had been coming into the Horse Brass for over 10 years. His interview was perfunctory. His first shift would be a Monday evening training shift with Theresa. Serving was different than being served, especially when the ship was full. There were a few ropes to be learned. Theresa came to work on that Monday afternoon. Clay introduced them, saying, "This is James. You're going to be training him tonight."

She just smiled; she knew him already. But she was taken aback when she saw James — he was wearing a tuxedo. During his following tenure as a waiter at the pub he wore normal waiter attire, casual. However, on his last night there as a waiter, he again wore a tuxedo. James had class.

Eventually, Theresa's career as a social worker was taking more and more of her time. She signed a formal termination notice and handed it to Don. He stared at it through the haze of his cigarette's smoke, then tore it up as he growled, "Oh, no you don't." Don convinced her to stay on to see if she could make things work out, but the same work pressures were there. A week later, another termination was put before Don, this time late in the evening. She was hoping more pints of bitter would cloud his thinking. They did not. The notice was ripped up. Finally, Don faced reality and accepted her resignation.

Her last night, coincidentally, was November 1st which was the date when Don and Bill had become owners of the Horse Brass. Theresa also had class. She arrived for her last shift wearing a spaghetti-strap black cocktail dress, a tiara and a small, frilly white waitress apron. She started serving customers and explained that her dress was appropriate for her last night as a waitress. She glanced over to the bar and saw Heidi, a waitress that usually worked only weekend shifts, having a cup of coffee. Theresa thought to herself, What's she doing here?

Rob Royster came in and he placed a big bouquet of flowers in her hands while another regular took off her apron. Heidi stepped in and took over the shift as the regulars placed a big spread of food on the regulars' table. It was quite a farewell party. The regulars gave her a collected sum as a parting gift. During all this, Don strolled in and faked being surprised by the affair. He asked Theresa to join him in the holodeck. There, he took her hand and explained that he had had a very difficult time trying to buy her a gift appropriate to her contributions to his pub. He went to many stores, but as with most men buying something for a woman, he did not have a clue as to what to buy. He had called other women for advice, even Theresa's closest friend, but was uncomfortable that he would not get it right. Don looked at her and said, "It finally just came to me."

"What's that, Don?"

Don managed to choke out, "I commissioned James Macko to paint your portrait, anywhere in the pub you want."

She had seen the portrait of Princess Diana. Theresa replied, "My, oh, my. Thank you . . . thank you, Don!" She threw her arms around him with a big hug. This was pub love in its purest form.

Awhile later, James met Theresa at the pub, and they found the perfect spot. Photographs were taken and used to paint an incredible image of her in her third place, her pub home. After the unveiling ceremony at the Horse Brass, she hung the painting in her other home, one of her most precious items. Theresa was not one to name-drop. But when guests asked about her portrait, she proudly stated, "James Macko did that portrait. Among his works is the memorial portrait of Princess Diana that hangs in the Princess of Wales pub in London."

And there were the visiting troubadours, those very talented in music and song who added life and mirth to Horse Brass nights, mostly on Fridays and Saturdays. The relationship between them and the ones they entertained was a close one. They, too, were regulars, part of the family that brought rock and roll, jazz, and country folk music to the Horse Brass. They performed by the piano or in front of the windows on the west side of the zoo. For some bands, Don would have his people clean out the zoo area, stacking up the tables and stools. That area then became a dance floor.

Don had heard about Bobby, a British piano entertainer and singer, Robert

Smith. He had a very lively routine that was perfect for the Horse Brass and British Pub Night sing-alongs. He went by the stage name, London Bobby.

In the 1800s, some London street traders wore trousers decorated at the seams with white pearl buttons, almost as a signature of their street-trading guild. A London merchant who plied the streets and was so-decorated became affectionately known as a Pearly. London Bobby's trademark, his performing garb, was a jaunty British cap and suit that had many sewn-on pearl buttons. Patrons at the Horse Brass looked forward to hearing and singing along with London Bobby, the Pearly. He was drawn to the Horse Brass as well, with fond memories of the place: "Of course, the best British pub in the United States is the Horse Brass Pub in Portland, Oregon. Over forty beers are on draft, many English imports and some of the best home brew. It has a very long bar. The decor is not polished brass and oak, it is real wood and looks like a pub and it has a piano!"[49]

Before, between, and after their sets, performers like London Bobby were often found tipping a pint at the regulars' table with Don. Entertainers that performed at the pub, including innumerable bagpipe players, had reputations that ranged from local to global. Some groups have since dissolved, some have passed from this life, but all have contributed to the making of the Horse Brass Pub. The following have performed at the pub; they were talented, but most importantly, they fit the pub as part of its family:

Back Alley	London Bobby
Big Thang	Lucky Dawgs
Bowden and Zenetto	Madrigal Singers
Buds of May	Martin Weller
The Calgary City Police Pipe Band	Michael Kahn
Captain Black and Company	Michael Wolfe
	Monte Ballou
The Chieftains	New Castle Jazz Band
Cock and Bull	Peter Yeates
Crush UK	Pope and Paul
David Rea	Portland Police Highland Guard
Edmonton Police Service Pipes and Drums	River City Jazz Band
Hard Days' Knights	Sean Slattery
Howling Gale	Steve Bradley
Larry and Paul	Tom May
	Tony Starlight

Some regulars had fame and recognition well beyond the pub. They included: a U.S. Senator from Oregon, a two-term mayor of Portland, Portland city commissioners, local TV and radio talk show personalities, and the scribes and leaders of the craft beer revolution. While they were quickly recognized, they could sit unpestered at the bar or regulars' table. Don knew some of them quite closely.

A publican himself, Mayor Bud Clark of Portland was often seen, sitting by Don at the bar discussing life, or maybe local issues with the regulars.

Fred Eckhardt, a distinguished author of books, publications and numerous articles about beer, was often seen in the Horse Brass sampling beer and inhaling the atmosphere of the pub.

The visits of the famous English beer writer and journalist, Michael Jackson, were less frequent owing to his home being in Britain. He was the author of several very influential books about beer and whiskey and a regular contributor of beer articles and essays to the British press. Michael Jackson was certainly a regular who made it known that the Horse Brass was one of his favorite pubs. That was not a trivial statement, considering the breadth of his travels and influence.

Many groups had frequented the Horse Brass over the years, starting with the Northwest Morgan Club formed when Jay Brandon was publican. There were other sports car clubs and many other groups whose character and spirit were in harmony with that found in the pub. Each was an extended family member and added their personality to the Horse Brass.

The Madrigal Singers from Reed College certainly helped make the pub eclectic on a somewhat random basis. The group that sang sea shanties on Monday nights added another dimension. The Wobblies came in monthly. Their focus has been forgotten, but some suspected that their name tied them to the North Wales Formation Drinking Team who had visited the pub. A group accurately dressed as British Red Coats during the American Revolution were seen in the zoo drinking beer from personal pewter tankards. Scottish pipe and drum bands from the United States and Canada added appropriate flair, but their visits were mostly done on an annual basis. A motorcycle club came in monthly. Other groups came into the pub but did not announce their affiliation or purpose as they casually conversed and enjoyed their surroundings.

Some groups came in to celebrate a birthday, wedding or anniversary. An event serendipitously occurred early one Tuesday morning, about 12:30 am. Theresa McAreavy was finishing the end of her normal Monday night shift. A group came in carrying a big cake. A spokesperson for the group said, "We're sorry to bother you, but we've been out on the town celebrating our friend's birthday. Could we have some plates?" For some establishments that served food, bringing in a cake could be frowned upon, but not at the Horse Brass. Theresa went back into the kitchen, all excited, and returned with plates, forks, and napkins—everything necessary for a proper birthday party in the pub. She had been working since 8 am the day before as a social services counselor, then on her shift at the pub since 5 pm, but did not mind one bit making this group feel at home for a special event. Two days later, Don received a letter that contained heartfelt thanks for the birthday party at the pub that Theresa had helped with. It reaffirmed his pub as the lounge of the village, its social center. He gave her the letter with a simple, "Theresa, thank you!"

Another group met for almost two years at the Horse Brass on Sundays. They were all freelance writers and artists for comic book publishers, or involved in this industry in one way or another. Katina, a relatively new regular, was among them. Most worked out of their homes. Their schedules were quite varied, but they could all meet on Sundays. Soon they named their weekly gatherings Beer Church Night. They certainly were a community, and they met for human companionship. Don overheard their conversations one night and went over to meet them. All he could do was smile in satisfaction. This was his church, alright, a church with levers.

For some of the regulars and the family of the pub, there were benefits beyond companionship and imbibing good beer; these were learning experiences at the elbow of the publican. From the occasional beer-drinking patron to regulars who called the pub their home, conversing with Don Younger could certainly be memorable. For many, this was one of the main reasons for a return visit or for making the Horse Brass their local.

Some meetings with Don proved to be more memorable, even instructive, leaving an indelible impression. This experience became a hallmark of the Horse Brass. A phrase was coined for it: being Younger'd. But a few unplanned things had to fall into place for a person to be Younger'd.

First, a person had to sit down at the bar by Don. Just taking an available stool for a good beer was all that was needed for the memorable event to occur. The second ingredient was beer, maybe accompanied by a shot of Scotch whiskey. These added to the warmth of the meeting and helped loosen the mind and tongue. Don would likely be minding his Ps and Qs, his pints and quarts, as a good publican should. Finally, good conversation had to "just happen" and had to include a topic of interest to Don at the moment, such as: beer, politics, sex, religion, women, a new pub, his pub, or sometimes just the person himself. Then the process began.

If the conversation were stimulating, as judged by Don, and the pint glasses neared empty, there would be a quick glance by Don at the bartender and a small, subtle signal, just a nod and two fingers barely raised off of the bar. This produced two pints of Younger's Special Bitter accompanied by two shot glasses of Macallan 12. This would be on the house, on Don. The bartender took special pains to pull the pub's cask-conditioned bitter to Don's standards. Being Younger'd had not always occurred in the pub. Quite often, Don's views were given within other taverns and pubs. Sometimes a person could even be Younger'd on a rented bus while traveling on a group excursion, or in the Horse Brass cooler discussing with a waitress a prepared English trifle that did not meet his standards for being served.

There was another form of being Younger'd, one when alcohol was not supplemented with blunt, verbal wisdom. These occasions were associated with bar hopping, pub crawls, and being "drunk under the table." People who had hung out, or had tried to hang out, with Don usually felt the effects of being Younger'd the next day, when they awoke with a throbbing head and blurred vision. After being Younger'd one morning, Don's group heard him proclaim, "Alcohol is the great leveler. If you can't hold your drinks, you don't know what you're doing."

Don appreciated differences of opinion. But he did not suffer fools gladly, at least those who had ideas that he considered foolish. Such ideas, if he thought they were founded on no more than sand, would bring his favorite expletives into the conversation to bring home his points. There were no personal attacks; that would have been out of character with the companionship fostered by Don and The Brass. To make his points, he embellished his "guidance" with peppery language, not for shock, but for emphasis. These words could be metaphors, adjectives or nouns, and they left the rapt listener with no doubt as to Don's sincerity. However, he never used such words when talking with a woman.

If the listener had made it this far, another glance from Don and the unobtrusive signal brought out more pints and shot glasses. Some recipients of Dons' guidance had appeared pretentious and pompous, boasting of important people they had known. When that occurred, Don would reach towards the floor, pretend to pick up something, and extend his empty hand towards his drinking companion. When asked what this was, Don would dryly say, "I think you dropped this name."

Finally, when Don had had his say and he thought further discussion unnecessary, the conversation would end. On occasion, this was triggered when a particularly attractive woman sat next to him on the other side. If this were one's first such experience with Don at the bar and one told the regulars about it, they would quickly respond, "Oh, you've been Younger'd."

Some regulars would say, "I've been Younger'd more than once. I remember exactly when they occurred and what we discussed. I'm better for it . . . I think." The recipients of Don's invective may not have agreed with him. Regardless, their name could now be added to the unwritten ledger of those who had been Younger'd by the publican of the Horse Brass Pub.

On more than one occasion, some members of the family of the pub were Younger'd en masse, without benefit of free beer or shots of scotch. The regulars' table, before it was called that, had been there for the sitting from the very beginning. Over the years, it had become a *Stammtisch* (German for a regulars' table found in a *Gasthaus*), but without being labeled as such. (A *Stammtisch* is traditionally designated with a different ashtray or flowered vase, as a signal to patrons. Even first-time customers know that a unique marker means that this table is reserved for *Gasthaus* regulars from the village, and they will sit elsewhere.) As the family of the Horse Brass grew and adopted the pub, they had just naturally assumed that this was their table. They usually arrived early before the pub was filled, and the table was available for them. They had occupied it often. However, the regulars' table was not an official designation, and tables were not reserved at the pub. They were there for the taking, on a first come, first served basis. One crowded evening, the regulars' table was occupied by other patrons of the pub. As the family of the pub strolled in, they had to sit elsewhere. A few regulars had taken this personally and had even quietly asked some new customers to move to another table, because they were sitting on their reserved stools. Don was at the bar and overheard the exchange. Even though polite, he immediately put a stop to it, "Don't you do that. Everybody is welcome here. This is a public house." Following that, when regulars sat at their partially-filled table, when the pub was crowded they would invite and welcome newcomers to sit with them. The newcomers were also gently brought into the conversation of the regulars, rather than being allowed to sit as a private group at one end of the table.

Even employees received a variant of being Younger'd, even before they were hired. If a person applied for a job at the Horse Brass, the interview by Don started there but adjourned to another tavern or two or three. Sometimes this could take the better part of the afternoon and include the evening. Drinks ordered by the job applicant at various taverns were covered by Don. At each, Don got to know the person better, and the person became more forthcoming as time went on. Drinks accumulated and the applicant's tongue was loosened. The hiring decision was made known, sometimes at the end of the interview day, sometimes the next day after Don had time to think it over. A longtime friend of Don's summarized this interview technique: "He used to take the waiters and waitresses to different places and just start drinking and drinking, get them to open up, to find out what they were really like, what their morals were. He didn't want anybody being a hooker out of the place, or selling drugs there, or someone who really didn't like serving people, that sort of thing. It was his way of interviewing. Some wait staff have said, 'Oh, yeah, when I came out here to apply for a job, the next thing you know, we were just old friends drinking at a tavern.' They'd been Younger'd in the process."

A waitress at the pub fondly recalls her introduction to Don and her employment at the Horse Brass. Don was attending another Great American Beer Festival in Denver, Colorado. As was usual, he was drawn to the Falling Rock Tap House where kindred spirits and real beer aficionados hung out during the festival. While there, he met a nice lady who was a talented singer performing at the Falling Rock. Between sets, they were introduced. She was captivated by this eccentric, intelligent man from the Horse Brass. She let Don know that she and her husband would soon be moving to Portland. Don jotted down his phone number, handed it to her, and said to be sure to look him up when they got into town. They did. After they arrived, she contacted Don and asked about possible work at the pub. He welcomed her and her husband to The Brass; it was as Don had described back in Denver. She was captivated again, as was her husband. The interview began around 10 am, then it was off to another tavern, then another. By 4 pm, they returned to the Horse Brass for a final drink after having been to seven taverns and pubs. She was hired. Don knew all he needed to know. They had been Younger'd without knowing it. Another waitress clued her in later that she was now a member of the Younger'd fraternity.

Don knew that the companionship found in The Brass was critically dependent on those that worked there, those that served others. He strongly felt that selecting his people was one of his most important jobs, if not *the* most important. Beer, music, events and trips were very much a part of the life of the pub, but good people were at its core. They had to have the good ethics that fit a British public house in order to sail in the Horse Brass. Certainly, this did not stop after being hired. Don continued the dialogue with all his employees to help ensure that the Horse Brass was maintained as a British public house. However, there were honest disagreements regarding food, beer, employee training, time off, music, and how to address valid complaints. Sometimes discussions happened immediately after rare unpleasant events. Tempers could flare, including Don's. His soul was in the pub; stewardship of the social center of the village was a very serious responsibility to him. As frustrations sometimes boiled over, there were quite a few firings in the late hours. The next day, these were almost always followed up with a phone call and a gruff, "Forget about last night. Come in to work today." Other times, people would just come in to work, along with Don, as if nothing had happened. A little sleep and less alcohol made more rational decisions possible. Both parties would feel that it was better not to discuss an inflammatory matter further. A "Let's get back to work" quickly healed open wounds. Being fired and re-hired was another form of being Younger'd.

There was a marriage at the Horse Brass made not only in Heaven, but in beer as well—Jon and Katina's. She was part of the Sunday Beer Church Night group. Katina was a Portland native and a teenager during the start of the craft beer revolution. Her stepfather and his friends were really into brewing beer at home; they had read Fred Eckhardt's book. She had fond memories of monthly gatherings at her home when basement brews were shared. Taste had been one thing, aroma quite another, not of beer but of hops when they were added to the boil. That aroma spread throughout the house. She did not like it, so much so that she asked her stepfather to avoid Portland's Blitz-Weinhard brewery in the car because that same boiled hops smell sometimes surrounded the brewery. When she turned 21, she started tasting microbrews legally and saw them from a different perspective, especially after a couple of pints. She had grown up in a craft beer culture and continued in it. She dated someone who frequented the Horse Brass and had won many medals at home brewing contests.

Jon, a Navy brat, came to Portland from New York State, arriving about the same time as Katina's 21st birthday. They did not meet until 12 years later at the Horse Brass. Jon had bartended at the Elephant and Castle, and for Don at the Horse Brass and the third Rose and Raindrop. Later, he hired on with a beer distributor for the Pacific Northwest. He had served beer; now he sold beer to those who served it. His distribution route included the Horse Brass, at the top of the list, twice a week. Naturally, he came in also for companionship. That included Don, and being Younger'd about what it meant to distribute good beer to good pubs.

For Jon and Katina, it was love and beer at first sight at the Horse Brass. She was two pints into the evening with friends, and he had a few pints of hard cider under his belt. They found that they had common interests; soon they sat as a pair at the regulars' table. They also had another thing in common—they had each been Younger'd the first time they had met Don. It was as if they had been initiated into an exclusive club of those who had had discussions with the publican.

Their companionship turned to love, then to marriage. They were married in the pub. Don escorted Katina down the Horse Brass aisle, past the bar into the zoo where a kilted Jon awaited with a piper and a minister. She wore a ring of small white flowers in her hair. Good craft beer was served at the reception in the pub. It all fit, perfectly.

Jon came into the Horse Brass one afternoon. His work in the beer distribution business was done for the day. He walked right up to where Don was sitting at the bar, said hello, flipped open his laptop computer, ordered a beer and started reviewing his client list. Don watched and said, "Here is where I thought you should be. You're doing a good job."

Jon's chest swelled. He took great pride in Don's compliment. Jon replied, "Thank you, Don." But he continued, "You know, I've always kind of dreamed about doing what you've done, opening a real pub and creating a warm comfortable environment. Damn, Don, I kind of envy your situation."

Jon thought he was offering a compliment. Don apparently only heard that Jon wanted to be him. That resulted in being Younger'd, starting with, "Fuck you, Jon!"

Absolutely taken aback, Jon replied, "What??"

Don followed with, "Don't you ever try to be Don Younger." He continued with a litany of other successful people in the craft beer and pub business, good people that Jon should never try to be. Don summarized, "Be the best Jon Reid you can be!"

Don calmed down, some, and Jon tried to explain where he was coming from. "Look, Don, I don't want to ever *be* you. I just want to be in your situation, to have what you have. I envy you and what you've done with yourself and the Horse Brass. I want to emulate you, but not be you."

Don sighed and took a long drag on his cigarette and said to Jon, "Oh, alright. But I want to tell you, most of the sales guys in the beer distribution business are assholes."

Jon looked shocked. "I'm a sales guy. What do you mean?"

Don was even more serious now. Almost lecturing, he answered, "Most sales guys want to steal everybody else's tap handle, to put the beers they sell in place of their competitors' beers. They want to squeeze the competition out of there." Then Jon received Don's piece-of-the-pie philosophy. For Don, it applied to beer sales and just about everything in the business world, and society in general. "Jon, everybody wants to go for a bigger piece of the pie. Don't go for a bigger piece. Make a bigger pie. When the pie gets bigger, everybody gets a bigger slice." They discussed this at some length. It took a while for Jon to internalize what Don had said. He would be Younger'd for five hours that night.

Jon went home to Katina and summarized his most memorable mental encounter with the famous Don Younger. He recounted the evening at The Brass with Don and finished with "Katina, remember what Oscar Wilde said,

'Be yourself; everyone else is already taken.' Well, Oscar is in good company with Don."

Don had Younger'd many others, taking the opportunity to imbue different variants of the same sage advice. Standing on one's own two feet was often inserted into conversations when Don thought appropriate.

Well before all the others, there was another regular at Old Belmont Square, a silent one that is absolutely required to sustain life—water. The family of the pub certainly knew about water. In addition to being in their bodies, it was in their beer. Water also flowed under the floor, under the regulars' table. The natural springs under Building Four of Old Belmont Square had been channeled by drainage tiles to the shallow swale outside the back door. It became a moat when the rains of Portland were heavy.

For eons, water has also had a spiritual dimension to it. Some people at the pub have thought that the unseen and unknown forces that emanate from flowing water underpin the regulars' table. Perhaps it has stimulated and softly guided the conversation and companionship above it. It, too, is a regular.

After Don's wake, Phil and Leslie Bourbeau were sitting at the regulars' table, reminiscing with their old friends. Well before Don's death, they had moved to Pacific City, Oregon, where they had found another regulars' table at the Sportsman's Pub•N•Grub and the frequent companionship of Rob Royster. Phil was still very active as a rehabilitation counselor for the Oregon Commission for the Blind. As a result, he frequently traveled the coastal highway between Pacific City and Lincoln City, sometimes twice a day, attending to clients and programs. Twists, turns, trees and rain—he knew that road very well. Discussion at the regulars' table turned to Don and his wake. All at the table had been there and had shared the crowded pub with many. After singing his "Ballad of the Horse Brass Pub," Tom May had given his remembrances of Don at the microphone near the piano and just naturally took on the role of master of ceremonies.

Phil recounted how Tom had spotted him in the crowd and invited him to the microphone, as another of Don's old friends. Phil said that he had taken a deep breath as he stepped forward and prepared to tell some personal stories about Don. As he gazed across the throng of people, he realized that all the faces near him were strangers. Those around the regulars' table were far across the pub from the microphone. With many people standing, the family of the pub was almost out of sight. There had been one story that he had wanted to share, but he could not bring himself to do so without the company of his pub family and their pub love closely surrounding him. So Phil had said a few things about Don being a great friend and related a few humorous anecdotes that spoke to Don's eccentric personality.

The regulars now nodded as they, too, remembered Phil's time at the microphone. Now Phil was prepared to tell his story about what had happened on that coastal highway. It was early morning on the day Don had died. Phil had learned of Don's death from a phone call by a member of the Horse Brass family in Portland. Phil had been shaken by the news. Don, his close friend and beloved publican of the Horse Brass, was gone.

Later, Phil was on the road to Lincoln City that rainy winter morning. He was alone, overwhelmed by memories of Don. He had to bring his car to a stop. Right in front of him, a large herd of beautiful elk were crossing the road. Elk were abundant in the coastal mountains, but he had never encountered them on the coastal highway before. Now it was just him and the elk. It was quite early, and there were no other cars on the road just then. The herd was large. A lone bull elk with an elegant set of antlers stood by the side of the road, in front of Phil's car, watching and supervising the crossing of the herd. The crossing took a while, and thoughts of Don's death consumed his time as he stared at those beautiful animals. All the elk finally crossed, but the bull elk stood there for a few more moments. He slowly swung his head and looked directly at Phil for a few seconds, but it seemed like forever. Time had stopped. The bull elk stared at Phil and spoke to him in a silent language, "It's OK, Phil."

Phil was absolutely transfixed. He exclaimed, "There you are! That's you!"

The regulars' table fell silent. A few turned and looked at the East Wall and the painting of Don in a London pub. Phil said he had never seen any elk on that frequent drive before or since. Ever. But they were there that morning, the day of Don's death.

At a revered spot at the bar where Don usually sat, near his ashes, close friends and regulars gather on occasion after "Last orders, please." Drinks are hoisted and toasts are made at this memorial to a dear friend who has moved on. All who loved Don know that they are in a place where his spirit remains, a place where Don could go and enjoy his mates and have a smoke, a beer, and a scotch.

Don had known that God was a regular at his pub. The regulars know that Don now sits where God's regulars sit, at His bar in a pub of the ages.

PART V

Tales from the Table

TALES FROM THE TABLE

Tales are often told over tables. The round wooden tables on cast iron legs at the Horse Brass Pub have surely overheard more than a few tales on both sides of the Atlantic. The bar and the regulars' table at The Brass have heard many. Some tales were friendly chat about the day's happenings, debate over politics, discussion of the frailties of love and marriage, or just bragging about the recent soccer wins of Manchester United or the Portland Timbers. Other stories recounted games played at the Horse Brass and community events. Many such stories have not stood the test of time, having evaporated from memories like so much spilled beer. Other tales, those that are defining, poignant, humorous or just plain interesting, have survived to be told again.

Before the Horse Brass was born, an English science fiction writer had compiled and published a collection of stories that he had written over the years. Arthur C. Clarke had ascribed these stories to regulars at a fictional English pub in London. The book was entitled *Tales from the White Hart*. He had frequented a real pub in London; the regulars there had included journalists and editors owing to the pub's proximity to the offices of Britain's national newspapers on and around Fleet Street. It had also been a gathering place for London's science fiction buffs and writers. This pub was camouflaged by his fictional White Hart pub, probably to keep curious readers from his cozy, quiet meeting place. Arthur Clarke was a prolific writer and published extensively throughout his life; his many works include *2001: A Space Odyssey*, which was made into a popular movie. Late in life, he was knighted for his services to English literature.

Regulars at the Horse Brass readily identified with Sir Arthur's fictional regulars at the White Hart. As in the White Hart pub, tales over tables were not in short supply; the banter, verbal jousting and engaging dialogue of Horse Brass regulars at their table paralleled that of White Hart regulars. As Sir Arthur explained in his preface to *Tales from the White Hart*, some of his stories were "intentionally unbelievable," others "unintentionally so." His tales ranged from "perfectly possible to the totally improbable." [50]

Sir Arthur's passing in 2008 was mourned by many readers around the world, including those at The Brass. The following tales from the regulars' table at the Horse Brass Pub, with all due respect to Sir Arthur, are written in his memory. They are true as told at the pub over a table and a pint, "perfectly possible." Sir Arthur would understand.

GIVE ME A BULL

It was a typical afternoon at the Horse Brass. Don was sitting at his usual spot talking to a customer. Brian Dutch was tending the bar. A few others were at the bar or tables, quietly conversing. It was time to start the evening shift, and Clay Connolly was a little late. Don took over as bartender and relieved Brian so he could get home to his wife, Betty. Don continued his conversation from the other side of the bar.

In those days, a new beverage had been introduced to the American market, Schlitz Malt Liquor. Its label had an image of a bull on it. In television ads, young men were prompted to order a "bull," not a beer. At the end of the ads, a large bull would crash into the bar as it shook and rumbled and patrons fled. All this apparently appealed to male beer drinkers. Because of the ads, some young men took to ordering Schlitz Malt Liquor by coming up to a bar, slapping it hard and demanding, "Give me a Bull!"

Caught up in the spirit of the moment, a compliant bartender would firmly plant a can of the malt beverage on the bar with the same gusto, saying, "Here's your Bull!" All this was apparently acceptable macho behavior in one's neighborhood tavern.

Clay arrived, washed up and walked behind the bar to take over his shift. Don was still there as a young man confidently strode in and up to the bar and threw down two dollars. Don was tending to something at the back bar, his back inadvertently turned to the new customer. The young man thought it appropriate to get Don's attention with a loud slap on the bar and an even louder demand, "Give me a Bull!"

Don flinched and hesitated for a moment as he collected his thoughts for an appropriate reply. He turned around with an emphasized, "Bull–*shit*!" Don then asked, "Just what the hell do you think you're doing?"

The young man arrogantly replied, "I was ordering a Schlitz Malt Liquor Bull. Do you have it or not?"

With a curt "Hold on," Don went back into the cooler, looked around and found a single case of the now-famous malt liquor. He returned to the bar, set the case in front of the customer and asked, "Is this it?"

"Yeah, that's it. You do have it."

Don said, "No, *I* don't have it. It's *yours*! I'm selling you this for your two bucks. Take it and get the hell out."

Wide eyed, the young man picked up the case and left. Without realizing it or intending to, he had disrespected the home of the publican and the home of the village. Such bull would not be part of the Horse Brass.

CALLAHAN'S FIREPLACE

Mike McCormick had been a regular since the earliest days of the Horse Brass. He was well-versed in its history and was well-known for his sometimes long-winded accounts of events at the pub and advice about life. Preparatory to his narratives, requested or not, he followed introductory sentences with, "To make a long story short," and then launched into a stump speech on the matter of the day.

He had been rummaging through the shelves in the science fiction section of the Looking Glass Bookstore in Southeast Portland. The name and cover of one especially caught his eye. He read the introduction and foreword, purchased the book and fell in love with it. Correctly sensing that other regulars at The Brass would likewise be captivated, he bought three more copies. He handed them out at the regulars' table. As they picked up the copies and thumbed through them, Mike excitedly started to describe the science fiction story within. When he gave his usual warning, "To make a long story short," they braced themselves for a lengthy soliloquy. It was, but this book report had their rapt attention and was worth every minute.

The regulars were avid readers: newspapers, historical texts, and novels. These literary habits provided fuel for conversation over their table at The Brass. Books were read and discussed at length. Many of the regulars at the Horse Brass had an added dimension; they were science fiction buffs. A good science fiction read made for a good discussion. Beyond that, the science fiction novel discovered by Mike was the right book at the right time.

Don Younger had been having a tough time. His first attempt to open another British pub in the heart of Portland was failing for reasons beyond his control. The name of the pub was absolutely perfect for rainy Portland, the City of Roses—the Rose and Raindrop. But other things were not so perfect. With much effort and heart invested and significant finances at risk, Don was in a considerable funk.

Mike found Don at his favorite spot at the bar with a beer in his hand. Don was staring off into space, deep in dejected thought, as he took a long drag on his cigarette. Mike slid the small science fiction paperback along the bar to him, advising, "Read this. You'll like it."

Don growled about the problems with the Rose and Raindrop and grumped that he did not have the time or the inclination to read a book, especially one of science fiction. Don raised his hand high over the bar and said, "I've got a stack of books this tall to read. I don't want another damn book."

Mike went on, "I know all about your problems with the Rose and Raindrop. Just read the book."

Don replied "Yeah, OK. Whatever." He took the book and headed out the back door into a dreary rain. Back at his house, he read the little paperback and brought it back a few days later. He slapped the book on the bar and pushed it over to Mike and said, "Thanks! This book put me into a new realm. The damn thing is science fiction, but it raised me up to an unbelievable level. It helped me get everything straight in my mind. OK, now where's the fucking fireplace?"

Mike slid the book back in front of Don and bluntly said, "You keep the book. I've got more copies."

Don walked off, leaving the paperback on the bar. Mike took this copy and had a small hole punched through the upper corner near the spine. A split ring was inserted through the hole with a loop of chain attached. A short time later, at Christmas, the book was given back to Don with 14 Horse Brass regulars' signatures within, all of those who had read the book. Mike firmly instructed, "Tie this to your bed post, and every six months read it again."

Over the coming months and years they would occasionally ask Don if he had read the book again. In his distinctive voice he would answer, "Yeah, dammit! I read the book again. I've come up with some fucking new attitudes."

Mike asked, "Oh? What the hell are we going to do now?"

Don retorted, "I still can't find a spot for the fucking fireplace!" He had whimsically thought about adding a fireplace to the Horse Brass, like the one in the book. But with offices above the pub, building and fire codes, the city or the landlord would not easily allow such a modification. But it was nice to think about. In the years to come, a common rhetorical comment from the regulars, even up until he died, was, "Don, where the hell are we going to put the fireplace?"

But, fireplace or not, the gospel found in that little book had to be spread. Mike personally purchased many copies of the book in the coming months and handed them out at the pub. Only a very few were ever returned. Like Don, Horse Brass patrons and customers kept their copies for occasional use when life seemed overwhelming, complex and confusing.

A heretofore unknown science fiction writer of considerable talent, Spider Robinson, had written a novel that had somehow captured the spirit of the Horse Brass without Spider ever having known of it. Seven years of college had prepared him for his literary career, but the job market at the time was a little tight, and he landed a job as a night guard at a sewer district pumping station out on New York's Long Island. Since not a lot of people were motivated to climb over the perimeter fence to do harm to a human waste pumping system, he had a lot of time on his hands to think and to write a science fiction story quite different from other science fiction stories swirling about at the time.

When the regulars first read *Callahan's Crosstime Saloon*, it gave them pause. The introduction was written by Ben Bova (editor at the time of the science fiction magazine, *Analog*); it was a little haunting to the Horse Brass regulars. It included his description of Spider's physical appearance when he had first walked into Ben's office at *Analog* in Manhattan: " . . . lank . . . bearded, long of hair . . . sort of grinning quizzically."[51]

They had been discussing the book and Spider Robinson's reported looks when Don walked in. He nodded at the regulars as he walked by, grinning at them, before settling in at his favorite spot at the bar. In real life, Spider and Don did not look alike, but they had matching characteristics. The written description of Spider tended to match that of their beloved publican. Don could certainly be described as lank, and he did have his trademark shoulder-length hair, a beard, and an interesting smile.

Spider's science fiction story centered on a fictitious saloon, Callahan's Place, set on Long Island. Some at the Horse Brass regulars' table had done some research and thought that Spider may have visited the very real North Star Pub. That pub was a distinctive place in Lower Manhattan, within a stone's throw of the Brooklyn Bridge. No doubt, colorful people frequented that pub.

In the story, the quite colorful regulars of Callahan's Place were introduced with their saloon handles: Big Beef McCaffrey, Fast Eddie (the blackjack wielding piano player), Spud Flynn, Slippery Joe Maser, Doc Webster, Shorty Steinitz, and Long-Drink McGonnigle. Just like the Horse Brass, Callahan's Place had very interesting characters, or more accurately, interesting people of good character. They were regulars that cared about each other. This drew a strong parallel with the regulars and their pub handles at the Horse Brass: The Mayor, The Emperor, Grizz, Hawk, Maid Marion, Frank the Knife, Munchkin, Meatloaf Bob and The Professor, to name just a few; each had a unique personality.

Some of the fictional visitors to Callahan's were of a science fiction bent, yet plausible in the minds of science fiction readers: aliens, time travelers, a telekinetic man, and telepaths. These characters brought their views of the human race, its problems, and their own solutions. Some were there to control the destiny of mankind. Their presence and dialogue prompted considerable discussion among Mike Callahan's regulars with differing views. This, by itself, made the story worth reading for regulars at The Brass because they, too, exchanged differing views on many topics. Time travelers and telepaths and aliens, in a bar on Long Island—it was not a typical science fiction setting. But the regulars at Callahan's were there to help folks with their problems and to provide absolution at the fireplace with shattered glasses.

The fictional twists and turns of the lives of those at Callahan's Place unfolded each night with Callahan himself behind the bar. As the publican, Callahan ensured proper behavior and camaraderie were maintained, as he meant it to be. With the same objectives, Don Younger was certainly the real life equivalent of Mike Callahan, sharing many of the same attributes; their views on life were similar.

All the Horse Brass regulars discussed at length the uncanny similarities between the fictional Callahan's Place and the real Horse Brass Pub. It was as if their pub had somehow channeled with Spider Robinson; as Spider wrote the book, the Horse Brass Pub was being built out and decorated. Don and Bill had purchased the pub from the Two Jays in 1976; the book was published in 1977. It was as if Spider Robinson had telepathy, like one of his characters, across the breadth of the United States.

Don Younger, ever the watchful publican, wanted his pub to be a friendly, welcoming home to his patrons, a cheerful place. In quite similar fashion, Callahan thought his place "should be merry." Don carefully culled those that were rude and those that disrespected his home. When somebody crossed Don's line of expected behavior, they were banned permanently. Like Don, Callahan culled his patrons. "If Callahan ever catches someone cheating on him; he personally ejects them forever."

Don Younger, with a steel trap mind and ever the fan of trivia, fostered Trivial Pursuit nights at the Horse Brass; Callahan had Punday Night at his Crosstime Saloon. Both games evoked groans and laughter. While puns and trivia were not the same thing, they both fostered a degree of mental acuity by patrons, regulars and publican. At Callahan's, disgusted regulars threw their glasses into the fireplace when someone made an awful pun; disgusted regulars at The Brass would certainly have thrown their glasses, if there had been a fireplace, in response to some of the trivia questions. Stimulated by the book, the regulars had several Pun Nights at The Brass, but they soon faded away. Good puns were hard to come by.

The Horse Brass would later have a special drink, Younger's Special Bitter, that was initially offered only at Don's pub. Callahan's Place also had a special drink, The Horse's Ass, available only at Mike's saloon. But that connection with the Horse Brass went deeper. In front of the OLCC, Jay Brandon had requested a special name for his pub, The Horse's Brass. After some back-and-forth with the staid commissioners, the name Horse Brass Pub was approved.

When the pub posted its proper name, some irreverent patrons had, on rare occasion, been overheard to say, "I'll meet you at the Horse's Ass."

Spider Robinson described the Third Annual Darts Championship of the Universe, held between patrons of Callahan's and a telekinetic visitor. The throwing distance was 30 feet. The design of the board was simple concentric circles like an archery target, but with a photograph of a despised political figure over the bullseye. Outside of the telekinetic visitor making the dartboard *want* the darts, the dart match at Callahan's was pretty much like dart matches at The Brass. PADA league championships, sometimes held at the Horse Brass, were about the same as the darts championship at Callahan's, complete with colorful characters and ample aiming fluid. While there were no pictures of political figures on the Horse Brass dart boards, pointed discussion at the regulars' table accomplished the same thing, using well-placed verbal darts aimed at disliked political figures.

A regular at the Horse Brass, Grizz, was on Mike McCormick's dart team. They were well into a league dart match against a visiting team, playing on Dart Board One. Grizz had just thrown. He went over to the bar and ordered a beer. Before the beer had been poured, it was Grizz's turn again. A single dead-center bullseye would win the doubles match. Now, all were waiting on him. Mike yelled, "Grizz, it's your turn! Get over here and finish this off with a bullseye."

Grizz had read *Callahan's Crosstime Saloon*. Standing at the bar, he turned around and let fly a single dart towards the board from the left side. While not 30 feet away, the distance was considerably more than the standard throwing distance. As if in slow motion, the dart players watched in amazement as Grizz's dart flew through the air and landed in the bullseye! Grizz picked up his pint of beer and casually asked, "There, does that count?"

Callahan's regulars had purpose—to help folks with their problems. This was right in line with Callahan's core values: "It was the place for absolution, all right—it was Callahan's stock in trade." Spider wove key threads into this Long Island saloon. "If you need to be here, you'll find it. When you're at Callahan's, you're at home. The kind of place you only hear about if you need to."

When this was discussed among the regulars at the Horse Brass, eyes widened. Don Younger had often described the essence of his pub and the British public house. His philosophy was embedded in the Horse Brass and advertised to all: "It's a bit of England where good companionship is the order of the day" and "When you walk through that door, you're a stranger no more—at the ol' Horse Brass!" Don felt strongly that the Horse Brass was his home and a home for others. The longtime regulars had a more profound term for what they found at their Horse Brass, pub love.

Serving others was held in high esteem by Don; to become an employee at the Horse Brass was quite an honor. This closely paralleled Callahan's, where it was a rare honor to be offered a job by Mike in his saloon, serving others. Their decisions to hire were not casual ones. An interview with Don included many pints that enabled him to look into the soul of a person. He hired people whose character fit the spirit of his pub family, just like Mike Callahan.

Human companionship described at Callahan's very closely matched that at the Horse Brass. Callahan reminded his employees and his regulars, ". . . there's nothing—if you don't have someone to share it with." Certainly, the Horse Brass regulars shared their lives with each other.

After having read *Callahan's Crosstime Saloon*, regulars and others at The Brass realized that, minus the time travelers, telepaths and aliens, Callahan's Place was an accurate metaphor for the Horse Brass Pub. A few glanced at the East Wall and wondered about telepathy. That wall held images of deceased regulars whose wakes had been held at the regulars' table; for some, the East Wall was thought to be a portal for those who had sat with them.

There was one big difference between Callahan's Place and the Horse Brass Pub. The fictional pub on Long Island had a large stone fireplace. In front of the fireplace, there was a chalk line on the floor. With proper cause, a regular or visitor would step up to that line as Callahan handed him a shot glass of strong whiskey. The patron would hold up the glass and propose a toast loud enough for all to hear, down the contents, and throw the glass into the fireplace, shattering the glass. The saloon would then erupt with confirming applause and cheers.

A toast at Callahan's Place was about what was happening in the life of the person proffering the toast, or, what was happening in the world: good riddance to a problem or unfaithful love, to a cured drug addiction, to progress, or to motherhood. Spider may have drawn on the toasting traditions of some cultures that thought that drinking again from the same glass after a toast diluted the toast. Don liked the idea of having a fireplace, with toasts and shattered glasses. It would have set the Horse Brass even further apart. But toasting followed by shattered shot glasses was not to be at the Horse Brass. But that was another matter altogether at the Rose and Raindrop.

There was an opportunity to test Spider Robinson's spirit-cleansing, fictional toasts in the non-fictional setting of Don's second Rose and Raindrop pub. The regulars had been on their tenth annual canoe trip down the Willamette River. These trips had been done on the first day of January every year, regardless of the weather. On New Year's Day, morning temperatures usually hovered around freezing, and the regulars were often basted with rain or snow showers. Mike McCormick would warm the cheerful group with gallons of his special blend, handed between floating canoes: strong hot tea, sugar, lemon, and a disproportionate amount of whiskey.

Don was not an outdoors type; he never went along on these damp, floating excursions. But he did support these canoe trips by his pub family, making sure that the Horse Brass was open early to warm them after their being exposed to the raw, winter elements. On this particular January day, there was a group of about a dozen folks. This time the Rose and Raindrop would warm them with drinks, toasts, and a fireplace.

Mike had foreseen the upcoming connection to Callahan's toasting tradition. Mel Hickman was managing the Rose and Raindrop. Mike asked Mel to buy a case of cheap shot glasses. Mel complied, except for the cheap part; Mel purchased shot glasses with considerable heft, thickness and cost.

Don and Mel were sitting at the bar when the damp, cold, weary travelers arrived. The fire was warm and welcoming. They asked Mel to charge their glasses with Irish whiskey. So did Don.

As Mel filled the glasses lined up on the bar, he notified Don of the total bill, and what each shot cost. Don said, "No, it's going to be a dollar each."

With furrowed brow, Mel looked at Don and said, "OK, boss, whatever you say."

Don placed a handful of quarters in an empty ashtray on the bar, and he gave the river rats instructions: "If you make a toast, toss back your drink, and chuck the glass into the fireplace, it'll cost you a buck. If you don't, you can pick up two quarters on the way out." These instructions came right out of *Callahan's Crosstime Saloon*. At Callahan's Place, customers did the same thing.

One in the group moved the couch and chairs, knelt down, and chalked a line on the floor in front of the fireplace. In turn, each stepped up to the line. They had all read *Callahan's Crosstime Saloon* and knew the meaning of the moment. Each made a special toast, some personal, some profound, then downed his whiskey in one fell swoop and chucked his heavy glass into the fireplace. The fireplace did its best to bounce glass shards back onto the floor. The place became a wonderful, glittering mess. The sparkling shards on the floor reflected the flames in the fireplace and added a surrealism sometimes found at Callahan's Place.

Don made his toast, shattered his glass in the fireplace, and loudly announced, "That felt good!" Spider Robinson and Mike Callahan were right.

By chance, Spider Robinson was in Portland that same New Year's Day. He knew nothing of the Horse Brass or Rose and Raindrop. By now he was a famous science fiction writer and was a guest on a local, call-in radio show. Bronco had been unable to join the river rats. He just happened to be listening to the radio at home when the host introduced Spider Robinson. Having read many of Spider's science fiction novels, including *Callahan's Crosstime Saloon*, he leaped for the phone and dialed as fast as he could. His call made it through, and he was put on hold. Soon, he was on the air with Spider. Bronco told him about the Horse Brass Pub and how it was just like Callahan's Place. Bronco could not see Spider, but he certainly heard Spider's smiles.

After Don's death, his sisters went into his bedroom to gather his things. They collected, folded and stacked them on the bed. There, at the end of a small loop of chain around his bedpost, hung a dog-eared paperback. They lifted it off, turned it over, and read the title: *Callahan's Crosstime Saloon*.

Retrieving the Rose and Raindrop

Portland needs another pub, thought Don. The Horse Brass was solidly embedded in the neighborhood near Mount Tabor. But he knew that some of his customers had to travel far to experience the companionship found at his pub. Don felt everyone should be able to take a short stroll to meet friends at a neighborhood pub.

A building that had housed a tavern on Southwest Beaverton-Hillsdale Highway needed a tenant. Ever the business entrepreneur, Don went to see the place. It was at a complex, sometimes dangerous, multiple-highway intersection, with much traffic. It was at times called "kamikaze corner" by white-knuckled drivers. A pub there could provide a brief respite on the way home, while letting the rush hour traffic thin out. Business looked promising, even though there was another pub right across the street. Don knew the owners of that pub very well. There were also homes and neighborhoods within walking distance. This would be the perfect place. But what to name it?

The Rose and Raindrop, of course. The first Rose and Raindrop, opened by Don and Bill in downtown Portland some years before, had succumbed to the unexpected vagaries and pressures of a new business. The second one would be different, or so they enthusiastically thought.

The lease was signed and an artisan retained to make the outdoor sign. It was perfect, a large translucent plastic sign, about four by six feet, backlit by fluorescent lights. On it was a real work of art—a big red rose, falling raindrops, and the pub's name in distinctive lettering. Everyone at the Horse Brass loved it, especially Don. The sign went up on the cupola of the building, the lights went on, and the second Rose and Raindrop was open for business.

Don secured a hard liquor license, and this pub was also stocked with wines, bottled beer, and beers on tap, all at significant investment. This was a joint venture. Some of the regulars had been offered the opportunity to invest in the new pub, and they had. Their names also appeared on the business license.

As expected, business started slowly. But it increased in the following months as the pub and its working manager, Mel, were discovered by the neighbors. The regulars at The Brass liked the Rose and Raindrop because they found Don's touch there, as well; some regulars frequented both pubs.

Don's lease payments for this pub, as at the Horse Brass, became a bit tardy in the following months. And there were other financial stresses on Don's central account. This landlord was not as understanding as Walter Tooze had been. Finally, enough was enough. Without much warning, less than a year later, the late payments were used as an excuse to padlock and chain the doors shut. Don, Bill and their partners were banned from the premises. They were served with no-trespass orders by the Washington County Sherriff, a sobering experience for all. An eviction notice was posted on the door and No Trespassing signs went up. Everything within was claimed by the landlord, including the pub sign on the roof.

The ugly news made it to the regulars' table at the Horse Brass. Their esteemed publican and a couple of their good friends were in a bind. To top it off, it was rumored that the landlord's next tenant planned to turn the place into a stripper bar. That fact may have prompted the eviction. While not as displeased as Don and Bill, the regulars' temperatures rose. Their table talk shifted from venting to the retrieval of the beer, wine and liquor stocks.

Unknown to Don, a few regulars became a beer-induced reconnaissance team. They went over to case the joint, even though they had been inside before. Now they were looking for a clandestine entry. It looked as if they might get into the building through the roof's cupola, which held vent fans, other equipment, and the pub sign. They peered in through the windows. It looked as if they could manage to get into the cupola through its small service door. They would have to smash through the overhead ceiling, above the bar, to be able to drop down and gather up the booze. But handing the alcohol stash out through the roof to a waiting getaway vehicle looked a bit tricky, day or night. Then it was back to The Brass for more beer and planning.

A few days later, on a Sunday, more pints stimulated a different retrieval plan. They could scramble over the roof to the cupola, enter it, and take down the Rose and Raindrop sign. That night, a "special forces" team formed out of the earlier reconnaissance team and other regulars.

One of them had recently purchased a new pickup truck. They would remove and load up the sign under the cover of darkness. But the many business signs around the pub shed some light over the area, as did the headlights of cars threading through the confusing intersection. They were especially worried about being seen through the large windows of McMenamin's Raleigh Hills Pub, right across the street.

The four-man Horse Brass team pulled into the parking lot of the closed pub. Unfortunately for them, the sign was backlit by fluorescent tubes within the cupola, and the lights were on inside the pub, as well. One in the group was quite familiar with the place and pointed out the best approach to get to the cupola.

There was a bit of good fortune. Traffic through the confusing intersection was relatively light as it was a Sunday evening. There would be fewer eyes to wander over and wonder about what was taking place. But what about the other pub?

McMenamin's pub, with its large windows, was open for business; there were happy customers and employees inside. They might get suspicious if they saw people nosing around a posted no-trespassing zone. They would have to be distracted.

The recovery team walked nonchalantly into to the pub and sat at the bar. Beers were ordered and a conversation was intentionally started. One person on the team was able to mimic accents and had subjected the Horse Brass regulars to this talent more than once. This time he pretended to be a Southerner, new to Portland, who was going up to Seattle. He said that he had heard about "this here McMenamin's beer."

The pub's staff and its customers appeared to be captivated, or annoyed, but certainly they were distracted. No one was looking out the windows. They were busy drinking beer and watching this apparent Southerner. The Horse Brass orator droned on, regaling his captive audience with Southern philosophy and jokes, stories of life on the plantation, and his family's recipe for grits.

The other three downed their beers, made some excuse, left the pub, and headed for the parked truck. They moved it to the edge of the Rose and Raindrop's roof. One stood watch while the other two climbed from the bed of the truck onto its cab, and from there onto the roof and its cupola.

A rectangular opening had been cut into the wall of the cupola to hold the sign which faced the busiest road. This was good for business, but bad for clandestine operations. The plastic Rose and Raindrop sign was held against the opening from the inside with a two-by-four frame. About a foot and a half behind the sign, fluorescent tubes had been mounted for backlighting.

The duo managed to squeeze in though the small, luckily-unlocked door of the cupola. Unluckily, the sign's lights were on. The lights had to go out, lest the two of them become moving silhouettes for passing motorists to see. The wires were found and their connections carefully loosened; in one clean jerk, both wires came off with some sparks and some four-letter expletives. Things went dark in the cramped cupola. In the dark, they felt for the retaining screws, found and removed them. The sign was carefully taken down, awkwardly slid through the small door, then handed down into the bed of the truck, out of sight.

The orating regular from The Brass was still successfully holding court; all eyes inside were on him. The euphoric retrieval team made their way back across the road and into the pub to have a quiet, celebratory beer. They quaffed their pints, stood up, and the "Southerner" bid his audience a fond farewell with an invitation to the plantation. "Y'all come down now, y'hear."

They walked out, dashed between moving cars, and jumped into the truck. Someone yelled, "Let's get the hell out of here." The sign was stored at one of the retrieval team member's new digs not far from the Horse Brass. Success!

Don was unaware of the tactical retrieval of his sign. He had to be told, possibly surprised. Another plot was hatched. Not long after, a housewarming backyard barbecue was planned. Don was invited, as was his brother, Bill. Guests arrived and were let in on the plan to present the sign to Don when he arrived. They waited and waited, but no Don. Two regulars were sent on another retrieval mission. Get Don!

He was not hard to locate. There he was at his favorite spot at the bar in The Brass, talking to Jack Joyce, owner and founder of Rogue Ales. Don was still feeling a bit down with the loss of his second Rose and Raindrop. Jack was trying to cheer him up. They told Don that his regulars were at the house-warming party and were waiting for him. Don assured them, gruffly, "Sure, sure, I know. I see them almost every day. Go on back. I'll be there in a little while."

When Don was enjoying conversation with a good friend over a beer at the Horse Brass, a little while could be anything but. He was not known for being on time. They continued to encourage Don to come back with them, using their best authoritative voices. "Don, you're coming with us. Now!"

Don resisted. One of the recovery team members just happened to have a set of handcuffs. He snapped one end onto Don's wrist with a loud click and held onto the other end, right in front of everyone. "Come with me. We're leaving."

Don said, "What the hell are you doing?! Take this damn thing off!"

"No. You're coming with me," was the commanding reply.

After a bit more grumbling, Don relented. "OK. OK, I'll go peacefully."

As they made their way out the back door, Jack Joyce called out, "I know a good attorney. He'll be down to bail you out in four or five hours."

Don drove his own car to the festivities, the hand cuff dangling from one wrist. His brother, Bill, had already arrived and had been let in on the surprise. When Don arrived at the house warming, a cheer went up. Someone handed him a beer, and everyone chatted as if nothing was out of the ordinary. The handcuffs were removed to make Don more comfortable—and more friendly.

With some difficulty, the retrieval of the sign had been kept very hush-hush. Now, wrapped in brown butcher paper, they hauled it in front of Don, balanced it upright and said that this was a present from all of them.

"For me? What the hell is it?" Don asked.

"Unwrap it," suggested Bill.

Don ripped the paper away. He just stood there as tears welled up in his eyes. The retrieval team described how the sign had "somehow just jumped off the building into the bed of their truck, then fell out in front of this house."

Don cried. He just plain cried. The group fell dead silent; they had not seen Don cry before. Here was their gruff, gravelly-voiced publican, one who could be a Dutch uncle with the best of them, unable to hide his emotion. Their late-evening raid had deeply touched him. Don composed himself and said, "Thank you. Thank you, all. This means so very much to me."

Much more than the Rose and Raindrop sign had been given that evening.

THE McCORMICK WALL

There were Christmas gift exchanges at the Horse Brass Pub, organized and promoted by Don Younger. People drew names, and the cost of a gift was not to exceed ten dollars. The spirit of giving was there, with a little humor thrown in for good measure.

Most certainly, members of the Horse Brass family had distinct personalities. Some had pub handles that spoke to these characteristics. Often, Christmas gifts received had something to do with them.

Mike McCormick liked to talk about any number of interesting things. "To make a long story short" usually indicated a long monologue to follow, which could make his listener's eyes glaze over. People loved Mike, but they realized that they had to have patience and another beer when he spoke.

One regular often winced when he heard, "To make a long story short." He had weathered many of Mike's monologues at the regular' table and had his opinions about them. One year, this patient regular received a Christmas gift made especially for him. This gift was ingenious, showed a good sense of humor, and was constructed by a skilled craftsman.

The gift-giver cut out three rectangles of plywood, each about two-feet high and a foot wide. He connected them with hinges so the three panels could be folded together for storage; unfolded, they could stand on a table. On one side of the panels were three, blown-up photographs that together made up an image of the East Wall; on the other side were enlarged photographs of other areas of the pub, taken looking west from the regulars' table. When the panels were set up on the table, a person sitting and facing east would see the image of the East Wall at about the same size as if looking directly at the wall. When facing west, looking at the other side of the panels, one felt like he was looking at the pub.

At the gift exchange, the recipient of many of Mike's monologues unwrapped his gift, dubbed by its creator The McCormick Wall. To demonstrate how it was to be used, he sat Mike on the east side of the regulars' table; he sat on the west side. When The McCormick Wall was set up between them, the panels completely hid Mike from his view, but his view of the East Wall on the panels remained.

A good laugh was had by all, even by Mike. He had mistakenly thought that the gift was his. But the giver proclaimed the rightful owner who said he would keep it behind the bar. It was to be used whenever necessary, whenever one heard, "To make a long story short."

THE PICKLING OF JOE MCGEE

Portland's famous Rose Festival and the United States Navy brought Ed Meyo to the Elephant and Castle pub. He had been an officer in the Navy, assigned to a ship of a visiting Rose Festival Fleet. The Elephant and Castle pub was very near the quay on the Willamette River. While in a friendly port, as sailors are wont to do, Ed and his shipmates had a few pints at the pub during the festival. He got to know the people of the pub and fell in love with Portland.

Some years later, after leaving the Navy, Ed made it back to Portland. He landed on a dart team playing out of the Elephant and Castle; that led him to the Horse Brass Pub. As it had for other first-time visitors, its warm interior and British charm reached out and pulled him in. He felt comfortable. Most importantly, he felt at home. He soon captained a PADA league team playing out of the Horse Brass.

While working on a master's degree at Portland State, Ed needed work to make ends meet. So he got a job at LSG (Lufthansa Service GmbH) Sky Chefs, an airline catering company. He worked as a supervisor for the loading trucks and met Arthur Hague, a food supervisor on the lines. Arthur also worked for Don Younger at the Horse Brass. Ed followed in Arthur's footsteps after interviewing with Don. That landed Ed in the pub's kitchen, behind the bar, and on the floor tending to patrons. He was not only at work, he was at home. He was a member of the family.

Later, something went amiss under the pub's floor; a water pipe had sprung a leak. This was not an easy fix as the pipe was beneath not only the wood floor, but also a slab of solid concrete. Jackhammers, pickaxes and shovels were used to get to the offending pipe. There, a tank-like junction for the plumbing was found which needed to be replaced. The area in front of the east end of the bar, by the shallow steps from the upper deck, became an ugly pit for awhile.

The work area was cordoned off with yellow tape and warning signs. Patrons and regulars merely stepped around the temporary obstruction and headed to the bar or their favorite table. The open pit was a topic of much discussion.

Resting in the pub one day during the repair work, Ed was reading "The Cremation of Sam McGee" by the English poet Robert Service. It struck him that he could write a poem of that type about the Horse Brass Pub, "The Pickling of Joe McGee." Pen in hand, he began writing a poem centered on the Horse Brass pit, the rusty tank junction, and the regulars. It was set to the rhyme and meter of Service's famous poem. Ed continued to work on his poem for some time. With pride, the nearly-finished poem was set before Don, who liked it very much. Don told Ed that when the poem was completed, they would do something special with it.

Then a tragic, accidental fire burned Ed most severely. Months of uncertain, painful recovery followed. With great difficulty, the poem was finally finished. The poem leaned towards the macabre, as did Service's. Appropriately, Ed presented a copy of the poem to Don at a Horse Brass Halloween party. It was suitably framed and hung in the pub with ceremony. Below the poem's title, Ed had written, "With apologies to Robert Service (Who is dead and in no position to sue, fortunately)".

With Ed Meyo's permission, his poem follows: (In the framed poem, each stanza has four lines. The eight-line format below, with author-selected breaks at rhythmic points, is used due to page size.)

The Pickling of Joe McGee

There are strange acts seen in the hours between
    the last orders and the sun,
On the southeast side where the streets ain't wide,
    in a pub when the work is done.
The smoke-dimmed lights have seen queer sights,
    but the queerest they did see
Came that night last May in the pale morning grey
    when we pickled Joe McGee!

Near to Tabor's hill you can get your fill
    of English beer and grub.
A dark, woody place when the rat's run his race,
    is the inn called the Horse Brass Pub.
It's a small spot and plain in the city of rain,
    yet some come from afar if they can.
The owner takes pride in the spirit inside:
    'tis a job for a Younger man.

There's a regular crew who go there for their brew,
    a group with a code of their own.
They're an odd enough band, but they're willing to stand
    by a pal when he's feeling alone.
People come and they go and you just never know
    of the diamonds there in the rough.
How it turned out that way no one really can say,
    but it did and that's good enough.

What year ago we first saw Joe,
    was a fact a few could recall.
Day after day he would come in and stay
    on a stool beside the wall.
A well-preserved man with a permanent tan,
    he stayed to himself at first,
But it didn't seem wrong that he came to belong—
    and we learned of his dreadful thirst.

We admired his style . . . still we talked all the while
    of his vast capacity.
Beer after beer, each would soon disappear
    with unique regularity.
Two pints of brew, then a trip to the loo;
    he repeated this steady refrain.
Ol' Joe, he could drink the way Einstein could think,
    yet it never besotted his brain.

I remember the date of the evening late —
    I'd been throwing some darts against Grizz.
It was close to two and with nothing to do,
    I just took a seat next to his.
Joe didn't look good as he slowly stood
    and spoke to the few of us there,
"I would just like to say a few words, if I may.
    There's a story I've needed to share."

"My friends," said he, "I am sure you'd agree
    that my drinking is one for the books."
Mike would pull on his briar, too polite to inquire.
    Others, too, I could tell from the looks.
"Somebody buy me a beer and you'll all get to hear,"
    he said with an ominous sigh.
"It's made for a life with a fair bit of strife.
    Really. Hell, why would I lie?"

"I think that it's due to the place where I grew,
    no water, you understand.
It's far from here — bleak, dry and sere.
    Just wastes, scrub brush and sand.
Well, I left from there to find someplace where
    life wasn't so goddammed parched.
I had to look, many years it's took.
    My God! The miles I've marched."

"I learned in time that whatever the clime,
    I could drink 'til I might burst.
A watering trough of fluids I'd quaff,
    but none would quench my thirst.
Only one thing came near and that thing was beer,
    it quickly became my crusade.
It is here in the West that I ended my quest.
    I came here. I liked it. I stayed."

"The gods gave me one gift: However many I lift,
    my mind stays amazingly clear.
I believe this because I just can't get a buzz;
    beer after beer after beer.
The optimal glass I found here at the Brass —
    an imperial pint drawn by Clay.
'Though I'd like to get high, my mouth always feels dry.
    That's the reason I drink this way."

"Now a vision's come clear that my end's drawing near.
    There's a favor I must ask of you.
Is there some way that here — amid friends — amid beer,
    you could plant me when my time is through?
It is cool here and dark and far from the stark
    and parching rays of the sun.
I could happily die if I'd never be dry
    in what follows when my days are done."

"There's no one behind to bury this rind
    when I shortly go to my fate.
I've no family, so the state will get me;
    they'll save money, they'll just cremate.
When my body is trash, I don't want to be ash;
    for me no dust to dust.
If I've got to be dead, why not buried instead?
    Some place quiet down under the crust."

"Please honor my plea and do this thing for me.
    A promise is all that I need.
If you all pledge your word — doesn't matter how slurred —
    I think I will finally be freed."
Joe looked at each one and before he was done,
    we had promised to all do our best.
A scant minute then passed before Joe breathed his last;
    just belched once and went to his rest.

Clay first called the boss and told of the loss.
    Don said that he'd be right down.
True to his word, he came quick as a bird;
    Joe still gripping his Newcastle Brown.
Then began a debate 'bout the one who sat late
    and the strange request he'd made.
We didn't know how, but we'd all made a vow
    that just couldn't be betrayed.

The answer came slow, then it just seemed to grow
    as Don stared at the main entrance planks.
"Up near the door, underneath the wood floor,
    lie a couple of old oil tanks.
Been empty for years," he said between beers.
    "I bet they're still there if we look.
We could use one to hide McGee's body inside—
    no one knows that they're under the nook."

The idea was good, so we pulled up the wood
    and set about digging Joe's grave.
Like armadillos we dug, the dirt heaped on the rug
    and we soon had a vertical cave.
There came a loud CLANK! We'd located a tank!
    It was time now to insert our dead.
Inside of the tun—free at last of sun—
    we laid Joe McGee to bed.

Before we could plug the hole we had dug,
    Rick said, "We're not finished yet.
I think that if I had lived my life dry,
    I'd sure like to finish it wet.
There's plenty of room to pour beer in Joe's tomb;
    were he here I'm sure he'd agree."
So as the dark night grew increasingly light,
    we pickled Joe McGee.

We quickly then filled the hole we had drilled;
    of the pit you could not see a trace.
After pounding it flat as a slow-dodging cat,
    the floorboards were laid into place.
We were all in a funk (and not a little bit drunk),
    so I mumbled a bleary so long.
Ed gave me a ride and though both of us tried,
    we just couldn't feel we had done wrong.

That was some months ago and now when the taps flow
    of a night at a vigorous rate,
If you sit very still and listen, you will
    hear a call from beyond, if you wait . . .
For at two, when the bell of last call sounds its knell,
    you can hear a sound from—well, down.
It's the voice of McGee, his spirit now free,
    "A pint, please, of Newcastle Brown."

There are strange acts seen in the hours between
    the last orders and the sun,
On the southeast side where the streets ain't wide,
    in a pub when the work is done.
The smoke-dimmed lights have seen queer sights,
    but the queerest they ever did see
Came that night last May in the pale morning grey
    when we pickled Joe McGee.

At the bottom of the framed poem was Ed's signed dedication to Don, dated 10-31-96: "To the Younger Man—Thanks for The Brass, a home and family of choice for all of us."

So Many Pubs, So Little Time

Young English lads, Bob, Bob and Raz, arrived at the Horse Brass full of enthusiasm. These regulars from the Prince of Wales pub were eager to see their twinned pub and the United States of America for the first time. Don Younger, Rick Maine, and the Horse Brass regulars gave them a hearty welcome. Rick renamed one of them Rob to keep confusion to a minimum. Their trip around the country just happened to coincide with Rick's graduation from college and his plan to take a vacation trip back to his hometown, Jamestown, North Dakota. The Brits initially planned to rent a car and camping trailer and just head out with a map, a general plan of sites to visit, with serendipity as their guide.

They had heard very much about the annual Thanksgiving Orphans' Dinner at The Brass. A few quick calculations revealed that they should be able to make their circumnavigation and arrive back at the pub in time for Thanksgiving.

Rick advised the visitors to buy a car, rather than renting one, and to purchase a tent and some camping gear. Also, with his help and that of the regulars, they just might find welcoming accommodations in friends' homes along the way. A patron at the pub just happened to have the perfect car for a comfortable driving tour of America, and he was willing to sell it for a very reasonable price. It had a few miles under its belt. So one of the lads became the proud owner of a gorgeous, midnight-blue 1969 Cadillac Coupe deVille with a big 375 horsepower V-8 engine, automatic transmission, posh leather seats and a classy vinyl top.

Being over 18 feet long and very wide, this grand touring car was something not often seen on narrow English country roads. Large American vehicles were sometimes seen on those roads, having been shipped over by assigned servicemen. To the locals, these oversized vehicles were known as "Yank Tanks." Now, the English travelers had one of their own, well-suited for the broad highways of America.

Rick suggested they stop in Jamestown since he was headed that way. Maybe he could meet them there. The more they discussed and planned their trip, the more Rick got involved. Finally, he changed his plans from a two-week vacation to an indefinite sabbatical, as Don grumpily called it, lest a two week vacation might turn into a two-week notice. Rick would be their tour guide en route to Jamestown. The Cadillac could certainly hold four people and the humongous trunk their camping gear, backpacks and luggage.

Everywhere they went along the way to North Dakota, they knew somebody, or somebody knew about the Horse Brass. In relay fashion, they were handed from one welcoming household to the next, being put up for a few days at each. It took the happy group two months to reach Jamestown, a trip that would take two or three days if driven directly.

They stayed quite a while there, meeting Rick's friends and relatives and the townsfolk. The locals fell in love with the roving Brits, and they with them. Rick noticed that they were starting to put down roots, some saying they wanted to move there and stay. They were impressed by the honest people and down-home simple life on the prairie. Local girls, some of them blonde and blue-eyed and of Scandinavian stock, might have influenced their thinking. They had not yet experienced a windy, 20-below winter day. Rick nearly had to force them out of town. After 18 days in Jamestown, Rick finally convinced them to get on with their trip. The trio hugged their newly-made friends and reluctantly left, aiming the big blue Cadillac towards New York City and hitting the accelerator of the big V-8. Rick left in the opposite direction.

Some weeks later, Bob, Rob and Raz found themselves in the Big Apple, saw the bright lights of Times Square, and visited Manhattan taverns and pubs. At one, they met a local chap, Eric Rosen. Their London accents got his attention. A few pints into the evening, Eric learned that they were camping somewhere in the city. Camping, in New York City?! That would never do.

He put the lads up at his apartment and showed them the sights. In the process, Eric learned very much about the Horse Brass in Portland and the Prince of Wales in London. Eric had been on many pub crawls in Manhattan, so this piqued his interest considerably. The travelers explained what great people were at The Brass and what a great pub it was and they would be back in Portland in time for the unique Thanksgiving Orphan's Dinner. Eric made careful note of that. He finally bid farewell to his English visitors. He told them he hoped to see them at the Horse Brass for Thanksgiving.

Eight months after they had started, they arrived back at The Brass just in time for the big Thanksgiving potluck. Attendance was the largest ever, over 200, and attendees included Eric Rosen from New York.

Of course, most of the regulars were there, Mike McCormick and Greg Bundy among them. Who better than them to tell the story of the Horse Brass to Eric? Over pints, Mike started to tell Eric the pub's history, hesitated and interjected, "To make a long story short." Eric had not heard that phrase from Mike before. So for more than a few minutes, Eric listened politely to Mike's detailed account, which included references to *Callahan's Crosstime Saloon*. Noted was that the book hung on the bedpost of the publican of the Horse Brass. Eric was told that the novel's author, Spider Robinson, may have frequented a pub in Lower Manhattan, the North Star Pub. Eric said that he had been to the North Star Pub.

Finally, in the following days, Bob, Rob and Raz said a fond farewell to all before heading back to England, there to raise a pint or two at the Prince of Wales and tell their stories. They invited their New York host and friend to visit the Prince of Wales, which he did. They showed Eric an exceptional time.

Don led a sizable contingent from the Horse Brass to visit the Prince of Wales over the Christmas/New Year's holiday season. There was considerable celebration, embellished all the more by fond tales told by Bob, Rob and Raz of their trip to America, especially their tour guide, Rick Maine, their "Yank Tank," and the people of Jamestown, North Dakota. On New Year's Eve, the Prince of Wales and the Horse Brass were both packed with celebrators. At about 4 am in England, after ringing in the New Year at the Prince of Wales, Don made a long-distance call to the Horse Brass and asked to speak to Rick. He knew Rick would be at the bar, about four hours before midnight Portland time. Rick answered, and over the background noise of merrymakers, he heard a barely intelligible, somewhat-slurred command, "I order you to come to England."

"What? Who is this? Don, is that you? Speak louder."

"It's me, yeah. I order you to come to England. Everybody here is talking about North Dakota."

"Do I come now?"

"No, no, no. But you've got to come."

Don returned to Portland. In a somewhat-clearer state of mind, he discussed Rick's upcoming trip to England. Rick now understood his mandate: to visit as many pubs as he could, so he could understand just what the hell a British pub is all about. With his mission made crystal clear, Don wanted to make sure everything was in order, such as travel plans, airline tickets, and passport. Rick was a detail man and assured Don that he was ready, and that he would be leaving April 26th and returning July 5th.

"Six weeks?!" exclaimed Don as he almost choked on his beer.

"Yep, that's what I booked if for."

This was to be another grumpily-agreed-to sabbatical, but one of investment in England and in the Horse Brass. Rick convinced Don that more than a couple of weeks were needed to do the job right. Don called the Prince of Wales and helped set things up with Terry and Debbie.

Rick was put up in a spare upstairs bedroom above the Prince of Wales. The first few days, Rick was overwhelmed with well-wishers, the regulars and the traveling trio. Rick had his mission, and they had theirs, which was to get the Yank "pissed." This they did quite well. While there, Rick learned more of Britain's slang as regards to drinking. A "piss up" was a drinking session.

With so many pubs and so little time, Rick had to set to his assigned task. It took him four days before he ventured as far as the South Wimbledon Tube Station, about a half-mile away. There certainly were many pubs within a half-mile radius of the Prince of Wales. He and some regulars checked them out. Their patrons joined them at the bar, proudly explaining their pubs and the public house in general.

Over 100 pubs and six weeks later, Rick had accomplished his mission and was getting ready to return. Over that time, he had worked a little behind the bar of the Prince of Wales, not for pay, but for the experience of properly serving pub patrons. A visitor working for pay in England, without a proper permit, could result in a considerable spot of bother. Rick did not push that limit, so as not to arouse any official suspicion. In six weeks, he pulled only four two-hour shifts behind the bar. There was no pay, except for use of the upstairs room.

Rick was having such a grand old time that he tried to extend his stay three more days. Debbie was going to help change his airline tickets and arrange for the rental of tuxedoes and top hats to attend Derby Day at Epsom Downs. It was pretty posh stuff, very upper crust, with beautiful ladies and handsome gentlemen all decked out to watch beautiful race horses. But it was not to be.

At first Don agreed when Rick called him at the Horse Brass about 3 am, Portland time. He thought Don would still be there, and he was. Two hours later, Don called back instructing Rick to get his ass back to the Horse Brass because of an emergency, and that he would explain later.

A day before his scheduled departure, a longtime Horse Brass employee, Theresa McAreavy, was to overlap with Rick at the Prince of Wales. The pub was to be the first stop on her first-ever tour of Europe. She was quite excited.

But she had a problem at Heathrow's customs desk, over two hours' worth. A grumpy British customs official looked at Theresa suspiciously and started asking a string of probing questions. Theresa tried to explain the purpose of her visit, the special relationship between the Prince of Wales pub that she planned to visit and the Horse Brass Pub in the United States where she worked. Work? Special relationship? This prompted the customs agent to discuss Theresa's situation with the chief immigration officer. Theresa saw two no-nonsense folks looking at her, talking and pointing.

The customs agent returned with a snide smile and bluntly accused Theresa. "The immigration officer and I agree. You're here to work, aren't you, luv?"

Theresa was flustered and replied, "No, no, no. I'm here on vacation. The man I work for at the Horse Brass Pub is here, Rick Maine. I spoke to him last night. He's coming to get me."

That did not reduce suspicions at all. "Rick, an American? What's he doing here?"

Theresa thought a little humor might help and answered, "Drinking." It did not. Theresa followed up with, "He's been here on vacation for six weeks."

Six weeks! The customs agent directed, "Wait here!"

She went out somewhere, returned and stated, "There's no Rick Maine here for you, luv. But I'd like to chat with him."

Just then, Rick had somehow managed to get through the arrivals area and came down the line. He had arrived late, driven to the airport by his mates at the pub. There had been an accident on the motorway. With great relief, Theresa grabbed him and pulled him into the conversation.

After much explanation, the focus shifted from Theresa to Rick. He was asked if he had been working at the Prince of Wales. Rick replied, "Hell, no! I drink too much."

The strict customs agent did not appreciate Rick's cavalier reply and called the Prince of Wales and spoke to Debbie. She was asked if Rick had been working there. Without any coordination with Rick, Debbie replied without hesitation, "Hell, no! He drinks too much."

Finally, the reasons for Theresa's and Rick's visits were believed, thanks to Debbie. They were let through, but the customs agent was not smiling.

When Rick and Theresa at last arrived at the Prince of Wales, filming was in progress of an episode of *The Bill*, a police detective drama on the "telly." From their upstairs quarters above the pub, they watched the actors as a fight scene was being directed in the car park. When filming finished, they went down to see a disgruntled Debbie behind the bar. She and Terry had known about the filming of *The Bill* at their pub. She had gotten up early, dressed nicely, and applied a fair bit of makeup, just in case she would be asked to act in a bit part. Unfortunately, she was not asked. However, Terry had acted in the scene, and Debbie was a bit miffed. Terry had not prepared at all. He was wearing his comfortable red flannel shirt and blue flannel pajama bottoms. Beer barrels were being delivered that day. Terry had been walking between the bar and the cellar to make sure his beer stocks were installed properly. The director saw Terry and asked if he wanted to be filmed, for a cash payment of 500 pounds. That was an easy question to answer. If he were actually a barman, he certainly could act the part, and the cash payment made the decision all the easier. With the pounds payment in pocket, Rick, Theresa and Terry and some regulars had a grand old time in London that night. Poor Debbie stayed behind, tending bar.

All good things had to come to an end. But Rick left with the experience of over 100 pubs under his belt, experience that he applied at the Horse Brass.

BUTT OF A JOKE

The regulars sat at their table one evening discussing their beloved publican. He had just walked by, and his physical shortcoming was again quite evident—his buttocks, or lack thereof. Don Younger had always been a thin man, so much so that he was posteriorly challenged. In his jeans, some thought he looked like one of those thin, rodeo cowboys. Another jested, "That figures. Cole Younger rode a horse alongside Jesse James. Thin butts must run in the family."

A beer-stimulated idea sprang from the group. A volunteer, Leslie Bourbeau, took the task of purchasing fake rubber buttocks from a costume shop on behalf of the pub's bowling team. On Halloween, she brought in the fake buttocks. With ballpoint pen, Don's pub family signed the rubber cheeks.

When Don came in that night, he was hailed and asked to come join them at the regulars' table. Like past Halloween festivities at the pub, he expected some irreverent gift or prank. Leslie stood and made some comments about Don's deficient backside. With that, she handed Don the solution. Being a good sport, he laughed along with them. He strapped on his gift outside of his jeans. With signatures showing, he perched on his favorite barstool. His new attributes hung out over the edge of his stool and were covered somewhat by his t-shirt. With his exposed, voluptuous backside, one of the regulars suggested that he looked ready to kneel down under the bar's sink and fix the plumbing. This drew cheers and raised pints in salute to the modified Don Younger, at least modified for that night.

When Don died, his sisters had found a copy of *Callahan's Crosstime Saloon* hanging on his bedpost. Above the headboard, they also found a set of signed rubber buttocks hanging on the wall.

CHEERS

It was a few minutes before closing time. "Last orders, please" had been announced by Rick Maine who was tending bar. Almost all the patrons had left by now. Rick noticed two attractive young women at a table in the upper deck; they had not left. He and the night crew were starting to clean up, getting things ready for opening later that day. Then in walked a stranger. He asked if the pub could stay open a little longer to serve him and his friends who would be arriving any minute. Rick politely declined, saying that the pub had to close. The stranger did a little name dropping. "My friend, Woody Harrelson, just got in on the red eye from LA. He just finished filming *Natural Born Killers.*"

Rick had heard exaggerations across the bar before. He knew that Woody Harrelson had played a bartender in the very successful TV sitcom, *Cheers*, a fictitious pub patterned after a Boston pub similar in many ways to the Horse Brass. Woody was Rick's acting alter ego. Rick looked at his watch and defiantly challenged the stranger. "If Woody Harrelson walks through that door in the next three minutes, I'll buy the beer."

Rick was smirking at the stranger when who should walk in but Woody Harrelson and a small entourage, all looking for a little relaxation in this famous Portland pub. From the last scenes in the movie, his head was shaved and he was wearing the iconic round, red-tinted sunglasses from the film. After everyone was in and had sat down at the regulars' table, Rick locked the wrought iron gate out front and locked all the doors. The Horse Brass was closed and became a private club on the fly. The attractive girls in the upper deck, having been invited there by a fellow bartender, were now locked in as well.

Rick poured a pitcher of ordered Guinness and set it and pint glasses before the late-night visitors. One pitcher was not enough, so another was served. Rick waved for the young ladies to come down. They did, very quickly, giggling with excitement; a real movie star and TV celebrity was at the table!

Woody took a few more sips, walked over to the bar, and offered to pay. Rick leaned over and said, "This place is more *Cheers* than *Cheers*."

Woody then walked around the Horse Brass, studied the décor, felt the charm, returned and nodded. "I've heard about this place. I believe it now. This place *is* more *Cheers* than *Cheers*."

311

The early morning wore on with much conversation about the Horse Brass and *Cheers*, more Guinness, and more conversation. Rick discussed with all the visitors, in detail, the Horse Brass, its regulars, its history. They drank, smoked and talked until 5 am.

Woody left convinced. The Horse Brass Pub was a real place that closely resembled the ambience of his TV pub. It fit the heart and lyrics in the *Cheers* theme song. At The Brass, people knew your name, and they were always glad when you came in.

THE CALGARY CITY POLICE PIPE BAND

It was the most festive time of the year in Portland, springtime and time for the annual Rose Festival. This was a long-standing tradition for the City of Roses; the first festival had taken place in 1907. Its centerpiece was the Grand Floral Parade, one of the largest such parades in the United States. Local marching bands from high schools and other organizations would be in the parade, sleeved among the many, flowered floats. One band came from much farther away, the Calgary City Police Pipe Band who played bagpipes and drums. They had impressively marched in this parade for many years. Some band members had found the Horse Brass Pub. That is all it took. The band soon made a tradition of coming into the Horse Brass to perform, and celebrate, the night before the parade.

The pub was packed with people eagerly awaiting the pipers. The music of bagpipes fit the pub. An elderly woman, a neighbor and longtime occasional patron, sat at a table near the pipers. She had attended their performances in years past and very much looked forward to hearing the pipes and seeing the policemen decked out in their plaid kilts and white leggings.

The performance met everyone's expectations. Eighteen pipers and six drummers had filled the Horse Brass. An expected piece was then played by a solo piper. Mournful and haunting, it touched the souls of all who had ever heard it, especially when it came from a lone bagpipe—"Amazing Grace." Partway into the melody, there arose a commotion and shouting at one of the tables. A person had fallen from a chair and lay on the floor. It was the elderly woman.

The music stopped abruptly. Two of the band members immediately knelt on the floor next to her. These were police officers from Calgary and had paramedic training. They worked hard to revive her and continued until a Portland ambulance with paramedics arrived to take over and move her quickly to the nearest hospital. The pub was silent as she was moved out to the ambulance on a gurney. Conversation did not start until the sound of the siren had faded. All they could do was hope and pray.

The following day the regulars learned that she had not survived her heart attack. They discussed this at their table, searching for meaning. Finally, one of them proposed a toast to her memory. They took some solace in that she had been taken from this world while in the embrace of the Horse Brass Pub, while a piper had played "Amazing Grace."

Another time, the Calgary City Police Pipe Band was in Portland again to march in the Rose Festival's Grand Floral Parade. They were once more playing at the Horse Brass the night before. As had happened in years past, Calgary's finest got caught up in the spirit of the pub, which included enjoying the company of Don and his regulars over many pints of beer.

It was a very rainy night. Portland was known for such weather, and this made the pub all the more cozy. The pub closed at 2:30 am, as required. Don called cabs for the large group, and the band members went outside to wait. Don joined them, pint in hand. Rather than wait in the rain on the sidewalk, they adjourned to the drive-through tunnel between the street and the rear parking lot. Still full of beer and merriment, they took to their pipes and continued to serenade the pub from the outside as employees cleaned up inside. Some neighbors were awakened, and they called the police to complain about the noise. Shortly, a police car showed up, and an officer stepped out and asked, "What's going on here, guys?"

One of the band members replied, "We're just waiting for our cabs."

The police officer could not help but notice their uniforms and asked, "Who are you?"

From within the group was heard, "We're the Calgary City Police Pipe Band. We're marching in the parade tomorrow. Well, actually, we're marching in the parade today."

Showing true Portland hospitality and respect for his uniformed brothers across the border, he made a radio call for every available police car in the area to come to the Horse Brass Pub. They were to use their flashing lights but not their sirens, as neighbors were already irritated. Don went in and called to cancel the cabs.

Over 20 Calgary band members had been driven back to their hotel in Portland police cars that early morning. When the last members of the band were seen to be safely tucked inside their hotel, a police officer looked at his watch and widened his eyes. Marshaling for the Grand Floral Parade would happen in a couple of hours.

Some of the Horse Brass regulars from the night before went to watch the parade. As the pipe and drum band from Calgary marched smartly by, one pub regular jumped out of the sidewalk crowd, walked alongside them for a few paces and asked, "Do you guys want a drink?"

They recognized the voice of the inquisitor as being from The Brass. From the head of the ranks, the Pipe Major replied, "Bugger off! I've got a hangover that won't quit, thanks to you blokes."

A Viking Ship

He was a big bear of a man. He was an iron worker, a blacksmith with arms like the large limbs of a tree. This strong, yet gentle, man had forged his life with that of the Horse Brass Pub. Don and the family of pub loved Grizzly Bear, calling him Grizz.

Lisa had met Grizz on one of the canoe trips made down the Willamette River each New Year's Day, no matter the weather. They confirmed their love by being wed at the Horse Brass, on the first day of January.

Tragically, an incurable disease later felled the large man in his prime. Of course, his wake was held in the pub, their home of choice. But that would not be his final sendoff. Lisa now had his ashes.

Grizz's lineage was English, but his spirit, way of life, and stature resembled that of the Vikings. The family of the pub approached Lisa and proposed a fitting farewell for Grizz, one suitable for a Viking chieftain. She agreed. A wooden funeral ship was made by skilled artisans who were close friends of Grizz, Mike Fitch and Doc Bruce. The ship was nearly five feet long, an excellent replica of a Viking ship. It had a single center mast, square sail, steering oar, and a dragon's head and tail high, on prow and stern. In keeping with their tradition, Lisa wanted to have the funeral on New Year's Day, but the weather was so bad that it was dangerous for people to drive. So Lisa postponed the funeral until they had good weather.

The day she chose was warm, with a clear blue sky. People gathered on the banks of the river at Sellwood Riverfront Park: co-workers, friends, family, those to whom he had taught his blacksmith skills (some were doctors and lawyers), motorcycle enthusiasts and members of his pub family. All branches of the military were represented by people who had served in them.

Lisa had earlier placed Grizz's ashes into a water-soluble bag. She carefully placed them in the Viking ship. The insides of the wooden ship had been soaked in a mixture of gasoline and charcoal lighter fluid. Road flare squibs were added for reliable ignition.

All moved out onto the floating wooden dock as the ship was sent towards the middle of the river, towed ingeniously by means of a weighted line, shot by an arrow over the ship. The archer needed just one flaming arrow. The ship ignited and caught fire, slowly at first. It was soon fully engulfed in flame with

317

a low roar that all could hear. Some people cheered, others cried. A Marine in full dress uniform gave their traditional battle cry, "Ooh-Rah!" Others saluted. Others stood respectfully silent. Grizz's funeral ship slowly sank out of sight.

While they watched, the floating dock became low in the water because of all the people on it. Unfortunately, many spiders had made their home under the dock. Between the planks, the little creatures now scurried up for their lives, scrambled across the dock and up people's legs. Some jumped from the dock to the shore while brushing off the spiders, some shrieked, others wearing shorts did a little jig on the dock while swiping at the clinging spiders.

It was a most memorable day. Grizz would have loved it!

Tin Foil Hat Night

Rick Maine's stories were always topics of some discussion at the regulars' table. He seemed to have a yen for things truly out of this world. Discussed were reports of sightings of UFOs, with varying degrees of certitude and belief. Moving lights in the night sky could have been of extra-terrestrial origin or the product of the hidden corners of the government. Rick, as did others around the country, had suspicions. One conjecture was that the government had an extra-terrestrial craft and the black-world folks were reverse-engineering it.

In the pub one evening, The Professor had overheard Rick in the Brits' area asking a well-known public figure about alien spaceships. A couple of days later, The Professor asked Rick, "What the hell was that all about?"

Rick recounted his conversation with the politician. The Professor then summarized the thoughts that hovered over the table. "Now we'll have to worry about damn space aliens."

A year or so later, it was getting close to Rick's birthday. As always, the regulars wanted to make this a good celebration. Rick was not at the pub one evening, so those around the regulars' table were able to plot in secret. Ideas for this special event were scarce, or trite, quite unusual for the regulars. Two very creative souls walked in, The Professor and Pope. Individually, they could come up with all kinds of ideas. Collectively, when their synergy kicked into high gear, there was no telling where the evening would end up.

Pope sat at his normal spot at the end of the table, The Professor right alongside. Others at the table asked them, "What should we do for Rick's birthday?"

Their eyes met and grins appeared. They huddled out of earshot, kicked around a few thoughts and broke out laughing.

The Professor spoke boldly, "Why don't we wear tin foil hats?"

Pope feigned seriousness. "Our brains will need protection from alien electromagnetic radiation. Hell, it's Rick's birthday. There's no telling who or what'll show up, or from where."

Terry, Debbie and a large group from the Princess of Wales pub arrived a few days later. This visit had been planned for some time. Most of them knew Rick well, either from his visits to their pub or from riding with him to Jamestown on their first visit to America. The visitors were brought in on the birthday plot. One slapped his leg and exclaimed, "That's smashing! That's an

319

excellent idea!" Pints were refreshed and toasts were made to the upcoming extra-terrestrial birthday party.

Rick normally arrived at the Horse Brass around 6 pm. The regulars and visitors planned to be sitting around their table, wearing tin foil hats and nonchalantly drinking beer when Rick walked in. They would assume deadpan faces, as if nothing were out of the ordinary. In the following days, everyone involved in the plot began making their tin foil hats. Actually, aluminum foil was used, but "tin foil" sounded better to them. Some were quite creative, using only aluminum foil. Others resorted to tightly covering real hats.

On the evening of his birthday, Rick walked in and sat at the regulars' table, much earlier than expected. As Rick sipped on a pint of beer, Greg walked in wearing a baseball cap, a cap well-coated in shiny, if crumpled, aluminum foil. Rick welcomed him, "How's it going Greg? What's with the hat?"

Greg sat down and tried hard to keep a stone cold face and quickly concocted a reply. "Oh, nothing really; it's just an old hat I found in my closet, from my high school days." Rick just assumed Greg had put on a special hat for his birthday.

As he chatted with Greg, regulars and the visiting Brits started to arrive. Each was wearing a tin foil hat. The Professor and his wife arrived with innovative creations on their heads. All those that came in worked hard to keep a straight face as they sat down and wished Rick a happy birthday. Rick smiled and said, "Oh, I get it."

A casual patron looked over from across the pub and asked a waitress, "What are the people at that table doing?"

She answered, "Oh, nothing special. They just want protection from extra-terrestrial radio waves."

The customer responded, "Well, that makes perfect sense, especially in here. Where can I get some tin foil?" The Professor had brought in four rolls of Reynolds' finest wrap and set them on the table. Soon, many of the uninitiated around the pub joined in the celebration.

Terry and Debbie came in late as they had tickets for a concert in Portland that night. Debbie had tin foil bows tied in her hair.

Those at the regulars' table laughed it up, at Rick's expense, of course. He took it all in good stride and offered a free beer for the best hat, as judged by him. When the night was over, some of the most original hats were placed on the high horizontal beams of The Brass.

As Rick's birthday approached the following year, he suggested that maybe just singing "Happy Birthday," followed by a toast at the regulars' table, would be a sufficient celebration. But it was too late. Another Horse Brass tradition had been started—Tin Foil Hat Night—for Rick's birthday.

Two metal millinery categories were created: hats made at home and hats made on the fly at the pub. To accommodate the latter, rolls of aluminum foil were placed on the table and offered around the pub, so other patrons could join in. This was the Horse Brass, after all. The size of the event grew to where a small, unbiased committee of regulars was formed to select the winners in each category. The winner of the made-at-home category was given an interesting trophy made of disparate, eclectic items glued together. The award was given with the proviso that it be returned at the next Tin Foil Hat Night with something new permanently affixed. As the birthday party and Tin Foil Hat Night grew, so did the rotating trophy. Award-winning hats were placed atop the pub's horizontal beams.

Tin Foil Hat Night for Rick's 60th birthday was particularly memorable. The regulars' area was full, each one wearing tin foil hats of ingenious design. In the run-up to the judging, a number of hat-wearing regulars circulated around the pub with rolls of aluminum foil. People conversing at tables were politely interrupted and asked if they would like to participate in the pub's 8th annual Tin Foil Hat Night. Most asked, "What the hell is Tin Foil Hat Night?"

When its origins were explained and Rick was pointed out, most accepted the roll of foil and set to work folding, rolling, crimping, cutting and forming. Across the sea of people, shiny foil hats started appearing on heads. As it turned out, there was a group of visiting Brits and a large local choral group sitting in the holodeck. One of the Night's promoters suggested to the singing group that they sing "Happy Birthday" to Rick.

Some minutes elapsed as over 20 people were organized by the choral director. Then, happy faces with tin foil hats crowded into to the regulars' area and began singing. It was not "Happy Birthday." It was an ad hoc take-off of a gospel song, "This Little Light of Mine," with Rick's name cleverly inserted.

Afterwards, the traditional "Happy Birthday" began. After the first "Happy birthday to you," the group parted, as practiced on the other side of the pub. The impromptu group made way for a saxophone player who was in the pub that evening with her instrument. As she came towards Rick and stood in front of him, the throaty sax set the tone and tempo for "Happy Birthday." When the song finished, the pub erupted into spontaneous applause. The serendipity of that evening had touched all. His tears could not be held back.

POPE

Not all tales from the table are happy ones. Some are sad, poignant. Such a story is one that involved "a" Pope, not "the" Pope. Pope was his pub handle. When that smiling face came in through the back door, he was always welcomed with, "Hi, Pope."

Like some of the regulars, Pope spent some time as an employee working in the kitchen for Don. This intelligent man quickly took to the tasks of preparing authentic English food. He was very happy to be able to please others through his cooking, plus he needed the money. He was a philosopher, as well, eager to discuss his views of life, love and politics over a pint at the regulars' table. He marched to a different drummer, but his rational, well-reasoned thoughts deserved and received attention.

Over a beer, the story of his pub handle came to light. There had been a party at his friend's home in the neighborhood, and he was invited. Upon arrival, he offered to help tote beer and food up to a second floor apartment and asked, "Who should I see? Who is running the party?"

The answer was, "Go see god at the top of the stairs. God runs things around here."

As he held a couple of cases of beer at the upstairs landing, he asked, "If you are god, who should I be?"

"You can be a pope." At and after the party, the name stuck.

Pope went on to other endeavors, leaving the kitchen staff, but he remained a true regular. He had been an avid dart player and would intently watch a game of Cricket being played on Board Number One, close by the regulars' table. The game involved scoring in only certain sectors of the dart board. In a tight game, when a sector was finally closed, one that the player had had trouble closing, Pope would utter a short statement, not particularly suitable for his pub handle. "Sum'bitch closed."

Pope was of middle age when a serious illness befell him. Those closest to him were aware, others not. Some patrons, who knew Pope well, were at the Washington State coast where they happened upon a regular of the Horse Brass, Hawk. He quickly informed them that he had just heard that Pope was in a hospital in Portland; which hospital was unknown. On the drive back to Portland, cell phone calls were made and the hospital identified. The two travelers decided to stop by to see Pope, to cheer him up.

As they entered the ward, they were greeted by some very somber nurses. The visitors asked to see him. What they received was a stern question, "Are you family?"

They honestly replied, "No. We're good friends and drinking buddies. We know him from the pub we frequent together, the Horse Brass."

The nurses looked at each other with eyes that spoke of bad news. One agreed to take them to Pope's room. What they found was tragic. Pope was in a coma. They could not awaken him despite a gentle hand on his arm, shaking it, while speaking directly into his ear, "Pope, we're here!"

There was no response despite repeated attempts. But they hoped that deep within he may have heard and understood. The nurses were questioned but, correctly, they did not provide information on Pope's condition or the doctor's prognosis. The visitors were part of Pope's pub family, not his blood family.

There was a dry-erase white board by all the equipment monitoring Pope's vital signs. The board was blank. On the outside chance that Pope would awaken later, they left him written messages on the board. They took turns and wrote, "Hi Pope, Sorry we missed you. You were asleep. See you at The Brass," and "Pope, Hurry up and get well soon so we can meet at The Brass. Bring your darts." They signed their names underneath; on their way out, they paused at the doorway to look back at Pope. Four hours later, Pope died, without family or friends by his side. But they had been there, his last visitors.

As had been done for other people special to the pub, a wake was held. It was very well attended, and food was brought out. The regulars' area was packed with those who mourned him and would speak about him. Pope's mother and sisters were there. As people spoke in testimony, their words touched the hearts of his family.

A toast was given in Welsh by a regular, a traditional farewell made at wakes in Wales, "*Nid yw dyn yn llwyddiannus yn cael ei farnu gan ei gyfoeth ond gan y nifer o ffrindiau sy'n mynychu ei angladd.*" Then he translated it, releasing its wisdom for all: "A man's success is not judged by his wealth but by the number of friends who attend his wake." Pope was judged well.

The two that had written on the white board back at the hospital went to offer their condolences to Pope's grieving mother and sisters. These regulars told his family that they thought that they might have been the last to see Pope alive, outside of hospital staff. His mother reached over and held their hands tightly then asked, "Were you the ones who left those kind words by his bedside?" She sincerely added, "That meant so much to me. Thank you. Thank you."

They said it was their privilege to have done so. "He was our friend."

These two glanced at each other, both thinking that if they had suspected that close family would be the next ones to see their words, they would have said something more profound, more eloquent. But they had written from their hearts, like friends would speak to each other in the Horse Brass. Pope's mother had seen that.

She saw even more about what her son had meant to the family of the pub. A longtime regular and friend of Pope's, James Macko, wrote a poem in his memory. It follows:

Ode to the Pope

A bright, young man I loved.
I did it easily.
Softly spoken times we spoke
Then laughed out loud
Against the cold we knew was there.
Warm, his laugh was warm
And short.
An adolescent boy was bubbling up.
It seemed he did it easily.
I'm used to putting words between my words,
But only spaces fill the voids.
I've lost them now.
His death has done it easily.
I think, therefore I drink.
I drink a toast to me tonight
For letting him get close enough to love.
I'll drink a toast tomorrow too,
To all the reasons not to drink.
I'll drink a toast to him.
Like him, I'll do it easily,
I think.

A small brass, engraved plaque now sits above Dart Board One in memory of Pope. When a difficult Cricket game sector is finally closed, to the relief of the players who knew Pope, they will give a quick look at the plaque and its engraved confirmation, and repeat, "Sum'bitch closed."

ALEX AND THE ANSWER

An avid dart player, Alex frequented the Horse Brass and often sat at the regulars' table. He lived in the neighborhood, but he hailed from back East. He was a strong man who worked at a big grocery store not far from the Horse Brass. For one festive affair at the pub, he and his brother had sported "greaser" hairdos, dressed up in black leather jackets. They intentionally looked very much like '50s street hoods from New Jersey.

Alex and others were unaware of his allotted time at the pub — and in this life. Tragically, a heart attack took him unexpectedly in his middle age. His family and his pub family were shocked. A wake was planned. His mother flew out to Portland.

After services at a nearby funeral home attended by his many friends from The Brass, she brought his ashes to the pub and set them on a table by the East Wall where she sat. Food, drink and testimonials followed. He was loved, and that was confirmed to his mother.

After testimonials and toasts, Peter Yeates, who had played The Brass many times, performed his tribute to Alex. The song Peter selected was a modified version of a popular song, "Living Next Door to Alice." Peter strummed along as he sang his version, substituting "Alex" for "Alice." When it came time for the refrain, those at the wake sang along loudly. Towards the end of the song, his mother chimed right in with the friends of her son, and she sang the refrain with real strength and feeling.

When the song was finished, she stood and thanked everyone for their kind consideration and that she was comforted that Alex was known and loved by many. She tearfully went on and spoke of the unexpected loss of his father, her husband, many years ago when Alex was a young boy. Like many who lose loved ones before their time, she had asked, Why?

She described the day after her husband's funeral. She said it was a calm, cold, crisp winter day. A veil of freshly-fallen snow covered everything under a crystal-clear blue sky. She described how she had walked out behind their home in the snow and silence, stood in the absolutely quiet cold, looked up and received an answer to her question.

Now, with her son taken from her, she had been asking the same question, Why?

She had not received the answer until Alex's wake at the Horse Brass. The warmth of the family of the pub had reached out and embraced her. Seeing and feeling the people that had touched her son, and the people he had touched, she spoke from the depths of her feelings. "All of you, this place, are the answer to my question."

PIED PIPER

It was a rainy fall evening on a weekend at the Horse Brass. What better place to be? What could be better on this cool, wet Portland day? This typical Portland weather had brought some special visitors to the pub. With the soaking rain, a few inches of water had accumulated just outside the back door. After braving the moat, two elderly couples came in to the warmth of the pub. This was their first visit. Like almost all first-time visitors, they stopped as they entered to take in what was for them a familiar scene. They were from England, as revealed by their distinct, lovely accents. The Horse Brass was also a bit crowded, and they looked around for a place to sit, as they stood between the bar and the regulars' table. They were also taking in the authentic decorations.

A woman in their group took particular interest in a black and white photograph. It was one of four, in a frame, mounted one above the other, hanging on the narrow wall at the end of the bar. The top three World War II photographs were of a Spitfire making a low pass over a British airfield, of a Spitfire parked on the ground surrounded by RAF fighter pilots, and of the nose of a parked U.S. B-17 bomber.

But it was the bottom photograph that had caught her eye; it showed young London lads aboard a train, grouped together, smiling with "thumbs up" gestures and heads hanging out a First Class carriage window. They were among many children to be evacuated from London. The boy with his head out of the top of the carriage's window wore a big, bright smile. He had large ears. With a very British accent, she exclaimed, "Look, luv, there's your picture!"

The man standing with her was her husband, and had those same distinctive ears. He looked over at the photograph and replied, "Yes, my dear, 'tis."

Some of the regulars were there, conversing at their table, and overheard her. One of the original regulars stood up and welcomed them warmly to the Horse Brass. They said that they had been to Vancouver, BC, and somewhere between England and there, they had heard much about a very English pub in Portland, Oregon. As Portland was already on their itinerary, they just had to stop in and see the place. They were not disappointed.

As they stood in crowded conversation, they offered a brief history. As a young boy, this man had been part of Operation Pied Piper, the evacuation of mostly children from urban areas to the countryside to avoid being bombed.

This photograph was quite well-known back in England. The gentleman informed them that, 50 years later, he had been on a British Broadcasting Corporation special feature about this epic evacuation, a byproduct of then-modern warfare.

Now, by luck or by chance, he was in the Horse Brass Pub.

Jay Brandon had stopped by *The Times* back in 1975 and looked over their archives of World War II photographs. One of the photographs he had selected to be copied was this picture of happy lads about to leave the city by train, for a war-driven adventure of their own. That wartime photograph had originated many miles away and years ago. It was there for one of those lads to happen upon at the Horse Brass.

Evacuation of children from London
Courtesy of The Times/Newssyndication.com

THANKS FOR TRYING

Don Younger was strolling through his pub, speaking with patrons, when he saw a close friend, a brewer, walk in. Don motioned him over, and they headed towards Don's favorite spot at the bar. They both sat down, and Don's friend ordered one of Oregon's craft beers, one made at his brewery. He held up his pint to the light and said, "Don, this is the best beer you've got in here."

Don set his cigarette down, held up his pint of award-wining Younger's Special Bitter, and replied, "Sure, if you want to believe that."

With laughter he responded, "Don, you know, beer touches people's lives in many ways. Their quality of life is better when people come into your pub and have a good brew. Especially if it's mine."

Don nodded and took a satisfying drag on his cigarette. "OK, whatever."

His friend continued, "Don, I had the opportunity to meet a past governor of Oregon, Victor Atiyeh. It was at a public event we attended. Did you know he was a public servant for over 30 years? You remember, he signed the Brewpub Bill back in the summer of '85."

"Yeah, I should know," replied Don.

"Well, I had a chance to meet him. He's a really nice man. He took the time to talk with me. Of course, we talked about beer. He told me a sad but really interesting story about Oregon beer."

With that, he retold the Governor's beer story to Don.

> Events had been planned across the state for Veterans Day, 1984. As in previous years, innovative leaders in Linn County had invited NASA astronauts to spend a week visiting high schools and motivating students. They would also be part of the large Veteran's Day parade in Albany, Oregon. During the visit, the astronauts had learned about microbreweries and the growing popularity of craft beer.
>
> Governor Atiyeh looked forward to attending the farewell luncheon for the visiting astronauts. He sat between Daniel Brandenstein and Judy Resnik; each had been into space the year before. They were invited to come forward to receive

gifts of appreciation made in Oregon. As she stood up, she whispered to Governor Atiyeh, "I hope it's beer."

Beer wasn't among the gifts. When Judy sat down, Governor Atiyeh requested, "Give me your address. I'll take care of it." The Governor personally bought and shipped the astronauts a case of special beer made at a Portland brewery. A week or so later, it was returned, along with an official note from a NASA administrative type with no sense of humor. The note explained that NASA, and the astronauts, could not accept the beer.

Later, the Governor received a special thank you from the astronauts for the beer. It was a framed collection of iconic NASA items. It included photographs of space shuttle launch, recovery and on-orbit operations, and mission patches for the most recent Challenger and Discovery missions that the astronauts had been on. They had signed above their printed names as Pilot and Mission Specialist, respectively. Centered above their signatures was printed: "Presented to Governor Atiyeh, With very best wishes. Thanks for the samples of one of Oregon's finest natural resources." Judy had lined through the words after "Thanks for," and had written "trying!"—"Thanks for trying!" to send her good beer made in Oregon.

Over a year later, six months after he had signed the Brewpub Bill, the Governor was in a weekly staff meeting. The door was flung open and a staff member shouted, "The Space Shuttle blew up!" Governor Atiyeh immediately went to his office and turned on the TV. There he saw replays of that terrible disaster. In the unfolding news reports the names of the astronauts aboard the Space Shuttle Challenger were sadly recounted. Governor Atiyeh looked over at the NASA gift that hung in his office and Judy Resnik's edited appreciation, "Thanks for trying!" She was among the astronauts lost in that tragedy.

It was hard for Don and his friend to know, or even speculate, but Judy Resnik's "I hope it's beer" and her edited "Thanks for trying!" could have had some influence on Governor Atiyeh when the Brewpub Bill crossed his desk eight months after her visit. They talked about this for a while, and how the Governor's signature had unleashed the craft beer revolution. Don elevated his pint and proposed a toast—"Here's to Judy. She knew it was about the beer."

The Ghost of Monte Ballou

It was a good night, a Friday night at the Horse Brass. Don Younger sat at his favorite place, surveying his home and speaking to friends. Good beer and conversation flowed. The regulars' table was full. Portland's rain moved unseen water beneath the floor under their table and filled the moat out back. Minding his step, an elderly gentleman gingerly stepped over the shallow water and came in through the back door. As he passed the table, banjo case in hand, regulars looked up to see the familiar, interesting face, lined and chiseled from age and a life in the world of professional music. The years and his passion, playing jazz in his famous band, had dimmed his hearing. He spoke loudly to compensate. As he walked by the regulars, he asked with a raspy voice, "You got any weed?"

They looked at him and each other but did not answer.

He waved his hand as he passed with, "Aw, I've been smoking that since the twenties."

A regular responded, "Whatever, Monte."

With that, a Portland jazz icon, known worldwide, made another grand entrance on a Friday night. Monte Ballou nodded to all as he headed to the piano to join a few members of his famous band. Everyone in the Horse Brass knew they would soon be treated to the best Dixieland Jazz this side of New Orleans. Monte had played with many jazz greats, Louis Armstrong among them.

Monte lived a few blocks west, towards the river. This was his neighborhood, and the Horse Brass was his local. He was among his family and friends.

In came a woman of equivalent age. She had had a little difficulty crossing the moat. She passed slowly by the regulars with the aid of a walker and her nurse. Her smile captivated them, as it had others for many years. She had sung in the same jazz haunts where Monte's Castle Jazz Band had played, which was formed by Monte over 40 years earlier in Portland. She made her way slowly and carefully to where Monte was standing. They hugged as longtime friends do. She kissed him on the cheek after he helped her sit near the piano. After a few rounds of really great jazz by Monte and his crew, singing and making his banjo come to life, her nurse and Monte helped her up to stand in front of the microphone. Frailty fell away as she belted out some songs with strength and feeling that raised eyebrows in amazement and appreciation. Combined, she and Monte had over 180 years in this world.

A regular, James Macko, a waiter for a time at the pub and also a natural artist, watched. He had been intrigued by Monte and his story since they had first met at the Horse Brass. During a break that night, James respectfully approached him. "Monte, I would like to paint your portrait."

In expected, crusty fashion, Monte replied loudly, "What the hell for?"

James said, as a true artist would, "You have a really interesting, craggy face."

Monte shot back, "What the hell does that mean?"

James replied, "Never mind, but would you agree to sit for me?"

Monte finally relented, saying, "Sure, as long as it doesn't require me to do anything more than sitting."

A time was arranged when he could meet Monte at his house a few days later. James came in with his trusty camera, shutter cable and tripod. He had Monte sit down on a chair where the light was good. James set up the camera and explained to Monte, "I'm going to take pictures of you. Then I'm going home, have the pictures developed and project the slides on the wall and select one. It will be like you're sitting for me, but when I get tired of you I can just turn the projector off, so I don't have to put up with you."

Monte understood and chuckled at that. James took some pictures but was not satisfied. Monte was just sitting, not doing anything, somewhat expressionless, just waiting to get it over with. With his thumb on the shutter-cable plunger, James instructed, "I want you to give me a certain look."

Monte asked, "What the hell look is that?"

James instructed, "Give me the look that says, Don't fuck with me, I'm a musician."

Monte threw his head back in laughter. As he lowered his head, his distinctive smile had not completely faded when James clicked the camera's shutter at just the right moment. The camera captured his smile and Monte's eyes, the essence that was Monte Ballou.

Back at his place, using that projected image, James roughed in Monte's captured expression on canvas to create an underpainting, a single-toned oil sketch upon which to do the final oil painting.

About a week after he photographed Monte, James came into the Horse Brass in the afternoon. The underpainting was still drying. He sat down at the regulars' table. There he learned that Monte had died, October 7, 1991, while the underpainting was still wet. With that very sad news, James announced to the table, "It's done. The painting's done."

Later, when it was dry, James framed the underpainting and presented it to Bill and the pub as *The Ghost of Monte Ballou*. It was hung on the wall by the piano. James explained to all that if Monte were still alive, he would have finished the portrait in full color. But Monte had passed while his underpainting was still drying. All nodded in understanding and agreed that this ghost-like image was an appropriate way to remember Monte.

Regulars and patrons later noticed that the captured image of Monte changed with the changing light in the Horse Brass. It depended on the time of day, whether it was cloudy or clear outside. At night, it was bathed in the pub's soft light. Sometimes Monte would almost disappear into the wall on which he rested. Other times, the lighting would sharpen his likeness. Somewhat amazingly, he would be there, or he would not be there . . . depending.

The Ghost of Monte Ballou
by James Macko
Courtesy of James Macko

THE LAST SMOKER

Horse Brass smoke was nearly as well-known as its publican and beer. Don Younger certainly enjoyed his cigarettes, frequently. Most of the pub's patrons also enjoyed smoking; smokers were welcome. The veil of smoke from burning tobacco hung in the air, almost like incense in this cathedral of beer. That smoke had come from people, breathed in and breathed out, and had seeped into the walls and ceiling over the years.

There were well-meaning folks across the State of Oregon who admonished its Legislature to change the smoking laws for the health of workers. For Don, these forces were hard to grapple with. He saw a smoking ban as a threat to individual liberty and the very pub itself. There was much arguing and gnashing of teeth on both sides of the debate: whether to ban smoking in restaurants, bars, taverns, and yes, pubs. Doom, gloom and dire predictions hung over the Horse Brass as a proposed new law appeared on Oregon's legislative agenda in June, 2007.

As the day of reckoning approached, a poster appeared in The Brass. It implored patrons to write to their elected state representatives, strongly opposing the proposed law. Don darkly pronounced that he would sell the Horse Brass, leave it all behind, before he would let the government prevent him smoking in his own pub! But it was all to no avail. This unstoppable force rolled over the land, as it had done in neighboring states. Oregon's Smokefree Workplace Law was enacted, to take effect January 1, 2009. After that, there would be no smoking in the Horse Brass. Fortunately, Don did not sell his pub. Rather, he grumpily waited for the unknown aftermath to unfurl.

A few months before the dreaded no-smoking date, the regulars' table was friendly and full of smokers. The topic that swirled around them was the approaching law, its impact on them and its impact on their pub, and Don. Jon and Katina were two of the regulars there that night. Katina was sitting on Pope's stool at the end of the regulars' table. As had the others, Katina had known him very well. Pope was gone now, but his spirit remained at the table. They discussed various reactions to the smoking ban. Katina participated but had not planned anything particular to say. But she blurted out, "Hey, why don't we have a last smoker?"

"What?"

Katina continued, "We could take a picture of Don and us around the table, all posing to resemble *The Last Supper*. We'll call it *The Last Smoker*. We can do it right before the smoking ban takes effect."

Eyes darted around the table. What a splendid idea! One of the regulars sat at the other end of the table, Aaron Barnard, who was an expert photographer. Aaron volunteered to photograph the epic scene. His wife, Diana, a longtime regular, would be in the photograph, of course. They, too, had met and married in the pub. Jon then commanded, "Let's do this."

If this were to happen, there had to be planning and commitment. Aaron cautioned, "This is not going to be one of those nights when we've been drinking too much beer, saying we're going to do something, and everybody forgetting about it the next day." A poll was taken at the table. With quickly-raised hands, everyone was "all in." Pope would surely have raised his hand, too.

First and foremost, who would represent whom? For Jesus, it was a no-brainer. He would be represented by Don. With his long hair, he already looked typecast for the part. Plus, who better to be at the most honored of places at the table than the publican of the Horse Brass?

What about the apostles? What better actors' guild for this production than the smokers at the regulars' table? Assignments were made by position in the painting. But who would represent the apostle of dubious character, Judas? Without any discussion, the table spoke in unison, "Rick Maine."

Rick readily agreed. He said he wanted to play the part. Rick thought he was appropriate for this role. In his earlier position as working manager at The Brass, he and Don had not always agreed on management issues and the direction of the pub. But they had always finished their "discussions" with a handshake and a beer.

Katina and Jon approached Don with the plan. He was reluctant to have anything to do with the smoking ban. They reasoned with Don that this was a fitting way to close out 2008. Obviously, he had to be part of the scene, the main character. Don asked the same question as to who would play Judas, and made his participation conditional. "I won't do it unless Rick is Judas."

In the following weeks a date was selected, based in part on availability of the actors and the closest proximity to New Year's Day. It was settled; it would be three days before the coming year. With telephone calls, e-mails, and meetings at the regulars' table, the assigned stand-ins confirmed that they would be there. Don was reminded to be there on the scheduled night and was again assured that Rick had agreed to be Judas. With his gruff voice, he replied, "Aw, what the hell. If Rick's here as Judas, I'll be here."

During the evening of December 29, 2008, there was a lot of fuss and scurrying about in the regulars' area, rearranging tables and stools in front of the East Wall. Each regular was given a small photocopy of *The Last Supper* with instructions on where to stand or sit and how to pose. Finally, everything was in order, despite the fact that directing them was like trying to herd cats. People were at their places, sitting at or standing behind the relocated tables with drinks and, most importantly, cigarettes. But the central figure was missing. The prime movers for the event, Katina and Aaron, said, "Everybody's in place. We need to get Don before he has another beer."

They knew where the stand-in for Jesus would be found. An onlooker volunteered to go and fetch him from his favorite place at the bar. Don was engaged in serious conversation and did not want to be interrupted. He had to be forcefully encouraged with, "Don. Don! Everybody's ready. They're waiting for you. Come on!"

Somewhat reluctantly, Don strolled over and slid behind the table and took his place in the middle of the apostles. Expecting that Don would want to get this over with quickly, they took advantage of his love of good looking women, placing Krissie on his left to keep him distracted. Krissie engaged Don with her beautiful smile. It was hard to get Don's attention and have him look towards the camera. All the while, people were directing Don to hold his arms out and apart, hands palm up, just as in *The Last Supper*, wherein Leonardo da Vinci painted Jesus at another Regulars' table, nearly 2,000 years earlier.

By this time, others in the pub realized that something special was happening. Out came a few cell phones, and pictures were snapped. One digital photograph quickly made its way onto the Internet.

Finally, some regulars behind the camera shouted, "Don! Don!" He looked towards the camera and Aaron rapidly took four pictures. One was selected; it would become famous as *The Last Smoker*. This photograph appeared in a number of venues, print and digital, including the February/March 2009 issue of the *Celebrator* and at *Willamette Week*'s website, posted December 31, 2008.[52]

A color print of this photograph was framed and appropriately mounted high on the East Wall of the Horse Brass Pub.

PART VI

Maintaining Course

Epilogue

The crew of the Horse Brass Pub — publican, bartenders, cooks, regulars, and those that wait and serve — inevitably changes as the hand of time moves. Future generations of the pub must look to its past to see the way ahead, never losing sight of what made the pub what it is. Sailing over changing seas and shoals, there is a constant, a single guiding star for this public house. It is fixed and permanent so that the Horse Brass Pub, this Portland church with levers, will not lose its way. That celestial beacon is the most fundamental of human needs: companionship.

The Horse Brass Pub is a work of art that is at once physical and spiritual. Don Younger painted on the canvas of his public house, a canvas first stretched by Walter Tooze and Jay Brandon. As he philosophically described while sitting at the bar in his waning years, ". . . it stops being the artist's work at a certain point and becomes the work of those who look at it. It's now well beyond me. It's now the viewers' responsibility to figure out what it means." This applies to viewers now and into the future.

One man that viewed Don's art was Martin Weller, singer, songwriter, guitarist, and leader of the three-man, British pop-rock band, Crush UK. They had played at the Horse Brass at the invitation of Don and at other venues around Portland. Martin and Don had first met during a performance in the Princess of Wales pub at its christening. Don had recognized their talent and loved their lyrics, honest and heartfelt stories of life, sung with a pop-rock beat. Don, the artist, painted a broad brushstroke on the pub's canvas with that invitation; Martin, a kindred artist, immediately felt and understood the very essence of the Horse Brass Pub.

Don hosted Martin and his band a number of times. During those years, Don lived near the Horse Brass. Of course, Martin stayed with Don, at Don's insistence. His band members stayed with Horse Brass regulars who readily volunteered their homes.

During Martin's first visit, Don laughed and boasted to Martin that he lived on a volcano. Standing outside his house on the shoulder of Mount Tabor, he pointed to the top and told Martin that they could get a good view of the city from up there. Don went on to say that Portland's weather was much like that found in England. It was mild, cloudy and rainy, but sometimes the sun

343

did shine. On those days, when the sun rose in the east, he said that Mount Tabor cast a shadow over his house, his neighborhood, and the Horse Brass Pub—they all lived in its morning shadow.

Then Don walked from his house to his Horse Brass home and relaxed upon his favorite bar stool. Martin and his band hiked up Mount Tabor. From the summit, they had a good view of the beautiful city of Portland. Off to one side, near the top, they also saw the ancient, blackened-rock caldera, a testimony to the mount's origins. Back down at the Horse Brass, Martin dubbed Don "Mountain Man."

Don replied, "Yeah, that's me . . . mountain man, whatever," then had proper pints of Younger's Special Bitter pulled and poured for his English visitors.

They moved over to the regulars' table later and met some of the pub's family. Crush UK performed that evening. The pub was full in anticipation and gave them a hearty welcome and rousing applause. There, in the zoo near the old piano and *The Ghost of Monte Ballou*, they felt the spirit of the Horse Brass, its vibrations coming from the people, the dark beams, the smoke-infused plaster—from everything.

The regulars eagerly told them of the pub's rich history, which threaded back to the homeland of the Crush UK members. They told stories about their eccentric publican. Each described what the pub meant to him, but what they had in common was that Don's pub home was also their home. Martin looked around and saw pints of beer on old wooden tables that had been in pubs in England, recognized the familiar horse brasses, heard the soft rustle of conversation, and said simply, "Mates, this place has a good vibe." All around him at the table nodded in agreement; the Horse Brass Pub indeed had a good vibe. More visits by Crush UK were to come.

Seven years after helping to celebrate Don's 25th anniversary as publican, Crush UK made their fourth visit to The Brass. Martin noted that Don did not look very happy, despite the wonderful vibe of his pub. Don grumpily told Martin that when January 1, 2009, rolled around in six months, smoking would be banned in all public establishments in Oregon. Don predicted dire consequences for his pub, and he took open umbrage at the intrusion into his own place. He loudly banged his empty pint glass down on the bar and announced that he was going to ". . . leave it all behind!"

Martin and his band returned to England. They were quite concerned about Don's intention to quit the pub. But there would be other concerns for them, as yet unknown; that would be the last time they saw Don.

He maintained contact with Martin by telephone. One topic of discussion during the following year was the impact of the no-smoking ban on The Brass.

Don told Martin that the general clientele of the pub now included gatherings of young non-smokers, while some smokers had quit coming. The regulars who smoked now went out back to light up. There, companionship continued in the parking lot, sometimes under the small rain cover that had been built especially for them. Don assured Martin that the vibe in his pub remained, and that business had actually increased. During one long-distance call, a perplexed Don asked rhetorically, "Martin, who knew?"

Later that same year, Martin was inspired to write a song about Don and the Horse Brass entitled "Who Knew." He sent Don the lyrics and a recording of him singing it at a public performance while accompanied by the music of Crush UK. Don absolutely loved it.

Martin wrote about the vibe of the Horse Brass during times of change, when the people of the pub change. He was stimulated by the no-smoking ban, since it did change the patronage of the pub somewhat. But something else may have guided Martin's hand, in a prophetic way. He had called Don from England in late January, 2011, to chat, having heard that he wasn't well. They talked for a while about health, wealth and the world, but Martin detected in Don's voice that something was amiss. A few days later, Martin received the very sad news that Don had died. The original hand-written lyrics of "Who Knew" lay on his desk before him. Martin hung up the phone and read them again, reflected, and then made a few changes. The words now had much greater meaning, and they were needed more than ever.

The Horse Brass will continue to sail on towards a distant, receding shore, the voyage its destination. Hopefully, the vibe of the pub will remain as the pub sails over unfolding charts, with a course scribed in the minds of the ever-changing crew: "It's a bit of England where good companionship is the order of the day."

Martin Weller's "Who Knew" is both chart and sailing orders for the next generations at the Horse Brass Pub. With his permission, the poignant lyrics appear on the final page of this book.

WHO KNEW
(Words and Music by Martin Weller, Copyright 2009)

Too much whiskey tears your throat apart
Three cigarettes for breakfast doesn't make it better

You've been lucky and good at your job
So we walked in the bar seven years later

It felt just the same
Some of the faces had changed
But the vibe remained

I could go back tomorrow and lead that life
But I got a home and a loving, if disapproving wife
You have to realize what it's all about
The American dream is hallowed, but somehow it all works

It felt just the same
Some of the faces had changed
But the vibe remained

January 1st 2009 that's when the Don said
he was going to "leave it all behind"
So if that was the last time
Let's raise a brew to the 'Mountain Man'
From me to you

It can't stay the same
Oh no, the faces will change
But I hope the vibe remains

It can't be the same
You know the old place will change
Maybe, somehow, the vibe will remain

References

1. White, Maggi. November 1, 1976. Walking shoes needed for Belmont tour. *The Community Press Downtowner*
2. Wendeborn, John. October 2, 1973. Firehouse tavern expands its music. *The Oregonian*
3. Northwest Magazine. May 12, 1974. *The Sunday Oregonian*
4. Minutes of the Recessed Meetings of the Council of the City of Portland. March 13, 1975, Calendar Number 715 (Portland Archives and Records Center)
5. Minutes of the Recessed Meetings of the Council of the City of Portland. March 20, 1975, Calendar Number 787 (Portland Archives and Records Center)
6. England On $10^{00} A Day (advertisement). March 14, 1976. *The Sunday Oregonian*
7. Bieber, George. October, 1996. The Beginning. *Brass Tacks*. Volume 5, Number 1
8. Eckhardt, Fred. 2002. Draft submission to *Celebrator Beer News* of conversations with Don Younger
9. Eckhardt, Fred. October/November 2002. A Conversation With Don Younger, A Publican's Perspective on the Craft-Beer Revolution. *Celebrator Beer News*
10. Watson, Mike. September 30, 2012. History of the Pub. *Beer Expert*. http://www.beerexpert.co.uk/HistoryOfThePub.html
11. Teeter, H. A., and W. M. Henabray. 1979. *English Pubs Through American Eyes*. TAPCO Ltd.
12. Prince, Tracy J. 2011. *Images of America, Portland's Goose Hollow*. Acadia Publishing
13. Ryerson, Michael. 2000-2012. expose yourself to art™. http://www.exposeyourselftoart.org
14. Richardson, David. February 21, 2007. *Shots of Portland*. Distilled Publishing
15. Culverwell, Wendy. July 20, 2012. A newer Old Lompoc. *Portland Business Journal*
16. Dalldorf, Tom. December 2001/January 2002. Portland's Horse Brass Pub Celebrates 25th Anniversary, Don Younger Honored by Beer Industry. *Celebrator Beer News*
17. Kriz, Tony. 2012. *Neighbors and Wise Men, Sacred Encounters in a Portland Pub and Other Unexpected Places*. Thomas Nelson
18. Wondrich, David. June, 2009. The Best Bars in America. *Esquire*

19. Foyston, John. May 11, 2009. Horse Brass tops Esquire's list of 2009's Best Bars in America. *The Oregonian*

20. Eßlinger, H. M. 2009. *Handbook of Brewing: Processes, Technology, Markets.* WILEY-VCH Verlag GmbH & Co. KGaA, Weinheim

21. Oregon Brewers Guild. December 20, 2012. The History of Craft Beer in Oregon. *Oregon Craft Beer.* http://oregonbeer.org

22. Morrison, Lisa. 2011. *Craft Beers of the Pacific Northwest.* Timber Press

23. Moen, Alan. 2001. An Interview with Don Younger. *Seattle Beer News.* http://seattlebeernews.com

24. Grant, Bert. 1998. *The Ale Master.* Sasquatch Books

25. Sadler, Russell. May 27, 1985. Brewpub bill gets casual dismissal. *The Oregonian*

26. Church, Foster. June 12, 1985. House approves Coors bill 45-15. *The Oregonian*

27. Cornell, Martyn. October 6, 2011. Wells gets Younger—which isn't as old as claimed. *Zythophile.* http://zythophile.wordpress.com

28. Oregon Brewers Guild. March 23, 2013. About the Oregon Brewers Guild. *Oregon Craft Beer.* http://oregonbeer.org

29. Campaign for Real Ale. June 30, 2013. Campaigning for real ale, pubs & drinkers' rights since 1971. CAMRA. http://www.camra.org.uk

30. Hall of Foam. July, 2006. Younger Publican. Portland Monthly

31. Oregon Public Broadcasting. November 5, 2007. Beervana. *Oregon Experience.* http://watch.opb.org/video

32. BestBars. September 29, 2010. DRAFT's 150 Best Beer Bars 2010. *Draft Magazine.* http://draftmag.com

33. Features. January/February 2012. America's 100 Best Beer Bars: 2012. *Draft Magazine.* http://draftmag.com

34. Abernathy, Jon. November 11, 2011. Lompoc Brewing (Portland). *The Brew Site.* http://www.thebrewsite.com

35. Headline Story, Sunrise Edition. December 25, 1983. Perilous storm puts NW on skids. *The Sunday Oregonian*

36. Osborn, Helen. 1999. *Britain's Oldest Brewery.* The Gresham Press

37. Osborn, Helen. 1991. *Inn and Around London, A History of Young's Pubs.* Surrey Fine Art Press Ltd.
38. Whicheloe, Clive. 2003. *Pubs of Merton (Past & Present).* Enigma Publishing
39. Bieber, George. October, 1996. Magic! *Brass Tacks*, Volume 5, Number 1
40. Obituary. October/November 2006. John Young: Britain's Oldest Brewery Chairman. *London Drinker.* Volume 28, Number 5
41. Melman, Yossi. 1986. *The Master Terrorist, The True Story of Abu-Nidal.* Adama Books
42. Goff, Amanda. May 8, 1997. Plans for local pub are driving drinkers to despair. *Putney and Wimbledon Times*
43. Butler, Martin. June, 1997. Prince of Wales, Morden Road SW19. *London Drinker.* Volume 19, Number 5
44. Goff, Amanda. June, 1997. Last Orders for Pub. *Putney and Wimbledon Times*
45. Ward, Natalie. December, 1997. Rescued pub changes its name in memory of Diana. *Putney and Wimbledon Times*
46. Jackson, Michael. September 20, 2006. John Young, Visionary chairman for four decades of Young's brewery. *The Independent*
47. Cask Marque Awards. February/March 2006. Young's Managers Celebrate 20 Years. *London Drinker.* Volume 28, Number 1
48. Butler, Martin. April/May 2011. Don Younger 1941 – 2011. *London Drinker.* Volume 33, Number 2
49. Smith, Robert. February 21, 2013. London Bobby's World Guide to Piano Pubs and Piano Bars. *London Bobby, Piano Entertainer.* http://londonbobby.com
50. Clark, Arthur C. 1957. *Tales from the White Hart.* Ballantine Books, Inc.
51. Robinson, Spider. 1977. *Callahan's Crosstime Saloon.* ACE Books
52. Jaquiss, Nigel. December 31, 2008. Smoky Bars: Horse Brass Regulars Say Goodbye to All That. http://www.wweek.com

Ed Keene, Keene Studio

After 27 years in the Air Force, Robert Wright had a second career in Washington D.C. He retired and returned to his hometown, Portland, Oregon. There, he published his memoirs. While in the Air Force, he had lived in England and had fallen in love with pubs. Later, he discovered Portland's Horse Brass Pub. Encouraged by the pub's regulars, he wrote its story.

CPSIA information can be obtained
at www.ICGtesting.com
Printed in the USA
FSOW01n0522070218
44115FS